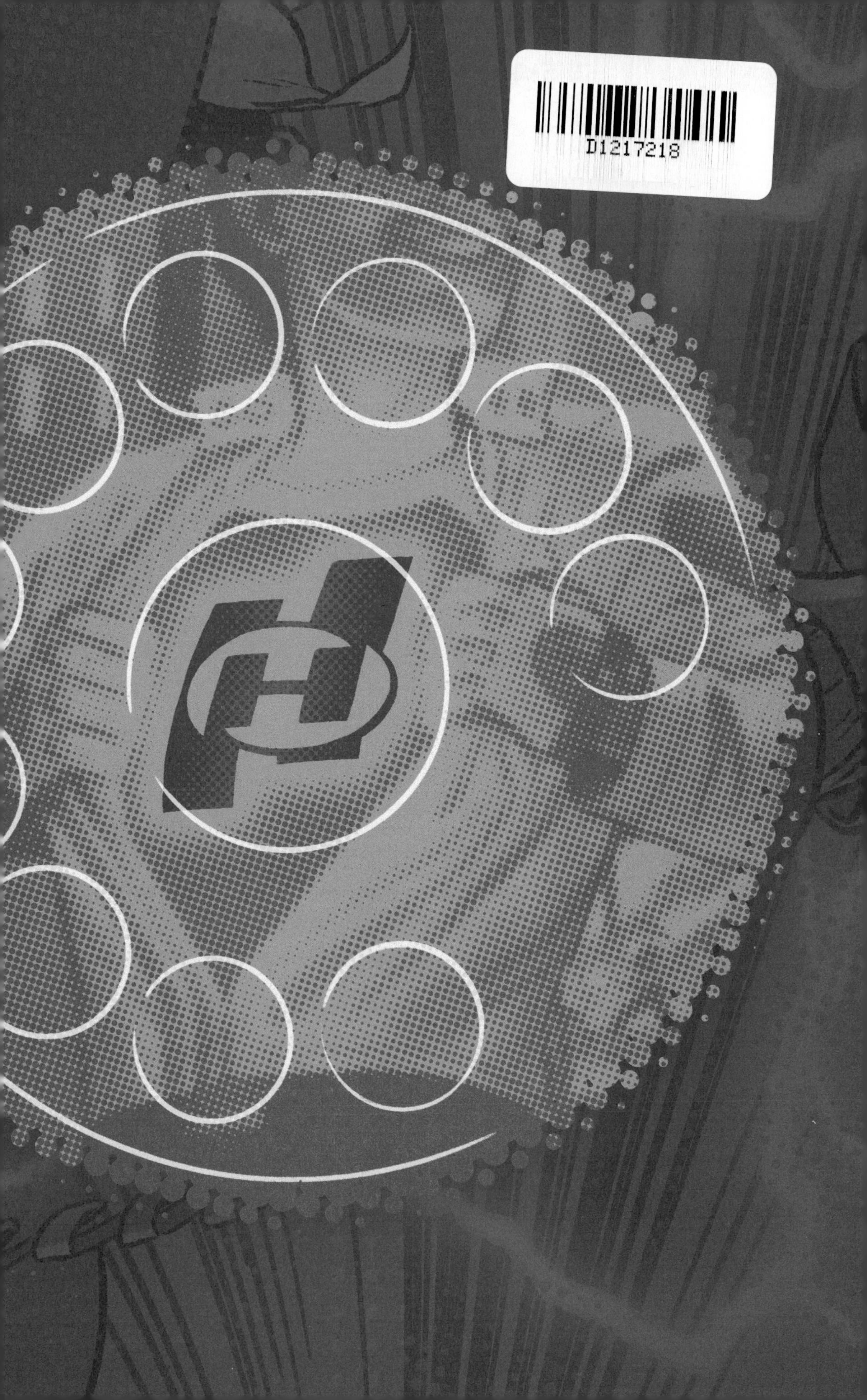

MIKE COTTON
ALEX ANTONE ANDY KHOURI
Editors – Original Series
ANDREA SHEA Assistant Editor – Original Series
JEB WOODARD Group Editor – Collected Editions
SCOTT NYBAKKEN Editor – Collected Edition
STEVE COOK Design Director – Books
CURTIS KING JR. Publication Design
KATE DURRÉ Publication Production

BOB HARRAS Senior VP – Editor-in-Chief, DC Comics
PAT McCALLUM Executive Editor, DC Comics

DAN DiDIO Publisher
JIM LEE Publisher & Chief Creative Officer
BOBBIE CHASE VP – New Publishing Initiatives & Talent Development
DON FALLETTI VP – Manufacturing Operations & Workflow Management
LAWRENCE GANEM VP – Talent Services
ALISON GILL Senior VP – Manufacturing & Operations
HANK KANALZ Senior VP – Publishing Strategy & Support Services
DAN MIRON VP – Publishing Operations
NICK J. NAPOLITANO VP – Manufacturing Administration & Design
NANCY SPEARS VP – Sales
MICHELE R. WELLS VP & Executive Editor, Young Reader

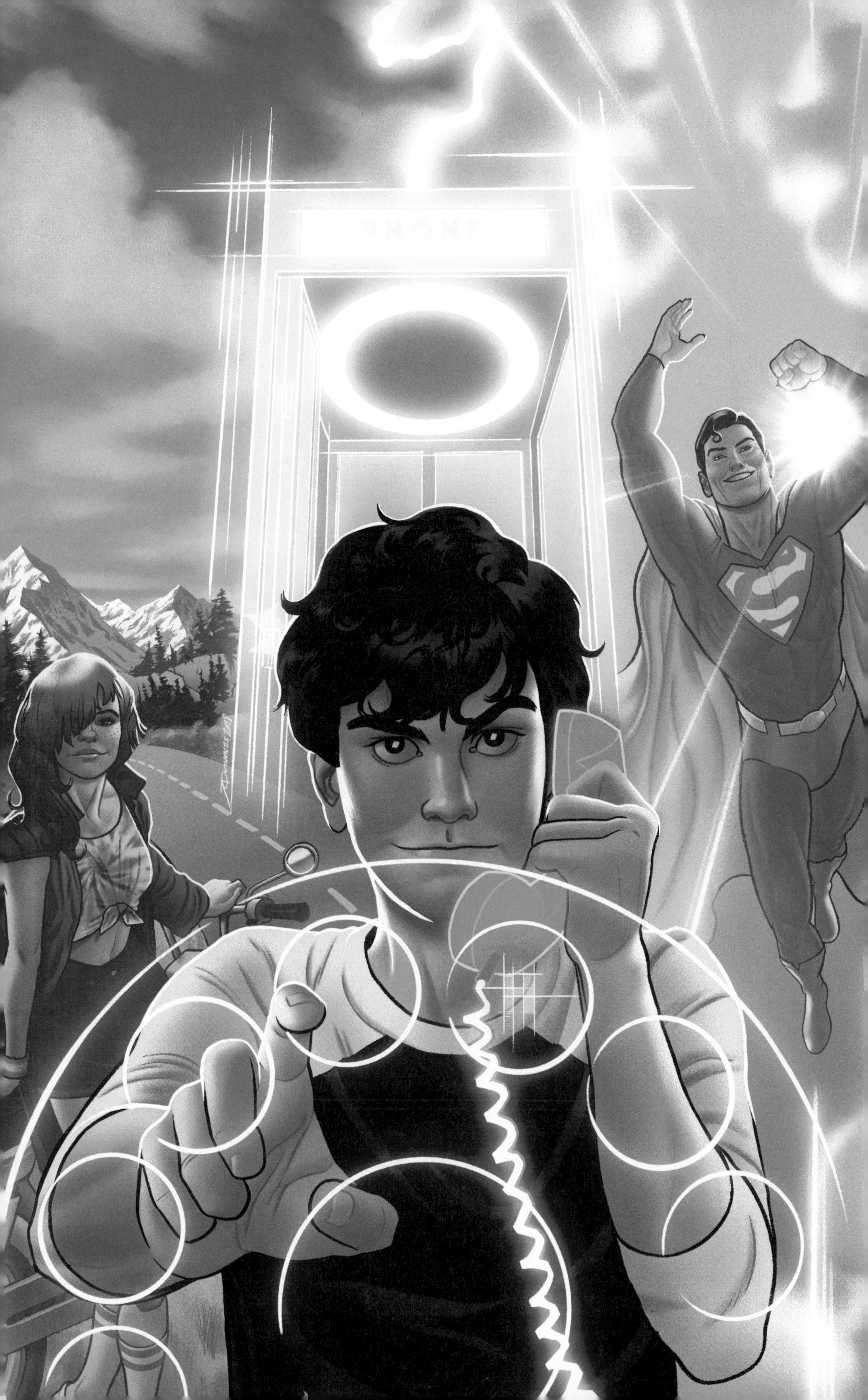
PHON

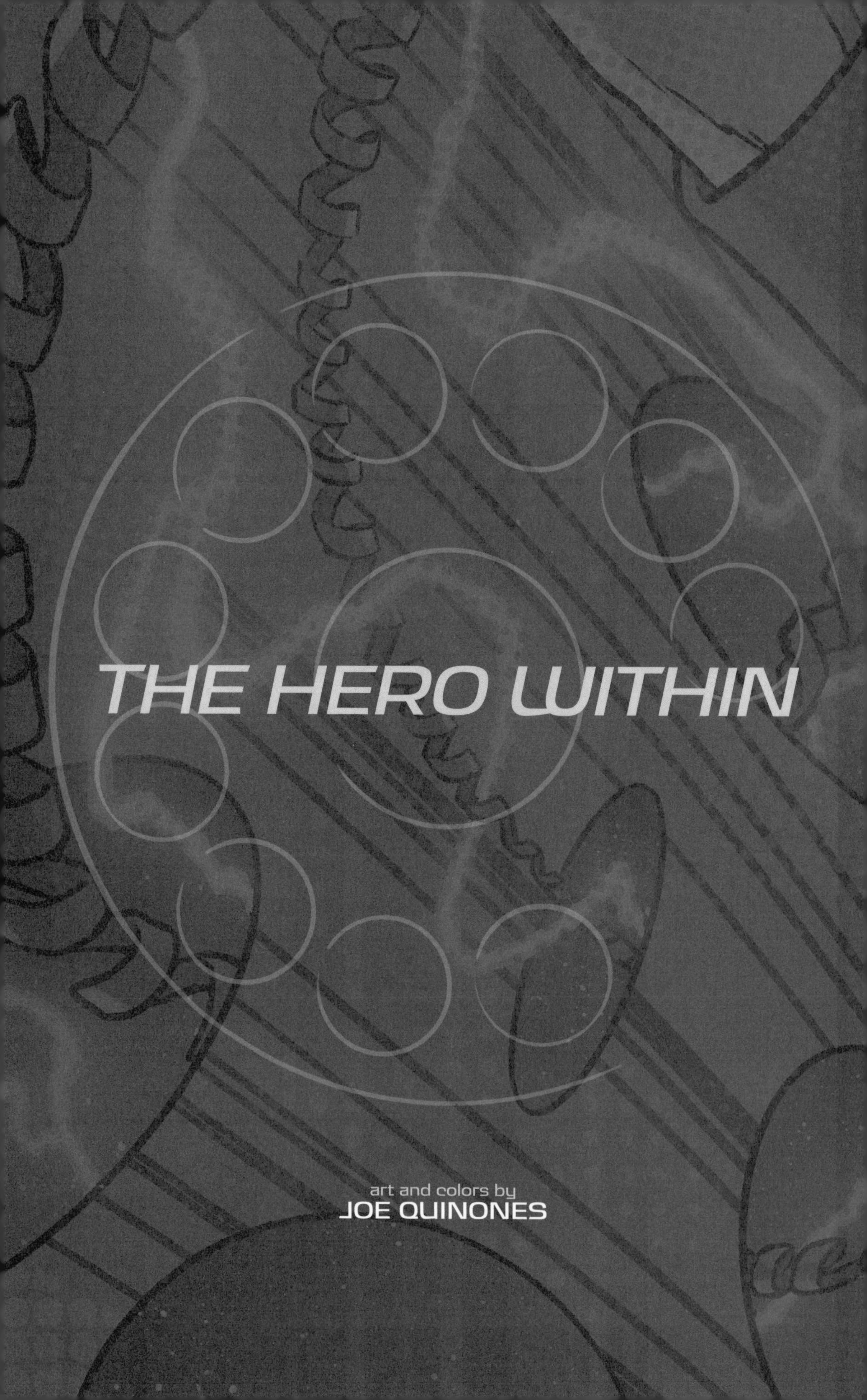

THE HERO WITHIN

art and colors by
JOE QUINONES

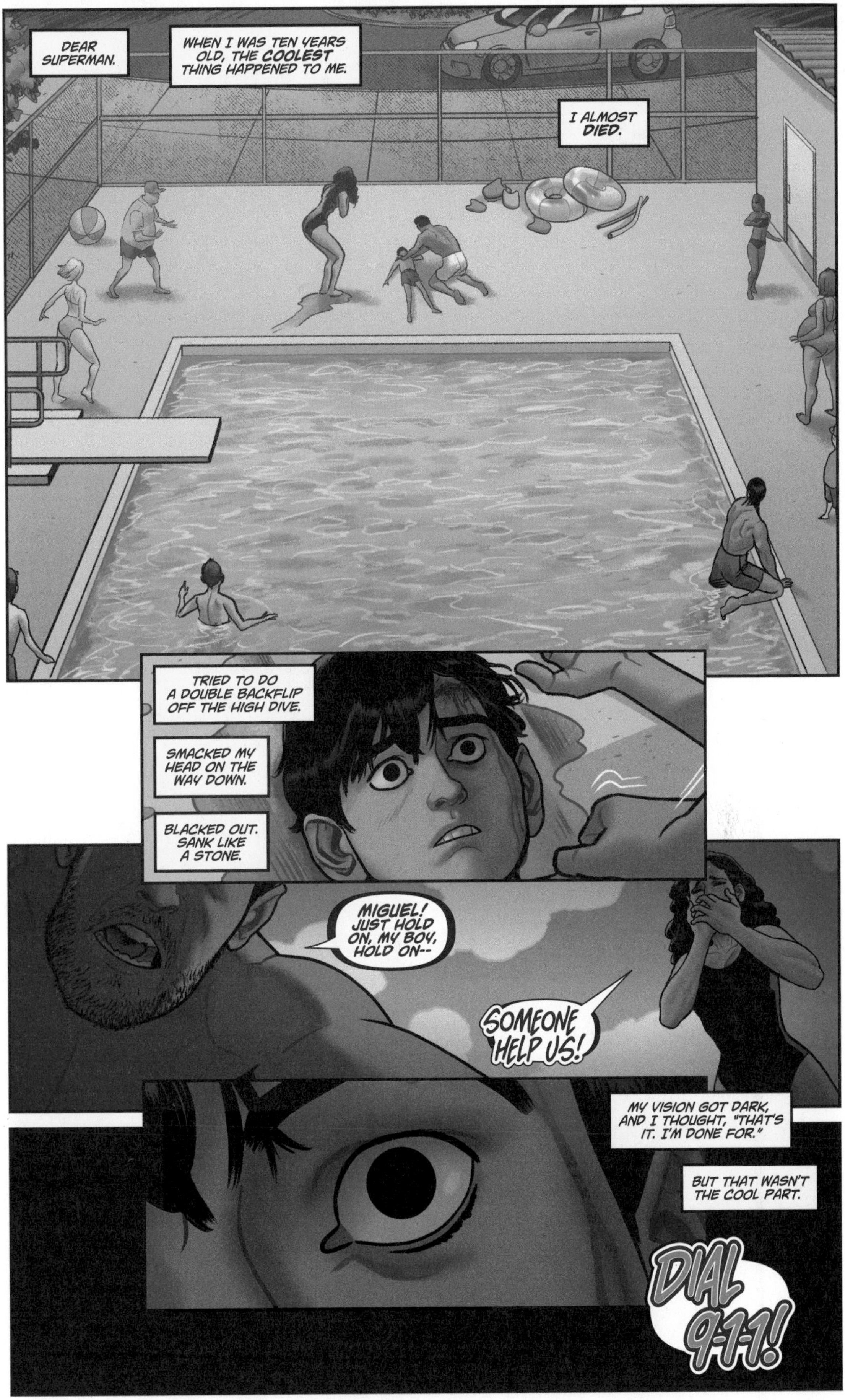
DEAR SUPERMAN.
WHEN I WAS TEN YEARS OLD, THE COOLEST THING HAPPENED TO ME.
I ALMOST DIED.
TRIED TO DO A DOUBLE BACKFLIP OFF THE HIGH DIVE.
SMACKED MY HEAD ON THE WAY DOWN.
BLACKED OUT. SANK LIKE A STONE.
MIGUEL! JUST HOLD ON, MY BOY, HOLD ON--
SOMEONE HELP US!
MY VISION GOT DARK, AND I THOUGHT, "THAT'S IT. I'M DONE FOR."
BUT THAT WASN'T THE COOL PART.
DIAL 9-1-1!

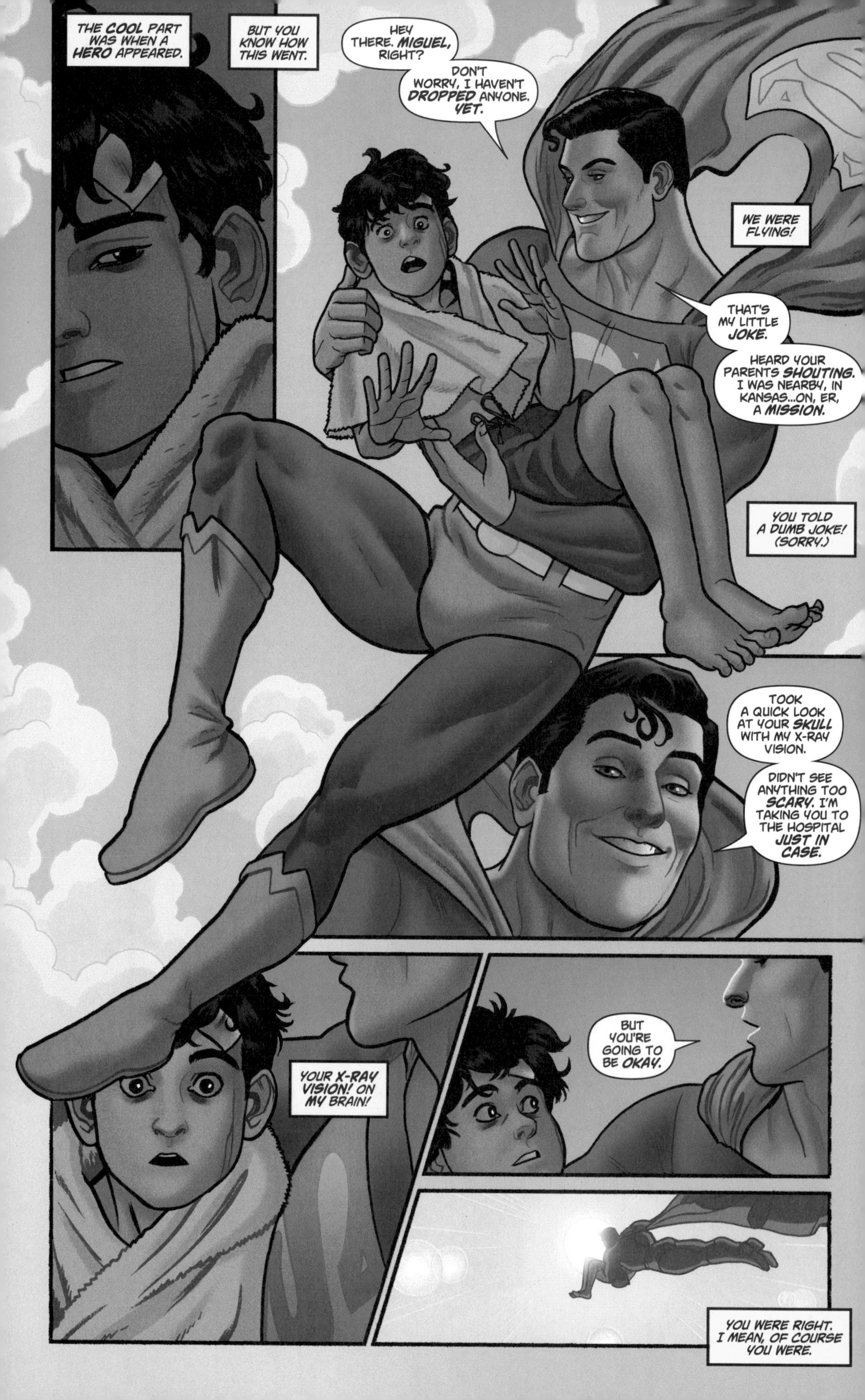
THE COOL PART WAS WHEN A HERO APPEARED.
BUT YOU KNOW HOW THIS WENT.
HEY THERE. MIGUEL, RIGHT?
DON'T WORRY, I HAVEN'T DROPPED ANYONE. YET.
WE WERE FLYING!
THAT'S MY LITTLE JOKE.
HEARD YOUR PARENTS SHOUTING. I WAS NEARBY, IN KANSAS...ON, ER, A MISSION.
YOU TOLD A DUMB JOKE! (SORRY.)
TOOK A QUICK LOOK AT YOUR SKULL WITH MY X-RAY VISION.
DIDN'T SEE ANYTHING TOO SCARY. I'M TAKING YOU TO THE HOSPITAL JUST IN CASE.
YOUR X-RAY VISION! ON MY BRAIN!
BUT YOU'RE GOING TO BE OKAY.
YOU WERE RIGHT. I MEAN, OF COURSE YOU WERE.

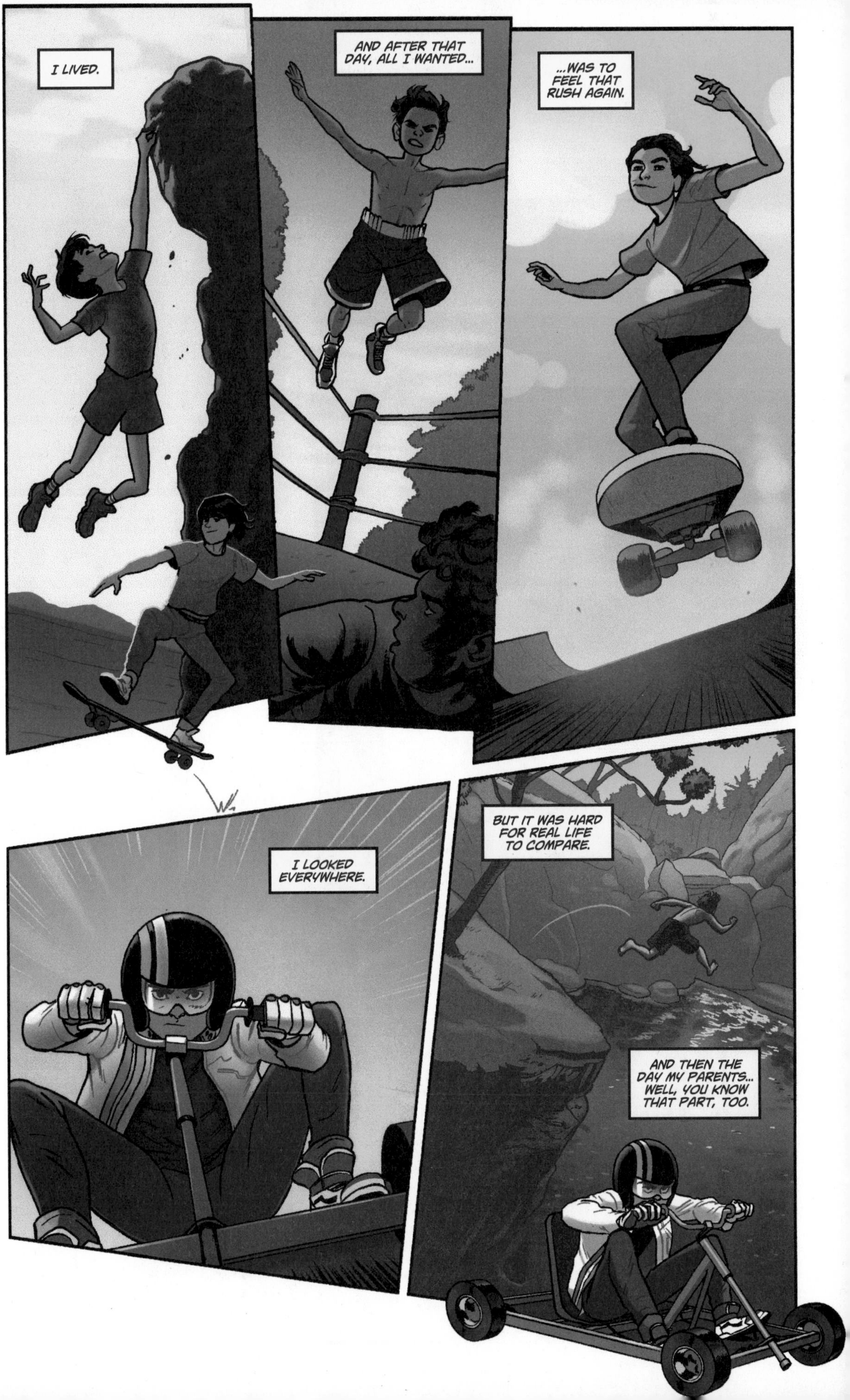
I LIVED.
AND AFTER THAT DAY, ALL I WANTED...
...WAS TO FEEL THAT RUSH AGAIN.
I LOOKED EVERYWHERE.
BUT IT WAS HARD FOR REAL LIFE TO COMPARE.
AND THEN THE DAY MY PARENTS... WELL, YOU KNOW THAT PART, TOO.

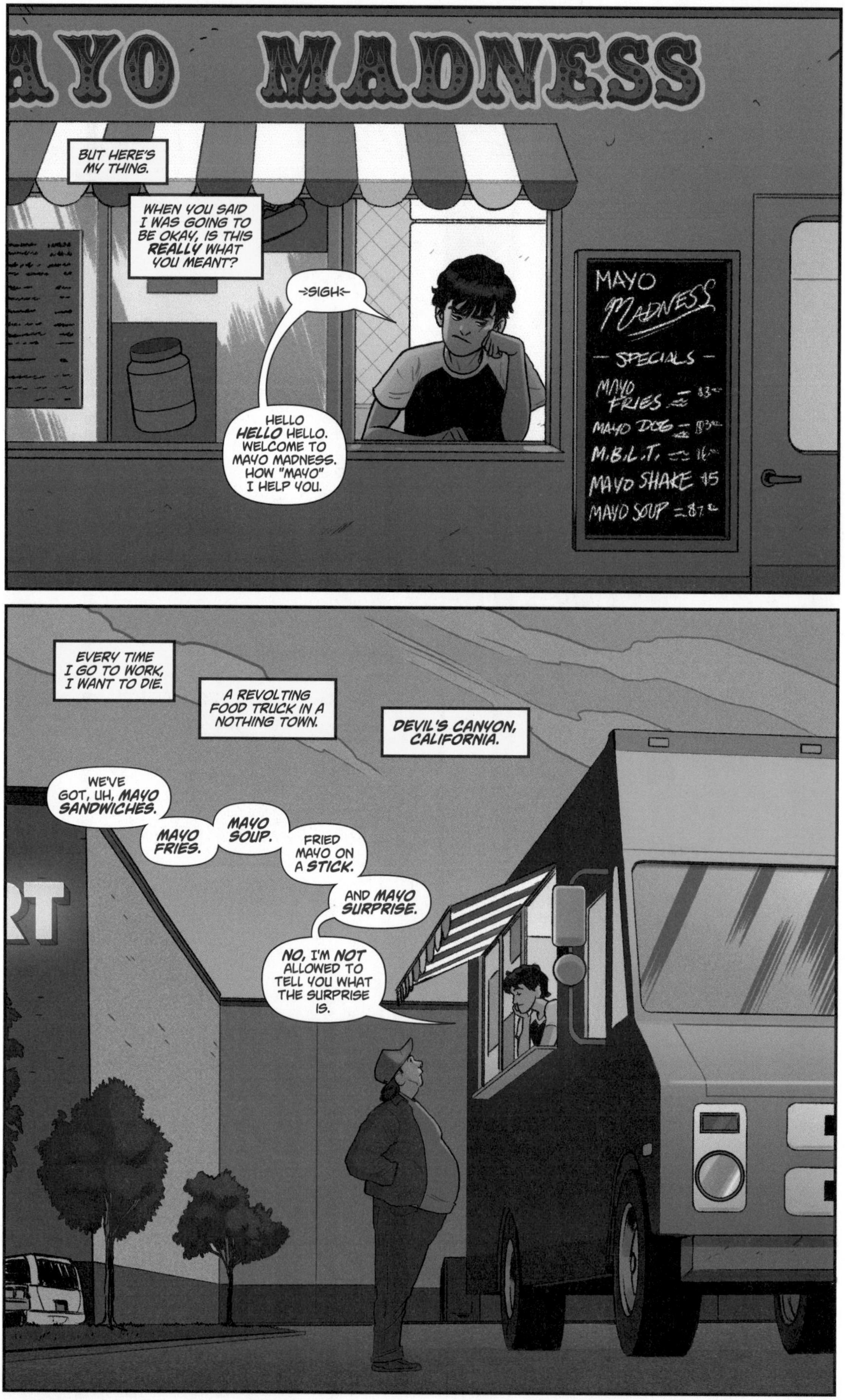
AYO MADNESS
BUT HERE'S MY THING.
WHEN YOU SAID I WAS GOING TO BE OKAY, IS THIS REALLY WHAT YOU MEANT?
SIGH
HELLO HELLO HELLO. WELCOME TO MAYO MADNESS. HOW "MAYO" I HELP YOU.
MAYO MADNESS
— SPECIALS —
MAYO FRIES
MAYO DOG
M.B.L.T.
MAYO SHAKE $15
MAYO SOUP
EVERY TIME I GO TO WORK, I WANT TO DIE.
A REVOLTING FOOD TRUCK IN A NOTHING TOWN.
DEVIL'S CANYON, CALIFORNIA.
WE'VE GOT, UH, MAYO SANDWICHES.
MAYO FRIES.
MAYO SOUP.
FRIED MAYO ON A STICK.
AND MAYO SURPRISE.
NO, I'M NOT ALLOWED TO TELL YOU WHAT THE SURPRISE IS.

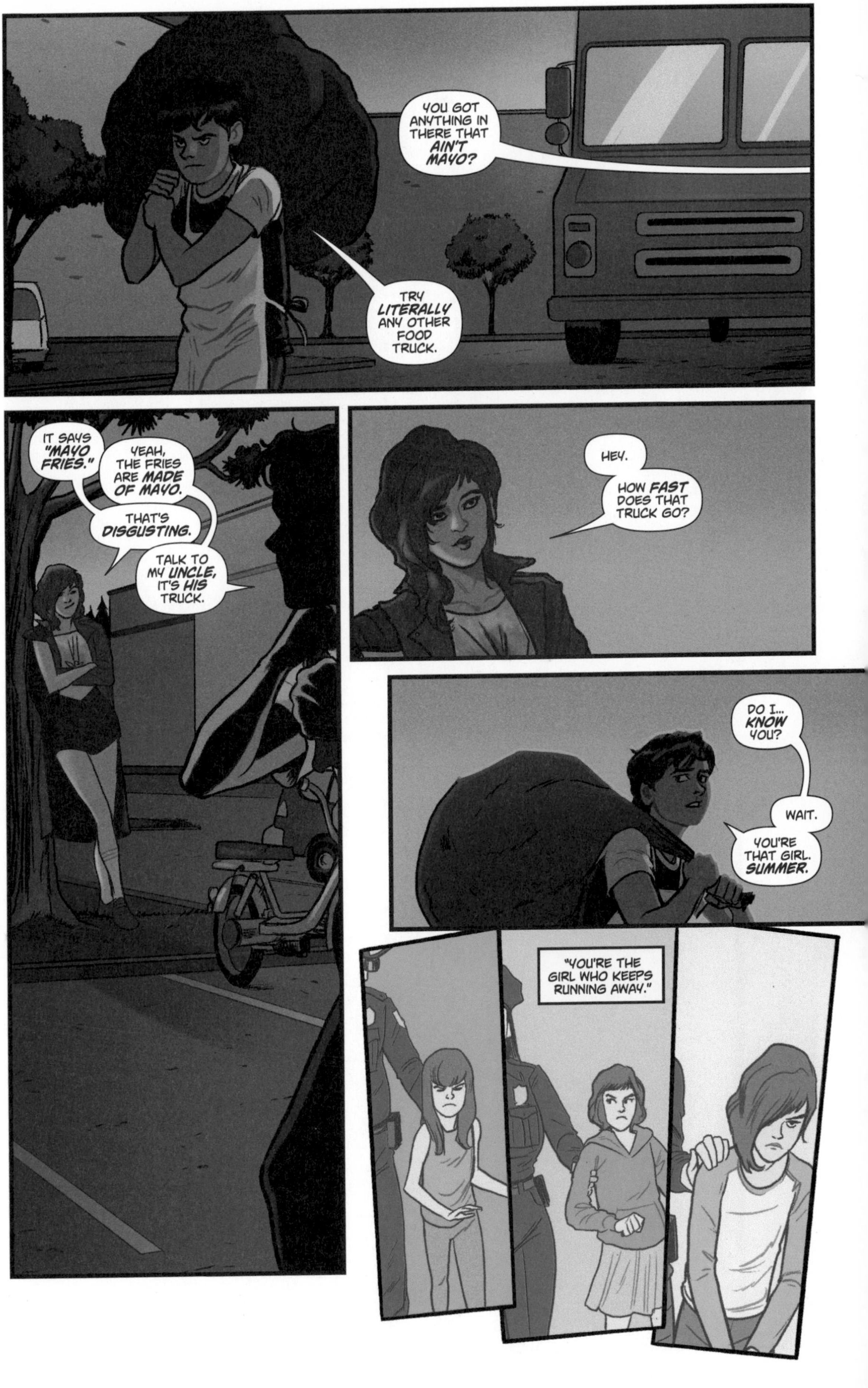
YOU GOT ANYTHING IN THERE THAT AIN'T MAYO?
TRY LITERALLY ANY OTHER FOOD TRUCK.
IT SAYS "MAYO FRIES."
YEAH, THE FRIES ARE MADE OF MAYO.
THAT'S DISGUSTING.
TALK TO MY UNCLE, IT'S HIS TRUCK.
HEY.
HOW FAST DOES THAT TRUCK GO?
DO I... KNOW YOU?
WAIT.
YOU'RE THAT GIRL. SUMMER.
"YOU'RE THE GIRL WHO KEEPS RUNNING AWAY."

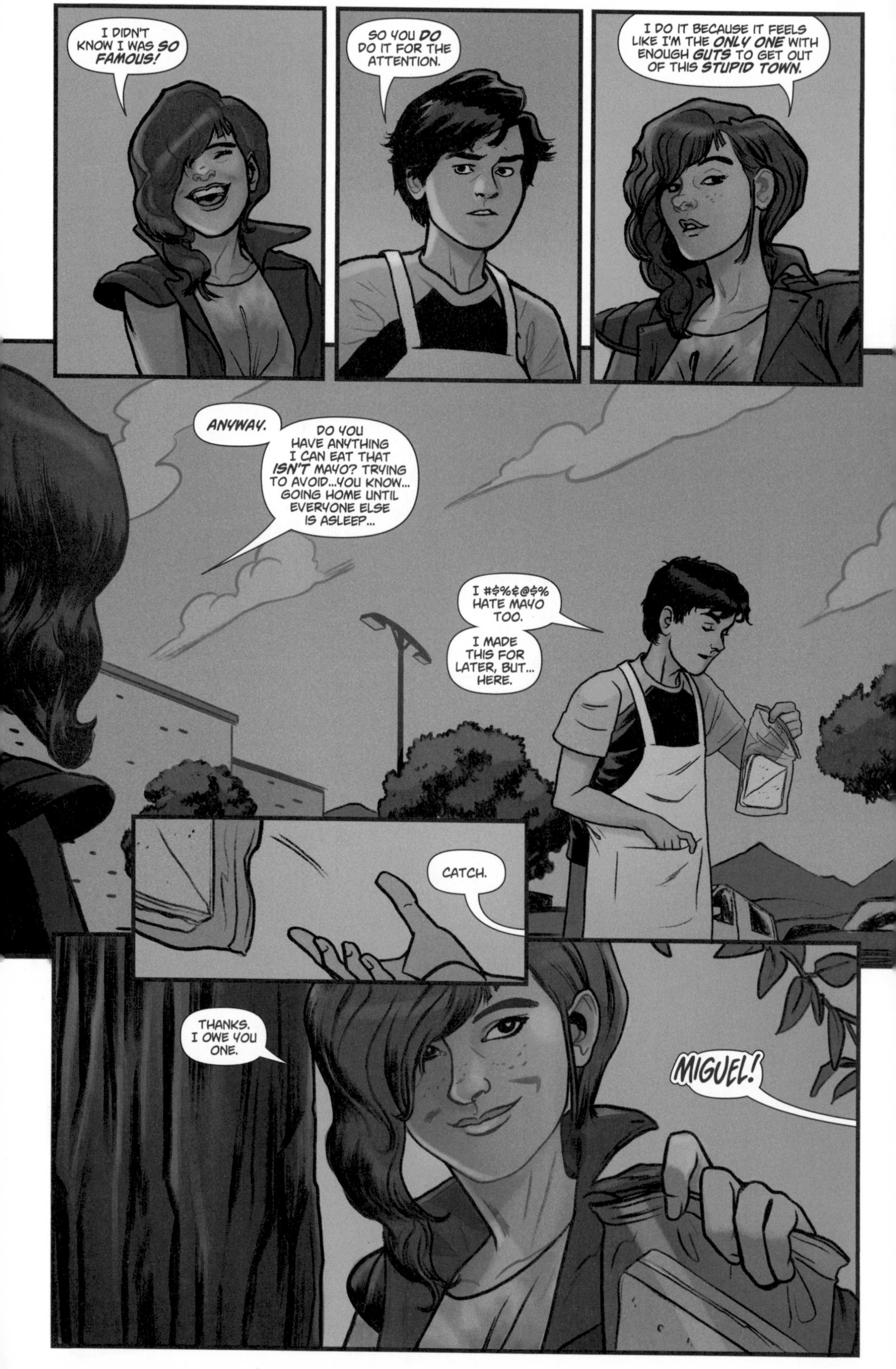
I DIDN'T KNOW I WAS SO FAMOUS!
SO YOU DO DO IT FOR THE ATTENTION.
I DO IT BECAUSE IT FEELS LIKE I'M THE ONLY ONE WITH ENOUGH GUTS TO GET OUT OF THIS STUPID TOWN.
ANYWAY.
DO YOU HAVE ANYTHING I CAN EAT THAT ISN'T MAYO? TRYING TO AVOID...YOU KNOW... GOING HOME UNTIL EVERYONE ELSE IS ASLEEP...
I #$%$@$% HATE MAYO TOO.
I MADE THIS FOR LATER, BUT... HERE.
CATCH.
THANKS. I OWE YOU ONE.
MIGUEL!

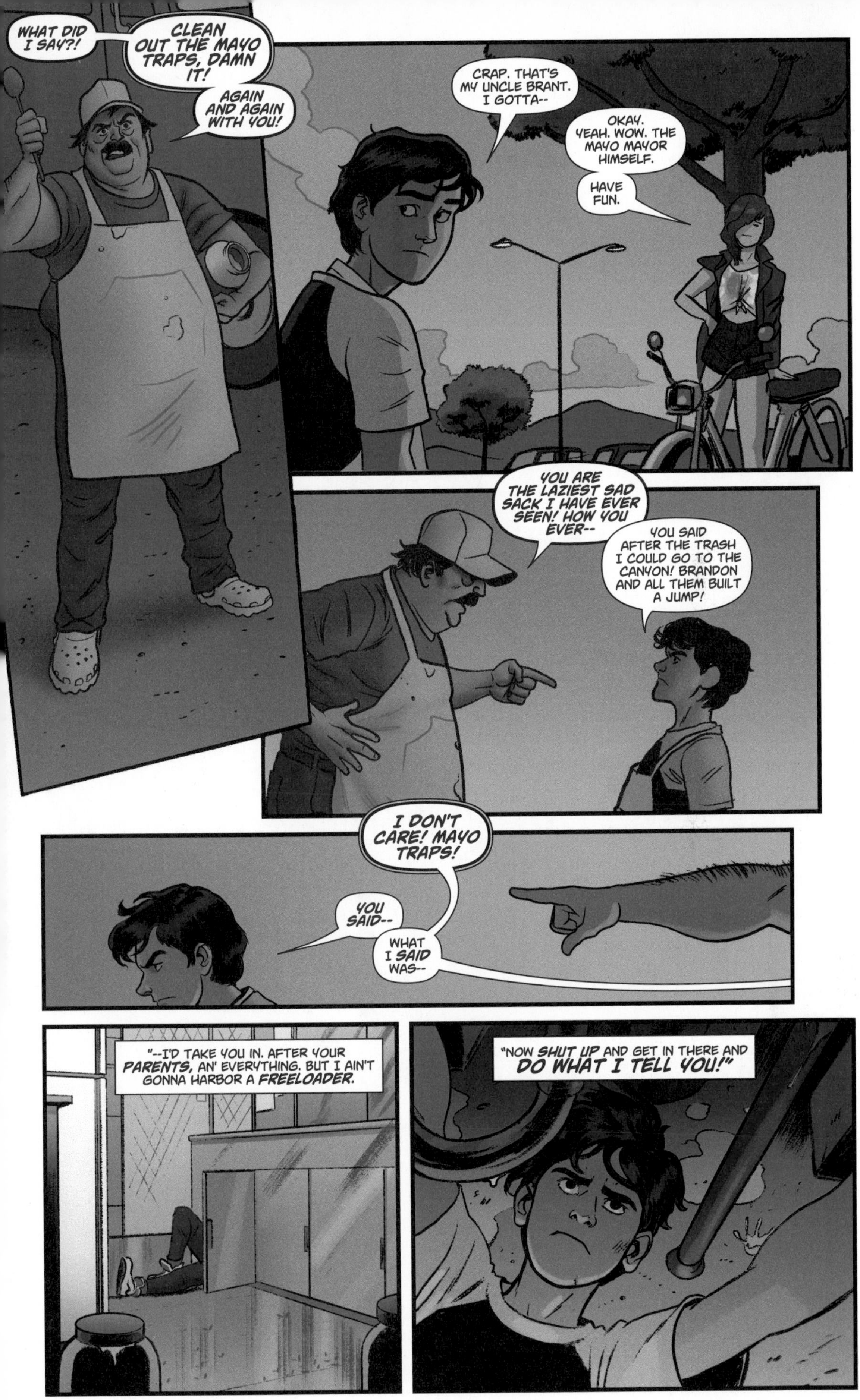
WHAT DID I SAY?!
CLEAN OUT THE MAYO TRAPS, DAMN IT!
AGAIN AND AGAIN WITH YOU!
CRAP. THAT'S MY UNCLE BRANT. I GOTTA--
OKAY. YEAH. WOW. THE MAYO MAYOR HIMSELF.
HAVE FUN.
YOU ARE THE LAZIEST SAD SACK I HAVE EVER SEEN! HOW YOU EVER--
YOU SAID AFTER THE TRASH I COULD GO TO THE CANYON! BRANDON AND ALL THEM BUILT A JUMP!
I DON'T CARE! MAYO TRAPS!
YOU SAID--
WHAT I SAID WAS--
"--I'D TAKE YOU IN. AFTER YOUR PARENTS, AN' EVERYTHING. BUT I AIN'T GONNA HARBOR A FREELOADER.
"NOW SHUT UP AND GET IN THERE AND DO WHAT I TELL YOU!"

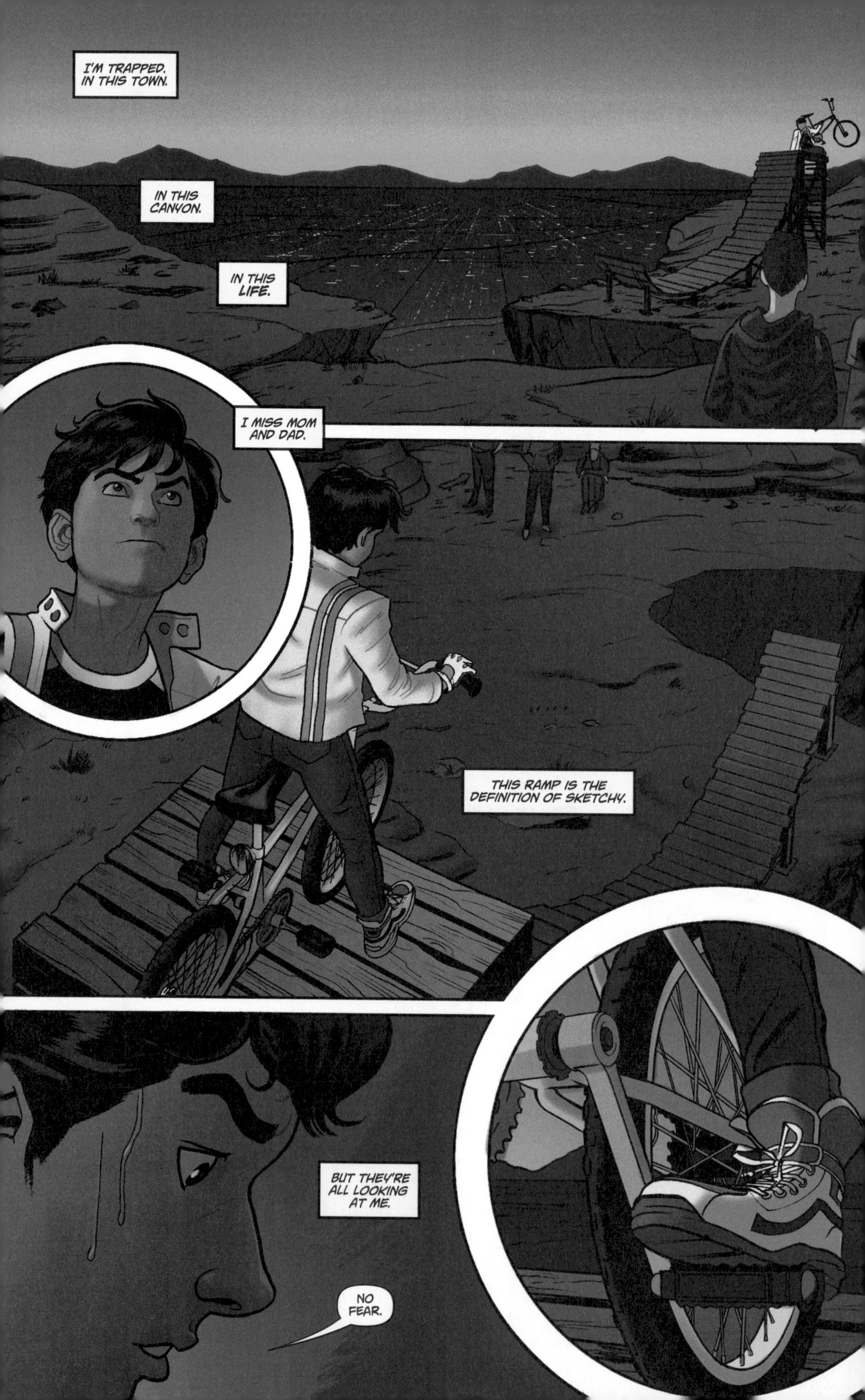
I'M TRAPPED. IN THIS TOWN.
IN THIS CANYON.
IN THIS LIFE.
I MISS MOM AND DAD.
THIS RAMP IS THE DEFINITION OF SKETCHY.
BUT THEY'RE ALL LOOKING AT ME.
NO FEAR.

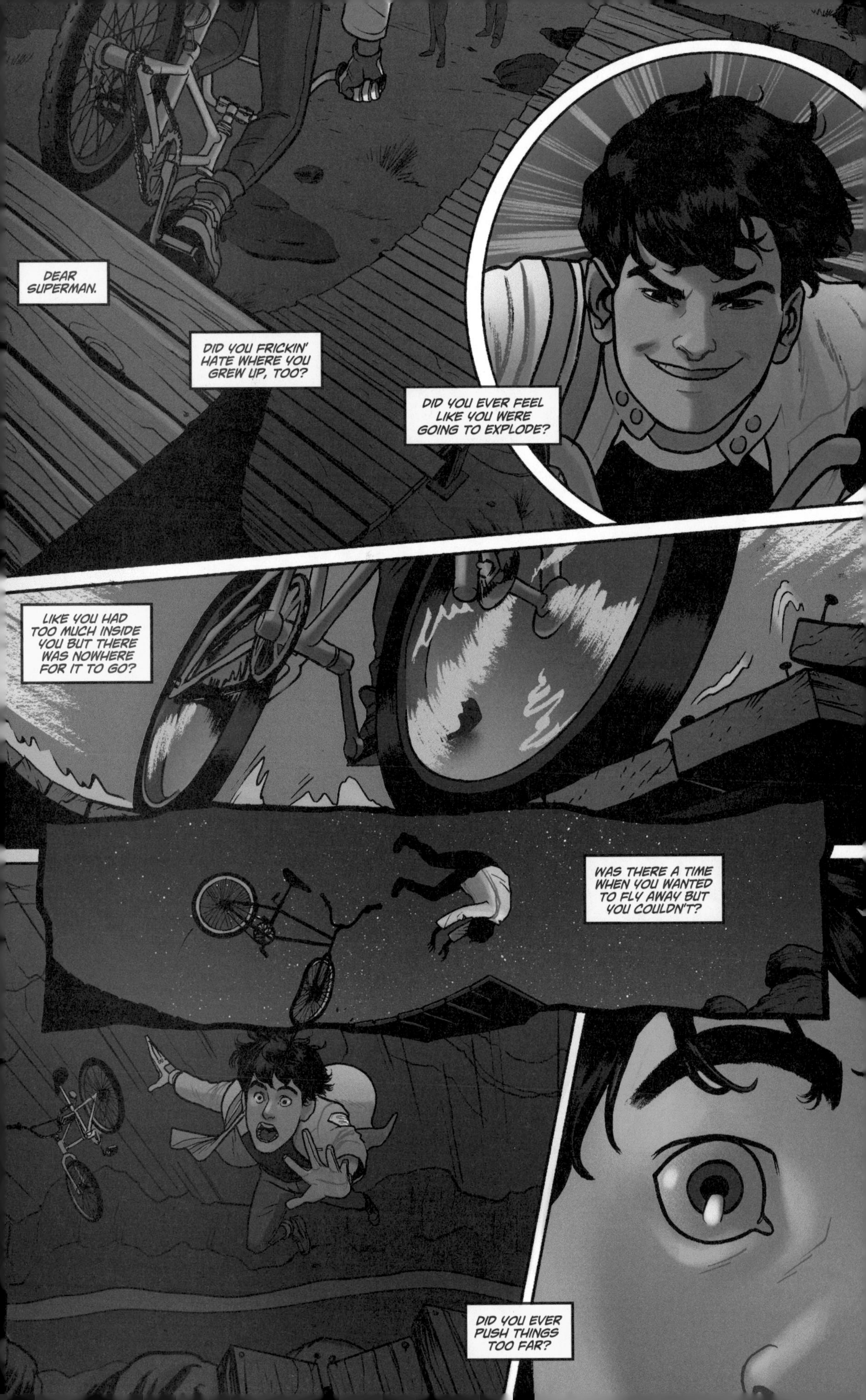
DEAR SUPERMAN.
DID YOU FRICKIN' HATE WHERE YOU GREW UP, TOO?
DID YOU EVER FEEL LIKE YOU WERE GOING TO EXPLODE?
LIKE YOU HAD TOO MUCH INSIDE YOU BUT THERE WAS NOWHERE FOR IT TO GO?
WAS THERE A TIME WHEN YOU WANTED TO FLY AWAY BUT YOU COULDN'T?
DID YOU EVER PUSH THINGS TOO FAR?

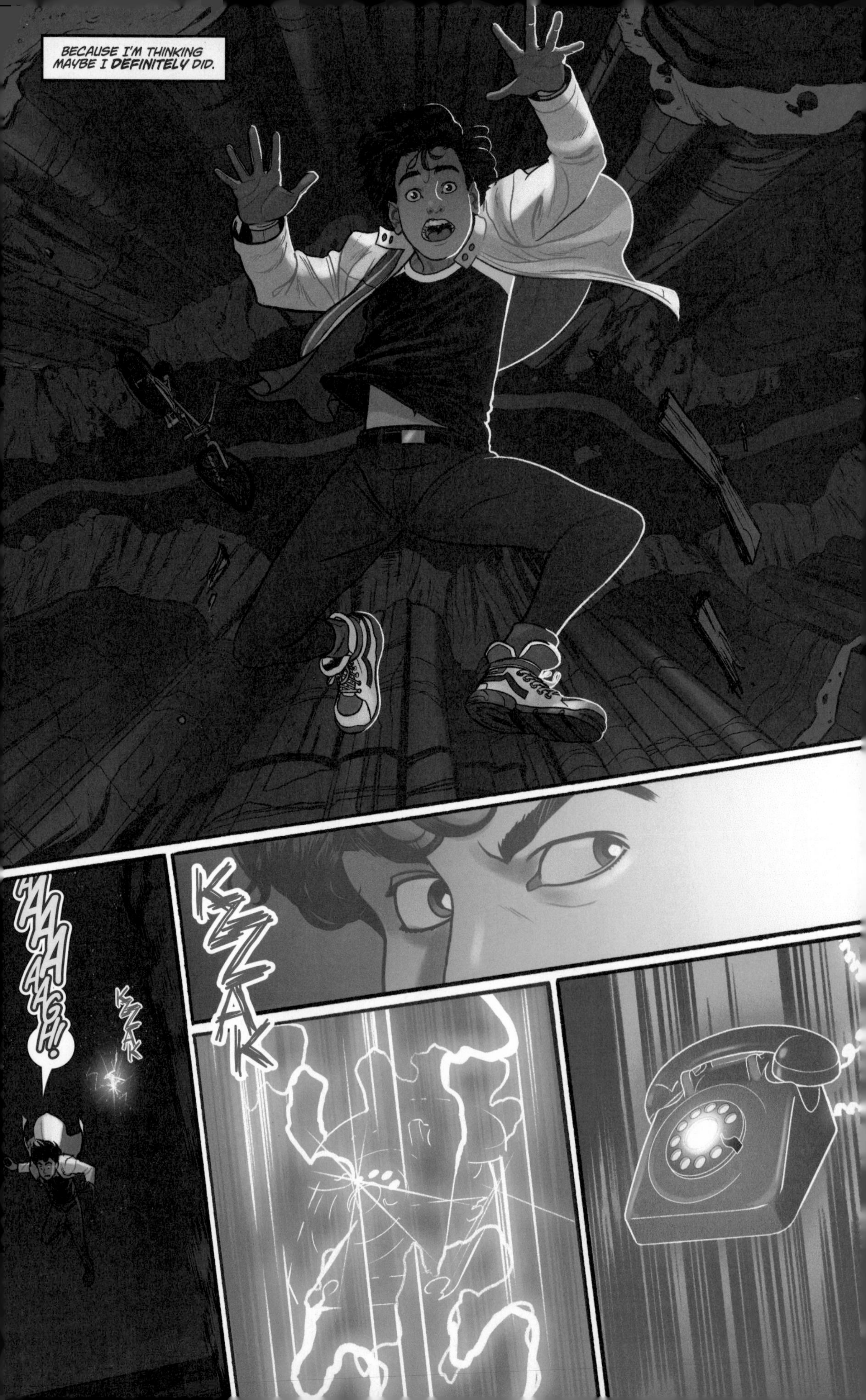
BECAUSE I'M THINKING MAYBE I DEFINITELY DID.
AAAAAGH!
KZZAK
KZZZAK

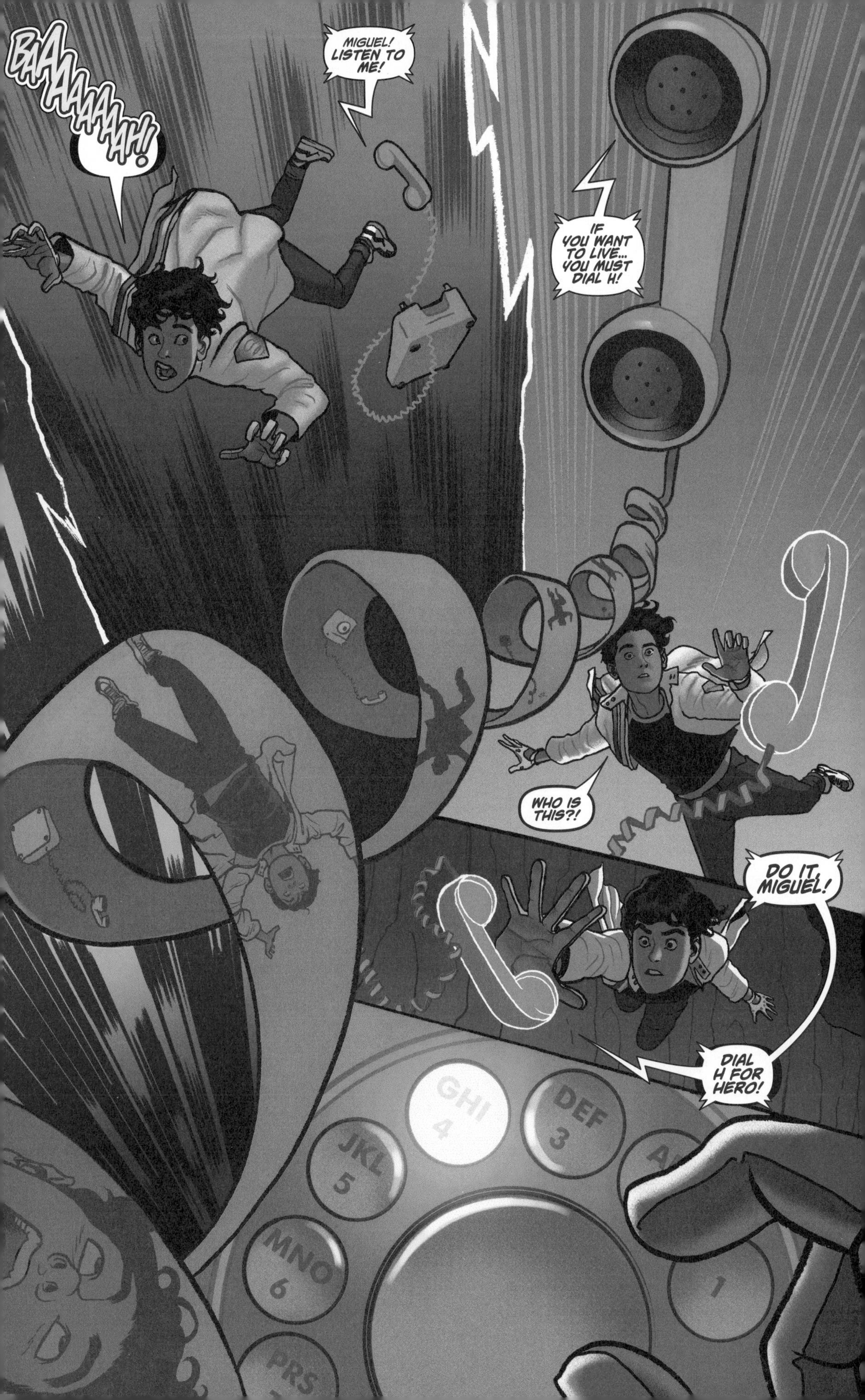
BAAAAAAAAAH!
MIGUEL! LISTEN TO ME!
IF YOU WANT TO LIVE... YOU MUST DIAL H!
WHO IS THIS?!
DO IT, MIGUEL!
DIAL H FOR HERO!
GHI 4
DEF 3
JKL 5
MNO 6
1
PRS

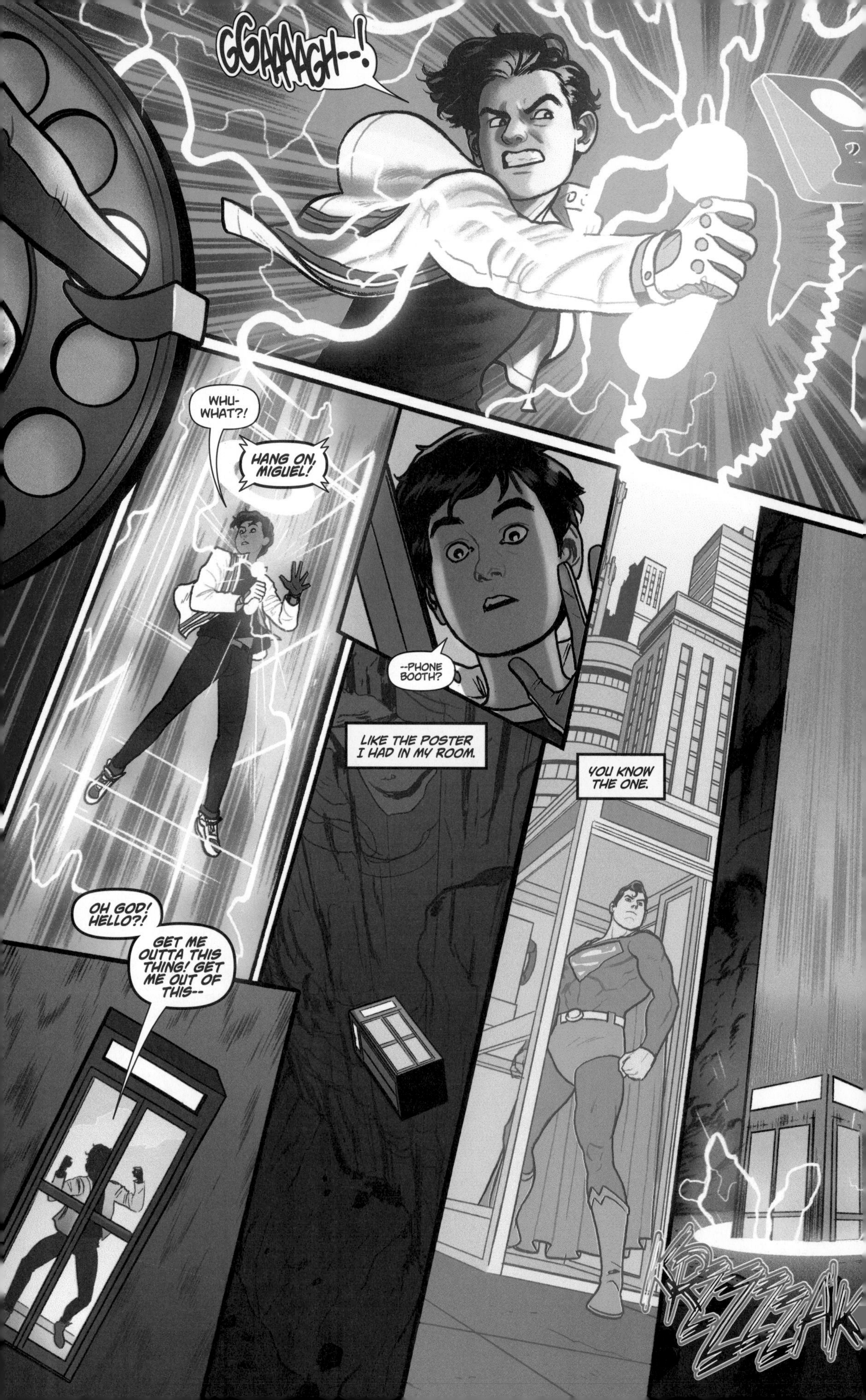
GGAAAAGH--!
WHU-WHAT?!
HANG ON, MIGUEL!
--PHONE BOOTH?
LIKE THE POSTER I HAD IN MY ROOM.
YOU KNOW THE ONE.
OH GOD! HELLO?!
GET ME OUTTA THIS THING! GET ME OUT OF THIS--

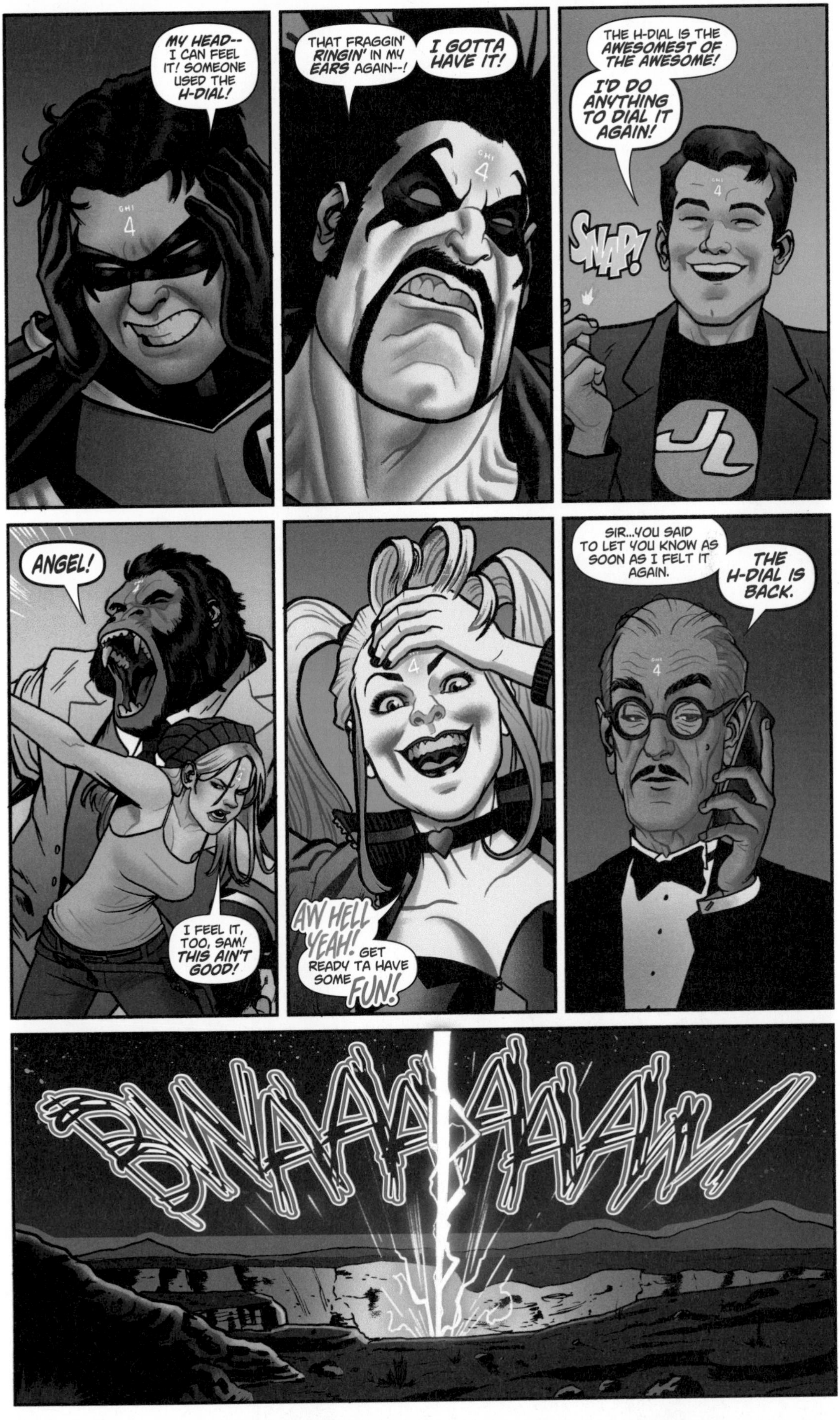
MY HEAD-- I CAN FEEL IT! SOMEONE USED THE H-DIAL!
THAT FRAGGIN' RINGIN' IN MY EARS AGAIN--!
I GOTTA HAVE IT!
THE H-DIAL IS THE AWESOMEST OF THE AWESOME!
I'D DO ANYTHING TO DIAL IT AGAIN!
SNAP!
ANGEL!
I FEEL IT, TOO, SAM! THIS AIN'T GOOD!
AW HELL YEAH! GET READY TA HAVE SOME FUN!
SIR...YOU SAID TO LET YOU KNOW AS SOON AS I FELT IT AGAIN.
THE H-DIAL IS BACK.

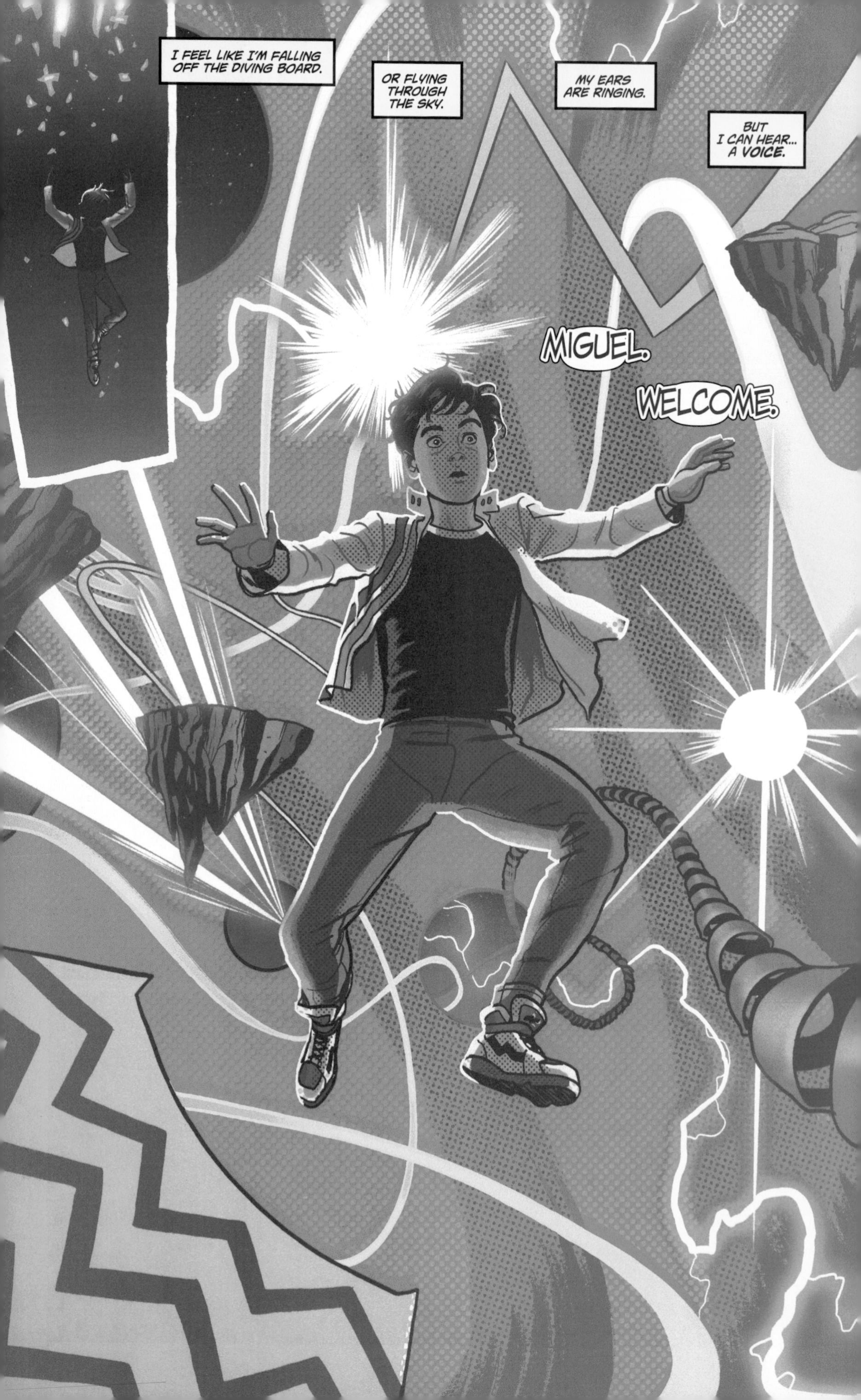
I FEEL LIKE I'M FALLING OFF THE DIVING BOARD.
OR FLYING THROUGH THE SKY.
MY EARS ARE RINGING.
BUT I CAN HEAR... A VOICE.
MIGUEL.
WELCOME.

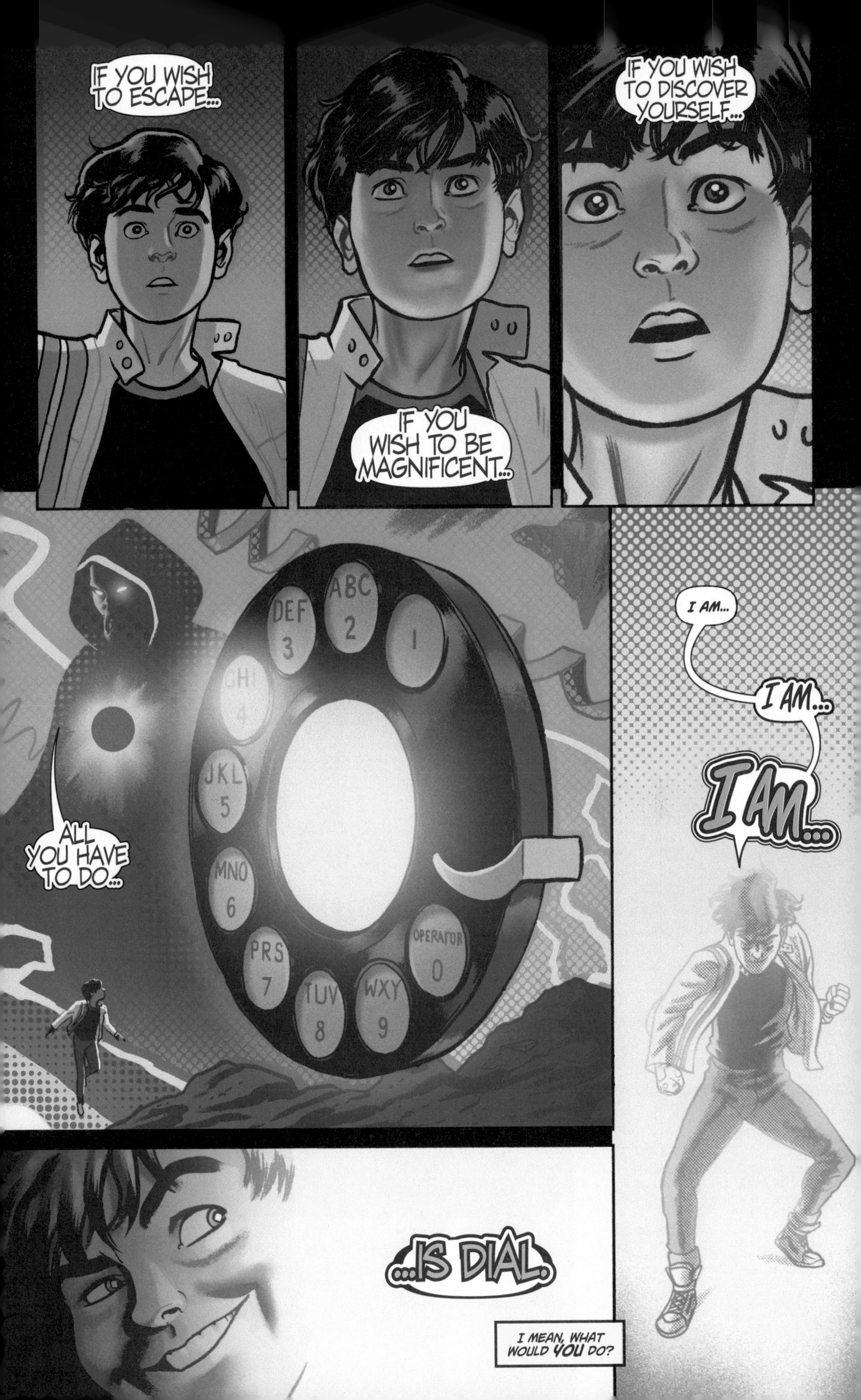
IF YOU WISH TO ESCAPE...
IF YOU WISH TO BE MAGNIFICENT...
IF YOU WISH TO DISCOVER YOURSELF...
ALL YOU HAVE TO DO...
ABC 2
DEF 3
GHI 4
JKL 5
MNO 6
PRS 7
TUV 8
WXY 9
OPERATOR 0
1
I AM...
I AM...
I AM...
...IS DIAL.
I MEAN, WHAT WOULD YOU DO?

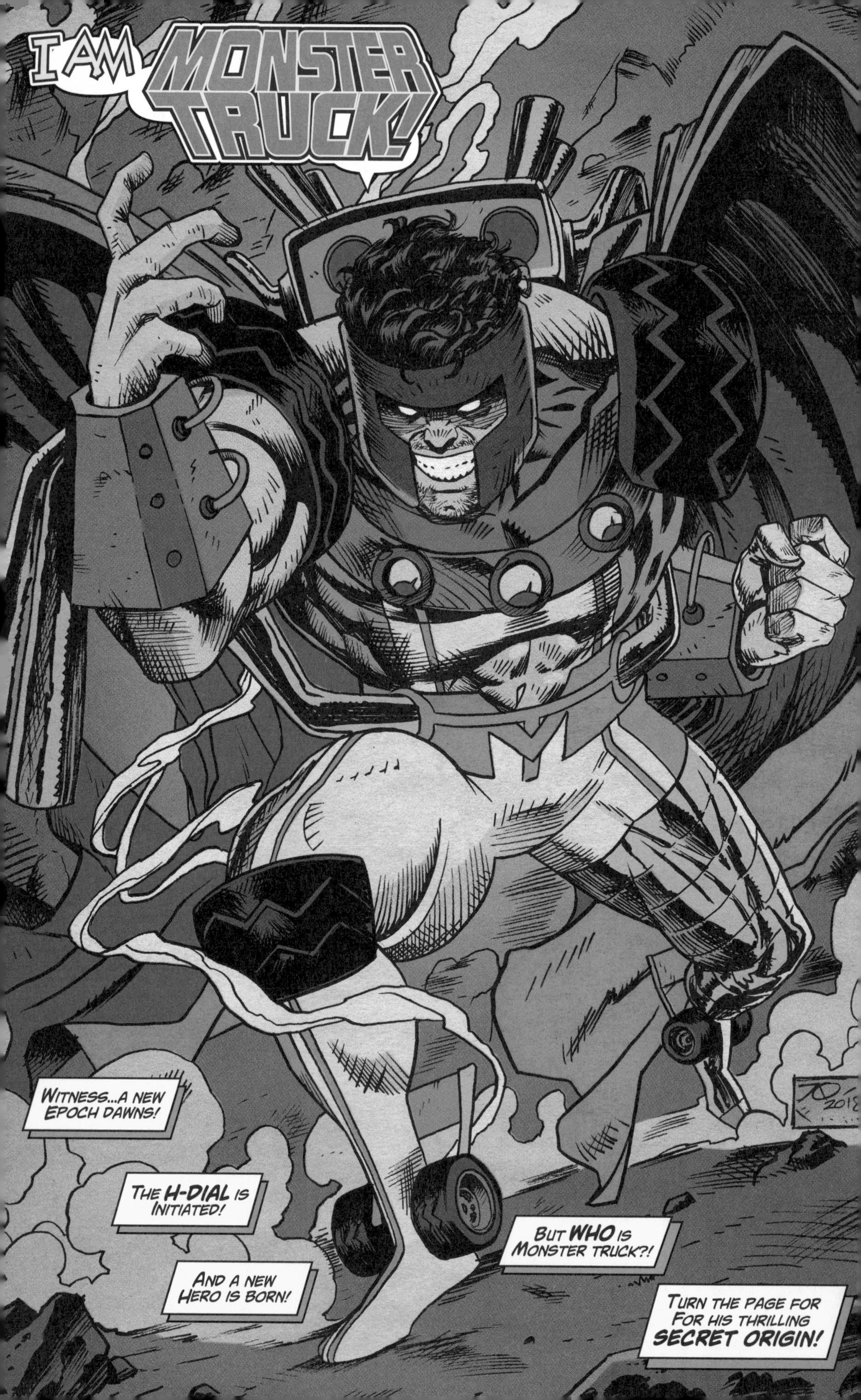
I AM MONSTER TRUCK!
WITNESS...A NEW EPOCH DAWNS!
THE H-DIAL IS INITIATED!
AND A NEW HERO IS BORN!
BUT WHO IS MONSTER TRUCK?!
TURN THE PAGE FOR FOR HIS THRILLING SECRET ORIGIN!

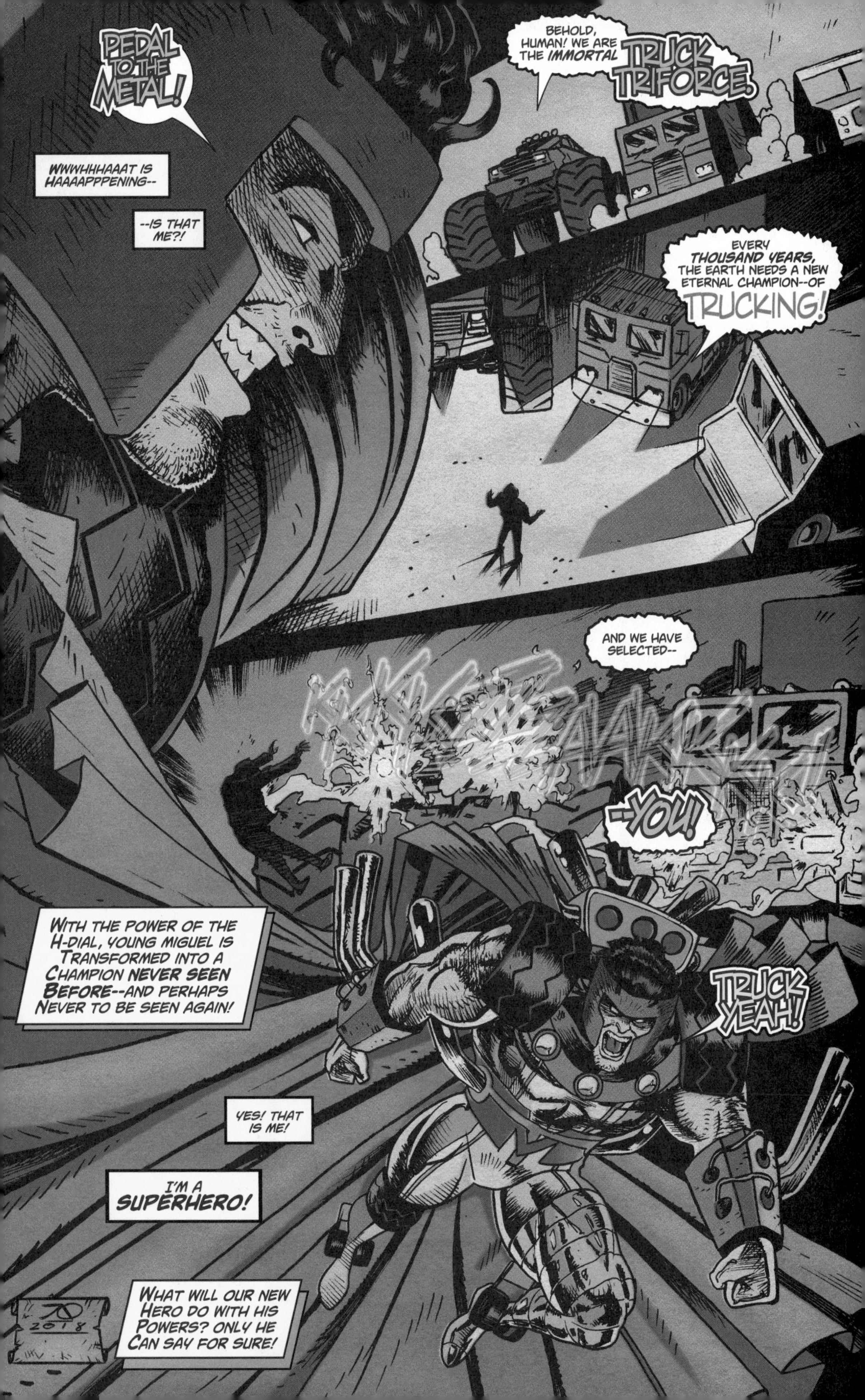

PEDAL TO THE METAL!
BEHOLD, HUMAN! WE ARE THE IMMORTAL TRUCK TRIFORCE.
WWWHHHAAAT IS HAAAAPPPENING--
--IS THAT ME?!
EVERY THOUSAND YEARS, THE EARTH NEEDS A NEW ETERNAL CHAMPION--OF TRUCKING!
AND WE HAVE SELECTED--
--YOU!
WITH THE POWER OF THE H-DIAL, YOUNG MIGUEL IS TRANSFORMED INTO A CHAMPION NEVER SEEN BEFORE--AND PERHAPS NEVER TO BE SEEN AGAIN!
TRUCK YEAH!
YES! THAT IS ME!
I'M A SUPERHERO!
WHAT WILL OUR NEW HERO DO WITH HIS POWERS? ONLY HE CAN SAY FOR SURE!
2018

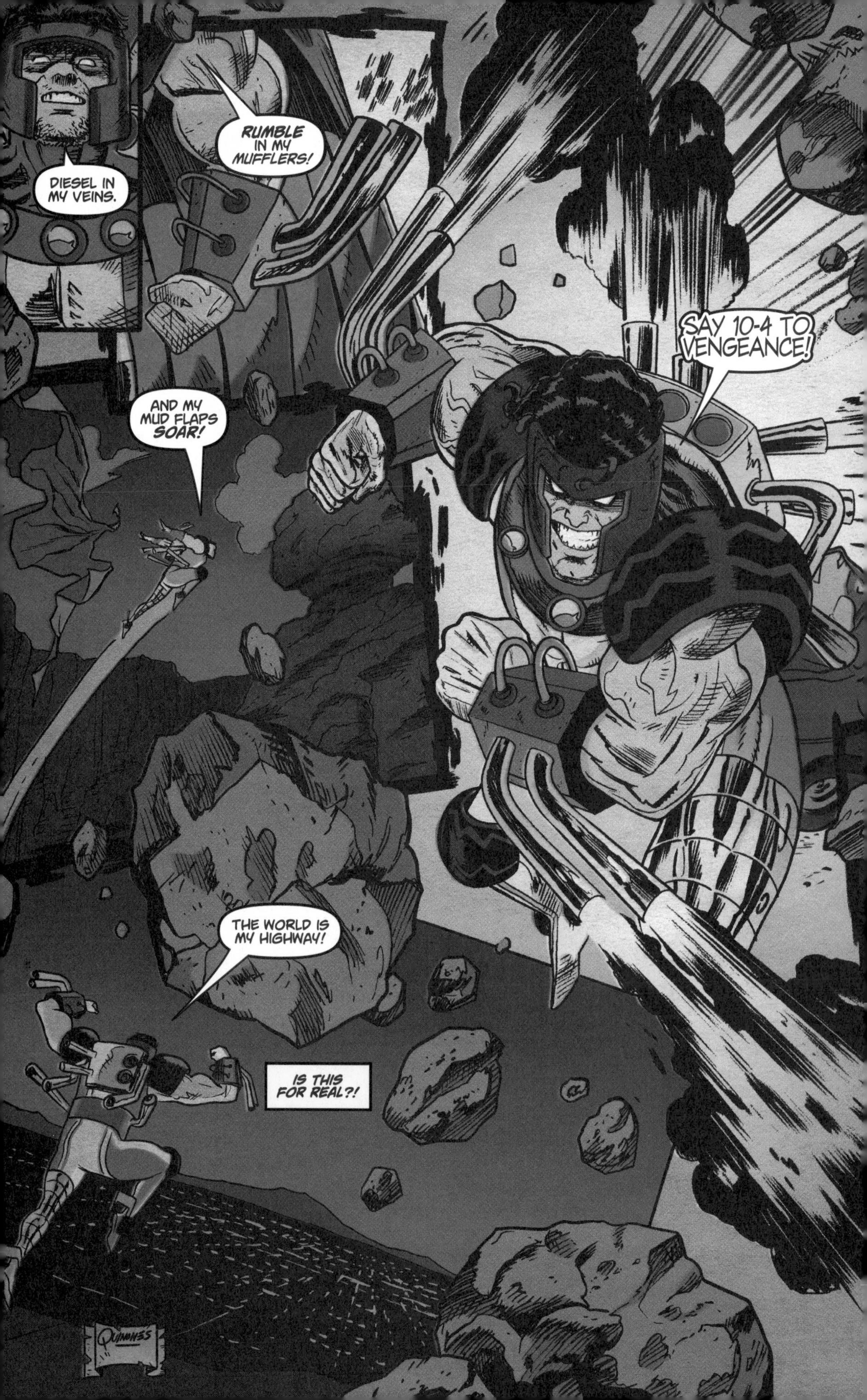
DIESEL IN MY VEINS.
RUMBLE IN MY MUFFLERS!
SAY 10-4 TO VENGEANCE!
AND MY MUD FLAPS SOAR!
THE WORLD IS MY HIGHWAY!
IS THIS FOR REAL?!
QUINONES

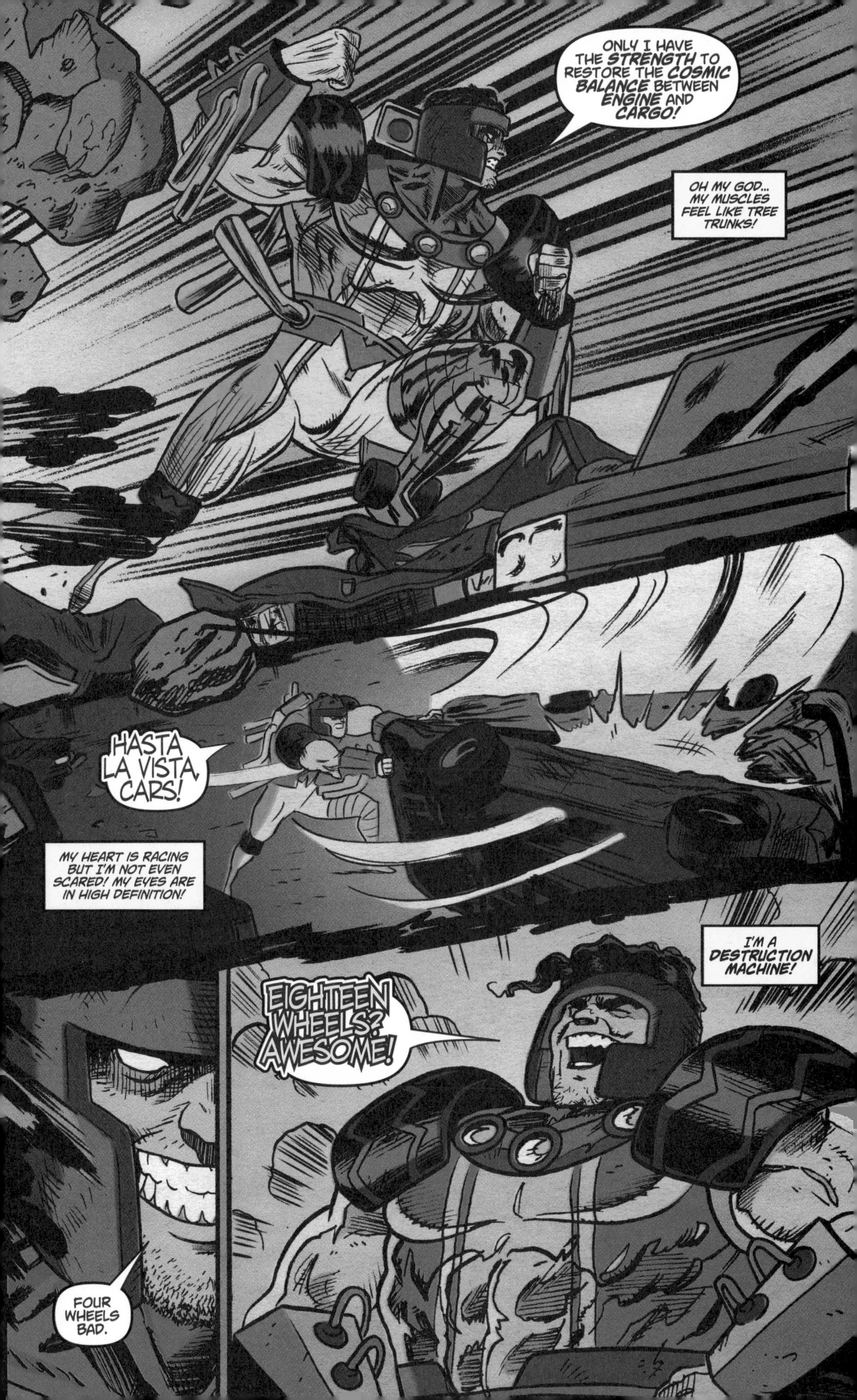
ONLY I HAVE THE STRENGTH TO RESTORE THE COSMIC BALANCE BETWEEN ENGINE AND CARGO!
OH MY GOD... MY MUSCLES FEEL LIKE TREE TRUNKS!
HASTA LA VISTA, CARS!
MY HEART IS RACING BUT I'M NOT EVEN SCARED! MY EYES ARE IN HIGH DEFINITION!
I'M A DESTRUCTION MACHINE!
EIGHTEEN WHEELS? AWESOME!
FOUR WHEELS BAD.

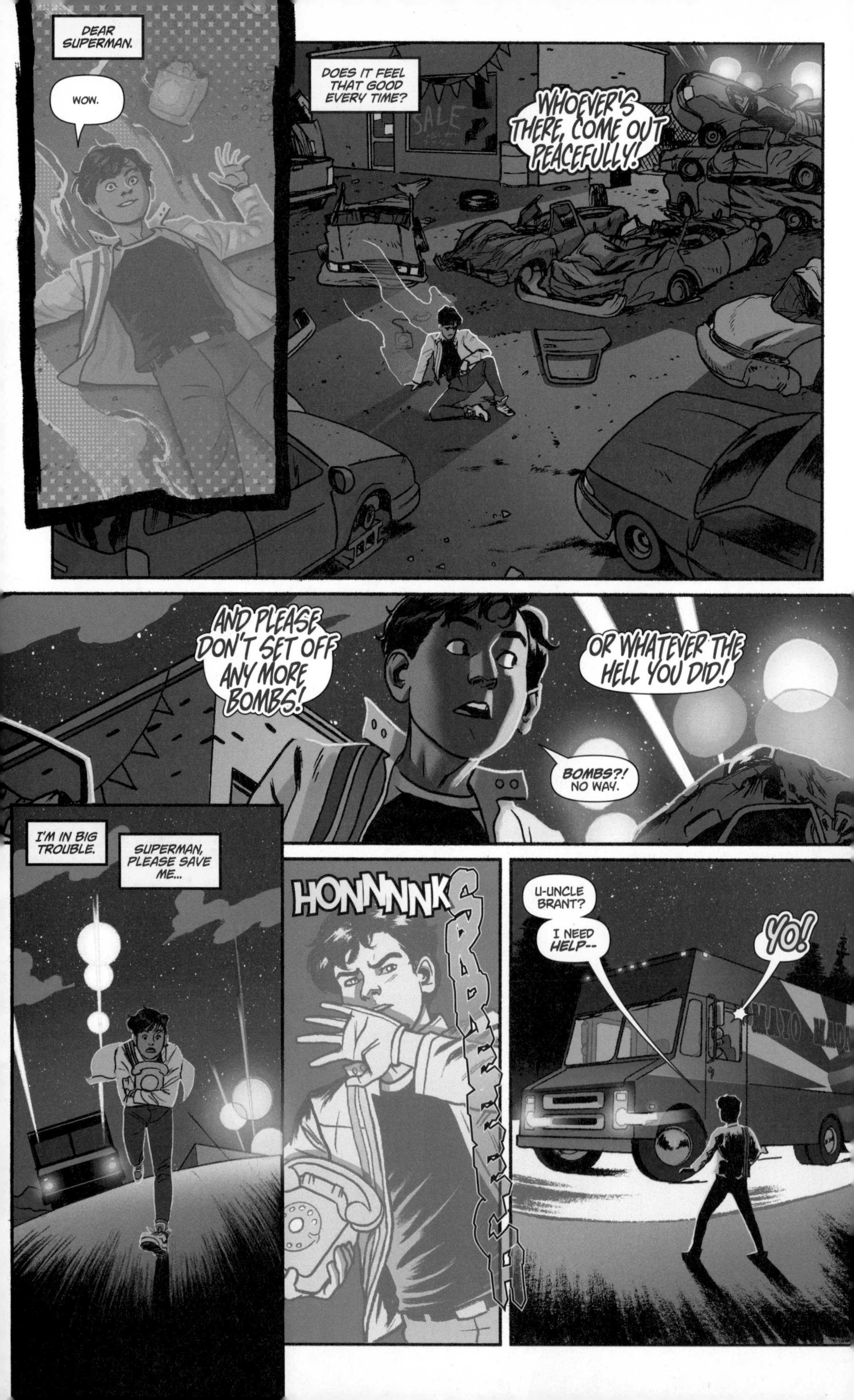
DEAR SUPERMAN.
WOW.
DOES IT FEEL THAT GOOD EVERY TIME?
SALE
WHOEVER'S THERE, COME OUT PEACEFULLY!
AND PLEASE DON'T SET OFF ANY MORE BOMBS!
OR WHATEVER THE HELL YOU DID!
BOMBS?! NO WAY.
I'M IN BIG TROUBLE.
SUPERMAN, PLEASE SAVE ME...
HONNNNNK
U-UNCLE BRANT?
I NEED HELP--
YO!

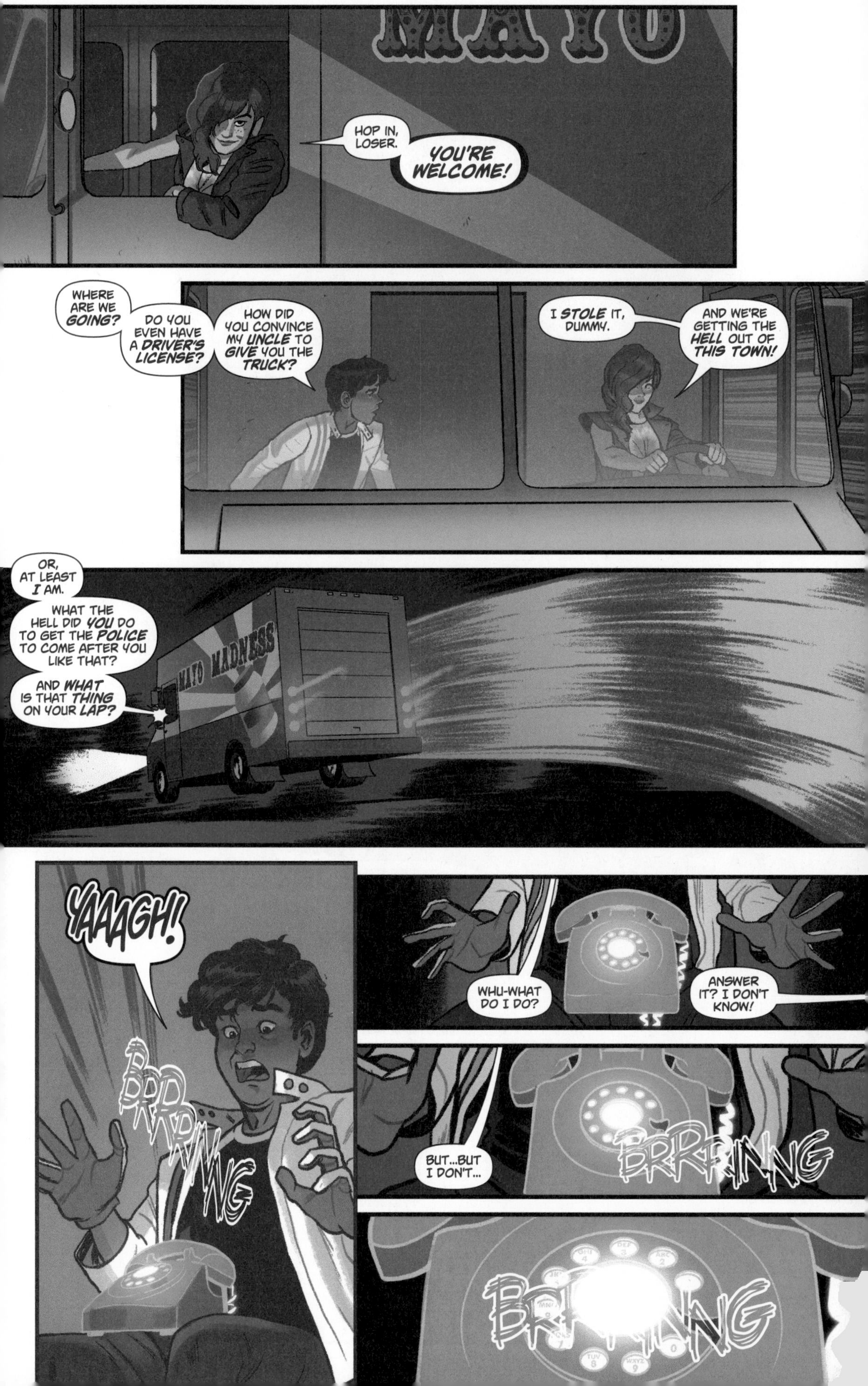

MAYO
HOP IN, LOSER.
YOU'RE WELCOME!
WHERE ARE WE GOING?
DO YOU EVEN HAVE A DRIVER'S LICENSE?
HOW DID YOU CONVINCE MY UNCLE TO GIVE YOU THE TRUCK?
I STOLE IT, DUMMY.
AND WE'RE GETTING THE HELL OUT OF THIS TOWN!
OR, AT LEAST I AM.
WHAT THE HELL DID YOU DO TO GET THE POLICE TO COME AFTER YOU LIKE THAT?
AND WHAT IS THAT THING ON YOUR LAP?
MAYO MADNESS
YAAAGH!
BRRRING
WHU-WHAT DO I DO?
ANSWER IT? I DON'T KNOW!
BUT...BUT I DON'T...
BRRRING
BRRRING

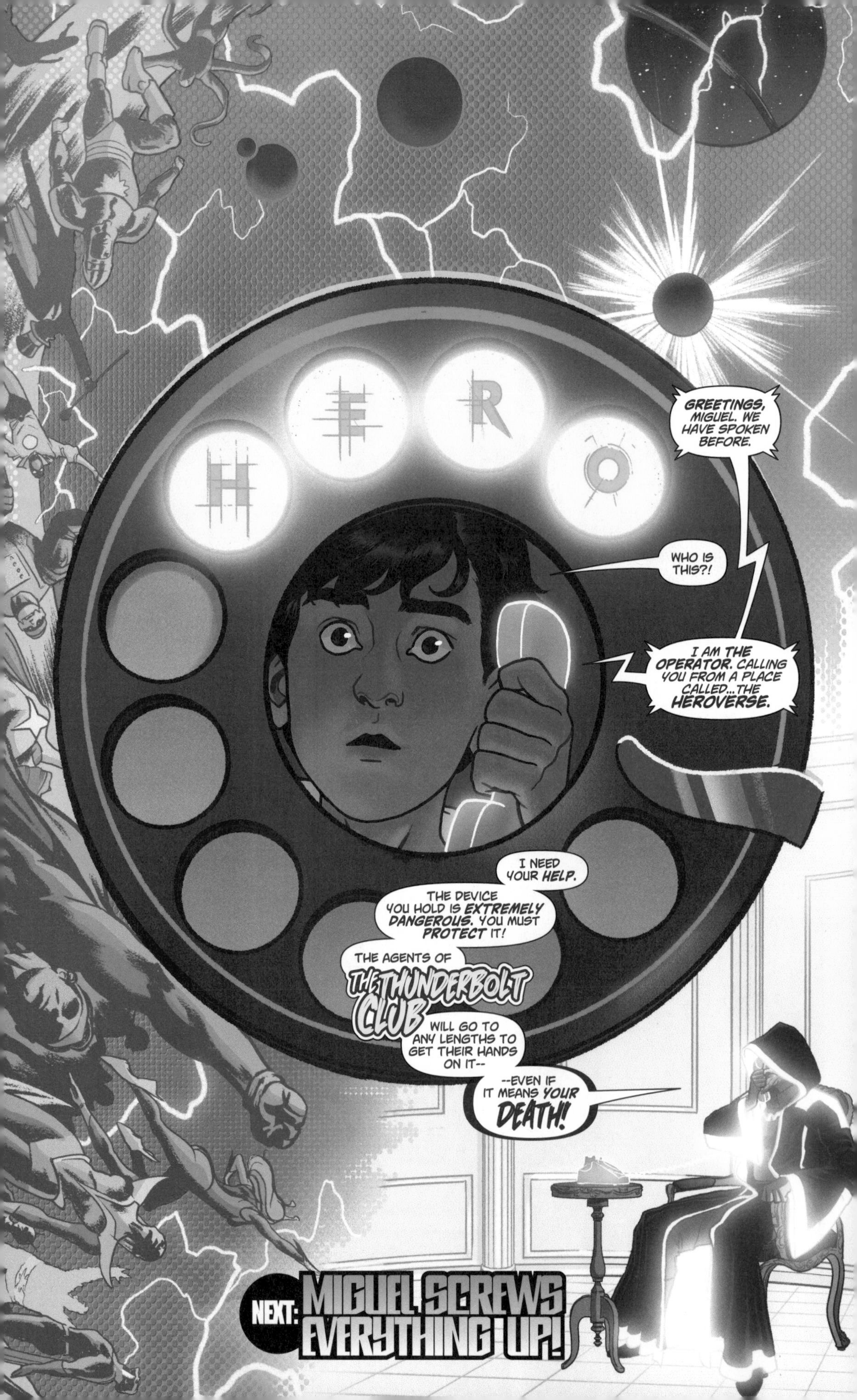
H E R O
GREETINGS, MIGUEL. WE HAVE SPOKEN BEFORE.
WHO IS THIS?!
I AM THE OPERATOR. CALLING YOU FROM A PLACE CALLED...THE HEROVERSE.
I NEED YOUR HELP.
THE DEVICE YOU HOLD IS EXTREMELY DANGEROUS. YOU MUST PROTECT IT!
THE AGENTS OF THE THUNDERBOLT CLUB WILL GO TO ANY LENGTHS TO GET THEIR HANDS ON IT--
--EVEN IF IT MEANS YOUR DEATH!
NEXT: MIGUEL SCREWS EVERYTHING UP!

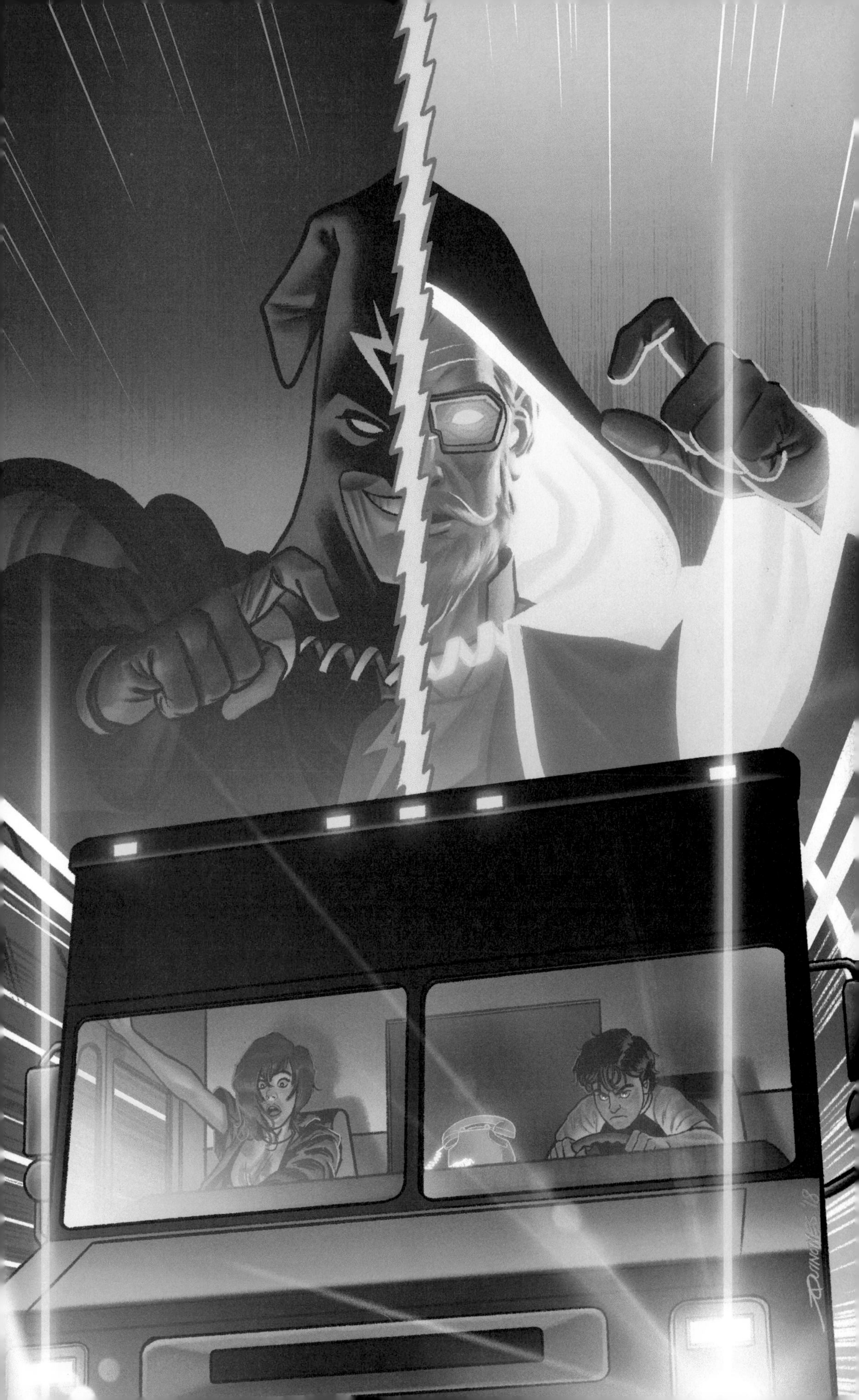
QUINONES '18

RIVER DEEP, MOUNTAIN HIGH

art by
JOE QUINONES
colors by
JORDAN GIBSON

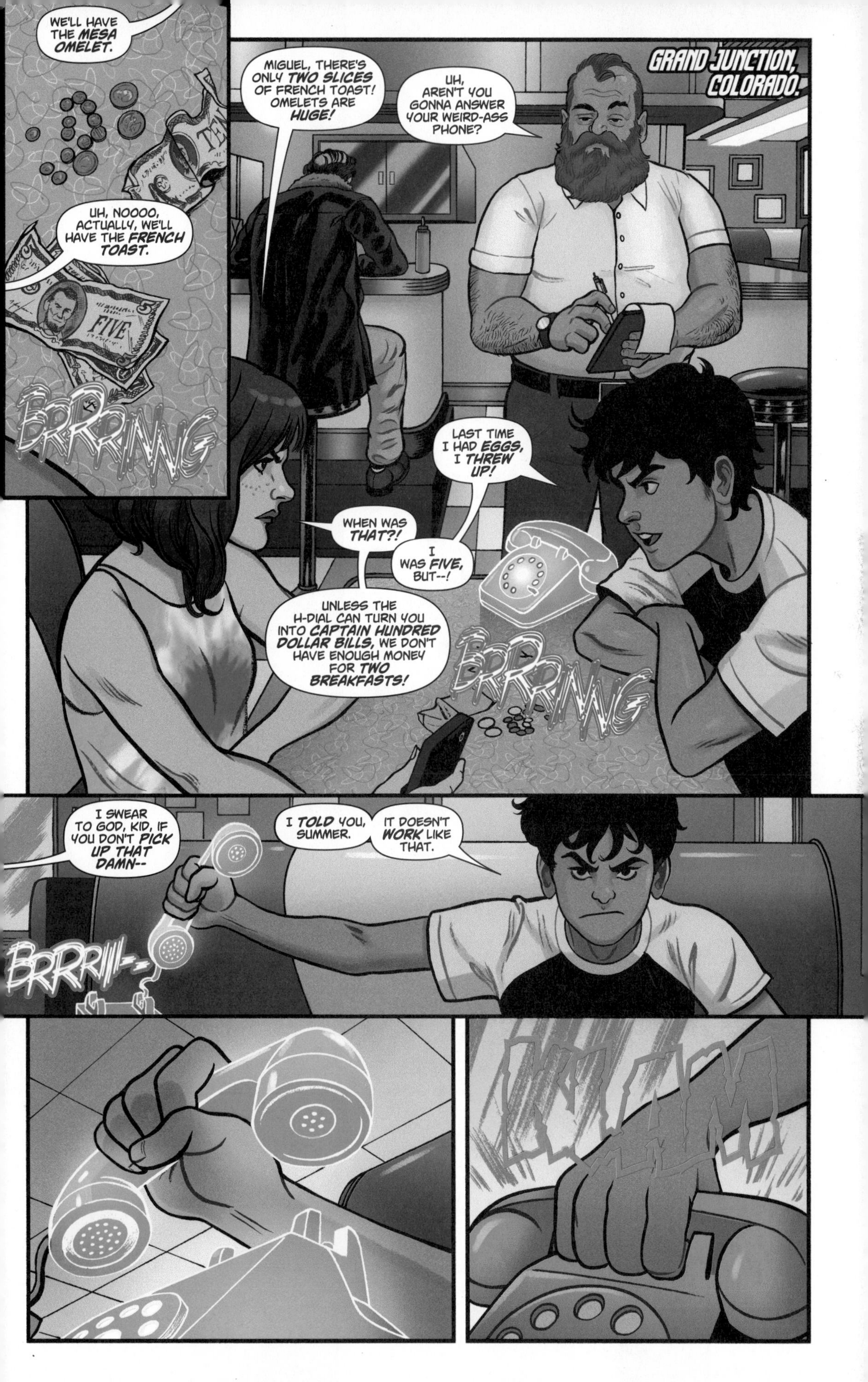
WE'LL HAVE THE MESA OMELET.
UH, NOOOO, ACTUALLY, WE'LL HAVE THE FRENCH TOAST.
BRRRINNG
GRAND JUNCTION, COLORADO.
MIGUEL, THERE'S ONLY TWO SLICES OF FRENCH TOAST! OMELETS ARE HUGE!
UH, AREN'T YOU GONNA ANSWER YOUR WEIRD-ASS PHONE?
LAST TIME I HAD EGGS, I THREW UP!
WHEN WAS THAT?!
I WAS FIVE, BUT--!
UNLESS THE H-DIAL CAN TURN YOU INTO CAPTAIN HUNDRED DOLLAR BILLS, WE DON'T HAVE ENOUGH MONEY FOR TWO BREAKFASTS!
BRRRINNG
I SWEAR TO GOD, KID, IF YOU DON'T PICK UP THAT DAMN--
I TOLD YOU, SUMMER.
IT DOESN'T WORK LIKE THAT.
BRRRIII--

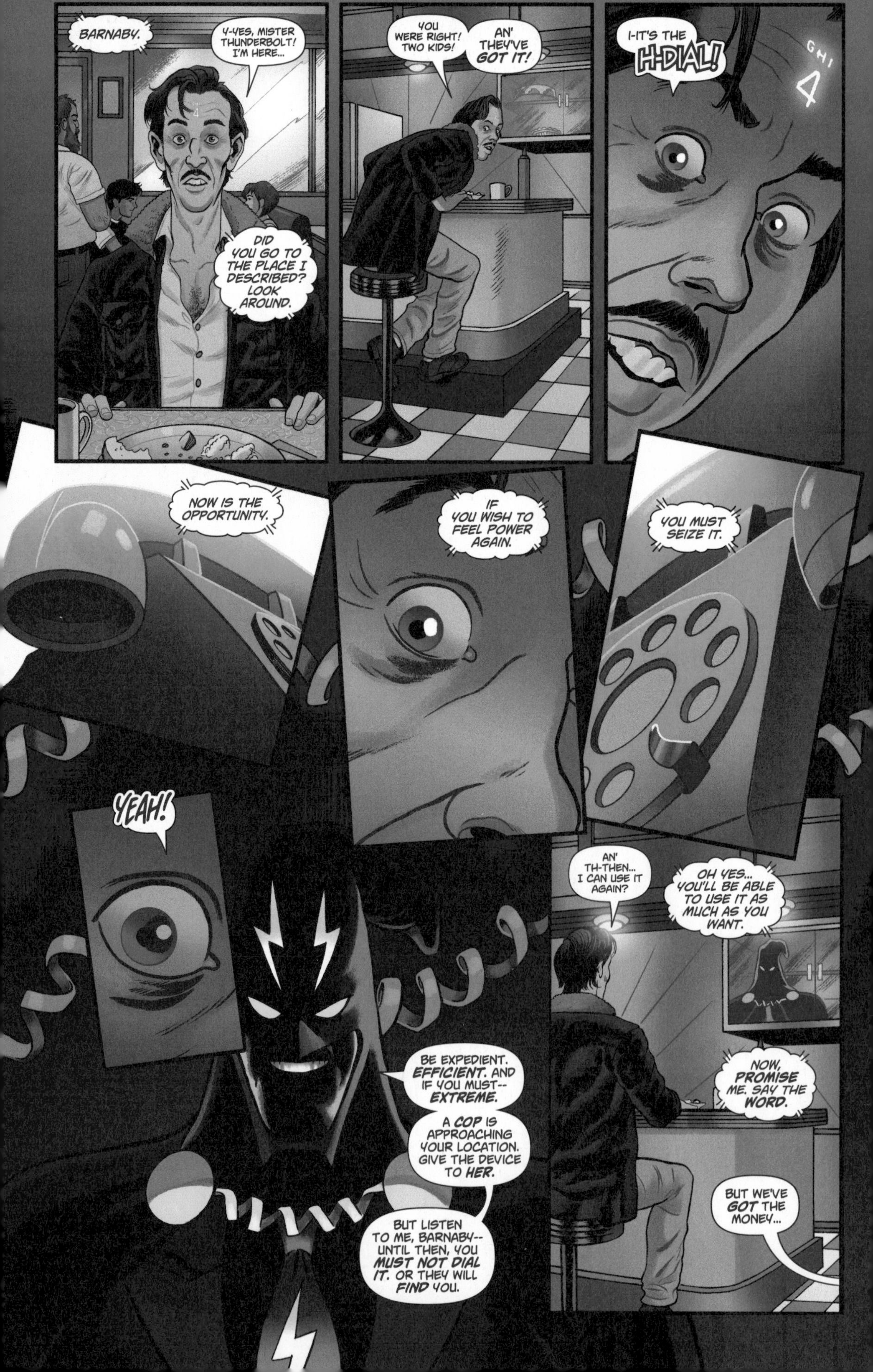
BARNABY.
Y-YES, MISTER THUNDERBOLT! I'M HERE...
DID YOU GO TO THE PLACE I DESCRIBED? LOOK AROUND.
YOU WERE RIGHT! TWO KIDS!
AN' THEY'VE GOT IT!
I-IT'S THE H-DIAL!
GHI 4
NOW IS THE OPPORTUNITY.
IF YOU WISH TO FEEL POWER AGAIN.
YOU MUST SEIZE IT.
YEAH!
BE EXPEDIENT. EFFICIENT. AND IF YOU MUST-- EXTREME.
A COP IS APPROACHING YOUR LOCATION. GIVE THE DEVICE TO HER.
BUT LISTEN TO ME, BARNABY-- UNTIL THEN, YOU MUST NOT DIAL IT. OR THEY WILL FIND YOU.
AN' TH-THEN... I CAN USE IT AGAIN?
OH YES... YOU'LL BE ABLE TO USE IT AS MUCH AS YOU WANT.
NOW, PROMISE ME. SAY THE WORD.
BUT WE'VE GOT THE MONEY...

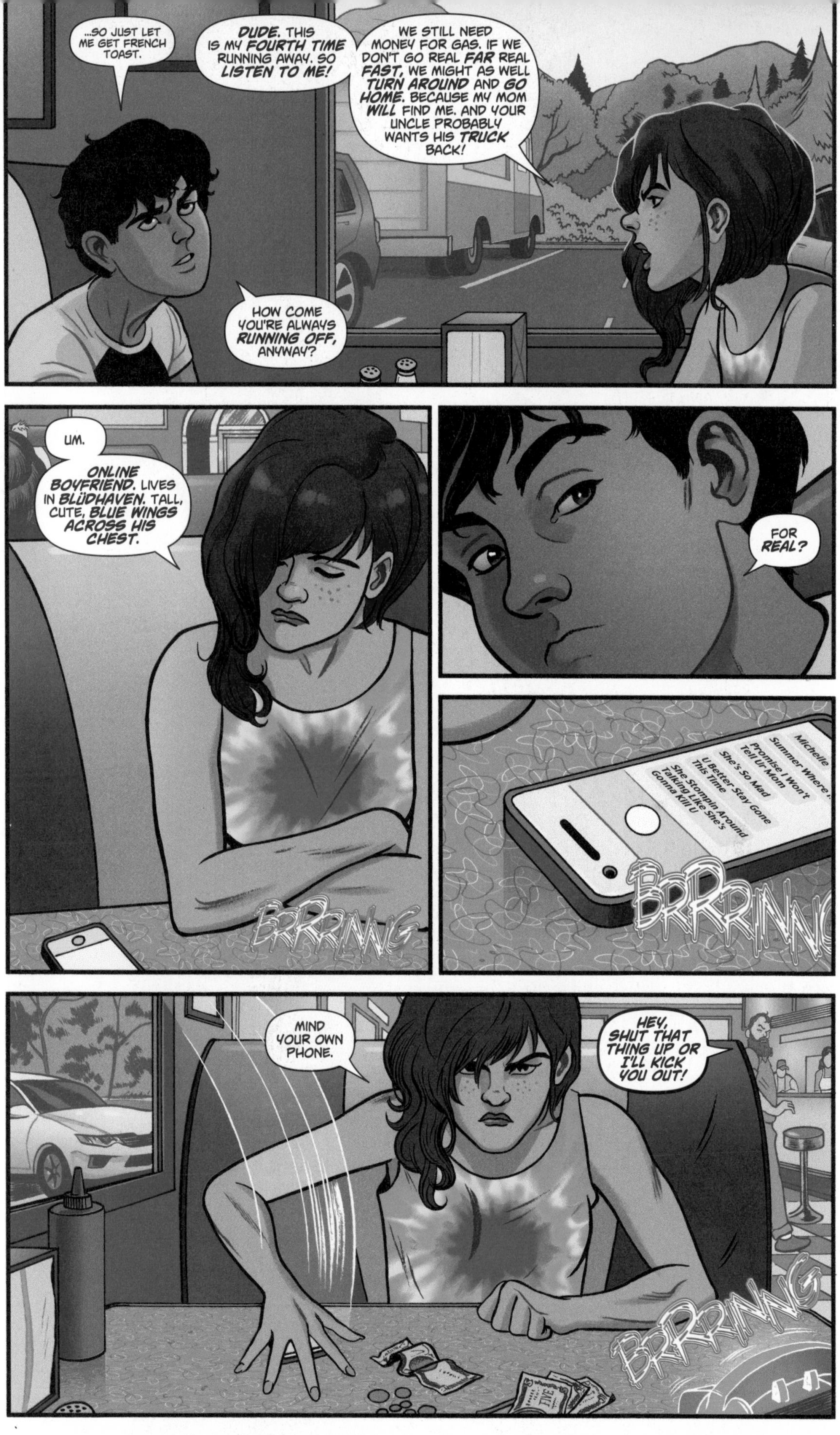

...SO JUST LET ME GET FRENCH TOAST.
DUDE. THIS IS MY FOURTH TIME RUNNING AWAY. SO LISTEN TO ME!
WE STILL NEED MONEY FOR GAS. IF WE DON'T GO REAL FAR REAL FAST, WE MIGHT AS WELL TURN AROUND AND GO HOME. BECAUSE MY MOM WILL FIND ME. AND YOUR UNCLE PROBABLY WANTS HIS TRUCK BACK!
HOW COME YOU'RE ALWAYS RUNNING OFF, ANYWAY?
UM.
ONLINE BOYFRIEND. LIVES IN BLÜDHAVEN. TALL, CUTE, BLUE WINGS ACROSS HIS CHEST.
BRRRING
FOR REAL?
Michelle
Summer Where I
Promise I Won't Tell Ur Mom
She's So Mad
U Better Stay Gone This Time
She Stompin Around Talking Like She's Gonna Kill U
BRRRRING
MIND YOUR OWN PHONE.
HEY, SHUT THAT THING UP OR I'LL KICK YOU OUT!
BRRRING

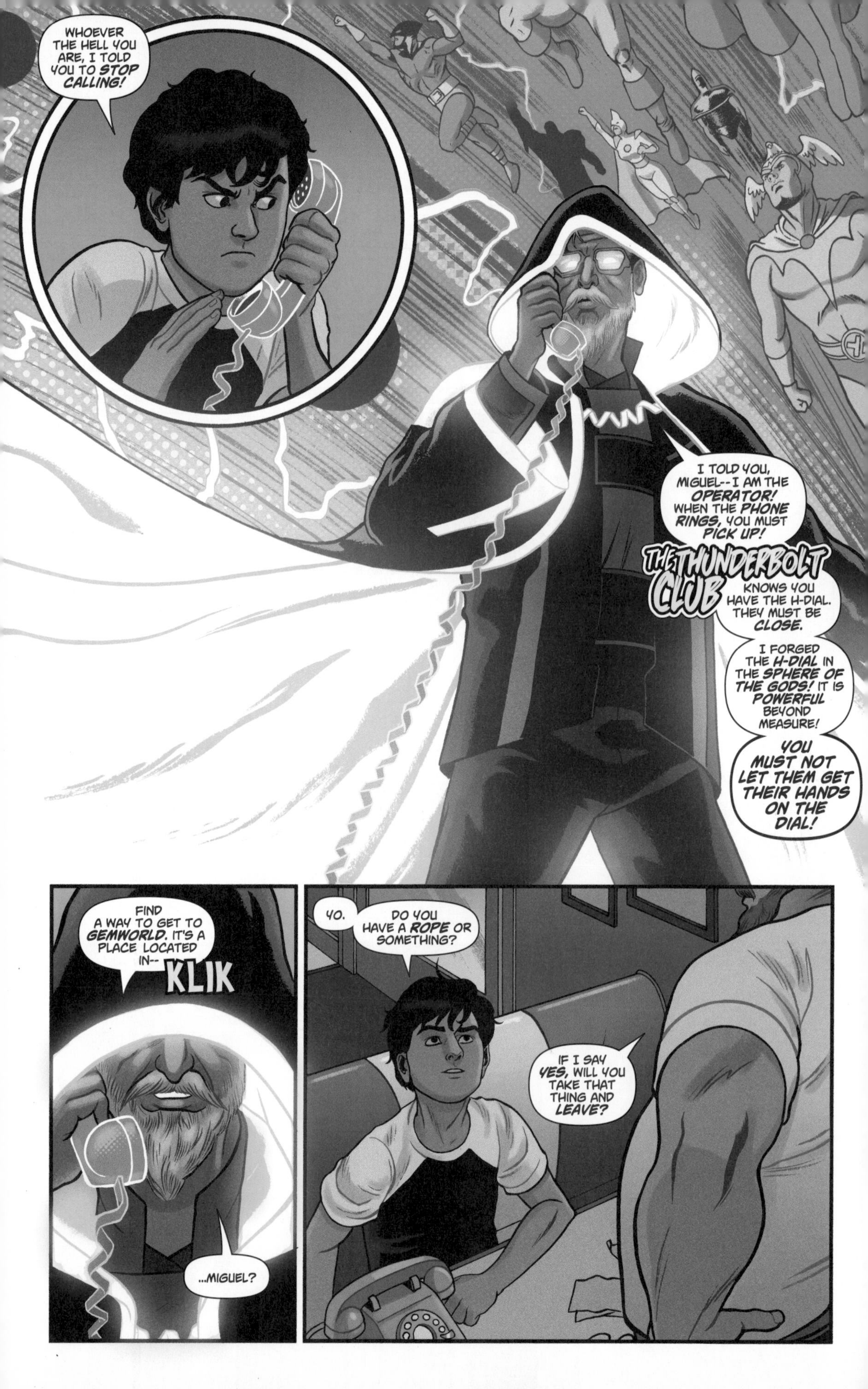

WHOEVER THE HELL YOU ARE, I TOLD YOU TO STOP CALLING!
I TOLD YOU, MIGUEL-- I AM THE OPERATOR! WHEN THE PHONE RINGS, YOU MUST PICK UP!
THE THUNDERBOLT CLUB KNOWS YOU HAVE THE H-DIAL. THEY MUST BE CLOSE.
I FORGED THE H-DIAL IN THE SPHERE OF THE GODS! IT IS POWERFUL BEYOND MEASURE!
YOU MUST NOT LET THEM GET THEIR HANDS ON THE DIAL!
FIND A WAY TO GET TO GEMWORLD. IT'S A PLACE LOCATED IN--
KLIK
...MIGUEL?
YO.
DO YOU HAVE A ROPE OR SOMETHING?
IF I SAY YES, WILL YOU TAKE THAT THING AND LEAVE?

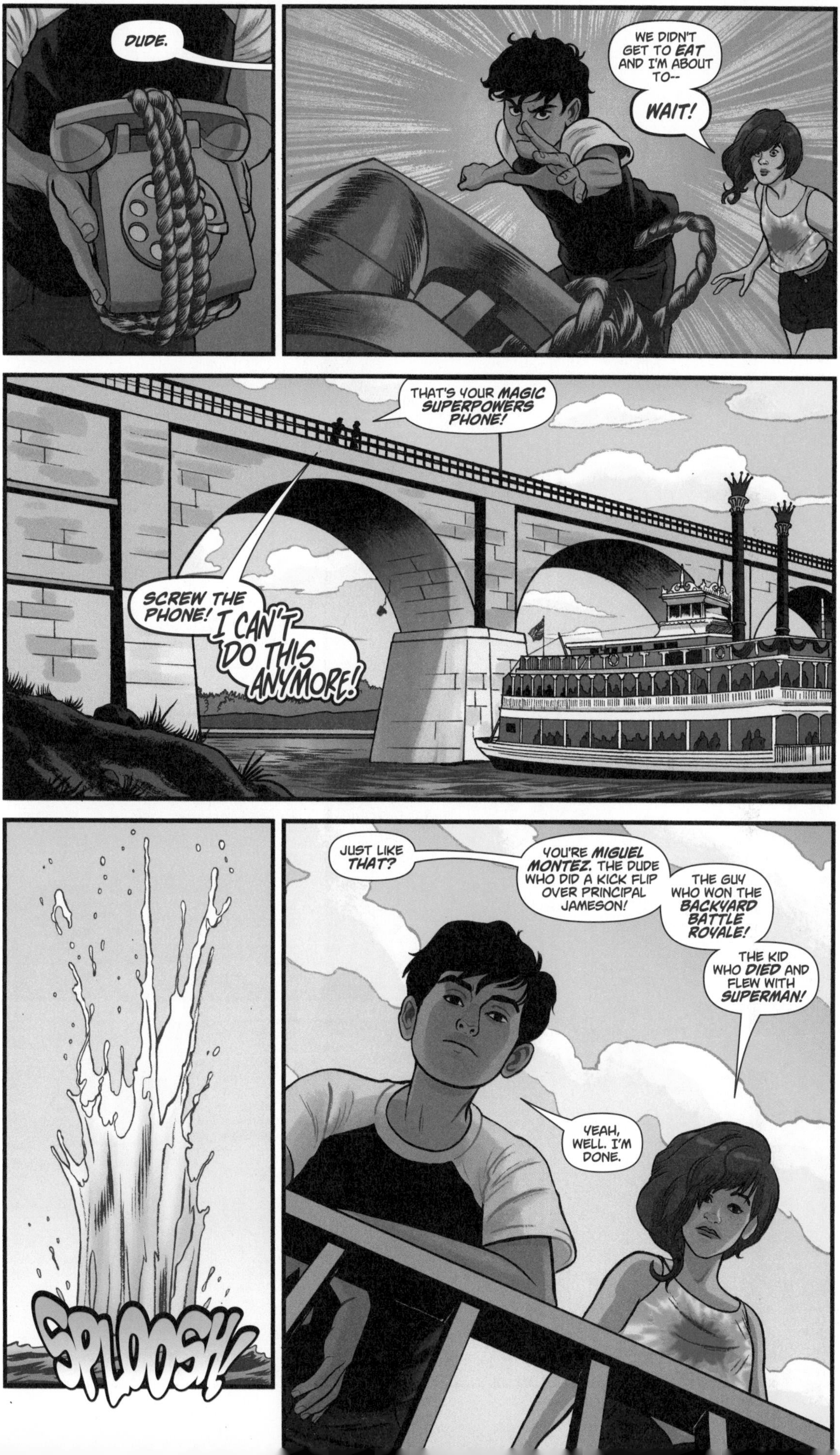
DUDE.
WE DIDN'T GET TO EAT AND I'M ABOUT TO--
WAIT!
THAT'S YOUR MAGIC SUPERPOWERS PHONE!
SCREW THE PHONE!
I CAN'T DO THIS ANYMORE!
SPLOOSH!
JUST LIKE THAT?
YOU'RE MIGUEL MONTEZ. THE DUDE WHO DID A KICK FLIP OVER PRINCIPAL JAMESON!
THE GUY WHO WON THE BACKYARD BATTLE ROYALE!
THE KID WHO DIED AND FLEW WITH SUPERMAN!
YEAH, WELL. I'M DONE.

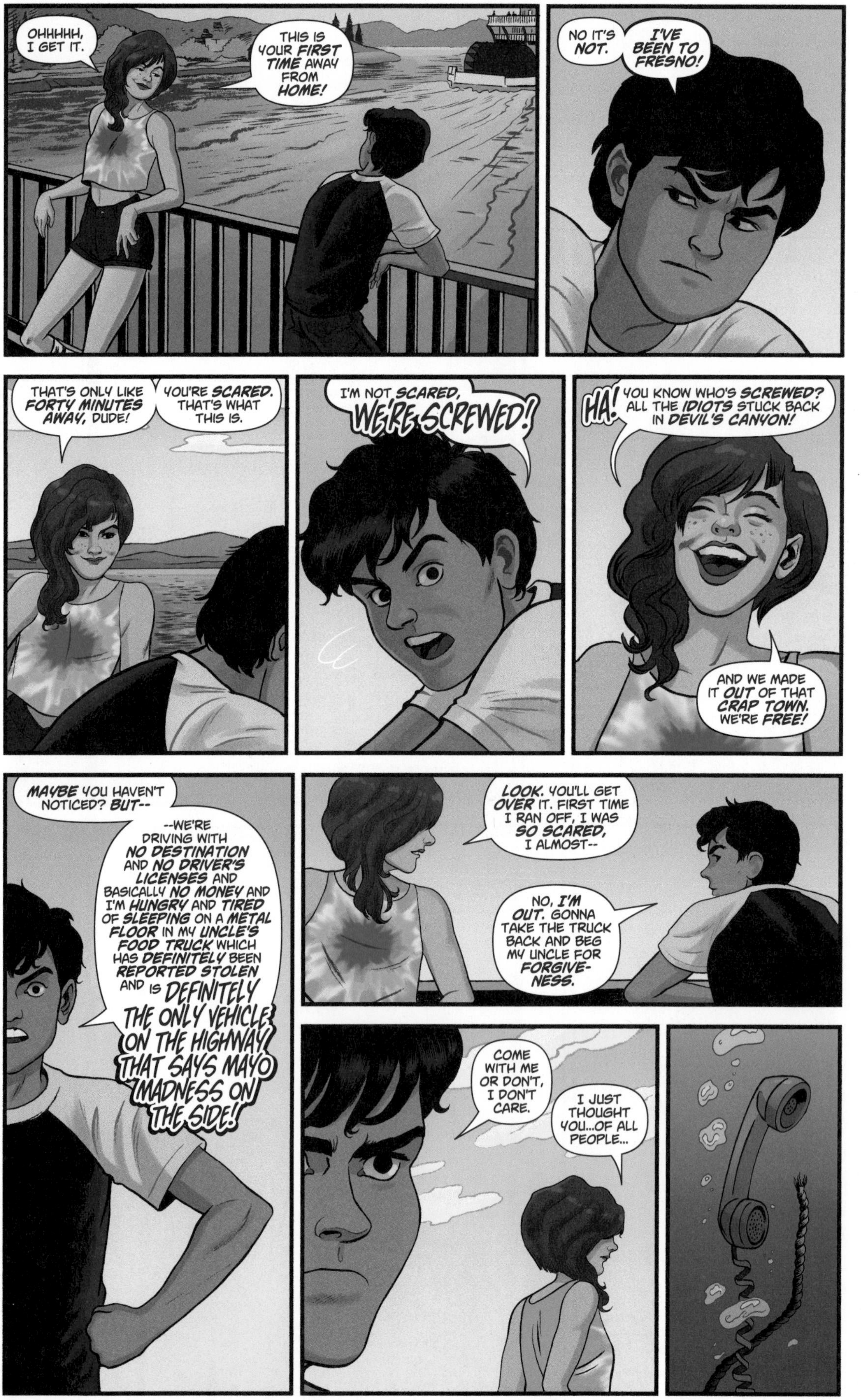
OHHHHH, I GET IT.
THIS IS YOUR FIRST TIME AWAY FROM HOME!
NO IT'S NOT.
I'VE BEEN TO FRESNO!
THAT'S ONLY LIKE FORTY MINUTES AWAY, DUDE!
YOU'RE SCARED. THAT'S WHAT THIS IS.
I'M NOT SCARED,
WE'RE SCREWED!
HA!
YOU KNOW WHO'S SCREWED? ALL THE IDIOTS STUCK BACK IN DEVIL'S CANYON!
AND WE MADE IT OUT OF THAT CRAP TOWN. WE'RE FREE!
MAYBE YOU HAVEN'T NOTICED? BUT--
--WE'RE DRIVING WITH NO DESTINATION AND NO DRIVER'S LICENSES AND BASICALLY NO MONEY AND I'M HUNGRY AND TIRED OF SLEEPING ON A METAL FLOOR IN MY UNCLE'S FOOD TRUCK WHICH HAS DEFINITELY BEEN REPORTED STOLEN AND IS DEFINITELY THE ONLY VEHICLE ON THE HIGHWAY THAT SAYS MAYO MADNESS ON THE SIDE!
LOOK. YOU'LL GET OVER IT. FIRST TIME I RAN OFF, I WAS SO SCARED, I ALMOST--
NO, I'M OUT. GONNA TAKE THE TRUCK BACK AND BEG MY UNCLE FOR FORGIVE-NESS.
COME WITH ME OR DON'T, I DON'T CARE.
I JUST THOUGHT YOU...OF ALL PEOPLE...

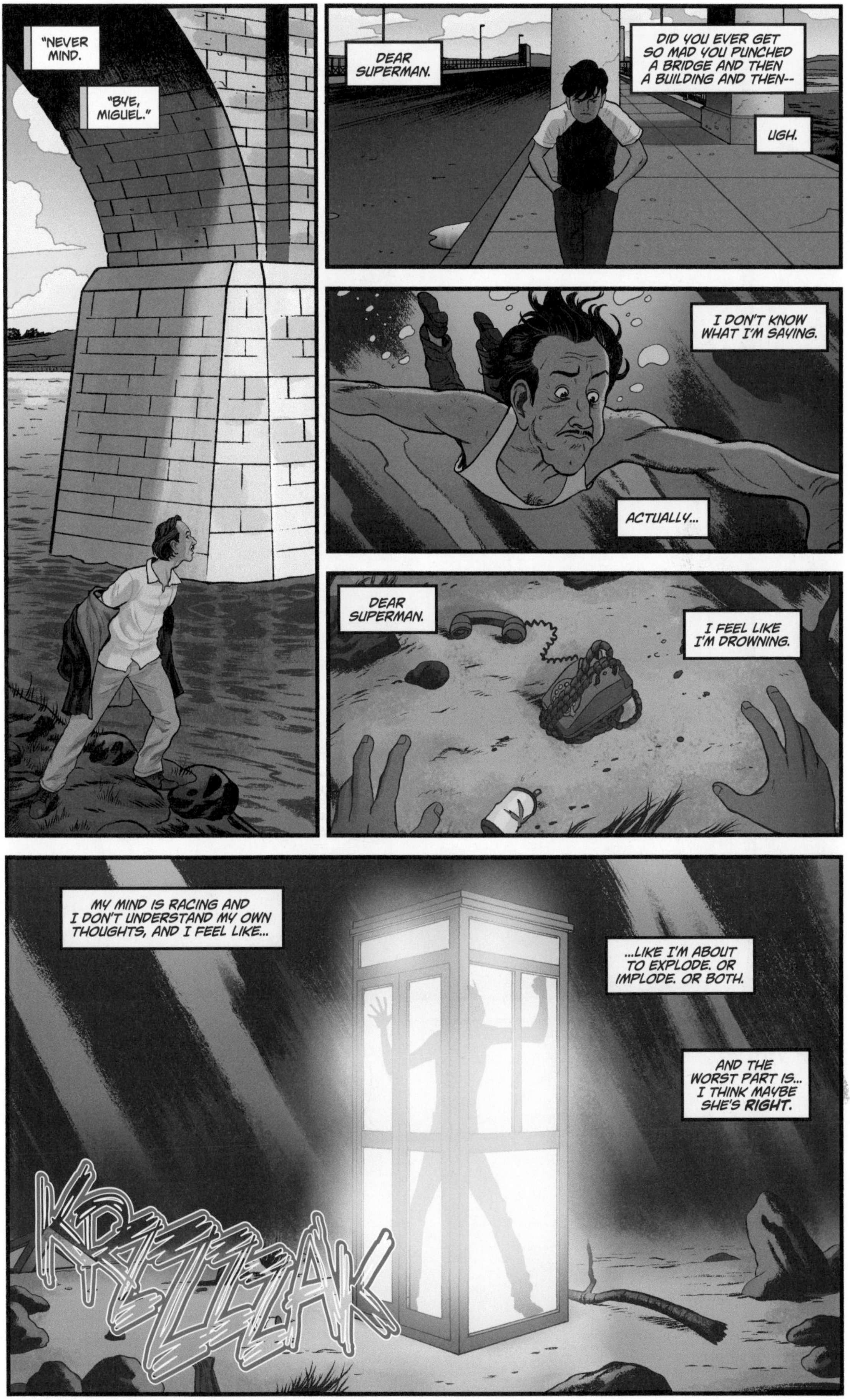
"NEVER MIND.
"BYE, MIGUEL."
DEAR SUPERMAN.
DID YOU EVER GET SO MAD YOU PUNCHED A BRIDGE AND THEN A BUILDING AND THEN--
UGH.
I DON'T KNOW WHAT I'M SAYING.
ACTUALLY...
DEAR SUPERMAN.
I FEEL LIKE I'M DROWNING.
MY MIND IS RACING AND I DON'T UNDERSTAND MY OWN THOUGHTS, AND I FEEL LIKE...
...LIKE I'M ABOUT TO EXPLODE. OR IMPLODE. OR BOTH.
AND THE WORST PART IS... I THINK MAYBE SHE'S **RIGHT**.
KRZZZZAK

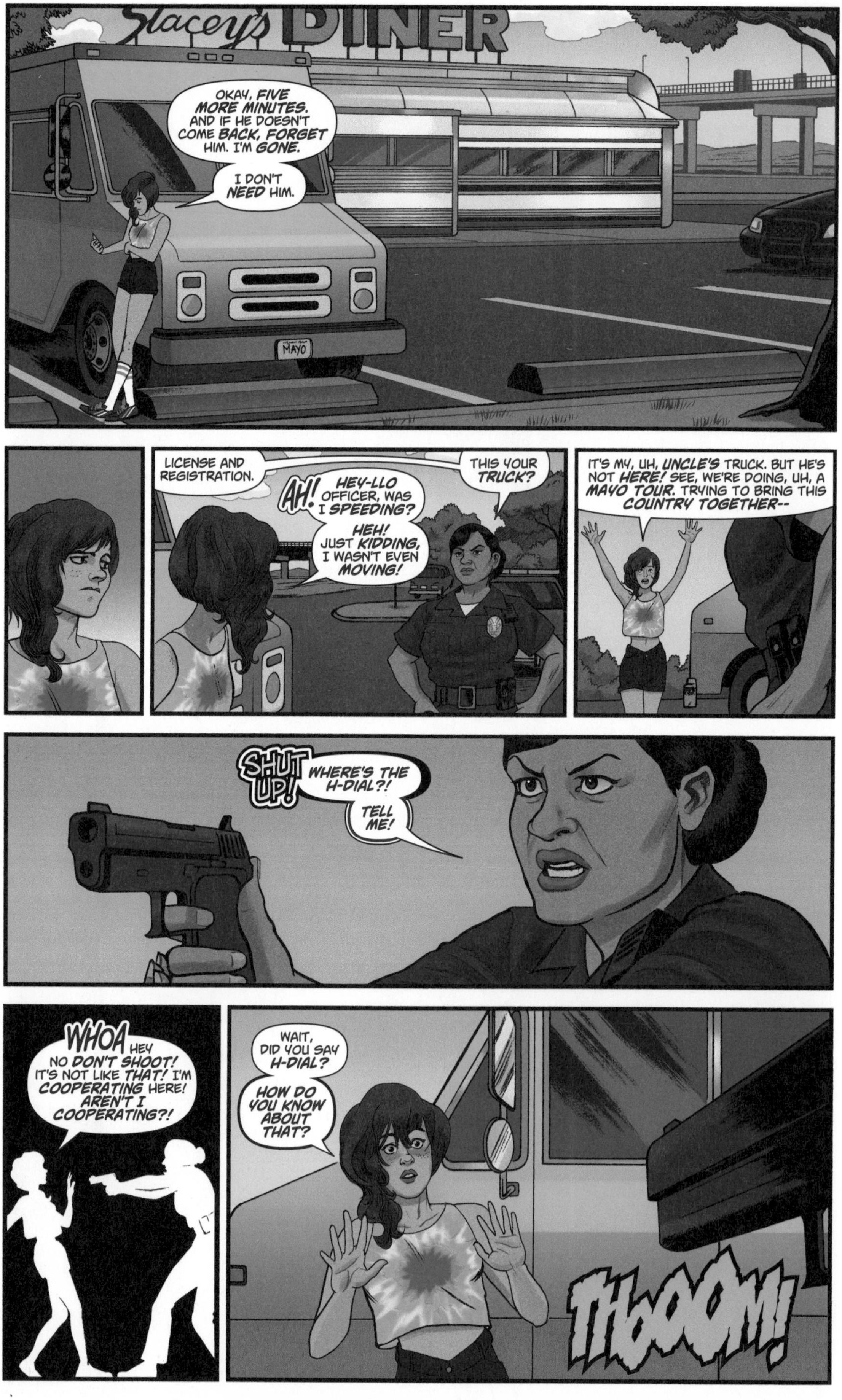
Stacey's DINER
OKAY, FIVE MORE MINUTES. AND IF HE DOESN'T COME BACK, FORGET HIM. I'M GONE.
I DON'T NEED HIM.
MAYO
LICENSE AND REGISTRATION.
AH! HEY-LLO OFFICER, WAS I SPEEDING?
HEH! JUST KIDDING, I WASN'T EVEN MOVING!
THIS YOUR TRUCK?
IT'S MY, UH, UNCLE'S TRUCK. BUT HE'S NOT HERE! SEE, WE'RE DOING, UH, A MAYO TOUR. TRYING TO BRING THIS COUNTRY TOGETHER--
SHUT UP!
WHERE'S THE H-DIAL?!
TELL ME!
WHOA HEY NO DON'T SHOOT! IT'S NOT LIKE THAT! I'M COOPERATING HERE! AREN'T I COOPERATING?!
WAIT, DID YOU SAY H-DIAL?
HOW DO YOU KNOW ABOUT THAT?
THOOM!

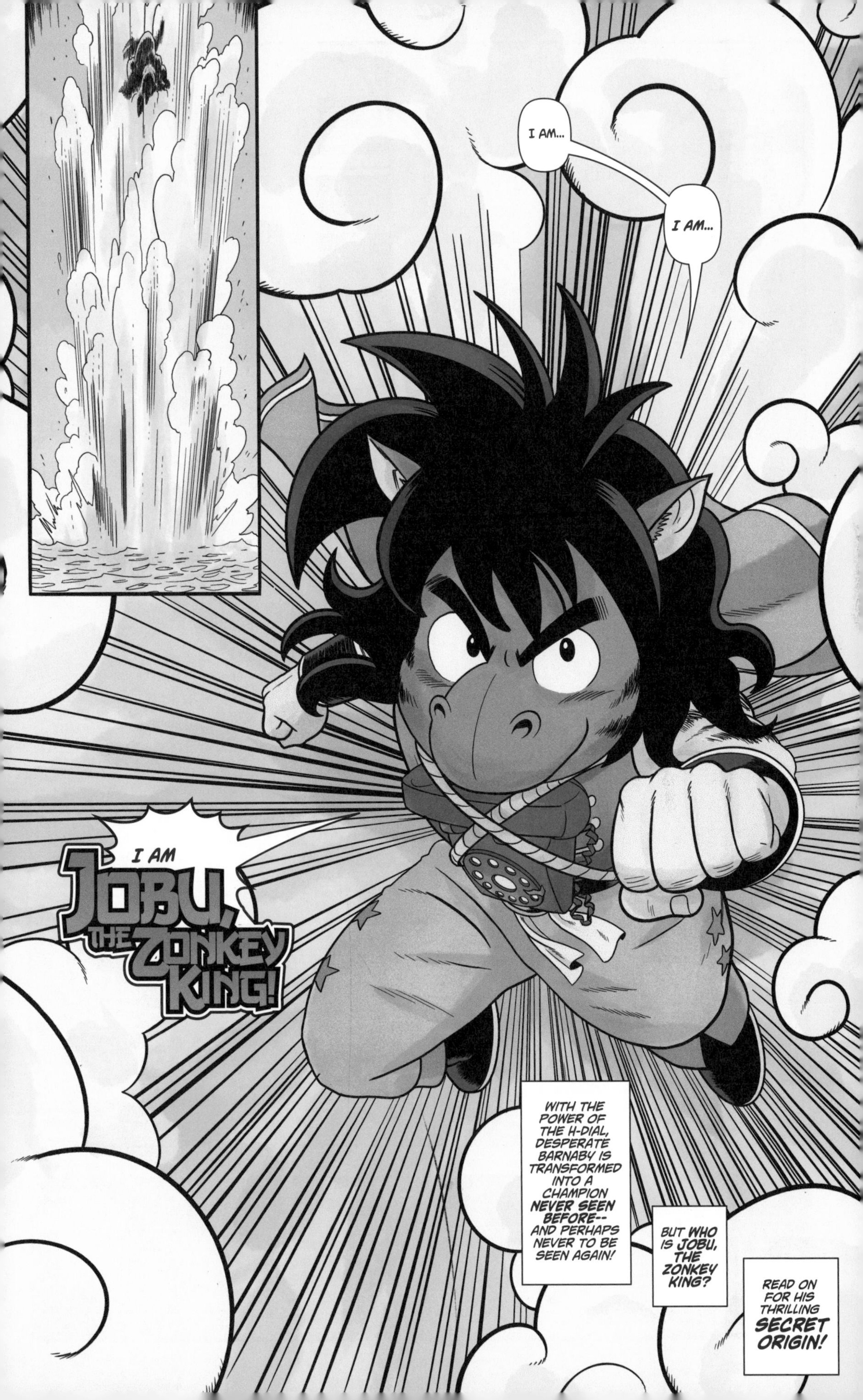
I AM...
I AM...
I AM
JOBU, THE ZONKEY KING!
WITH THE POWER OF THE H-DIAL, DESPERATE BARNABY IS TRANSFORMED INTO A CHAMPION NEVER SEEN BEFORE-- AND PERHAPS NEVER TO BE SEEN AGAIN!
BUT WHO IS JOBU, THE ZONKEY KING?
READ ON FOR HIS THRILLING SECRET ORIGIN!

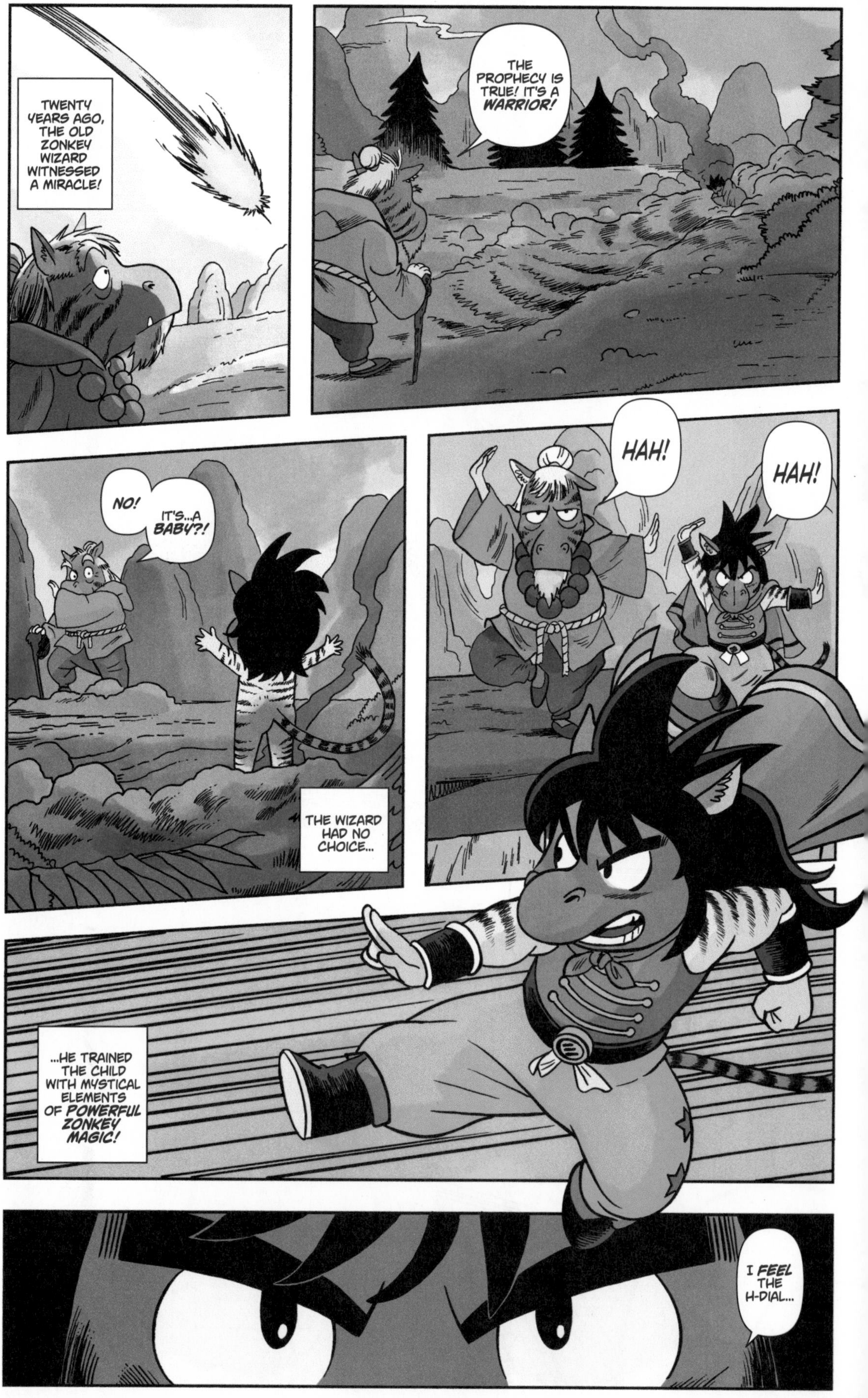
TWENTY YEARS AGO, THE OLD ZONKEY WIZARD WITNESSED A MIRACLE!
THE PROPHECY IS TRUE! IT'S A WARRIOR!
NO!
IT'S...A BABY?!
THE WIZARD HAD NO CHOICE...
HAH!
HAH!
...HE TRAINED THE CHILD WITH MYSTICAL ELEMENTS OF POWERFUL ZONKEY MAGIC!
I FEEL THE H-DIAL...

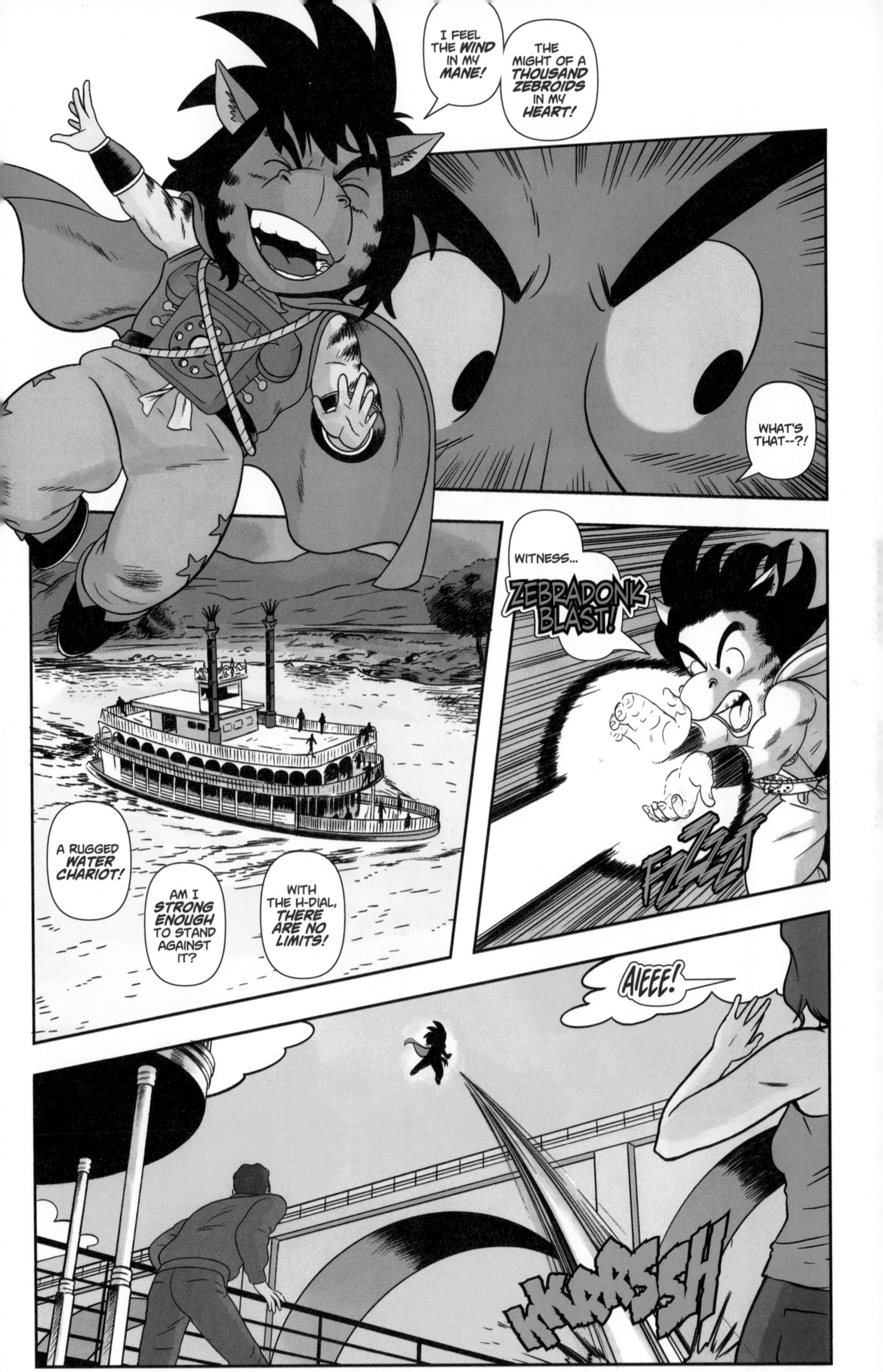

I FEEL THE WIND IN MY MANE!
THE MIGHT OF A THOUSAND ZEBROIDS IN MY HEART!
WHAT'S THAT--?!
A RUGGED WATER CHARIOT!
AM I STRONG ENOUGH TO STAND AGAINST IT?
WITH THE H-DIAL, THERE ARE NO LIMITS!
WITNESS...
ZEBRADONK BLAST!
FZZZZT
AIEEE!
KKRRSSH

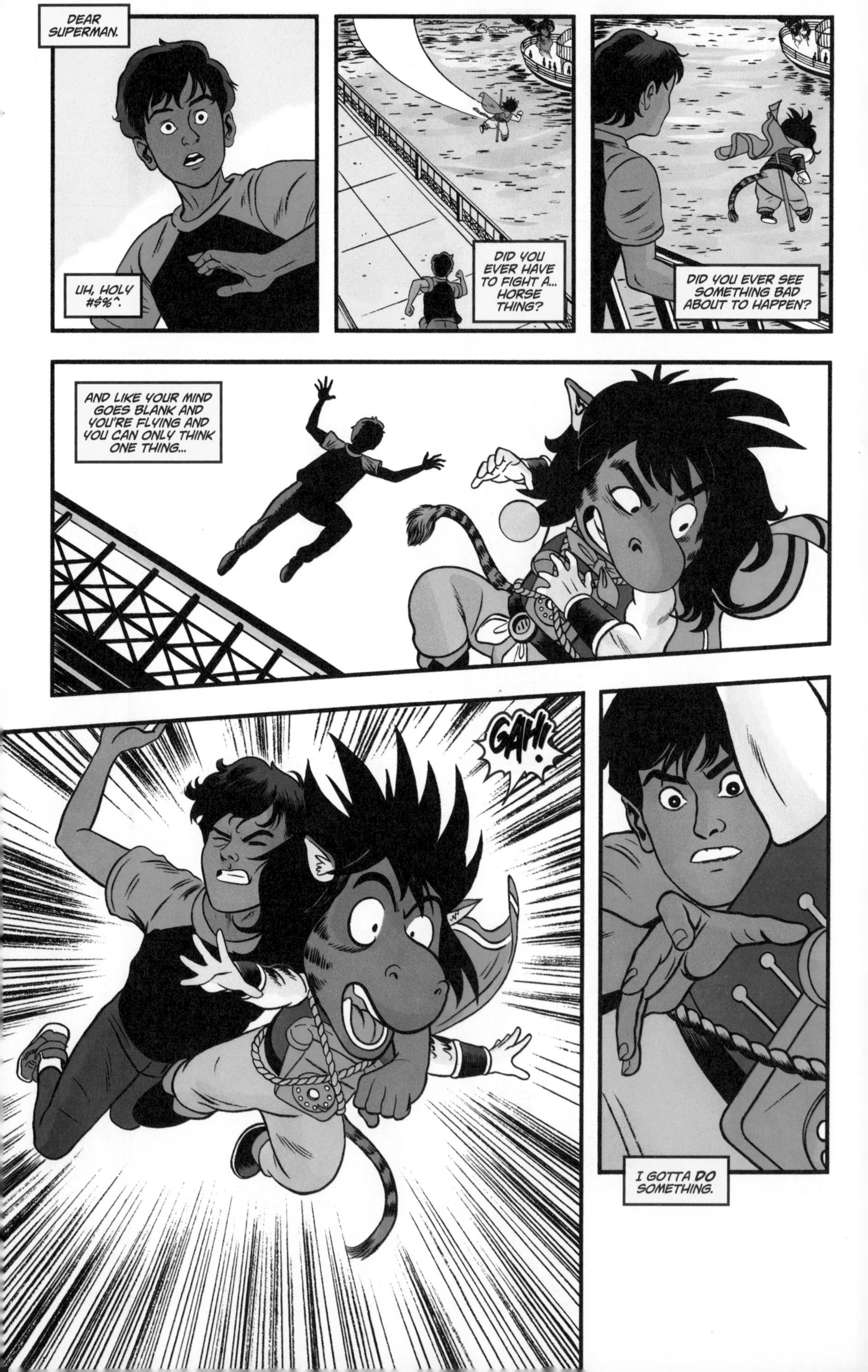
DEAR SUPERMAN.
UH, HOLY #$%^.
DID YOU EVER HAVE TO FIGHT A... HORSE THING?
DID YOU EVER SEE SOMETHING BAD ABOUT TO HAPPEN?
AND LIKE YOUR MIND GOES BLANK AND YOU'RE FLYING AND YOU CAN ONLY THINK ONE THING...
GAH!
I GOTTA DO SOMETHING.

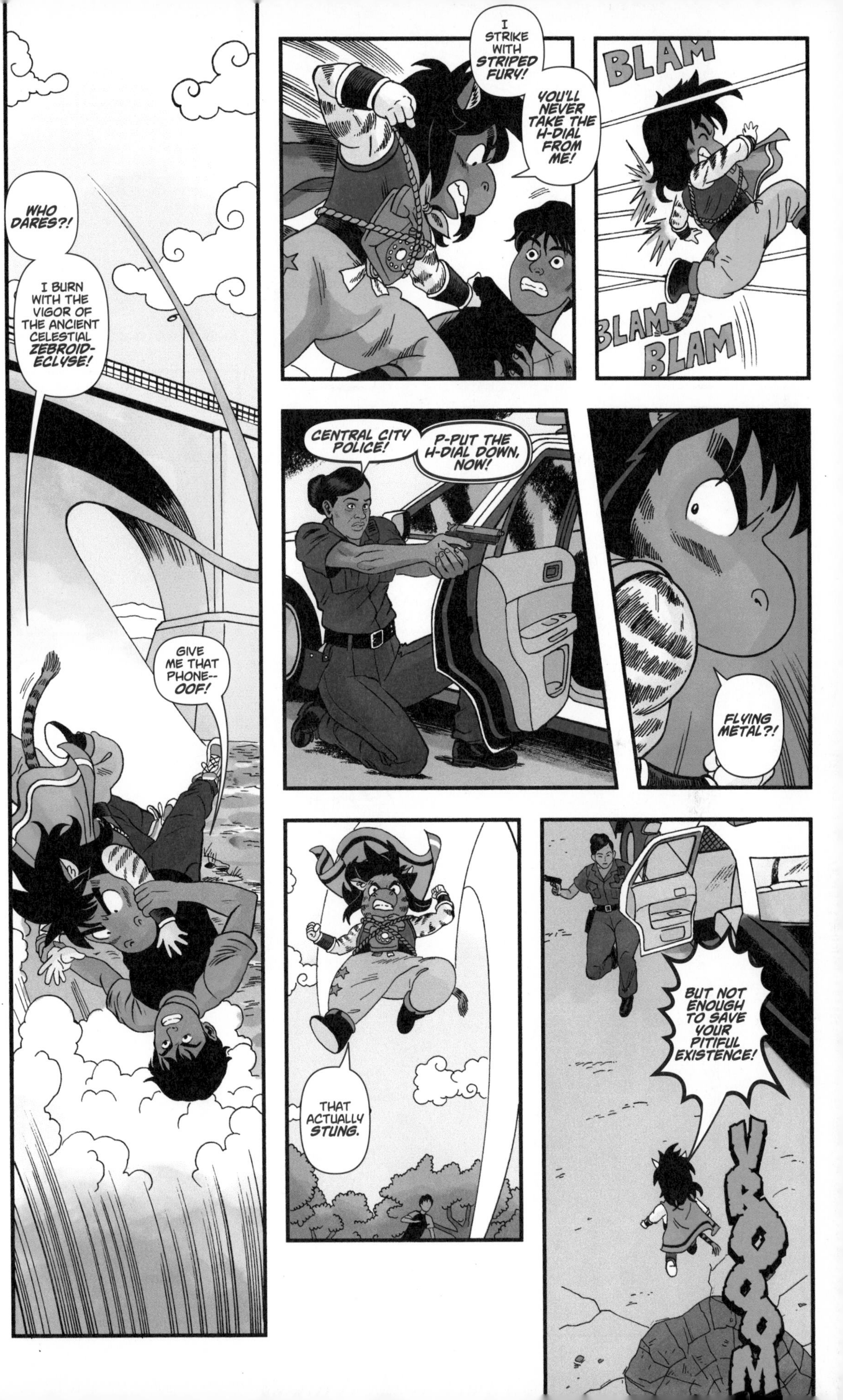
WHO DARES?!
I BURN WITH THE VIGOR OF THE ANCIENT CELESTIAL ZEBROID-ECLYSE!
GIVE ME THAT PHONE-- OOF!
I STRIKE WITH STRIPED FURY!
YOU'LL NEVER TAKE THE H-DIAL FROM ME!
BLAM
BLAM
BLAM
CENTRAL CITY POLICE!
P-PUT THE H-DIAL DOWN, NOW!
FLYING METAL?!
THAT ACTUALLY STUNG.
BUT NOT ENOUGH TO SAVE YOUR PITIFUL EXISTENCE!
VROOM

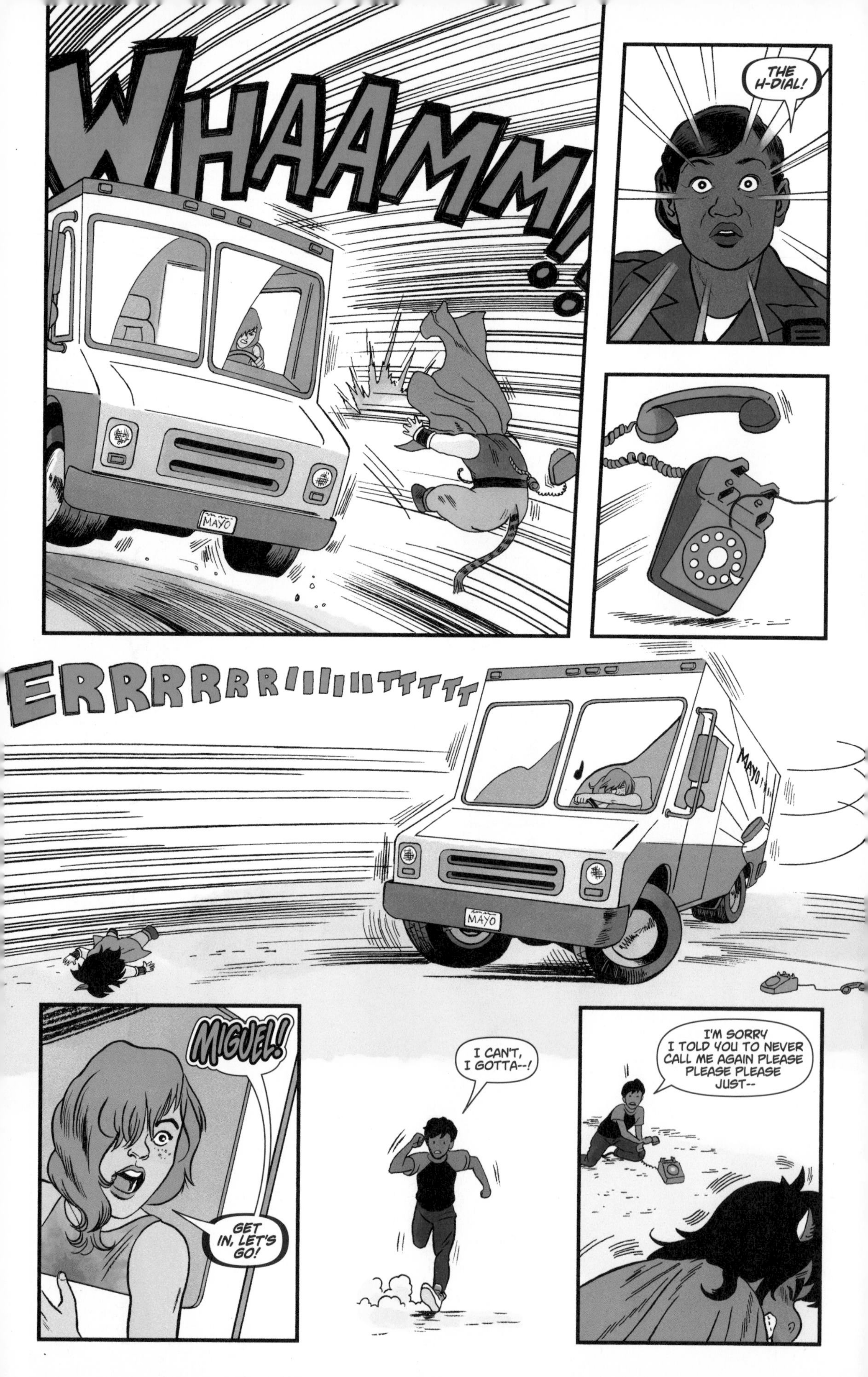
WHAAMM!!
THE H-DIAL!
MAYO
ERRRRRRIIIIIIITTTTTT
MAYO
MIGUEL!
GET IN, LET'S GO!
I CAN'T, I GOTTA--!
I'M SORRY I TOLD YOU TO NEVER CALL ME AGAIN PLEASE PLEASE PLEASE JUST--

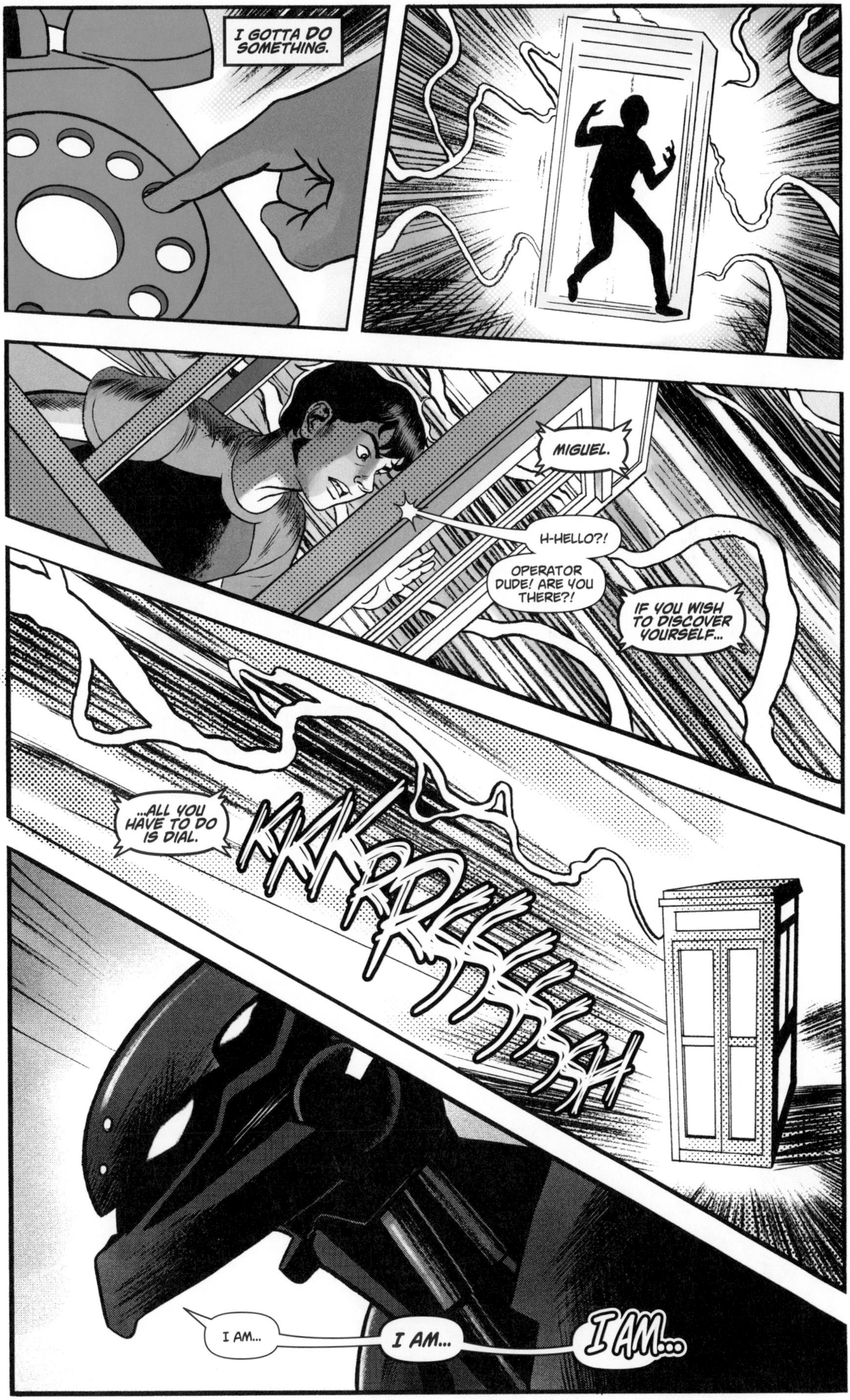
I GOTTA DO SOMETHING.
MIGUEL.
H-HELLO?!
OPERATOR DUDE! ARE YOU THERE?!
IF YOU WISH TO DISCOVER YOURSELF...
...ALL YOU HAVE TO DO IS DIAL.
KKKRRSSSHHSSSH
I AM...
I AM...
I AM...

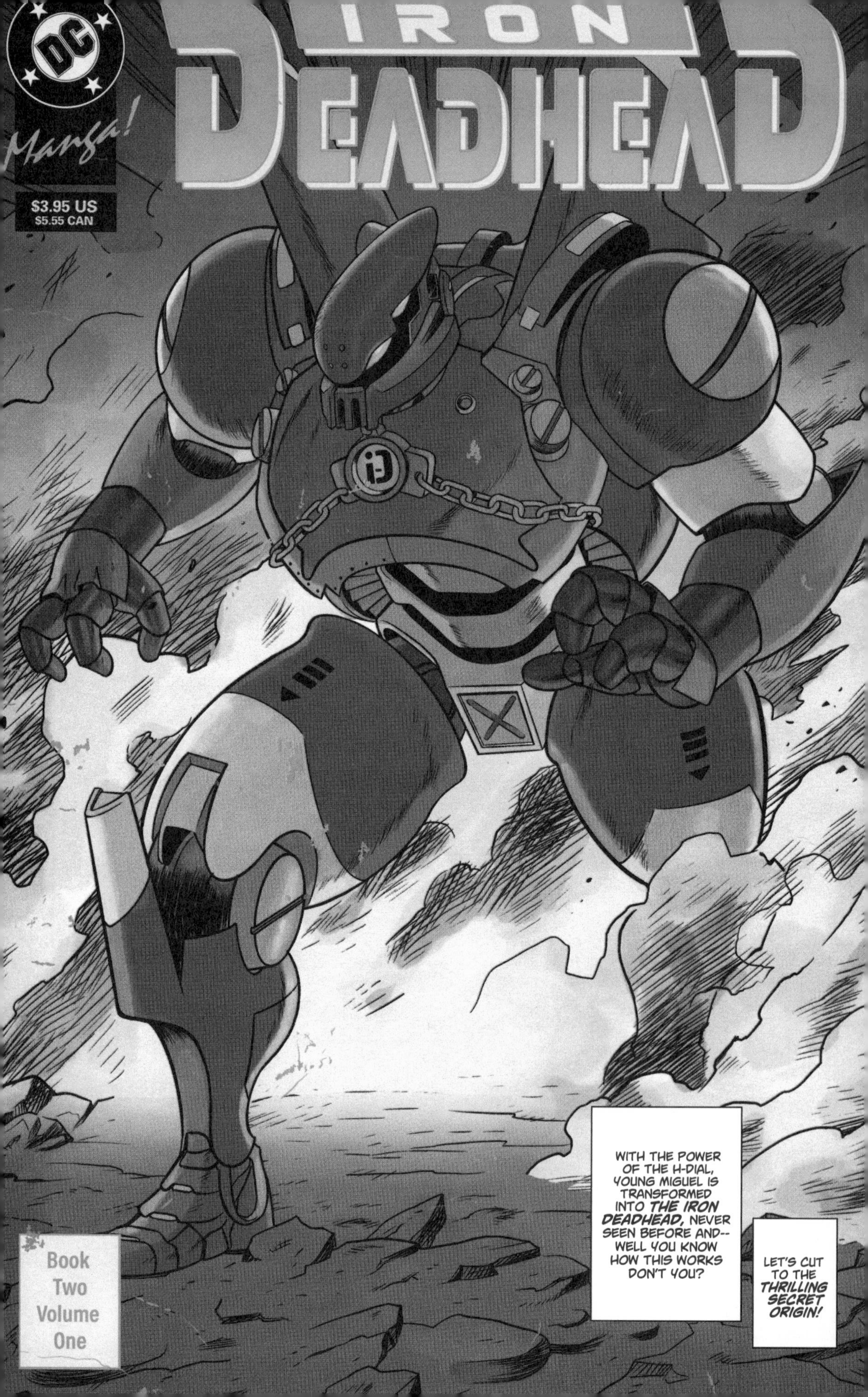

IRON DEADHEAD
DC
Manga!
$3.95 US
$5.55 CAN
Book Two Volume One
WITH THE POWER OF THE H-DIAL, YOUNG MIGUEL IS TRANSFORMED INTO THE IRON DEADHEAD, NEVER SEEN BEFORE AND-- WELL YOU KNOW HOW THIS WORKS DON'T YOU?
LET'S CUT TO THE THRILLING SECRET ORIGIN!

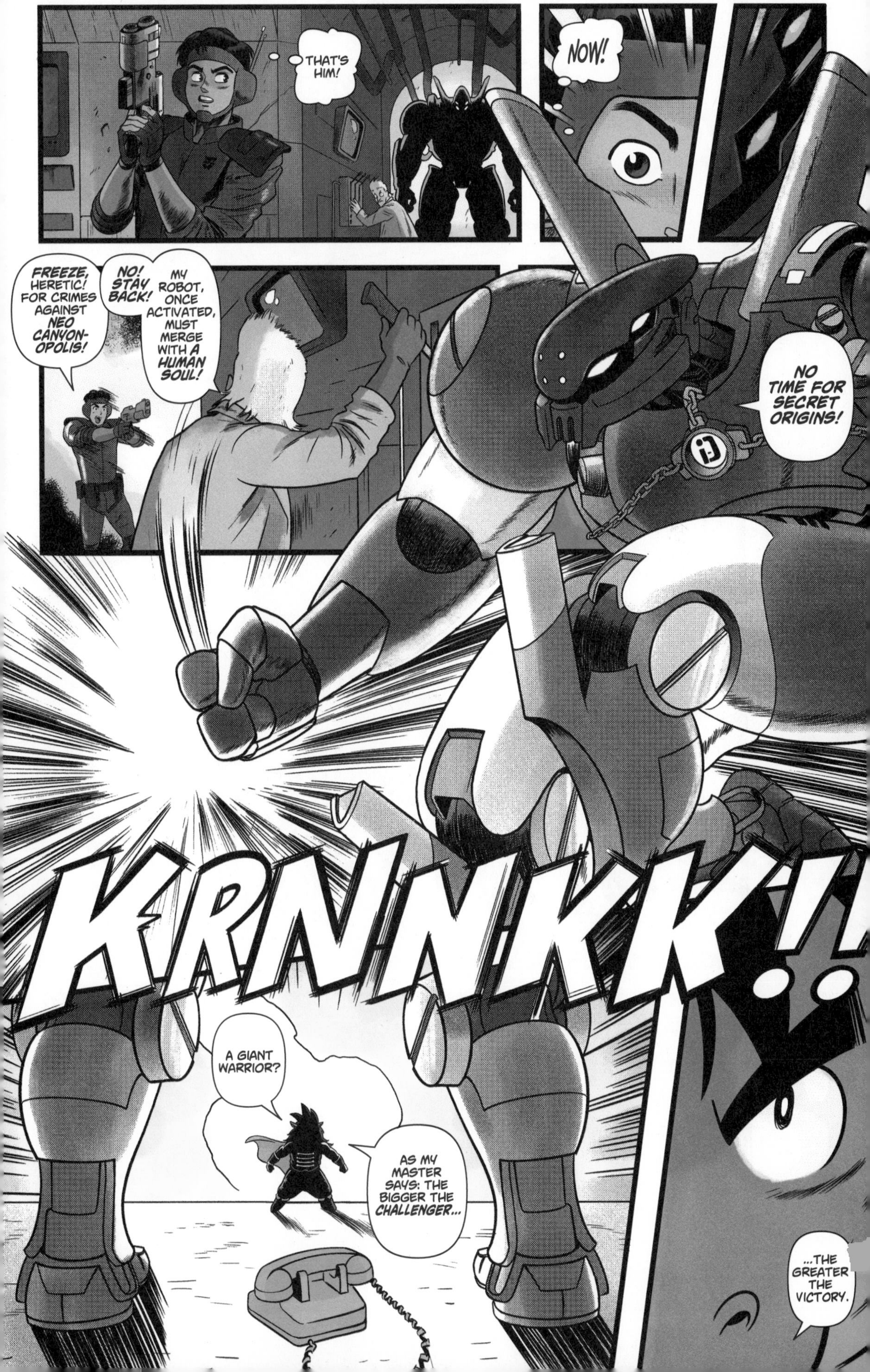
THAT'S HIM!
NOW!
FREEZE, HERETIC! FOR CRIMES AGAINST NEO CANYON-OPOLIS!
NO! STAY BACK!
MY ROBOT, ONCE ACTIVATED, MUST MERGE WITH A HUMAN SOUL!
NO TIME FOR SECRET ORIGINS!
KRNNKK!!
A GIANT WARRIOR?
AS MY MASTER SAYS: THE BIGGER THE CHALLENGER...
...THE GREATER THE VICTORY.

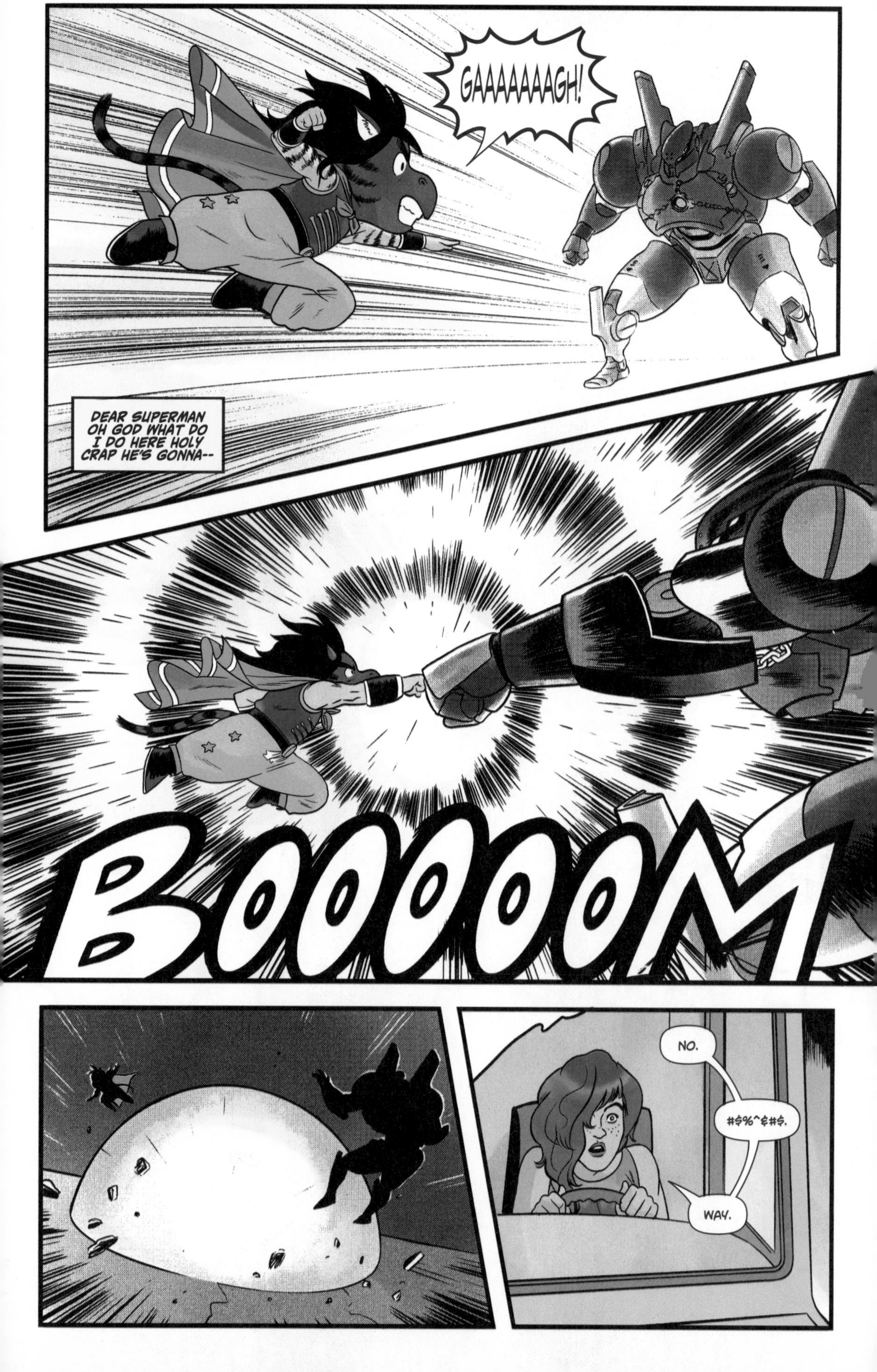
GAAAAAAAGH!
DEAR SUPERMAN OH GOD WHAT DO I DO HERE HOLY CRAP HE'S GONNA--
BOOOOOM
NO.
#$%^¢#$.
WAY.

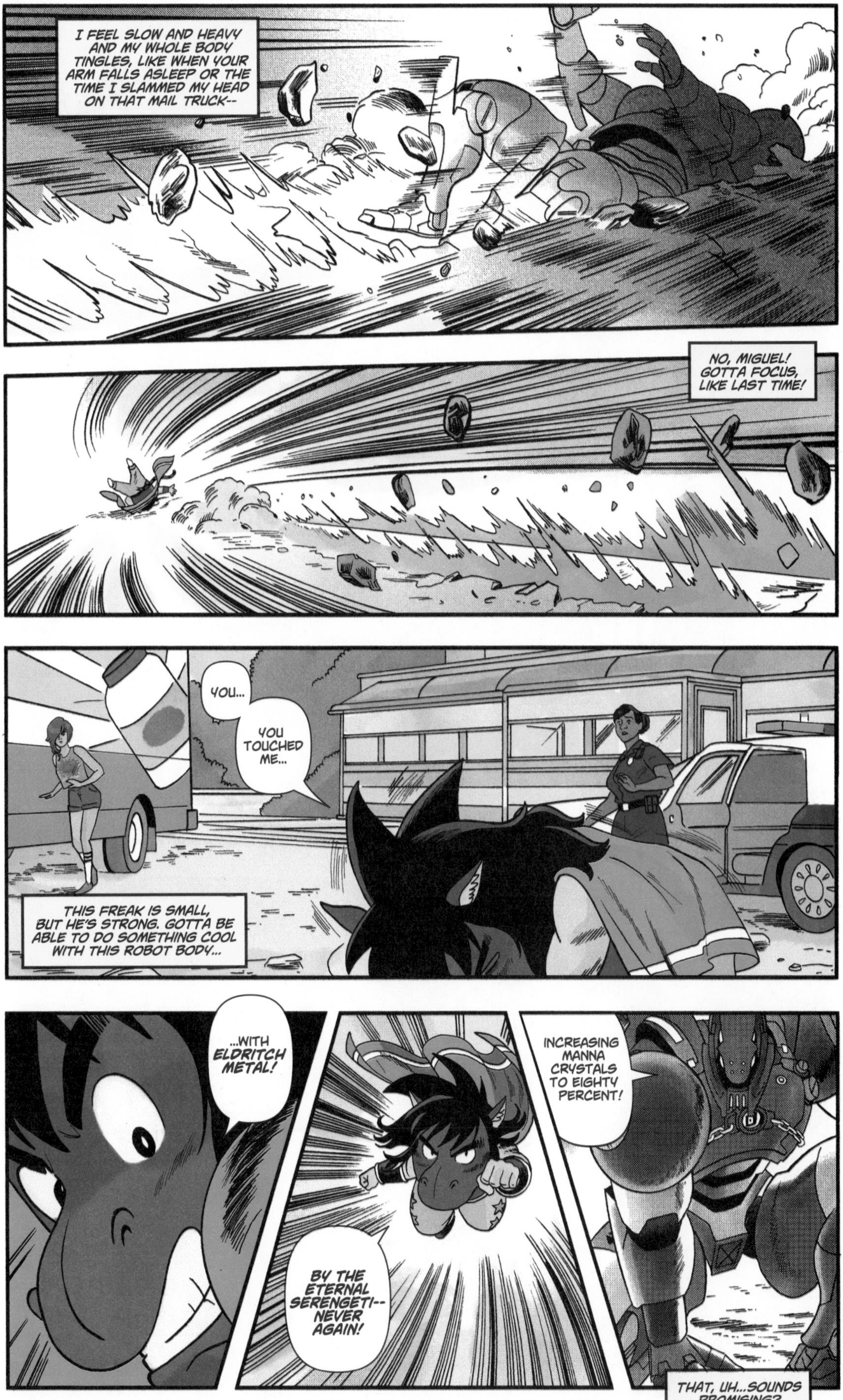
I FEEL SLOW AND HEAVY AND MY WHOLE BODY TINGLES, LIKE WHEN YOUR ARM FALLS ASLEEP OR THE TIME I SLAMMED MY HEAD ON THAT MAIL TRUCK--
NO, MIGUEL! GOTTA FOCUS, LIKE LAST TIME!
YOU...
YOU TOUCHED ME...
THIS FREAK IS SMALL, BUT HE'S STRONG. GOTTA BE ABLE TO DO SOMETHING COOL WITH THIS ROBOT BODY...
...WITH ELDRITCH METAL!
BY THE ETERNAL SERENGETI-- NEVER AGAIN!
INCREASING MANNA CRYSTALS TO EIGHTY PERCENT!
THAT, UH...SOUNDS PROMISING?

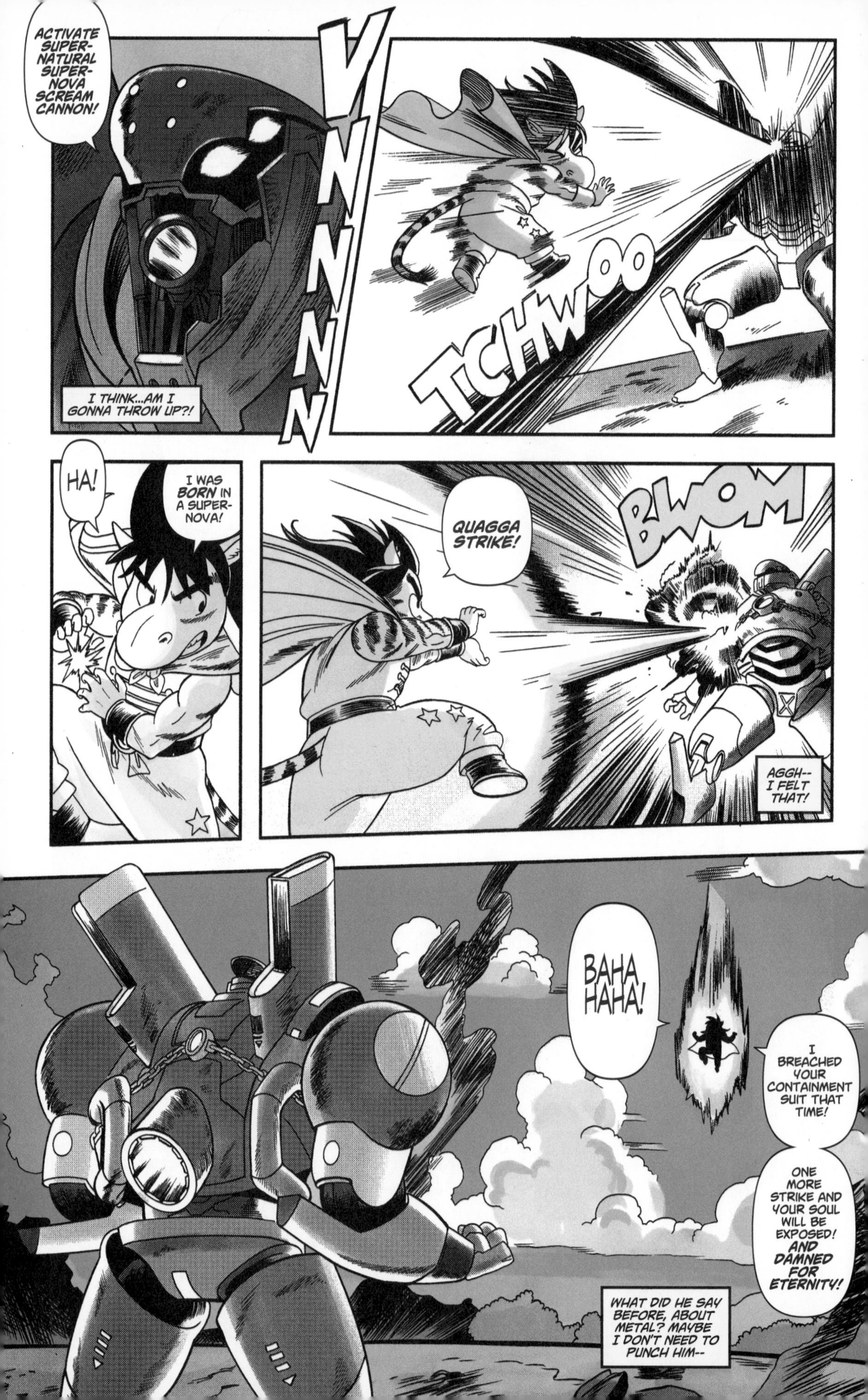
ACTIVATE SUPER-NATURAL SUPER-NOVA SCREAM CANNON!
I THINK...AM I GONNA THROW UP?!
VNNNNNN
TCHWOO
HA!
I WAS BORN IN A SUPER-NOVA!
QUAGGA STRIKE!
BWOM
AGGH-- I FELT THAT!
BAHA HAHA!
I BREACHED YOUR CONTAINMENT SUIT THAT TIME!
ONE MORE STRIKE AND YOUR SOUL WILL BE EXPOSED! AND DAMNED FOR ETERNITY!
WHAT DID HE SAY BEFORE, ABOUT METAL? MAYBE I DON'T NEED TO PUNCH HIM--

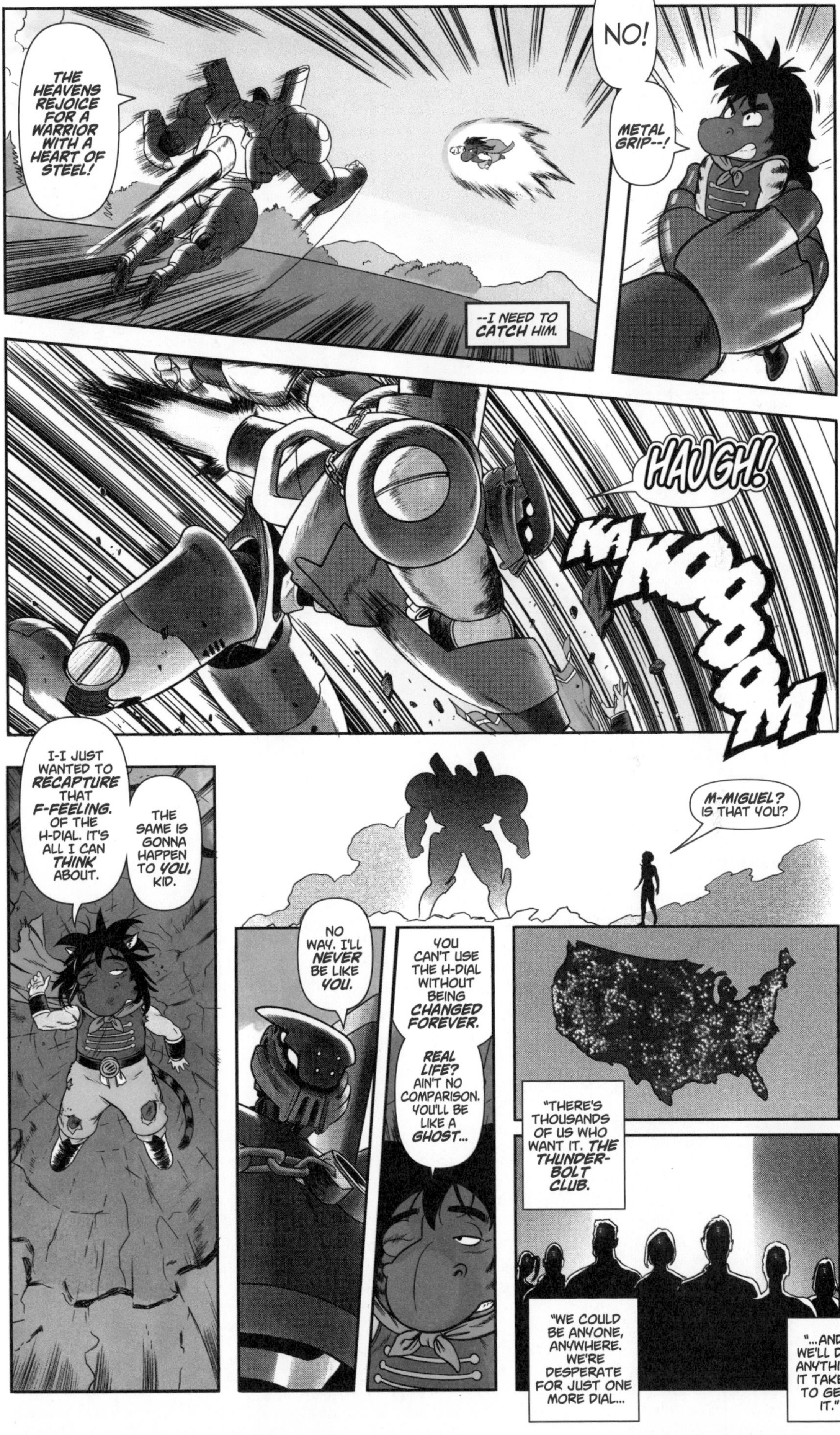
THE HEAVENS REJOICE FOR A WARRIOR WITH A HEART OF STEEL!
NO!
METAL GRIP--!
--I NEED TO CATCH HIM.
HAUGH!
KAKOOOOM
I-I JUST WANTED TO RECAPTURE THAT F-FEELING. OF THE H-DIAL. IT'S ALL I CAN THINK ABOUT.
THE SAME IS GONNA HAPPEN TO YOU, KID.
M-MIGUEL? IS THAT YOU?
NO WAY. I'LL NEVER BE LIKE YOU.
YOU CAN'T USE THE H-DIAL WITHOUT BEING CHANGED FOREVER.
REAL LIFE? AIN'T NO COMPARISON. YOU'LL BE LIKE A GHOST...
"THERE'S THOUSANDS OF US WHO WANT IT. THE THUNDER-BOLT CLUB.
"WE COULD BE ANYONE, ANYWHERE. WE'RE DESPERATE FOR JUST ONE MORE DIAL...
"...AND WE'LL DO ANYTHING IT TAKES TO GET IT."

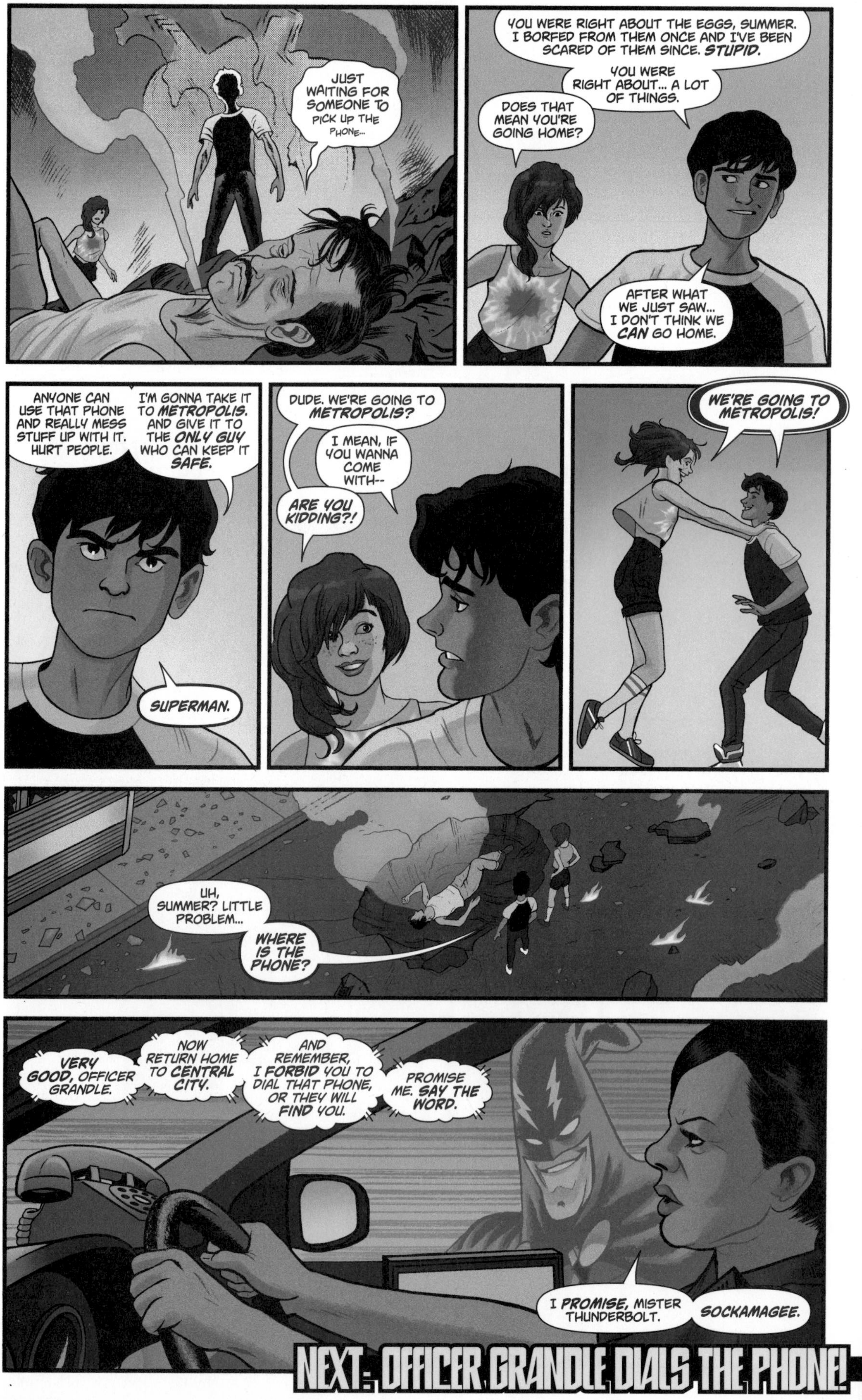
JUST WAITING FOR SOMEONE TO PICK UP THE PHONE...
YOU WERE RIGHT ABOUT THE EGGS, SUMMER. I BORFED FROM THEM ONCE AND I'VE BEEN SCARED OF THEM SINCE. STUPID.
YOU WERE RIGHT ABOUT... A LOT OF THINGS.
DOES THAT MEAN YOU'RE GOING HOME?
AFTER WHAT WE JUST SAW... I DON'T THINK WE CAN GO HOME.
ANYONE CAN USE THAT PHONE AND REALLY MESS STUFF UP WITH IT. HURT PEOPLE.
I'M GONNA TAKE IT TO METROPOLIS. AND GIVE IT TO THE ONLY GUY WHO CAN KEEP IT SAFE.
SUPERMAN.
DUDE. WE'RE GOING TO METROPOLIS?
I MEAN, IF YOU WANNA COME WITH--
ARE YOU KIDDING?!
WE'RE GOING TO METROPOLIS!
UH, SUMMER? LITTLE PROBLEM...
WHERE IS THE PHONE?
VERY GOOD, OFFICER GRANDLE.
NOW RETURN HOME TO CENTRAL CITY.
AND REMEMBER, I FORBID YOU TO DIAL THAT PHONE, OR THEY WILL FIND YOU.
PROMISE ME. SAY THE WORD.
I PROMISE, MISTER THUNDERBOLT.
SOCKAMAGEE.
NEXT: OFFICER GRANDLE DIALS THE PHONE!

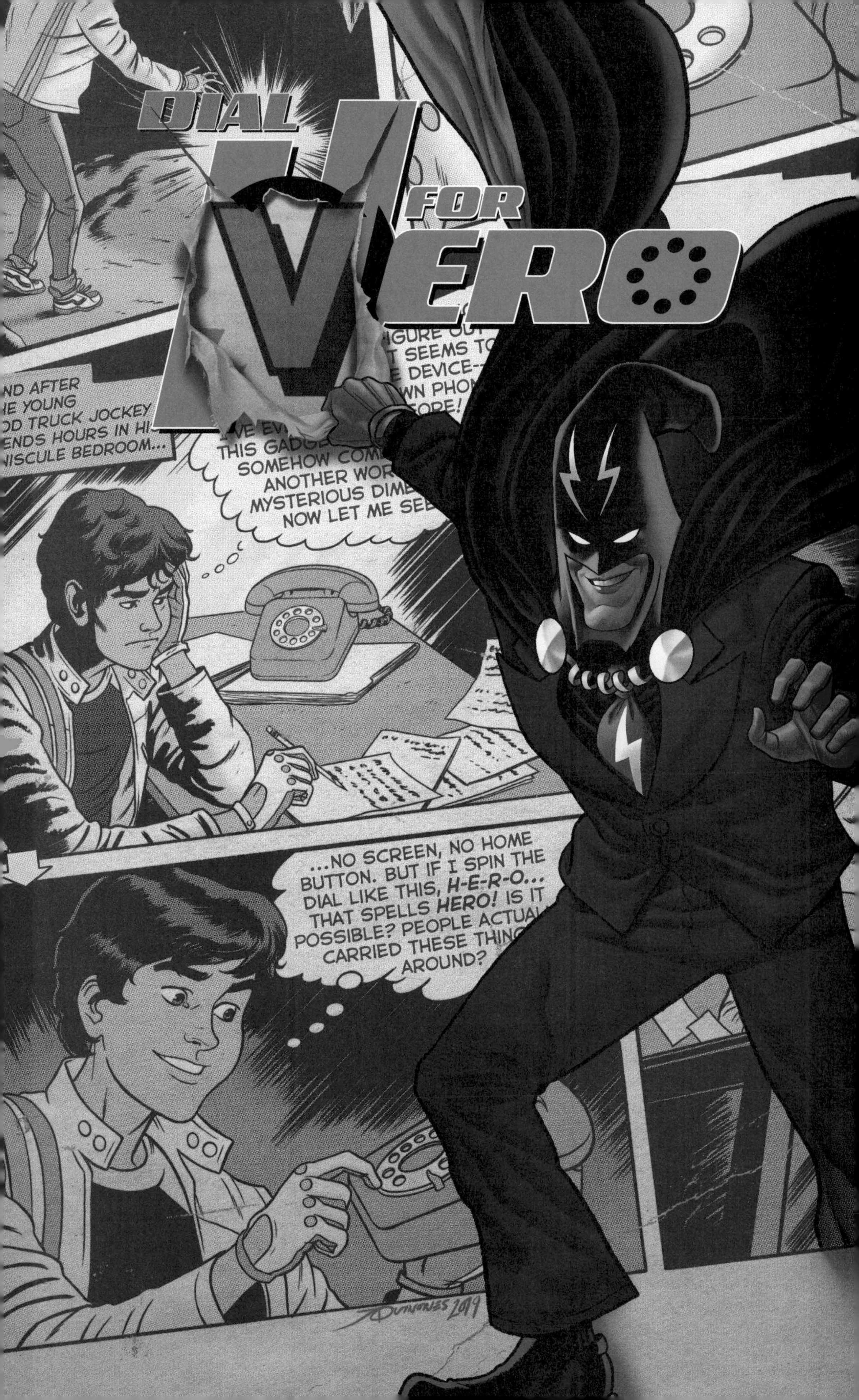

DIAL
FOR
ERO
ND AFTER
HE YOUNG
OD TRUCK JOCKEY
ENDS HOURS IN HI
NISCULE BEDROOM...
IGURE OUT
T SEEMS TO
E DEVICE--
WN PHON
ORE!
VE EVI
THIS GADGE
SOMEHOW COM
ANOTHER WOR
MYSTERIOUS DIME
NOW LET ME SE
...NO SCREEN, NO HOME BUTTON. BUT IF I SPIN THE DIAL LIKE THIS, H-E-R-O... THAT SPELLS HERO! IS IT POSSIBLE? PEOPLE ACTUAL CARRIED THESE THING AROUND?

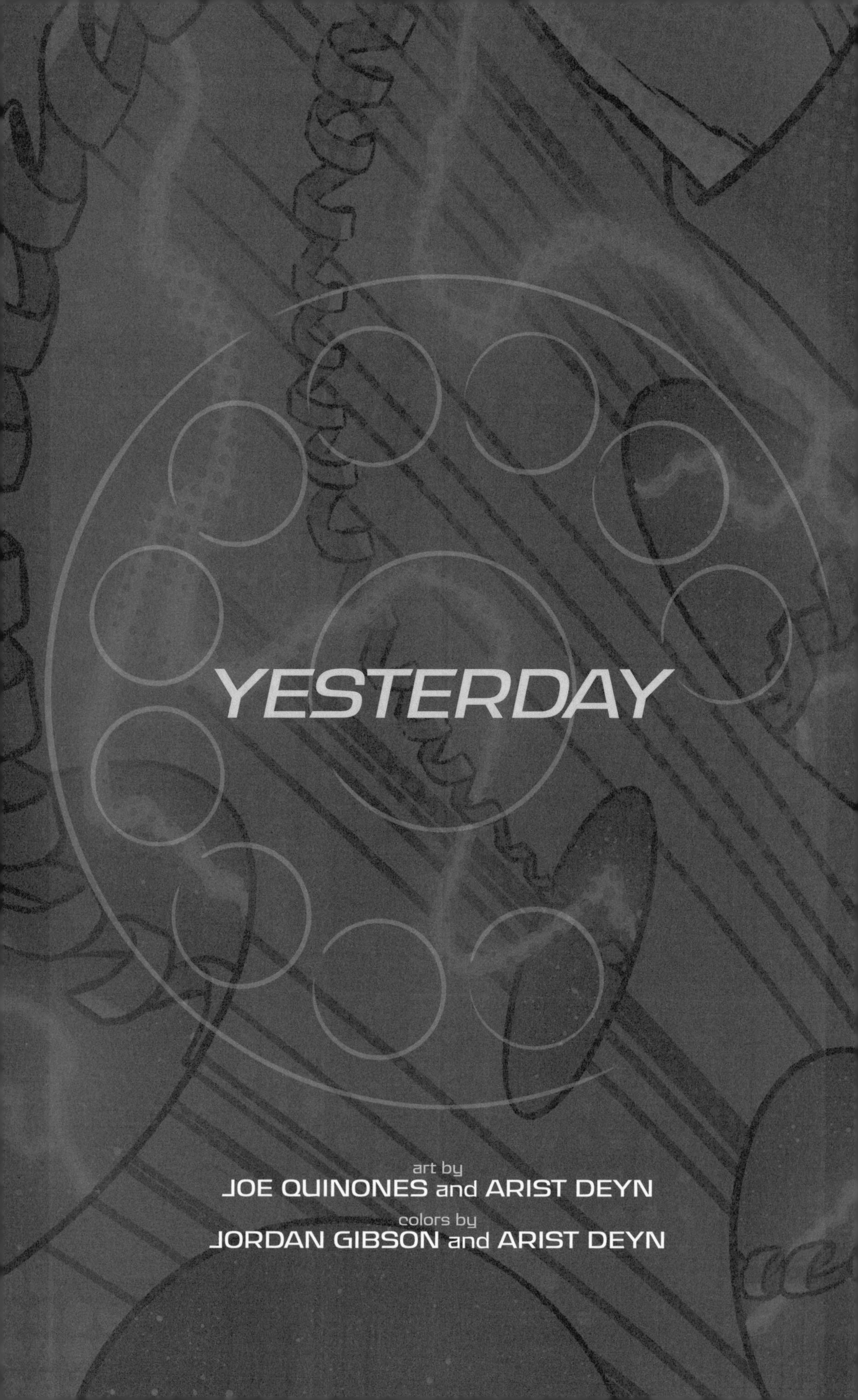

YESTERDAY

art by
JOE QUINONES and ARIST DEYN

colors by
JORDAN GIBSON and ARIST DEYN

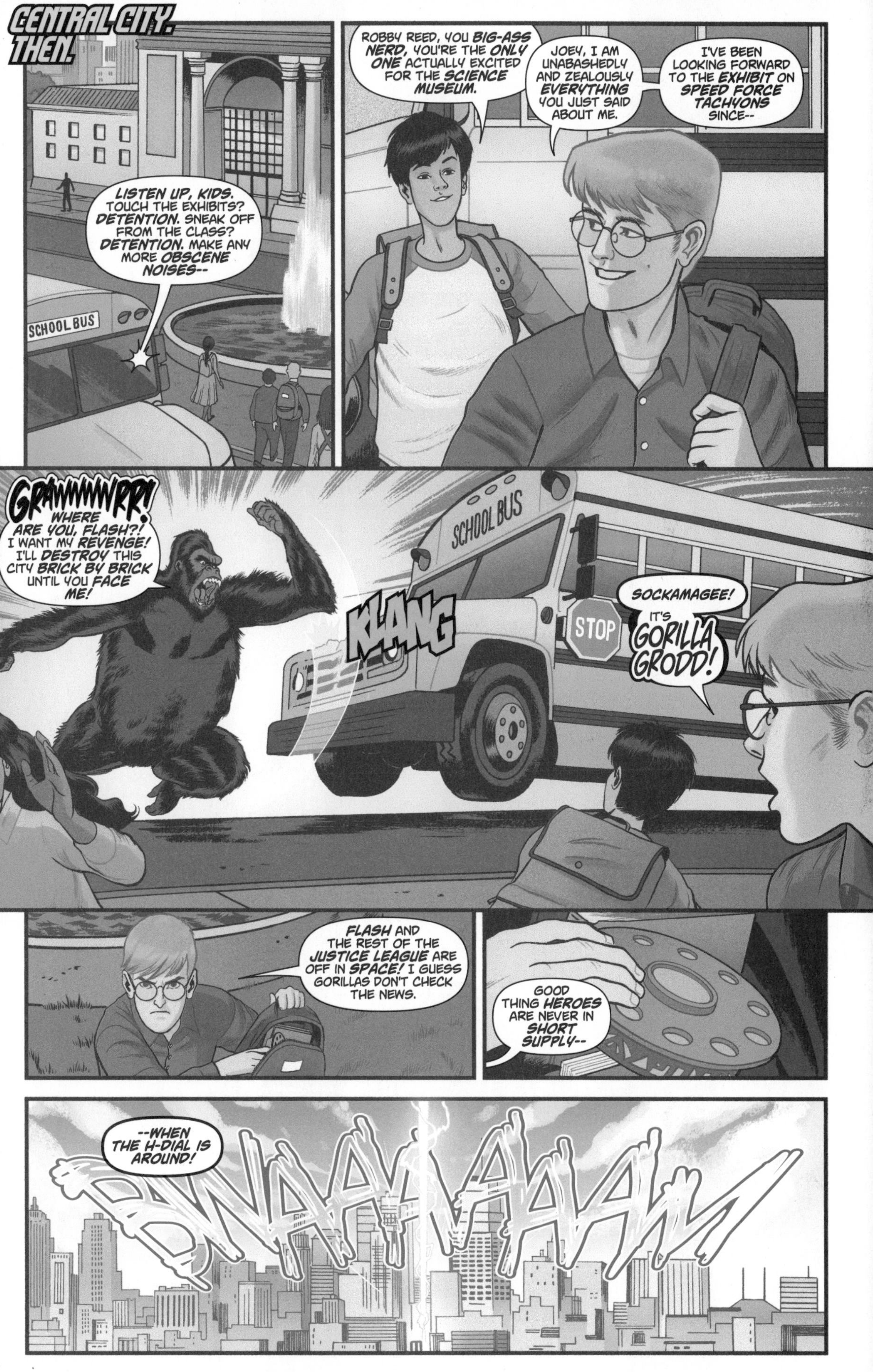
CENTRAL CITY. THEN.
LISTEN UP, KIDS. TOUCH THE EXHIBITS? DETENTION. SNEAK OFF FROM THE CLASS? DETENTION. MAKE ANY MORE OBSCENE NOISES--
SCHOOL BUS
ROBBY REED, YOU BIG-ASS NERD, YOU'RE THE ONLY ONE ACTUALLY EXCITED FOR THE SCIENCE MUSEUM.
JOEY, I AM UNABASHEDLY AND ZEALOUSLY EVERYTHING YOU JUST SAID ABOUT ME.
I'VE BEEN LOOKING FORWARD TO THE EXHIBIT ON SPEED FORCE TACHYONS SINCE--
GRAWWWWRR!
WHERE ARE YOU, FLASH?! I WANT MY REVENGE! I'LL DESTROY THIS CITY BRICK BY BRICK UNTIL YOU FACE ME!
SCHOOL BUS
KLANG
STOP
SOCKAMAGEE!
IT'S GORILLA GRODD!
FLASH AND THE REST OF THE JUSTICE LEAGUE ARE OFF IN SPACE! I GUESS GORILLAS DON'T CHECK THE NEWS.
GOOD THING HEROES ARE NEVER IN SHORT SUPPLY--
--WHEN THE H-DIAL IS AROUND!
BWAAAAAAW

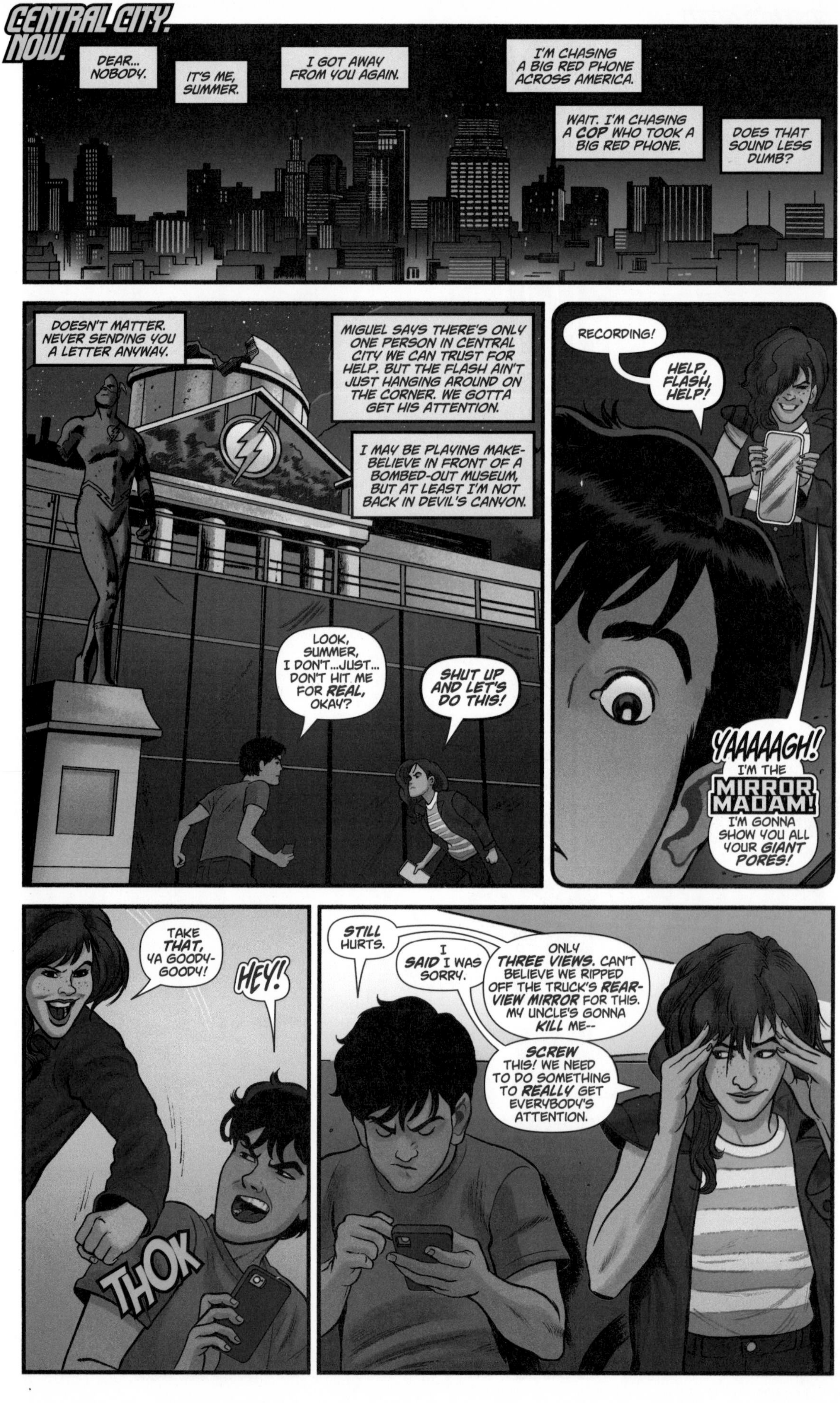
CENTRAL CITY. NOW.
DEAR... NOBODY.
IT'S ME, SUMMER.
I GOT AWAY FROM YOU AGAIN.
I'M CHASING A BIG RED PHONE ACROSS AMERICA.
WAIT. I'M CHASING A COP WHO TOOK A BIG RED PHONE.
DOES THAT SOUND LESS DUMB?
DOESN'T MATTER. NEVER SENDING YOU A LETTER ANYWAY.
MIGUEL SAYS THERE'S ONLY ONE PERSON IN CENTRAL CITY WE CAN TRUST FOR HELP. BUT THE FLASH AIN'T JUST HANGING AROUND ON THE CORNER. WE GOTTA GET HIS ATTENTION.
I MAY BE PLAYING MAKE-BELIEVE IN FRONT OF A BOMBED-OUT MUSEUM, BUT AT LEAST I'M NOT BACK IN DEVIL'S CANYON.
LOOK, SUMMER, I DON'T...JUST... DON'T HIT ME FOR REAL, OKAY?
SHUT UP AND LET'S DO THIS!
RECORDING!
HELP, FLASH, HELP!
YAAAAAGH! I'M THE MIRROR MADAM! I'M GONNA SHOW YOU ALL YOUR GIANT PORES!
TAKE THAT, YA GOODY-GOODY!
HEY!
THOK
STILL HURTS.
I SAID I WAS SORRY.
ONLY THREE VIEWS. CAN'T BELIEVE WE RIPPED OFF THE TRUCK'S REAR-VIEW MIRROR FOR THIS. MY UNCLE'S GONNA KILL ME--
SCREW THIS! WE NEED TO DO SOMETHING TO REALLY GET EVERYBODY'S ATTENTION.

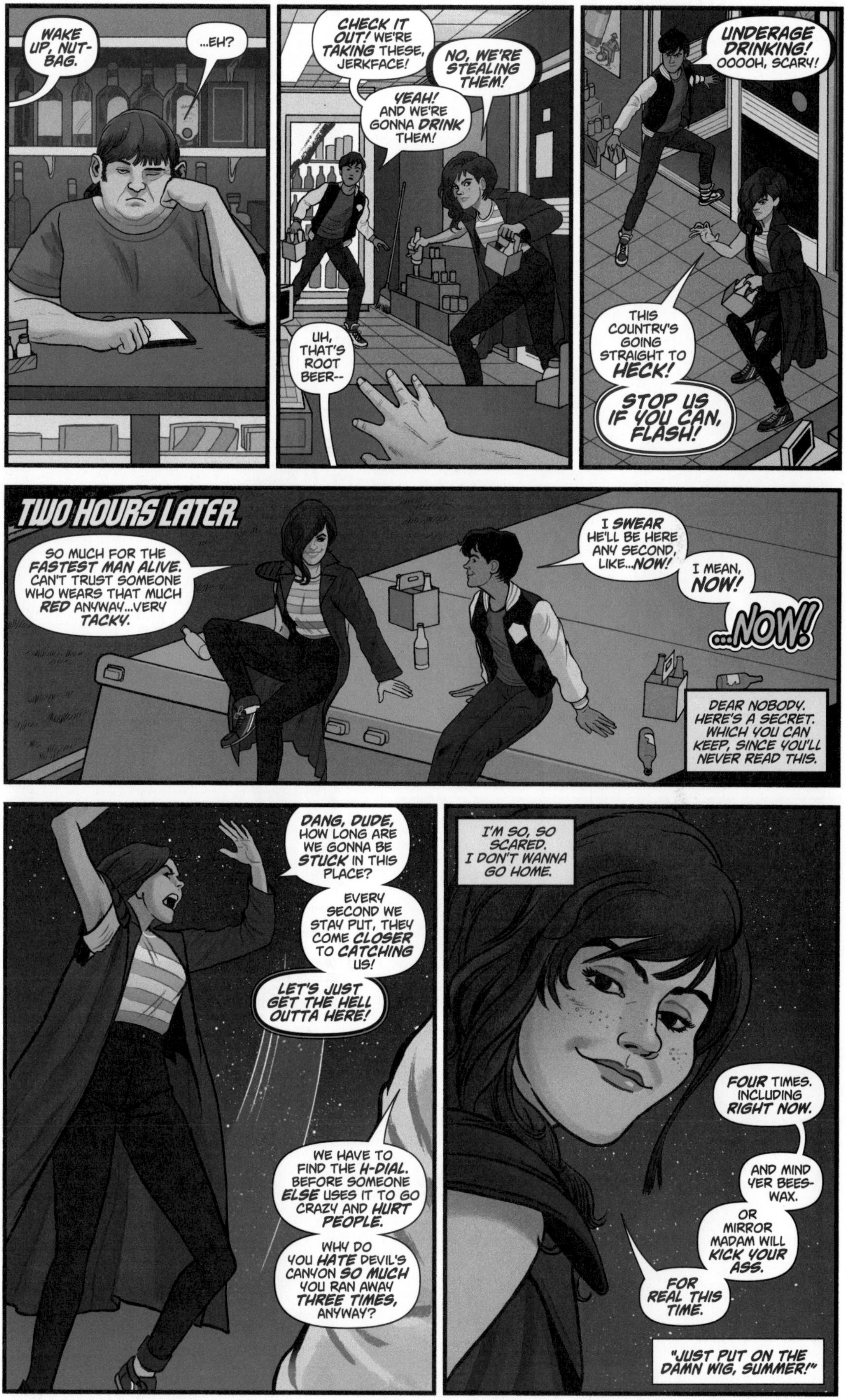
WAKE UP, NUT-BAG.
...EH?
CHECK IT OUT! WE'RE TAKING THESE, JERKFACE!
NO, WE'RE STEALING THEM!
YEAH! AND WE'RE GONNA DRINK THEM!
UH, THAT'S ROOT BEER--
UNDERAGE DRINKING! OOOOH, SCARY!
THIS COUNTRY'S GOING STRAIGHT TO HECK!
STOP US IF YOU CAN, FLASH!
TWO HOURS LATER.
SO MUCH FOR THE FASTEST MAN ALIVE. CAN'T TRUST SOMEONE WHO WEARS THAT MUCH RED ANYWAY...VERY TACKY.
I SWEAR HE'LL BE HERE ANY SECOND, LIKE...NOW!
I MEAN, NOW!
...NOW!
DEAR NOBODY. HERE'S A SECRET. WHICH YOU CAN KEEP, SINCE YOU'LL NEVER READ THIS.
DANG, DUDE, HOW LONG ARE WE GONNA BE STUCK IN THIS PLACE?
EVERY SECOND WE STAY PUT, THEY COME CLOSER TO CATCHING US!
LET'S JUST GET THE HELL OUTTA HERE!
WE HAVE TO FIND THE H-DIAL. BEFORE SOMEONE ELSE USES IT TO GO CRAZY AND HURT PEOPLE.
WHY DO YOU HATE DEVIL'S CANYON SO MUCH YOU RAN AWAY THREE TIMES, ANYWAY?
I'M SO, SO SCARED. I DON'T WANNA GO HOME.
FOUR TIMES. INCLUDING RIGHT NOW.
AND MIND YER BEES-WAX.
OR MIRROR MADAM WILL KICK YOUR ASS.
FOR REAL THIS TIME.
"JUST PUT ON THE DAMN WIG, SUMMER!"

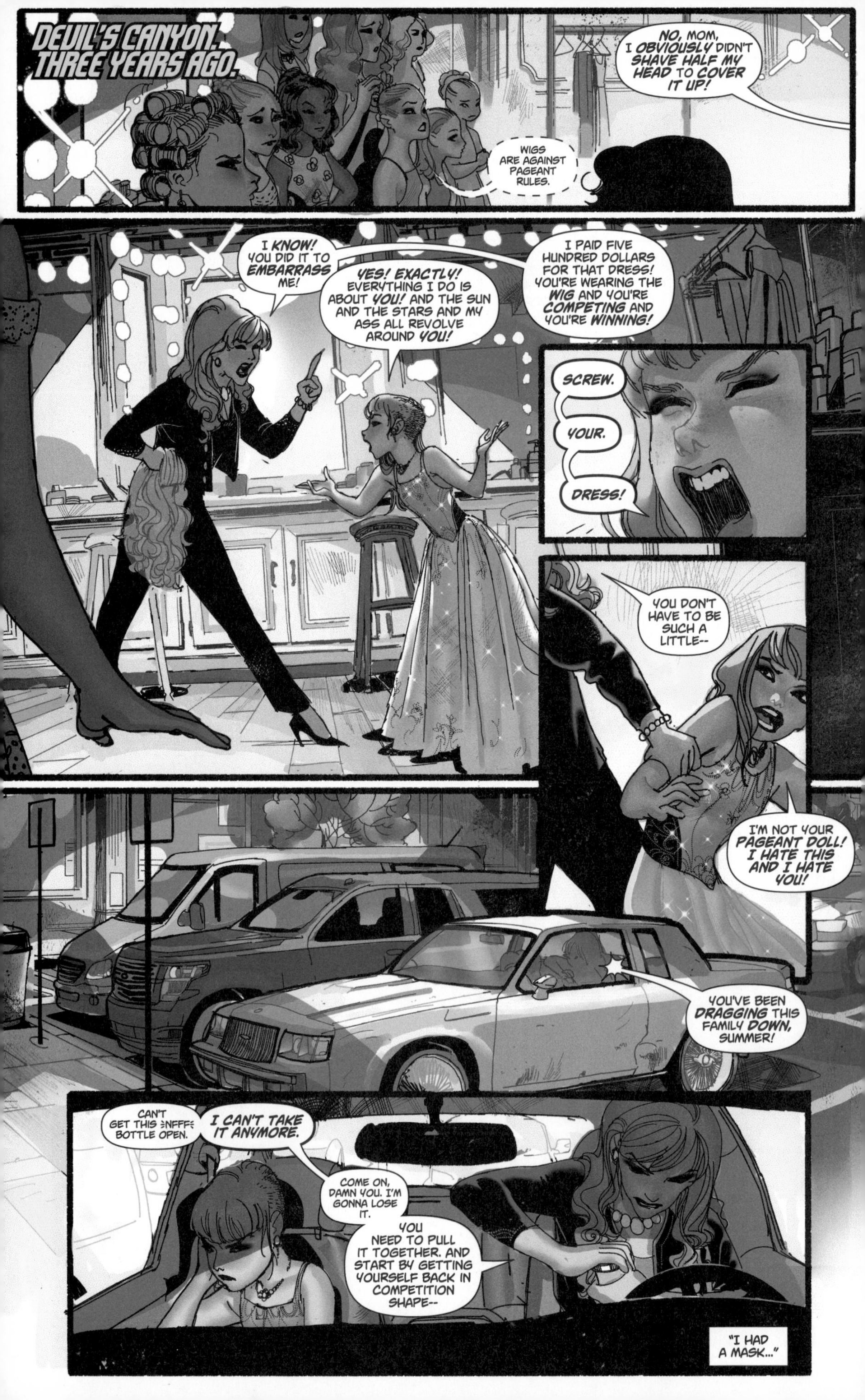

DEVIL'S CANYON. THREE YEARS AGO.
NO, MOM, I OBVIOUSLY DIDN'T SHAVE HALF MY HEAD TO COVER IT UP!
WIGS ARE AGAINST PAGEANT RULES.
I KNOW! YOU DID IT TO EMBARRASS ME!
YES! EXACTLY! EVERYTHING I DO IS ABOUT YOU! AND THE SUN AND THE STARS AND MY ASS ALL REVOLVE AROUND YOU!
I PAID FIVE HUNDRED DOLLARS FOR THAT DRESS! YOU'RE WEARING THE WIG AND YOU'RE COMPETING AND YOU'RE WINNING!
SCREW.
YOUR.
DRESS!
YOU DON'T HAVE TO BE SUCH A LITTLE--
I'M NOT YOUR PAGEANT DOLL! I HATE THIS AND I HATE YOU!
YOU'VE BEEN DRAGGING THIS FAMILY DOWN, SUMMER!
CAN'T GET THIS SNFFF BOTTLE OPEN.
I CAN'T TAKE IT ANYMORE.
COME ON, DAMN YOU. I'M GONNA LOSE IT.
YOU NEED TO PULL IT TOGETHER. AND START BY GETTING YOURSELF BACK IN COMPETITION SHAPE--
"I HAD A MASK..."

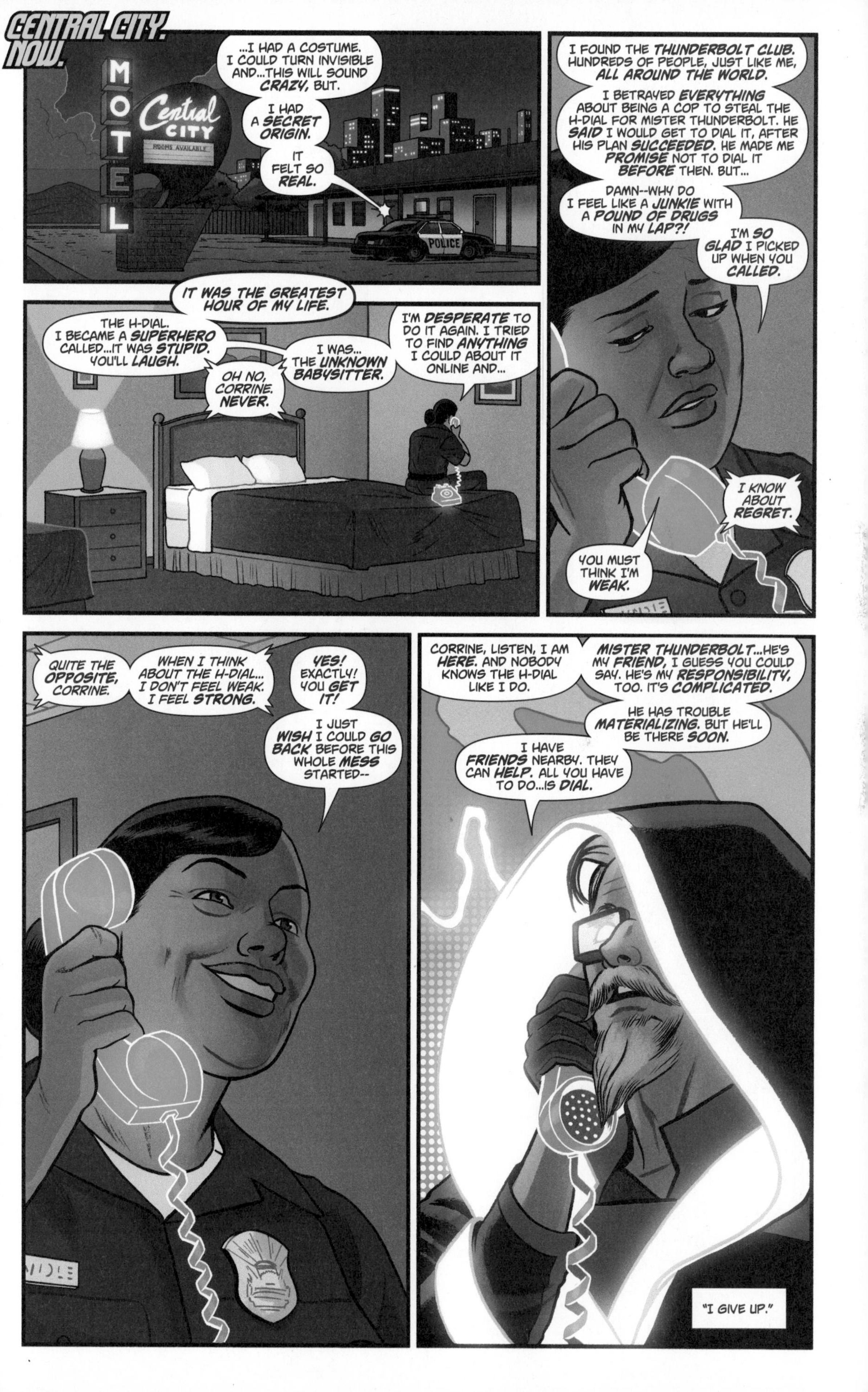
CENTRAL CITY. NOW.
MOTEL
Central CITY
ROOMS AVAILABLE
...I HAD A COSTUME. I COULD TURN INVISIBLE AND...THIS WILL SOUND CRAZY, BUT.
I HAD A SECRET ORIGIN.
IT FELT SO REAL.
POLICE
I FOUND THE THUNDERBOLT CLUB. HUNDREDS OF PEOPLE, JUST LIKE ME, ALL AROUND THE WORLD.
I BETRAYED EVERYTHING ABOUT BEING A COP TO STEAL THE H-DIAL FOR MISTER THUNDERBOLT. HE SAID I WOULD GET TO DIAL IT, AFTER HIS PLAN SUCCEEDED. HE MADE ME PROMISE NOT TO DIAL IT BEFORE THEN. BUT...
DAMN--WHY DO I FEEL LIKE A JUNKIE WITH A POUND OF DRUGS IN MY LAP?!
I'M SO GLAD I PICKED UP WHEN YOU CALLED.
IT WAS THE GREATEST HOUR OF MY LIFE.
THE H-DIAL. I BECAME A SUPERHERO CALLED...IT WAS STUPID. YOU'LL LAUGH.
I WAS... THE UNKNOWN BABYSITTER.
OH NO, CORRINE. NEVER.
I'M DESPERATE TO DO IT AGAIN. I TRIED TO FIND ANYTHING I COULD ABOUT IT ONLINE AND...
YOU MUST THINK I'M WEAK.
I KNOW ABOUT REGRET.
QUITE THE OPPOSITE, CORRINE.
WHEN I THINK ABOUT THE H-DIAL... I DON'T FEEL WEAK. I FEEL STRONG.
YES! EXACTLY! YOU GET IT!
I JUST WISH I COULD GO BACK BEFORE THIS WHOLE MESS STARTED--
CORRINE, LISTEN, I AM HERE. AND NOBODY KNOWS THE H-DIAL LIKE I DO.
MISTER THUNDERBOLT...HE'S MY FRIEND, I GUESS YOU COULD SAY. HE'S MY RESPONSIBILITY, TOO. IT'S COMPLICATED.
HE HAS TROUBLE MATERIALIZING. BUT HE'LL BE THERE SOON.
I HAVE FRIENDS NEARBY. THEY CAN HELP. ALL YOU HAVE TO DO...IS DIAL.
"I GIVE UP."

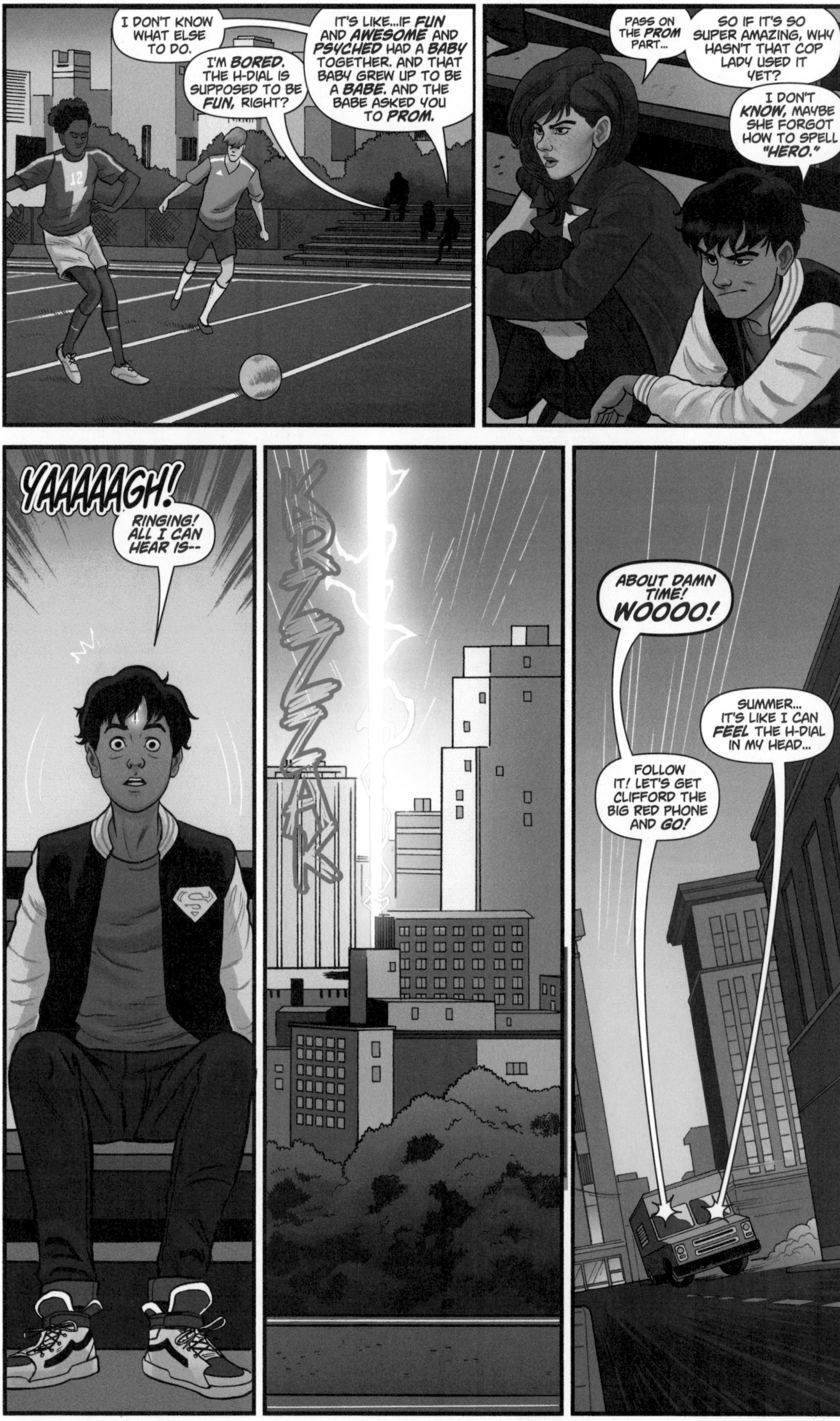
I DON'T KNOW WHAT ELSE TO DO.
I'M BORED. THE H-DIAL IS SUPPOSED TO BE FUN, RIGHT?
IT'S LIKE...IF FUN AND AWESOME AND PSYCHED HAD A BABY TOGETHER. AND THAT BABY GREW UP TO BE A BABE. AND THE BABE ASKED YOU TO PROM.
PASS ON THE PROM PART...
SO IF IT'S SO SUPER AMAZING, WHY HASN'T THAT COP LADY USED IT YET?
I DON'T KNOW, MAYBE SHE FORGOT HOW TO SPELL "HERO."
YAAAAAGH!
RINGING! ALL I CAN HEAR IS--
KRZZZZAK
ABOUT DAMN TIME! WOOOO!
SUMMER... IT'S LIKE I CAN FEEL THE H-DIAL IN MY HEAD...
FOLLOW IT! LET'S GET CLIFFORD THE BIG RED PHONE AND GO!

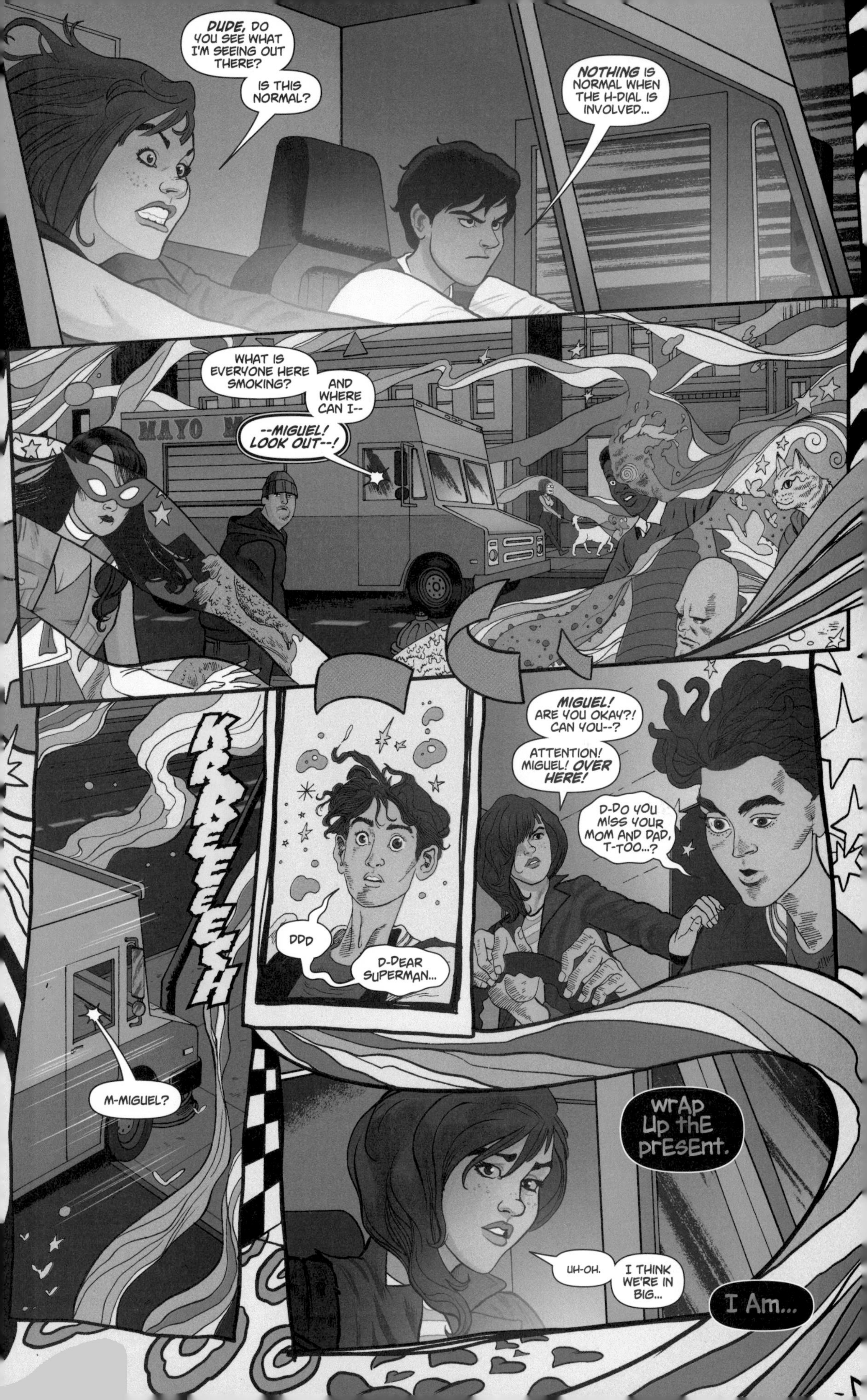
DUDE, DO YOU SEE WHAT I'M SEEING OUT THERE?
IS THIS NORMAL?
NOTHING IS NORMAL WHEN THE H-DIAL IS INVOLVED...
WHAT IS EVERYONE HERE SMOKING?
AND WHERE CAN I--
--MIGUEL! LOOK OUT--!
MAYO
KRBEEEESH
DDD
D-DEAR SUPERMAN...
MIGUEL! ARE YOU OKAY?! CAN YOU--?
ATTENTION! MIGUEL! OVER HERE!
D-DO YOU MISS YOUR MOM AND DAD, T-TOO...?
M-MIGUEL?
wrAp Up thE prESEnt.
UH-OH.
I THINK WE'RE IN BIG...
I Am...

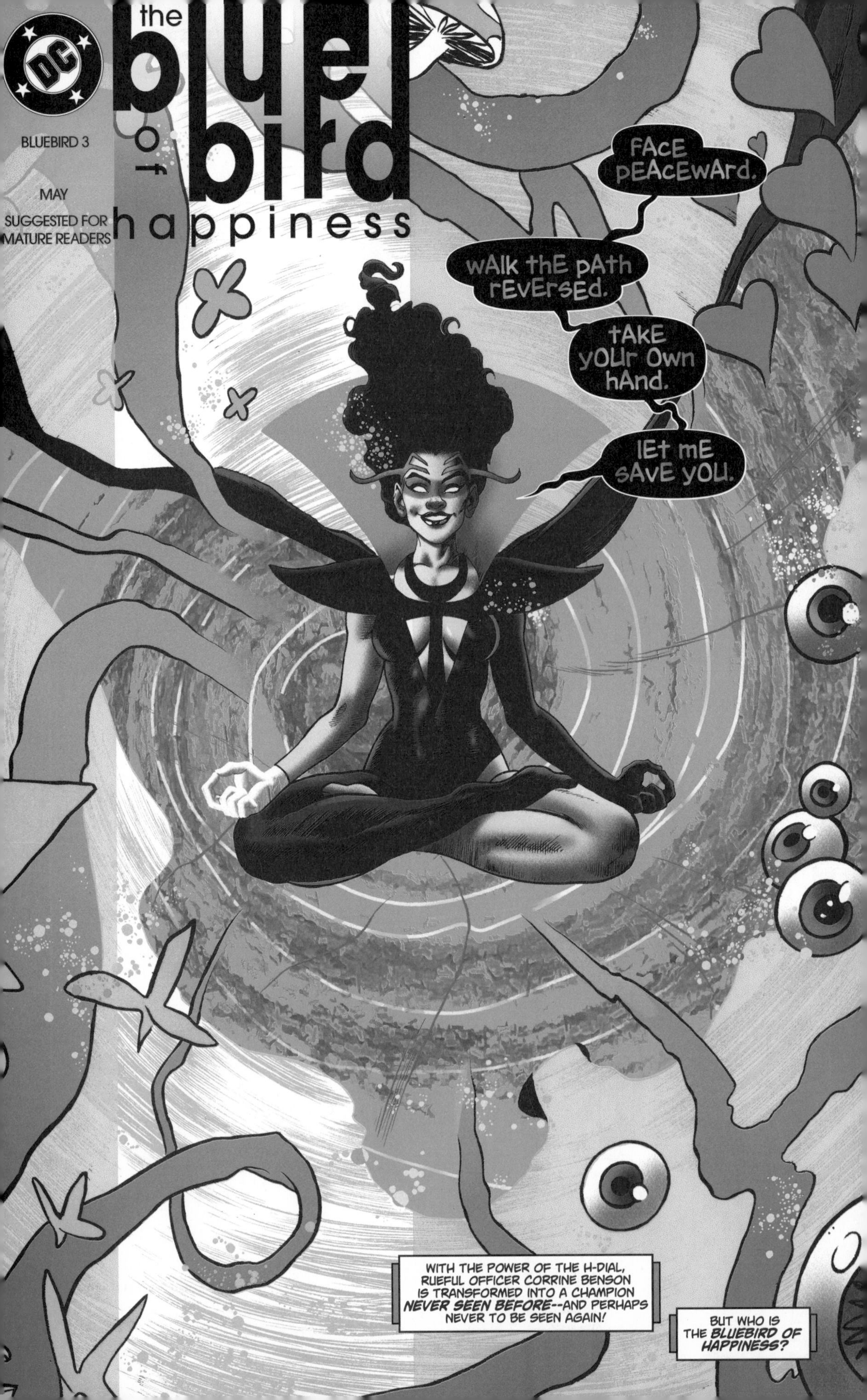
the bluebird of happiness
BLUEBIRD 3
MAY
SUGGESTED FOR MATURE READERS
FACE PEACEWARD.
WALK THE PATH REVERSED.
TAKE YOUR OWN HAND.
LET ME SAVE YOU.
WITH THE POWER OF THE H-DIAL, RUEFUL OFFICER CORRINE BENSON IS TRANSFORMED INTO A CHAMPION *NEVER SEEN BEFORE*--AND PERHAPS NEVER TO BE SEEN AGAIN!
BUT WHO IS THE *BLUEBIRD OF HAPPINESS?*

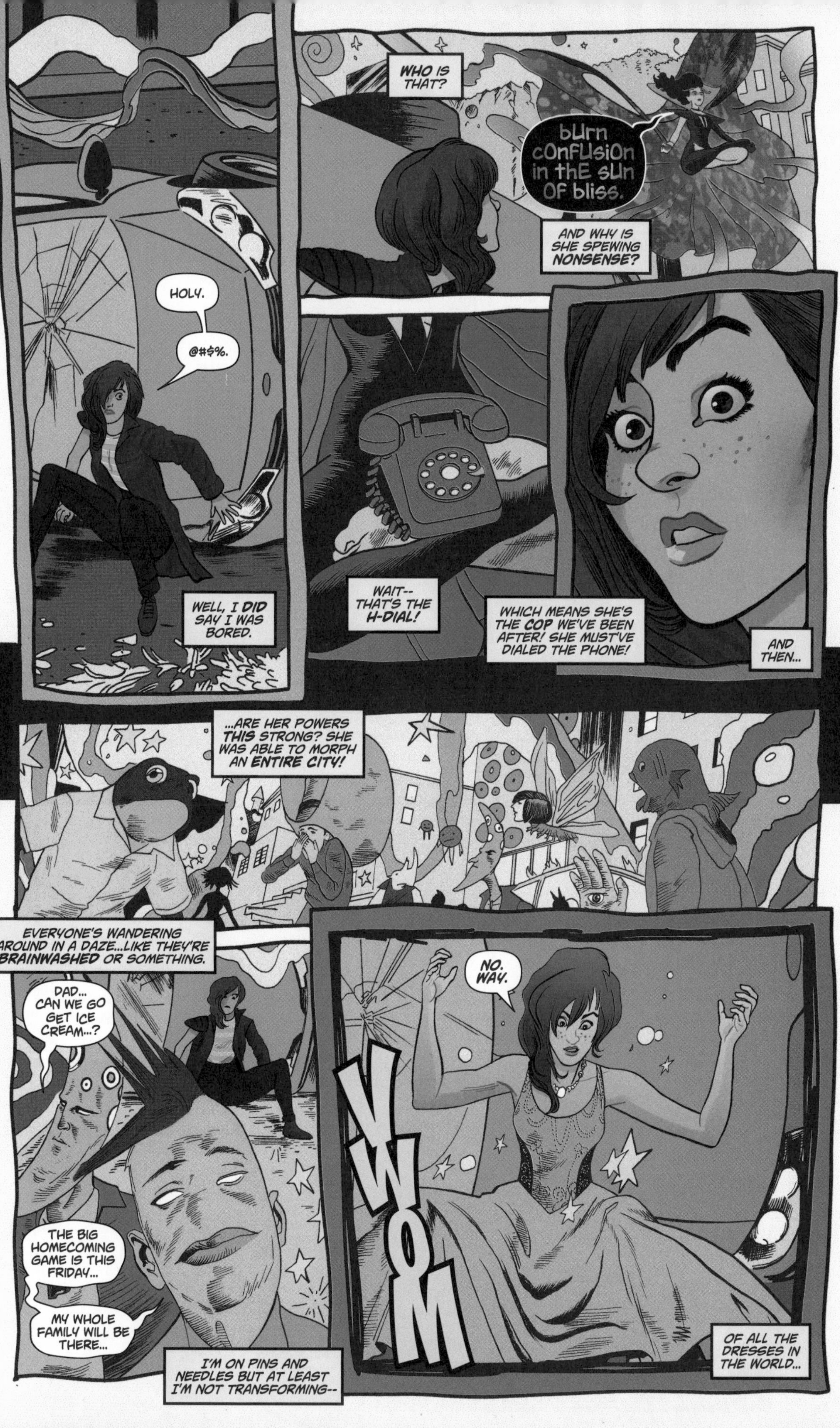

HOLY.
@#$%.
WELL, I DID SAY I WAS BORED.
WHO IS THAT?
burn confusion in the sun of bliss.
AND WHY IS SHE SPEWING NONSENSE?
WAIT-- THAT'S THE H-DIAL!
WHICH MEANS SHE'S THE COP WE'VE BEEN AFTER! SHE MUST'VE DIALED THE PHONE!
AND THEN...
...ARE HER POWERS THIS STRONG? SHE WAS ABLE TO MORPH AN ENTIRE CITY!
EVERYONE'S WANDERING AROUND IN A DAZE...LIKE THEY'RE BRAINWASHED OR SOMETHING.
DAD... CAN WE GO GET ICE CREAM...?
THE BIG HOMECOMING GAME IS THIS FRIDAY...
MY WHOLE FAMILY WILL BE THERE...
I'M ON PINS AND NEEDLES BUT AT LEAST I'M NOT TRANSFORMING--
NO. WAY.
VWOM
OF ALL THE DRESSES IN THE WORLD...

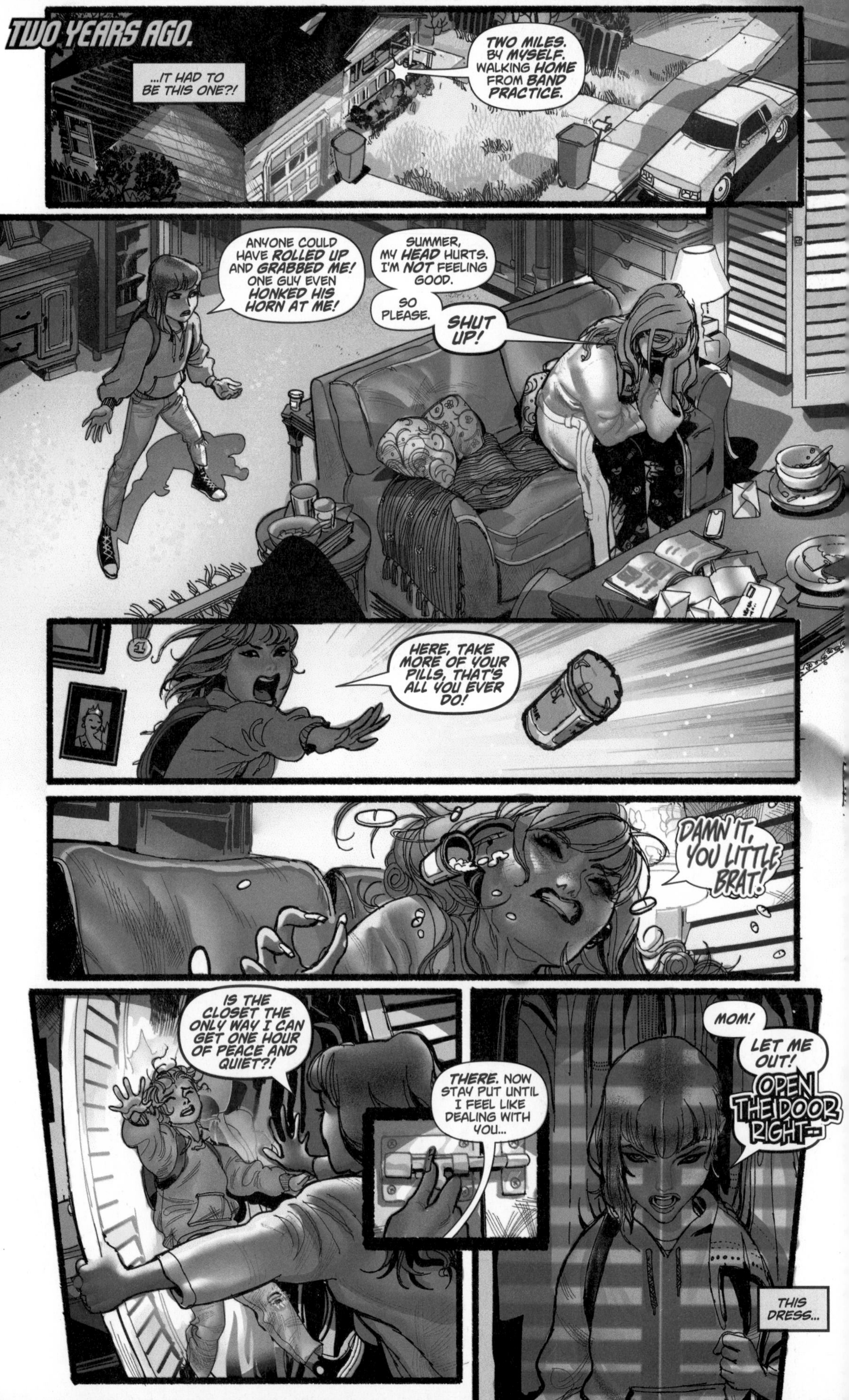
TWO YEARS AGO.
...IT HAD TO BE THIS ONE?!
TWO MILES. BY MYSELF. WALKING HOME FROM BAND PRACTICE.
ANYONE COULD HAVE ROLLED UP AND GRABBED ME! ONE GUY EVEN HONKED HIS HORN AT ME!
SUMMER, MY HEAD HURTS. I'M NOT FEELING GOOD.
SO PLEASE.
SHUT UP!
HERE, TAKE MORE OF YOUR PILLS, THAT'S ALL YOU EVER DO!
DAMN IT, YOU LITTLE BRAT!
IS THE CLOSET THE ONLY WAY I CAN GET ONE HOUR OF PEACE AND QUIET?!
THERE. NOW STAY PUT UNTIL I FEEL LIKE DEALING WITH YOU...
MOM!
LET ME OUT!
OPEN THE DOOR RIGHT--
THIS DRESS...

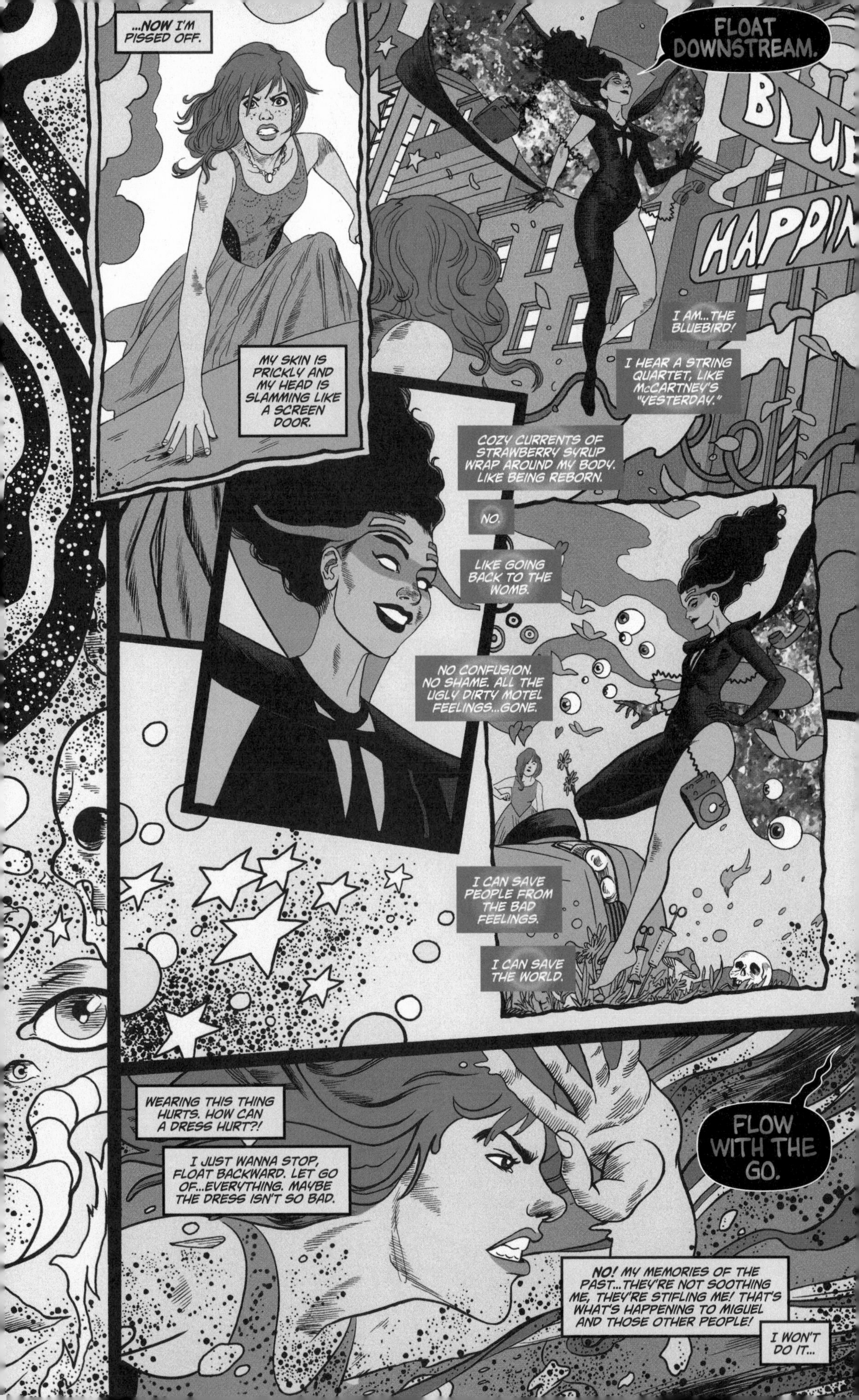
...NOW I'M PISSED OFF.
FLOAT DOWNSTREAM.
MY SKIN IS PRICKLY AND MY HEAD IS SLAMMING LIKE A SCREEN DOOR.
I AM...THE BLUEBIRD!
I HEAR A STRING QUARTET, LIKE McCARTNEY'S "YESTERDAY."
COZY CURRENTS OF STRAWBERRY SYRUP WRAP AROUND MY BODY. LIKE BEING REBORN.
NO.
LIKE GOING BACK TO THE WOMB.
NO CONFUSION. NO SHAME. ALL THE UGLY DIRTY MOTEL FEELINGS...GONE.
I CAN SAVE PEOPLE FROM THE BAD FEELINGS.
I CAN SAVE THE WORLD.
WEARING THIS THING HURTS. HOW CAN A DRESS HURT?!
I JUST WANNA STOP, FLOAT BACKWARD. LET GO OF...EVERYTHING. MAYBE THE DRESS ISN'T SO BAD.
FLOW WITH THE GO.
NO! MY MEMORIES OF THE PAST...THEY'RE NOT SOOTHING ME, THEY'RE STIFLING ME! THAT'S WHAT'S HAPPENING TO MIGUEL AND THOSE OTHER PEOPLE!
I WON'T DO IT...

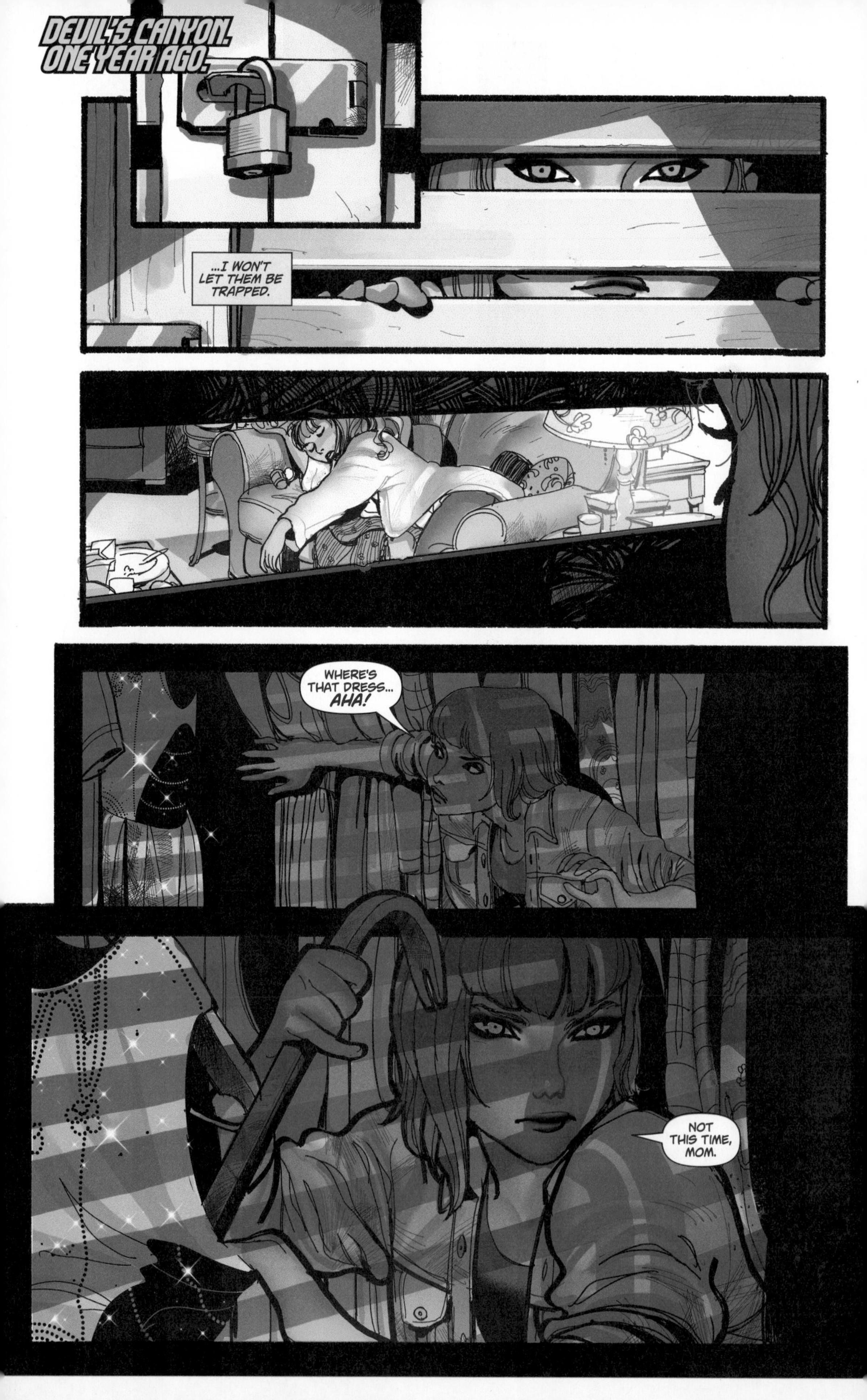
DEVIL'S CANYON. ONE YEAR AGO.
...I WON'T LET THEM BE TRAPPED.
WHERE'S THAT DRESS... AHA!
NOT THIS TIME, MOM.

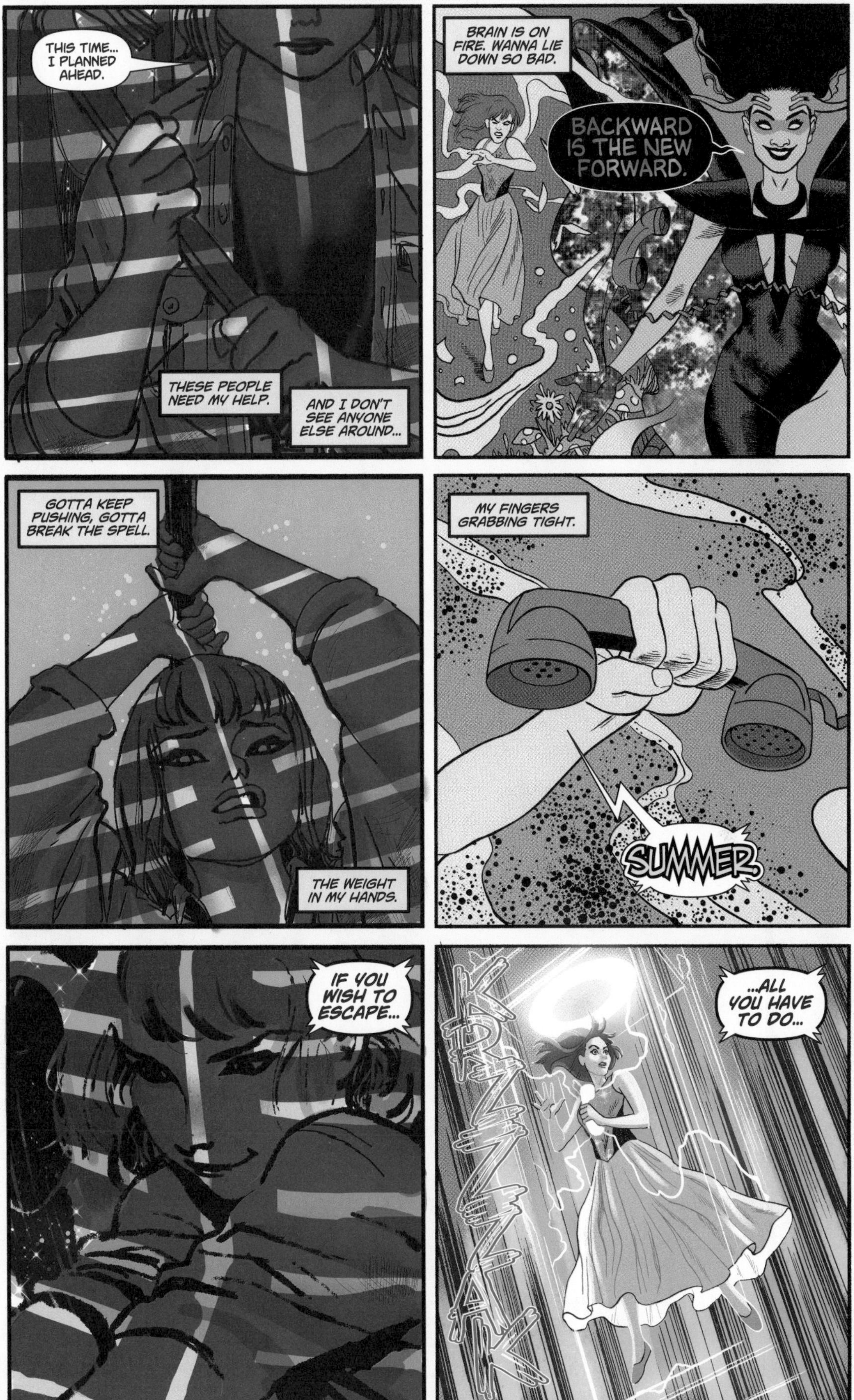
THIS TIME... I PLANNED AHEAD.
THESE PEOPLE NEED MY HELP.
AND I DON'T SEE ANYONE ELSE AROUND...
BRAIN IS ON FIRE. WANNA LIE DOWN SO BAD.
BACKWARD IS THE NEW FORWARD.
GOTTA KEEP PUSHING, GOTTA BREAK THE SPELL.
THE WEIGHT IN MY HANDS.
MY FINGERS GRABBING TIGHT.
SUMMER.
IF YOU WISH TO ESCAPE...
...ALL YOU HAVE TO DO...

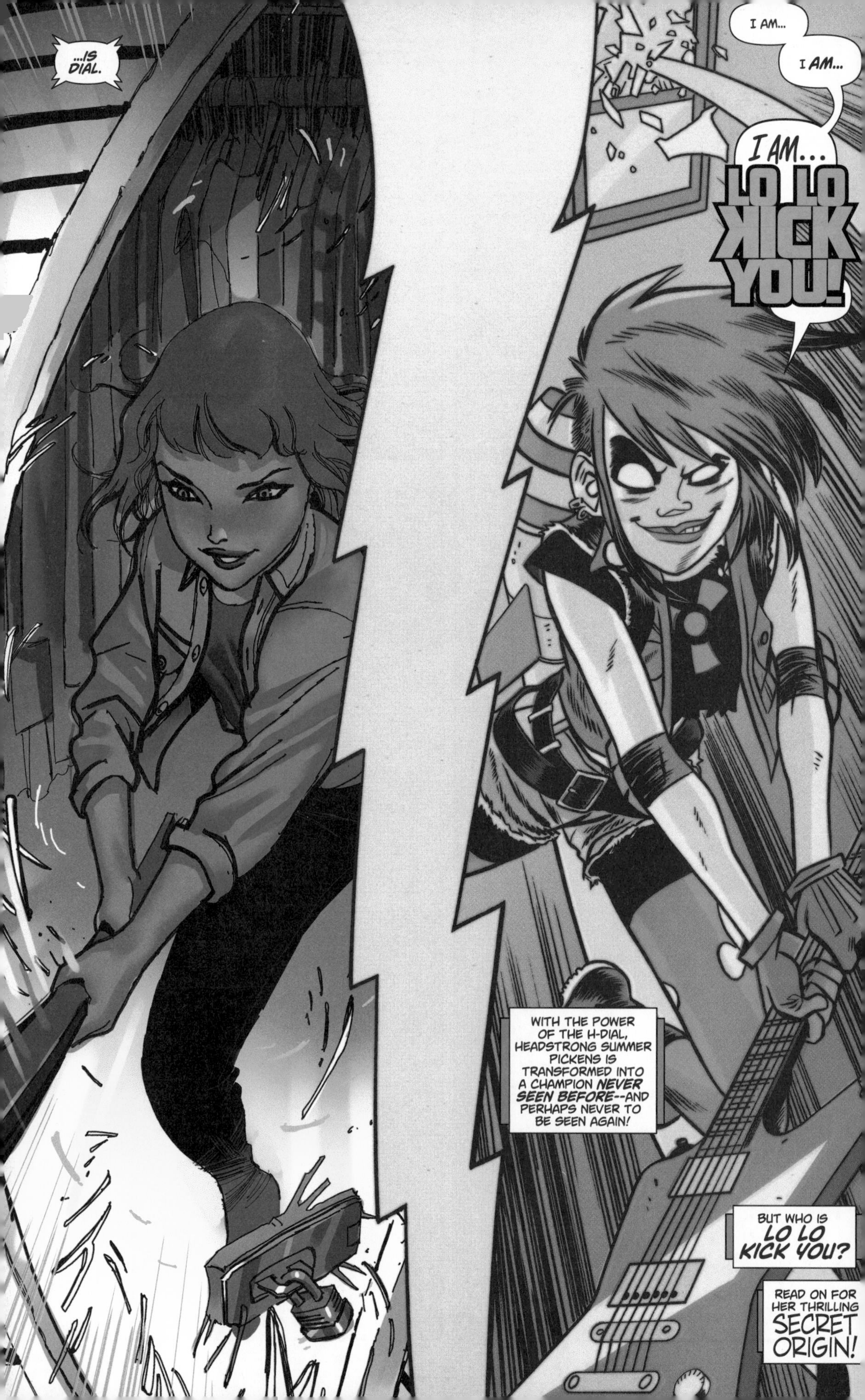
...IS DIAL.
I AM...
I AM...
I AM... LO LO KICK YOU!
WITH THE POWER OF THE H-DIAL, HEADSTRONG SUMMER PICKENS IS TRANSFORMED INTO A CHAMPION NEVER SEEN BEFORE--AND PERHAPS NEVER TO BE SEEN AGAIN!
BUT WHO IS LO LO KICK YOU?
READ ON FOR HER THRILLING SECRET ORIGIN!

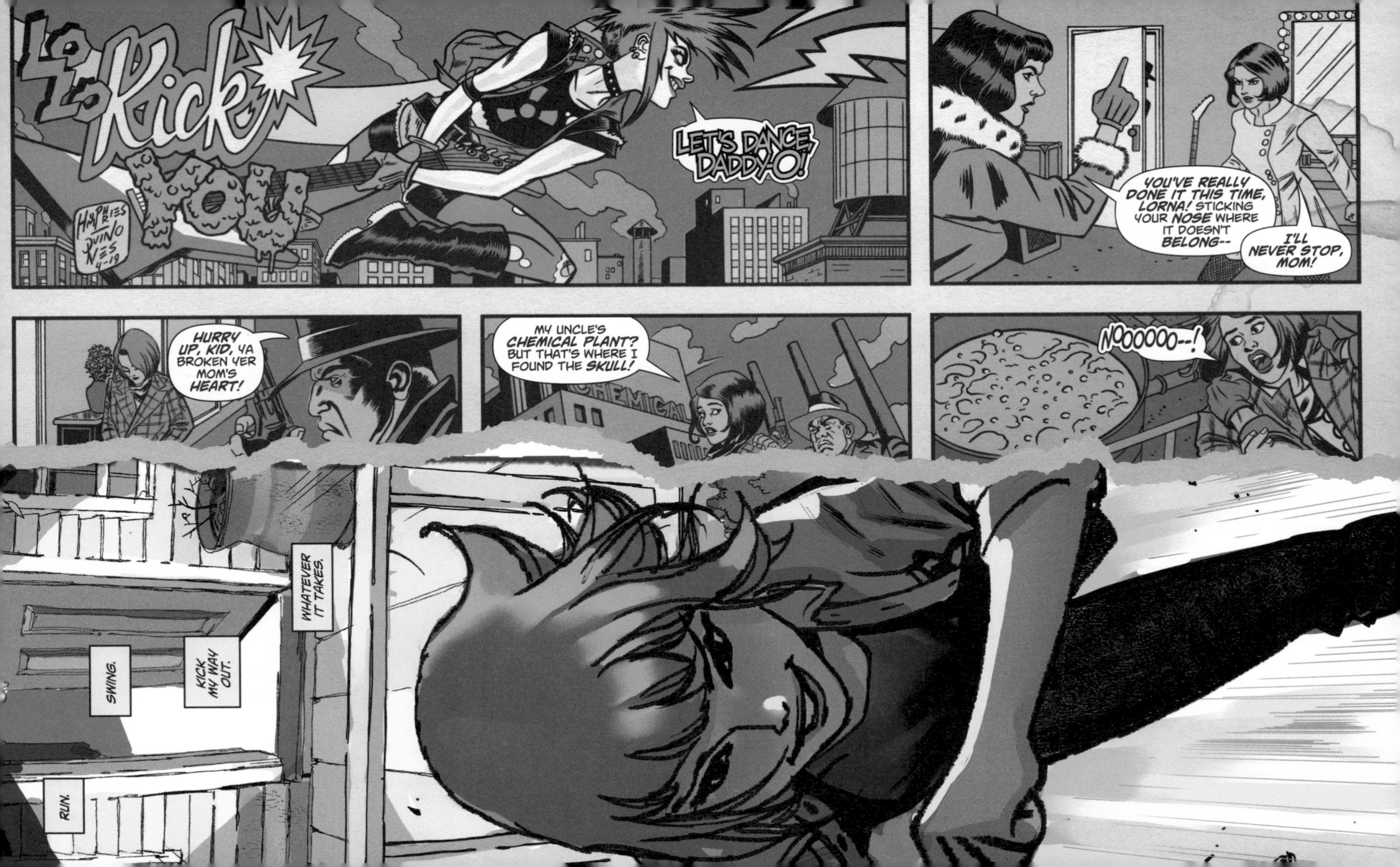
Lo Kick You
LET'S DANCE, DADDY-O!
YOU'VE REALLY DONE IT THIS TIME, LORNA! STICKING YOUR NOSE WHERE IT DOESN'T BELONG--
I'LL NEVER STOP, MOM!
HURRY UP, KID, YA BROKEN YER MOM'S HEART!
MY UNCLE'S CHEMICAL PLANT? BUT THAT'S WHERE I FOUND THE SKULL!
CHEMICAL
NOOOOOO--!
RUN.
SWING.
KICK MY WAY OUT.
WHATEVER IT TAKES.

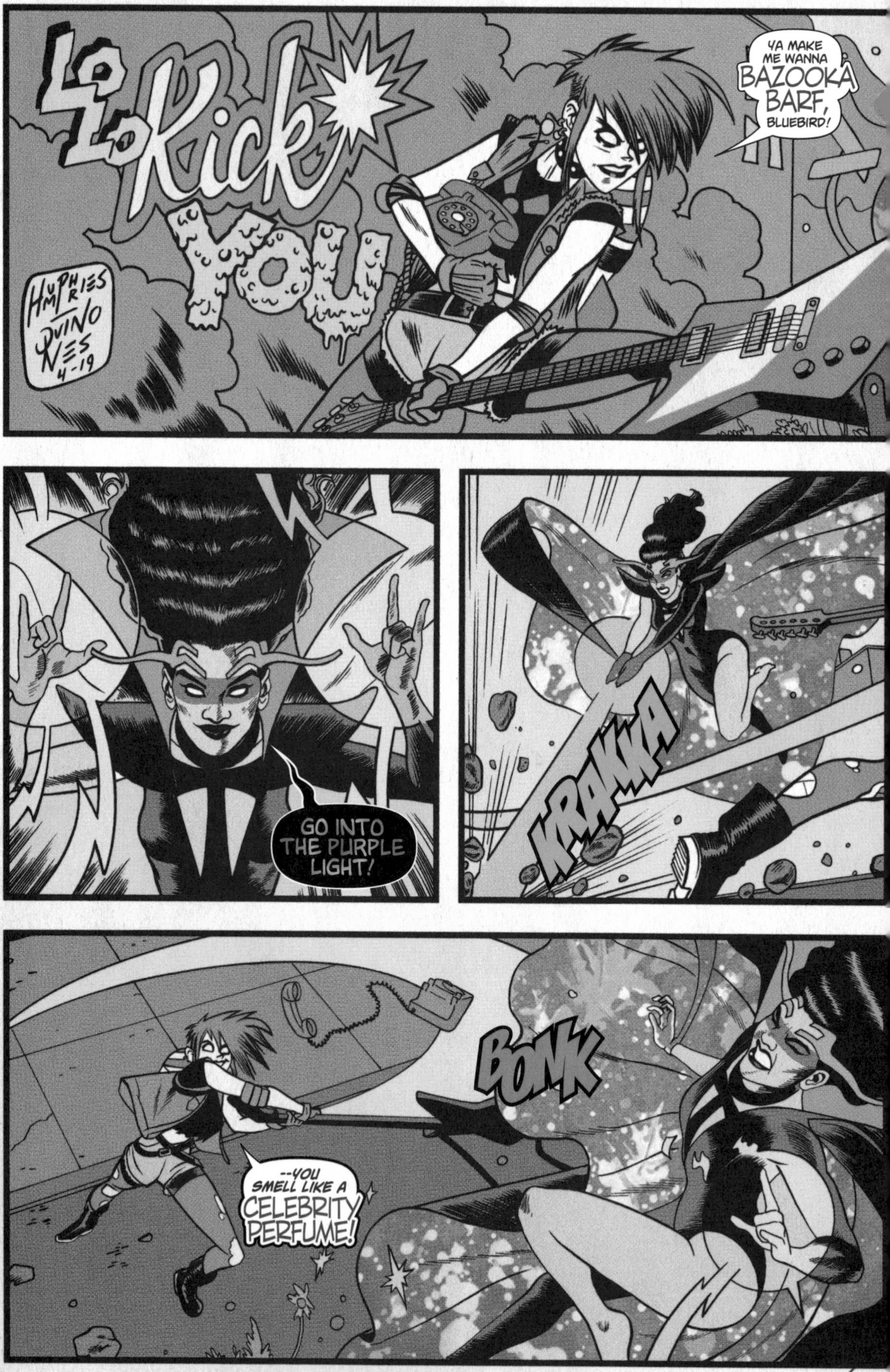
LO LO KICK YOU
HUMPHRIES QUINONES 4-19
YA MAKE ME WANNA BAZOOKA BARF, BLUEBIRD!
GO INTO THE PURPLE LIGHT!
KRAKKA
BONK
--YOU SMELL LIKE A CELEBRITY PERFUME!

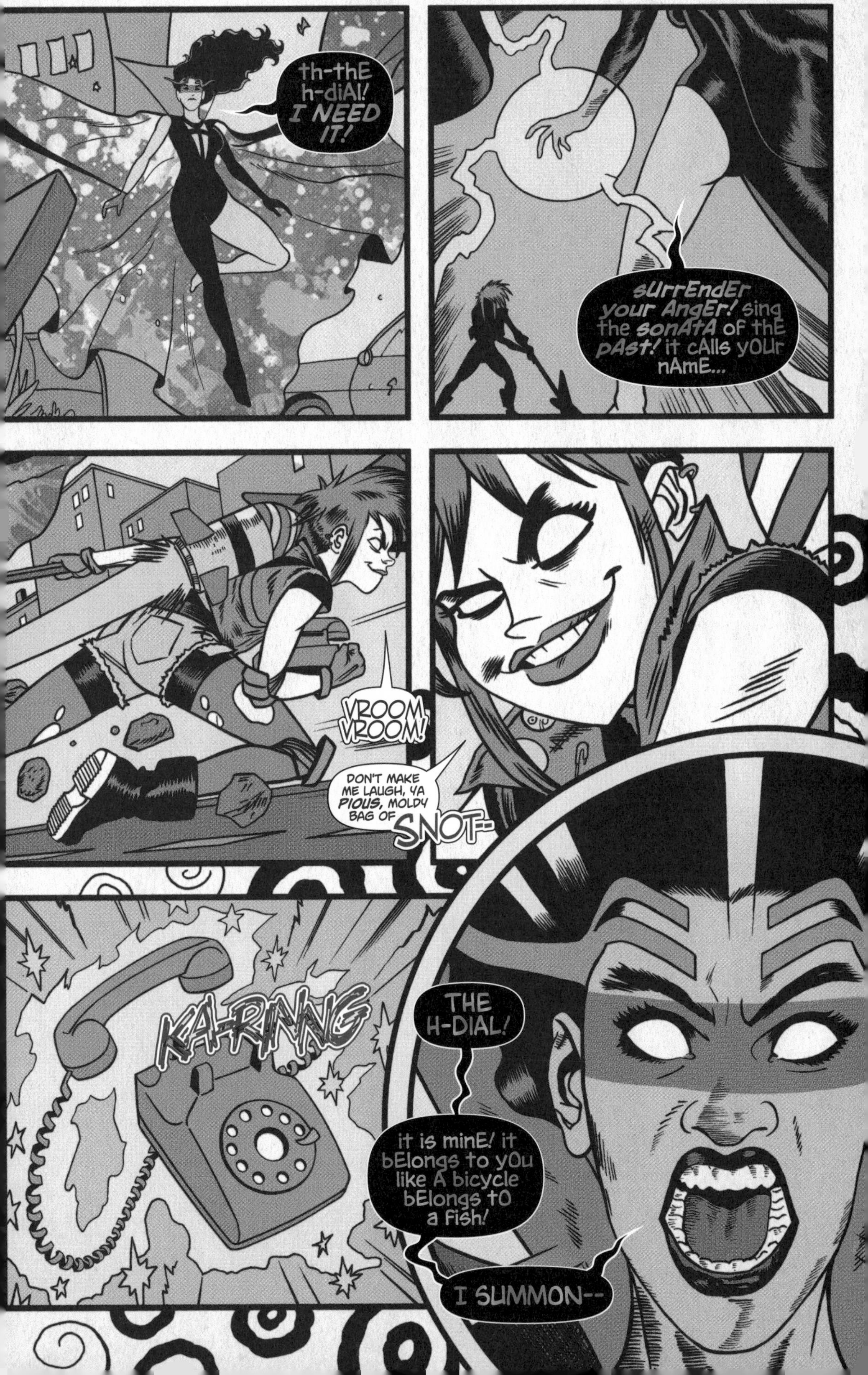

th-thE h-diAl! I NEED IT!
sUrrEndEr your AngEr! sing the sonAtA of thE pAst! it cAlls yOUr nAmE...
VROOM VROOM!
DON'T MAKE ME LAUGH, YA PIOUS, MOLDY BAG OF SNOT--
KA-RING
THE H-DIAL!
it is minE! it bElongs to yOu like A bicycle bElongs tO a fish!
I SUMMON--

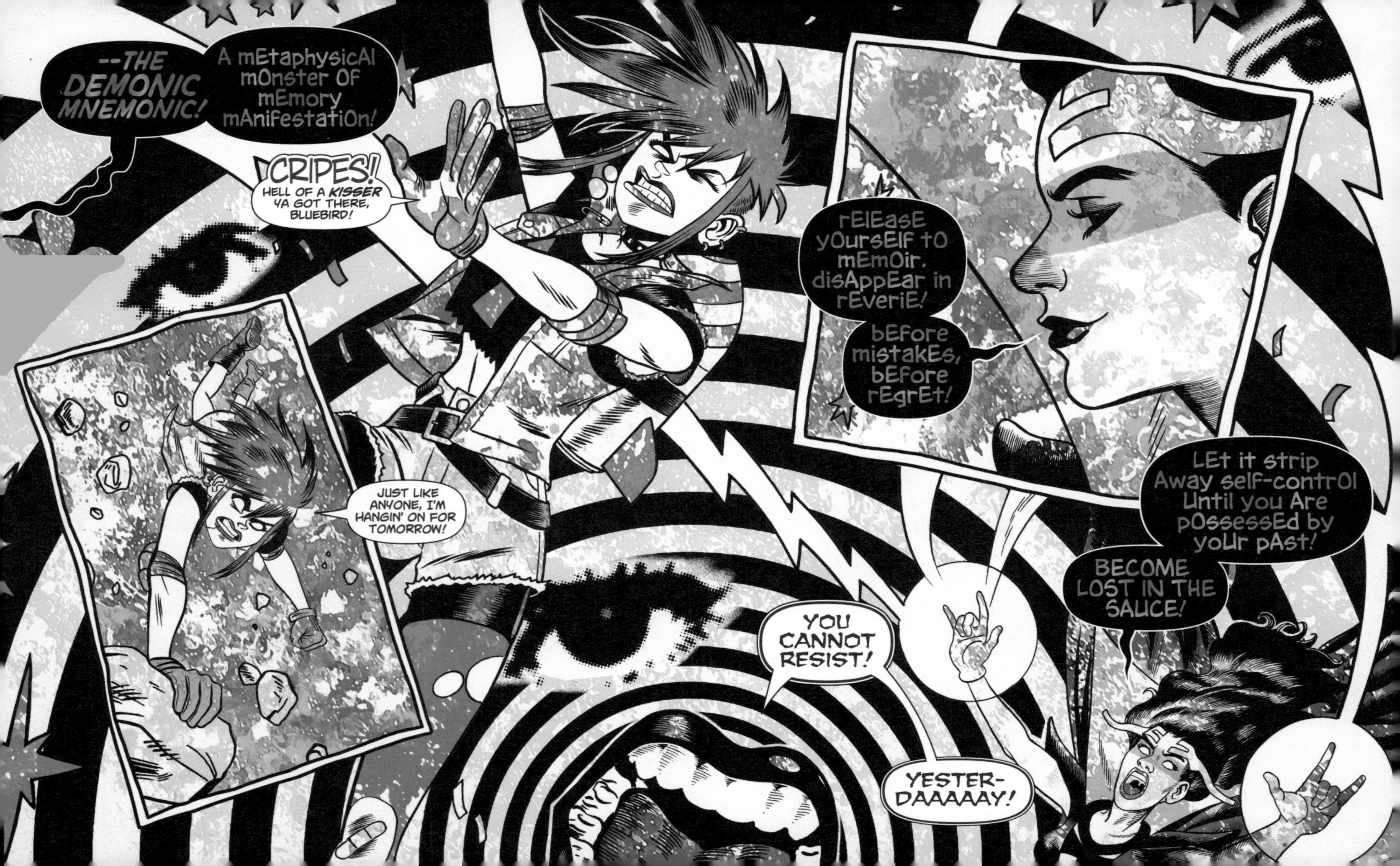
--THE DEMONIC MNEMONIC!
A mEtaphysicAl mOnster OF mEmory mAnifestatiOn!
CRIPES! HELL OF A KISSER YA GOT THERE, BLUEBIRD!
JUST LIKE ANYONE, I'M HANGIN' ON FOR TOMORROW!
rElEasE yOursElf tO mEmOir. disAppEar in rEveriE!
bEfore mistakEs, bEfore rEgrEt!
LEt it strip Away self-contrOl Until you Are pOssessEd by yOUr pAst!
BECOME LOST IN THE SAUCE!
YOU CANNOT RESIST!
YESTER-DAAAAAY!

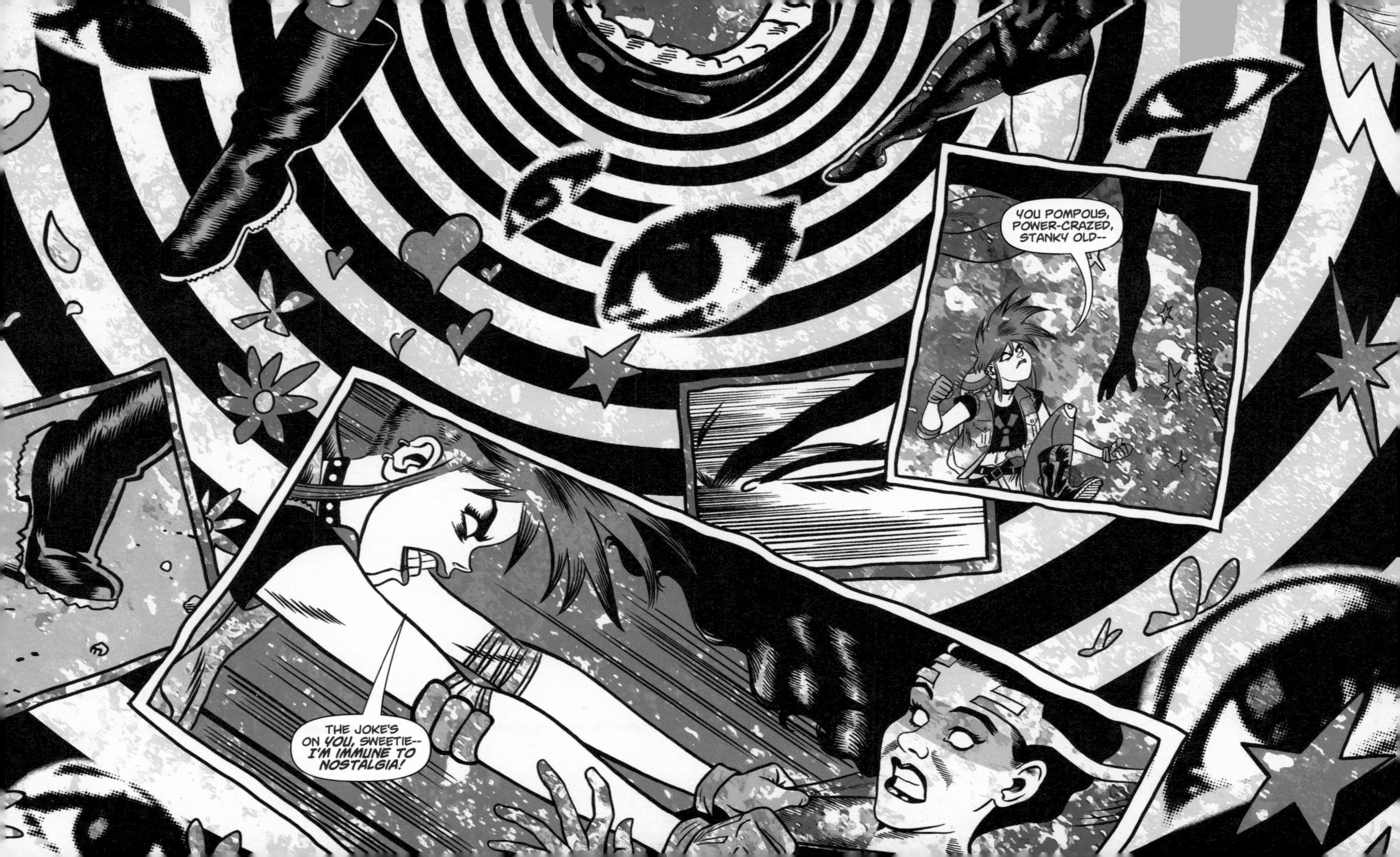
YOU POMPOUS, POWER-CRAZED, STANKY OLD--
THE JOKE'S ON YOU, SWEETIE-- I'M IMMUNE TO NOSTALGIA!

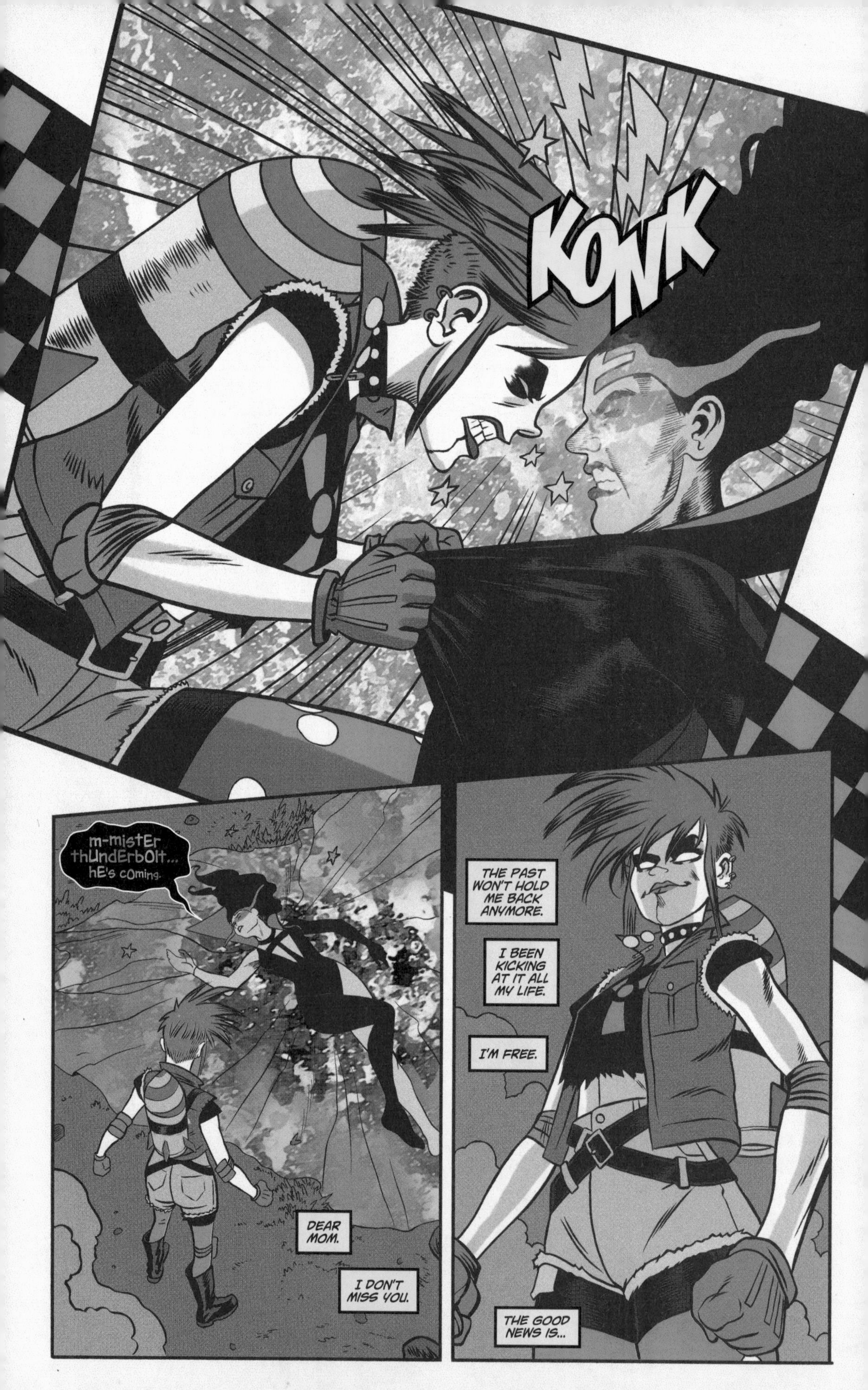
KONK
m-mister thunderbolt... he's coming.
DEAR MOM.
I DON'T MISS YOU.
THE PAST WON'T HOLD ME BACK ANYMORE.
I BEEN KICKING AT IT ALL MY LIFE.
I'M FREE.
THE GOOD NEWS IS...

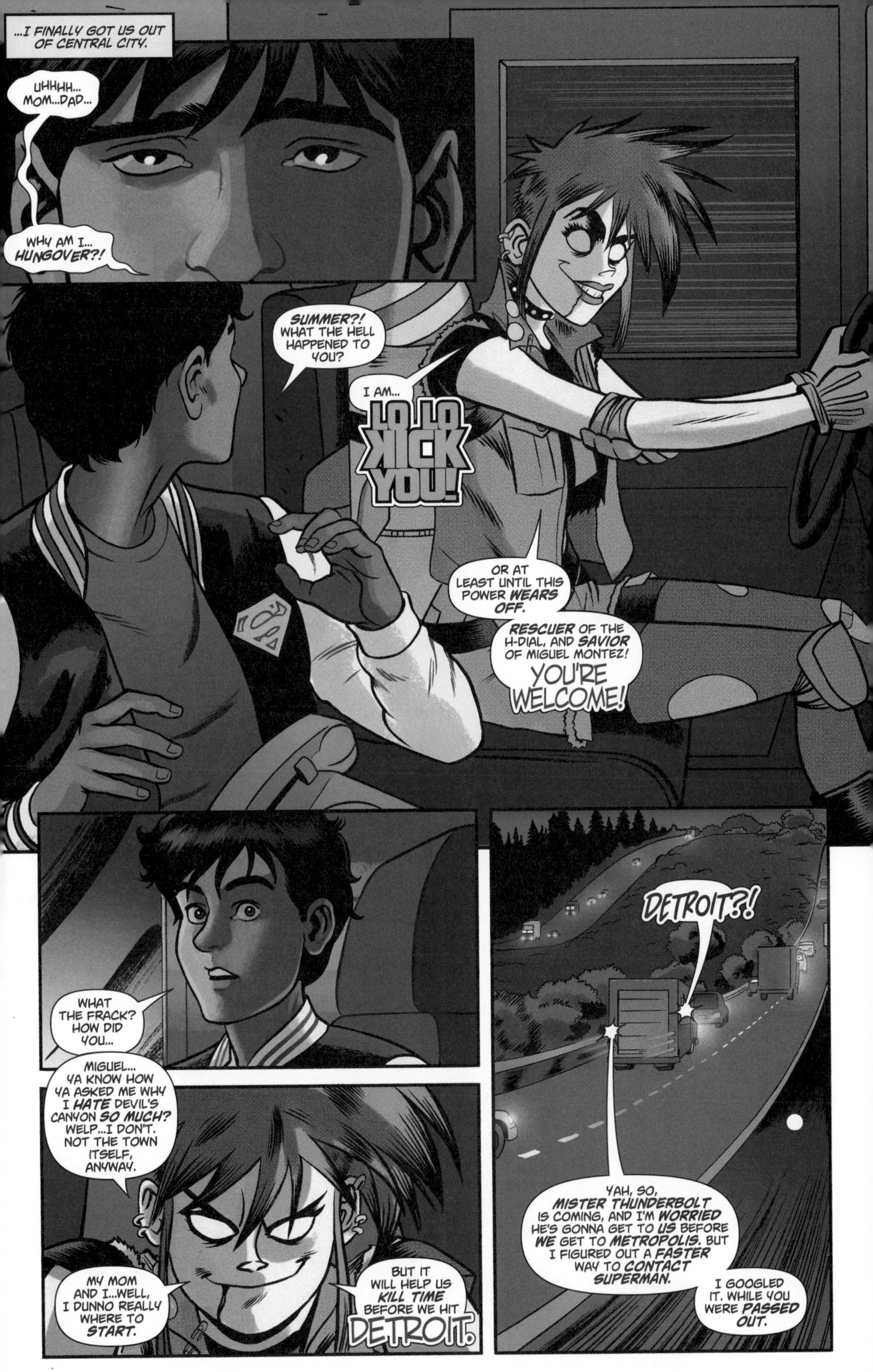

...I FINALLY GOT US OUT OF CENTRAL CITY.
UHHHH... MOM...DAD...
WHY AM I... HUNGOVER?!
SUMMER?! WHAT THE HELL HAPPENED TO YOU?
I AM...
LO LO KICK YOU!
OR AT LEAST UNTIL THIS POWER WEARS OFF.
RESCUER OF THE H-DIAL, AND SAVIOR OF MIGUEL MONTEZ!
YOU'RE WELCOME!
WHAT THE FRACK? HOW DID YOU...
MIGUEL... YA KNOW HOW YA ASKED ME WHY I HATE DEVIL'S CANYON SO MUCH? WELP...I DON'T. NOT THE TOWN ITSELF, ANYWAY.
MY MOM AND I...WELL, I DUNNO REALLY WHERE TO START.
BUT IT WILL HELP US KILL TIME BEFORE WE HIT
DETROIT.
DETROIT?!
YAH, SO, MISTER THUNDERBOLT IS COMING, AND I'M WORRIED HE'S GONNA GET TO US BEFORE WE GET TO METROPOLIS. BUT I FIGURED OUT A FASTER WAY TO CONTACT SUPERMAN.
I GOOGLED IT. WHILE YOU WERE PASSED OUT.

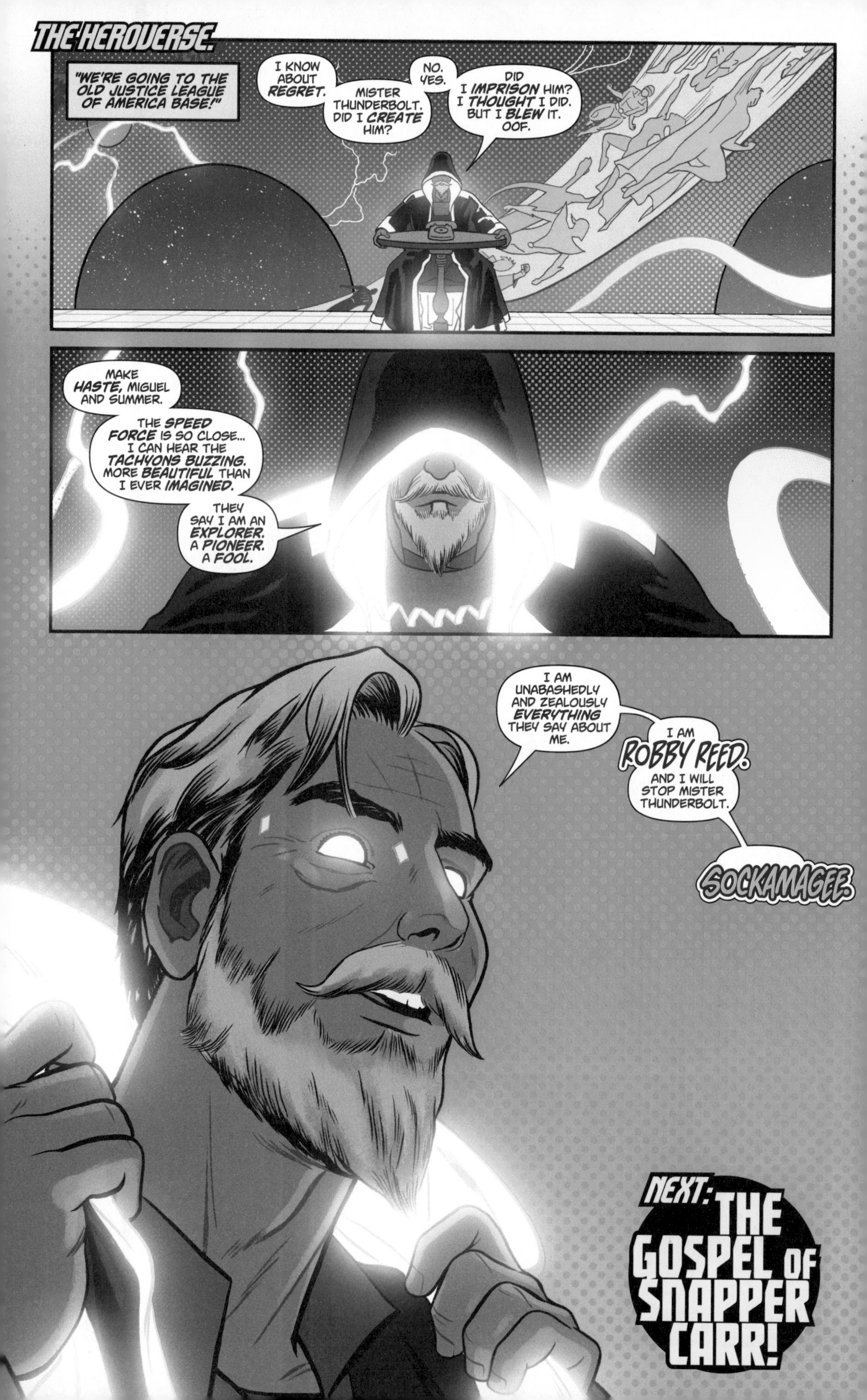
THE HEROVERSE.
"WE'RE GOING TO THE OLD JUSTICE LEAGUE OF AMERICA BASE!"
I KNOW ABOUT REGRET.
MISTER THUNDERBOLT. DID I CREATE HIM?
NO. YES.
DID I IMPRISON HIM? I THOUGHT I DID. BUT I BLEW IT. OOF.
MAKE HASTE, MIGUEL AND SUMMER.
THE SPEED FORCE IS SO CLOSE... I CAN HEAR THE TACHYONS BUZZING. MORE BEAUTIFUL THAN I EVER IMAGINED.
THEY SAY I AM AN EXPLORER. A PIONEER. A FOOL.
I AM UNABASHEDLY AND ZEALOUSLY EVERYTHING THEY SAY ABOUT ME.
I AM ROBBY REED.
AND I WILL STOP MISTER THUNDERBOLT.
SOCKAMAGEE.
NEXT: THE GOSPEL OF SNAPPER CARR!

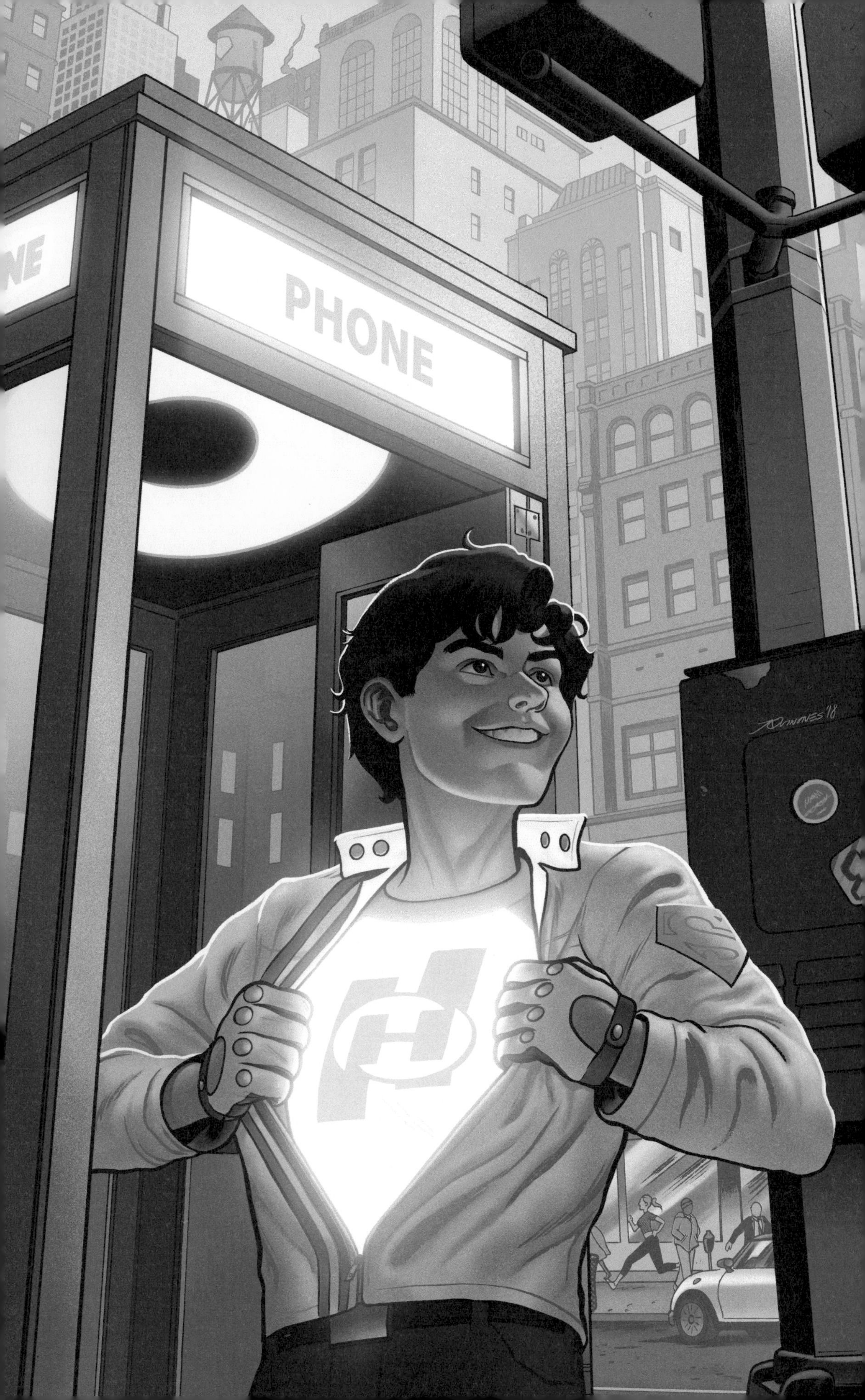
PHONE

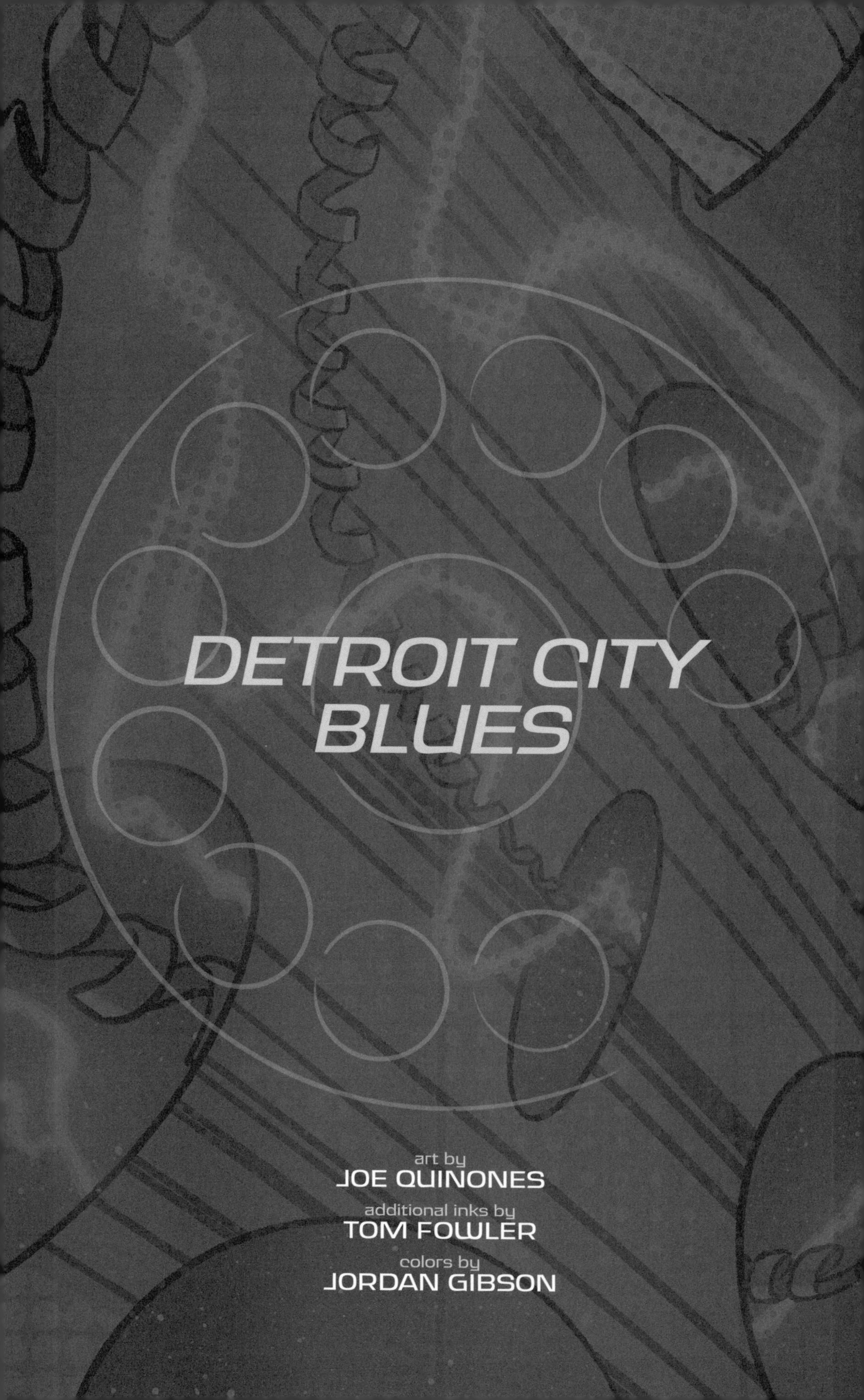

DETROIT CITY BLUES

art by
JOE QUINONES
additional inks by
TOM FOWLER
colors by
JORDAN GIBSON

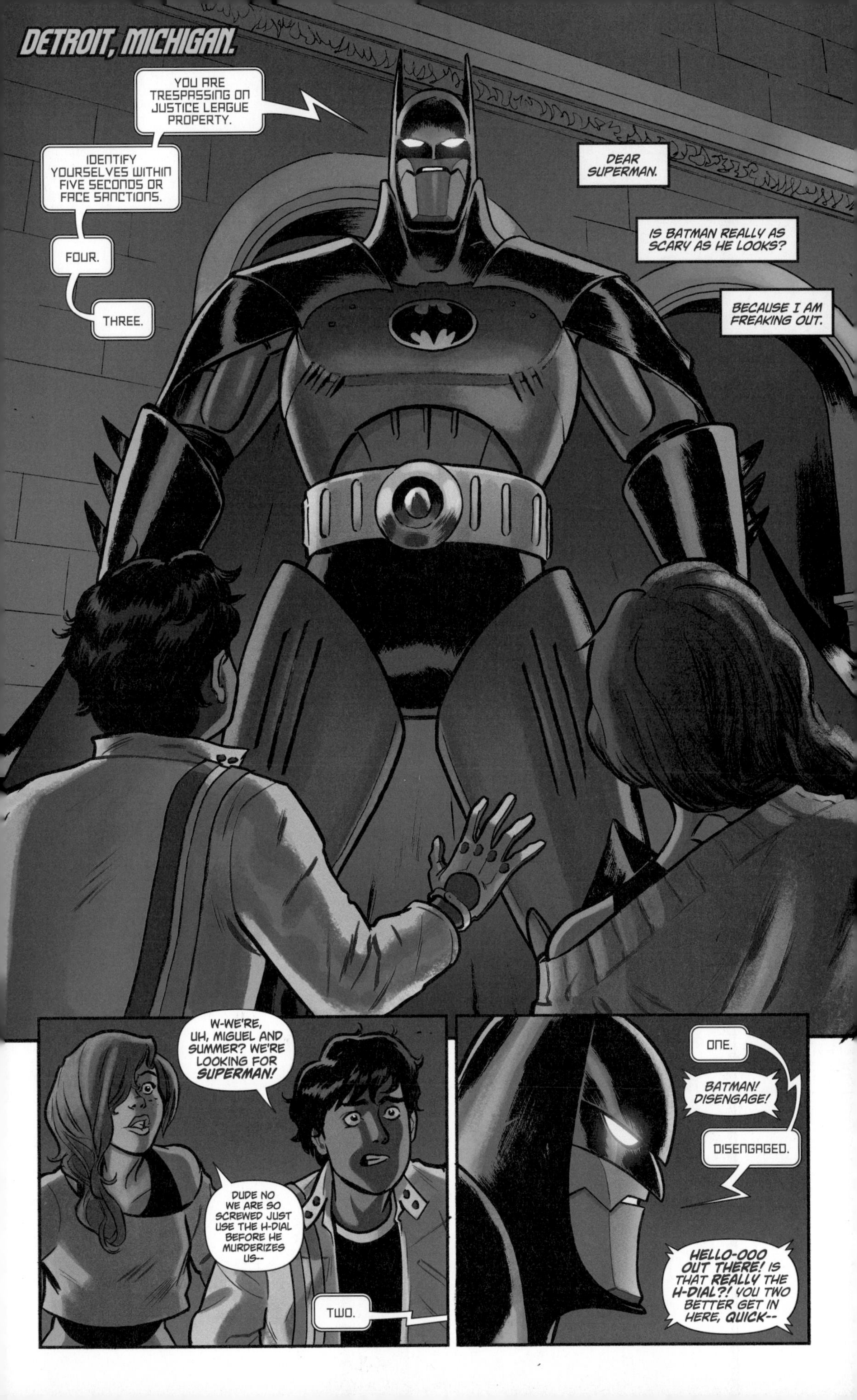
DETROIT, MICHIGAN.
YOU ARE TRESPASSING ON JUSTICE LEAGUE PROPERTY.
IDENTIFY YOURSELVES WITHIN FIVE SECONDS OR FACE SANCTIONS.
FOUR.
THREE.
DEAR SUPERMAN.
IS BATMAN REALLY AS SCARY AS HE LOOKS?
BECAUSE I AM FREAKING OUT.
W-WE'RE, UH, MIGUEL AND SUMMER? WE'RE LOOKING FOR SUPERMAN!
DUDE NO WE ARE SO SCREWED JUST USE THE H-DIAL BEFORE HE MURDERIZES US--
TWO.
ONE.
BATMAN! DISENGAGE!
DISENGAGED.
HELLO-OOO OUT THERE! IS THAT REALLY THE H-DIAL?! YOU TWO BETTER GET IN HERE, QUICK--

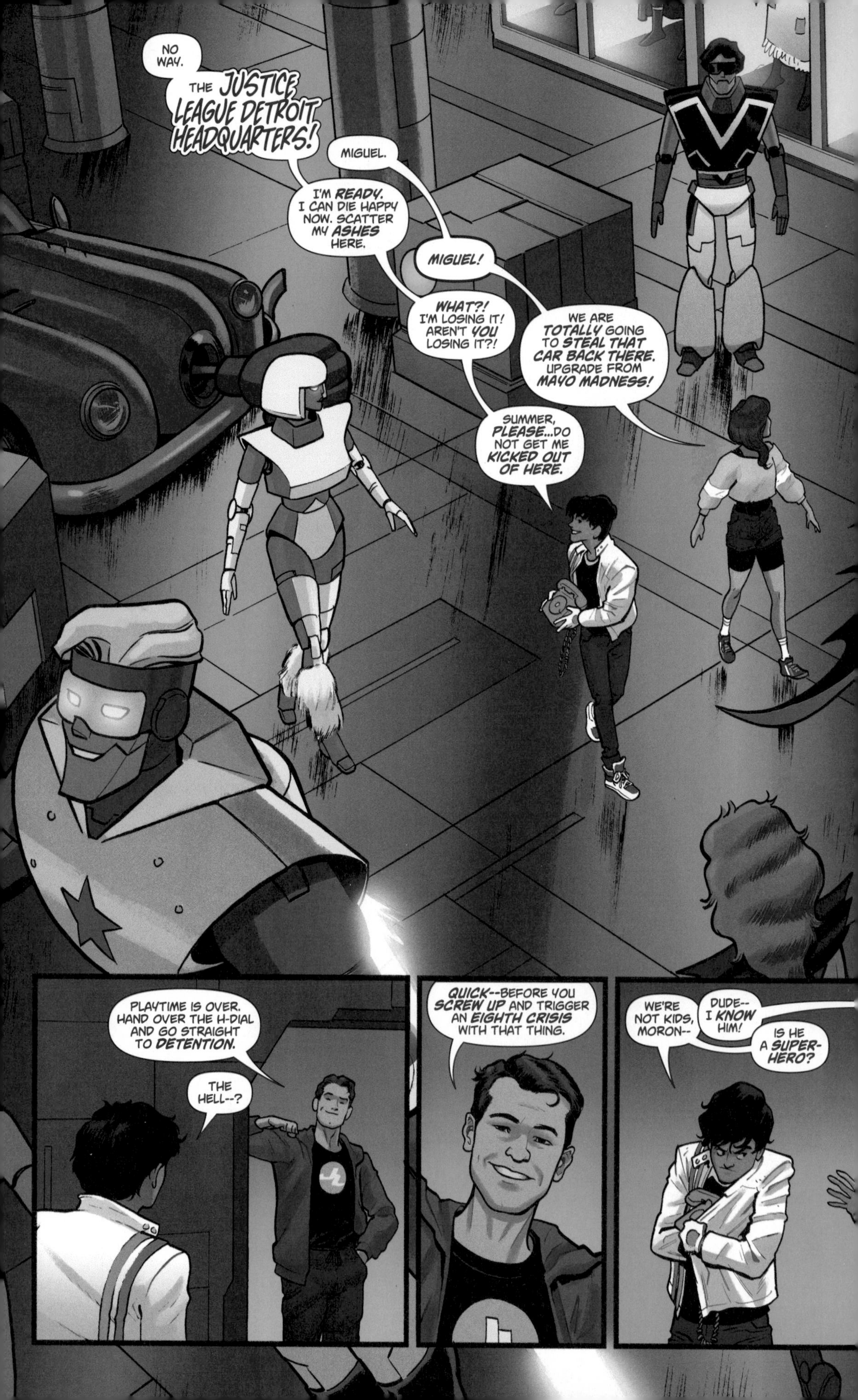
NO WAY.
THE JUSTICE LEAGUE DETROIT HEADQUARTERS!
MIGUEL.
I'M READY. I CAN DIE HAPPY NOW. SCATTER MY ASHES HERE.
MIGUEL!
WHAT?! I'M LOSING IT! AREN'T YOU LOSING IT?!
WE ARE TOTALLY GOING TO STEAL THAT CAR BACK THERE. UPGRADE FROM MAYO MADNESS!
SUMMER, PLEASE...DO NOT GET ME KICKED OUT OF HERE.
PLAYTIME IS OVER. HAND OVER THE H-DIAL AND GO STRAIGHT TO DETENTION.
THE HELL--?
QUICK--BEFORE YOU SCREW UP AND TRIGGER AN EIGHTH CRISIS WITH THAT THING.
WE'RE NOT KIDS, MORON--
DUDE-- I KNOW HIM!
IS HE A SUPER-HERO?

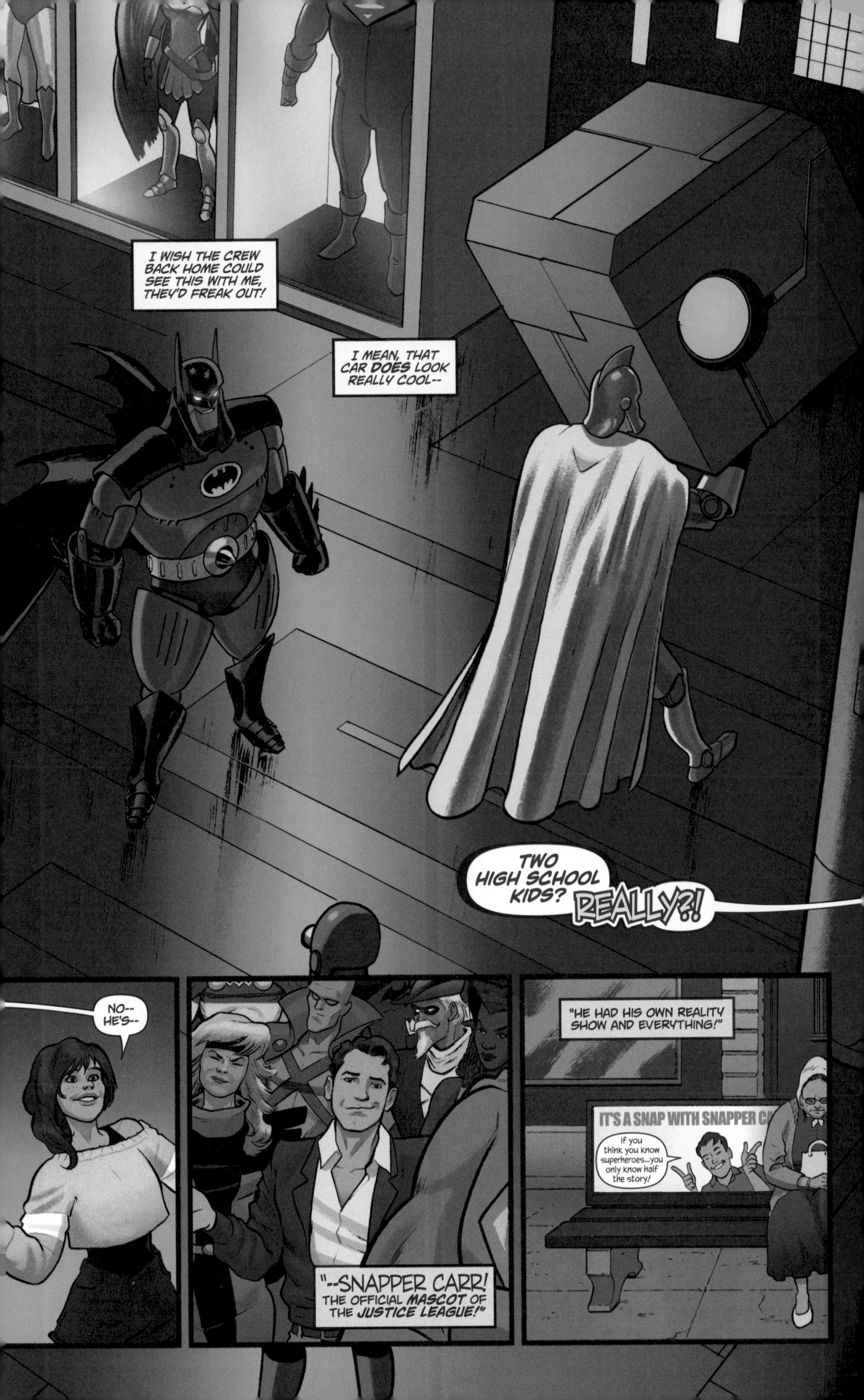
I WISH THE CREW BACK HOME COULD SEE THIS WITH ME, THEY'D FREAK OUT!
I MEAN, THAT CAR DOES LOOK REALLY COOL--
TWO HIGH SCHOOL KIDS? REALLY?!
NO-- HE'S--
"--SNAPPER CARR! THE OFFICIAL MASCOT OF THE JUSTICE LEAGUE!"
"HE HAD HIS OWN REALITY SHOW AND EVERYTHING!"
IT'S A SNAP WITH SNAPPER CA
If you think you know superheroes...you only know half the story!

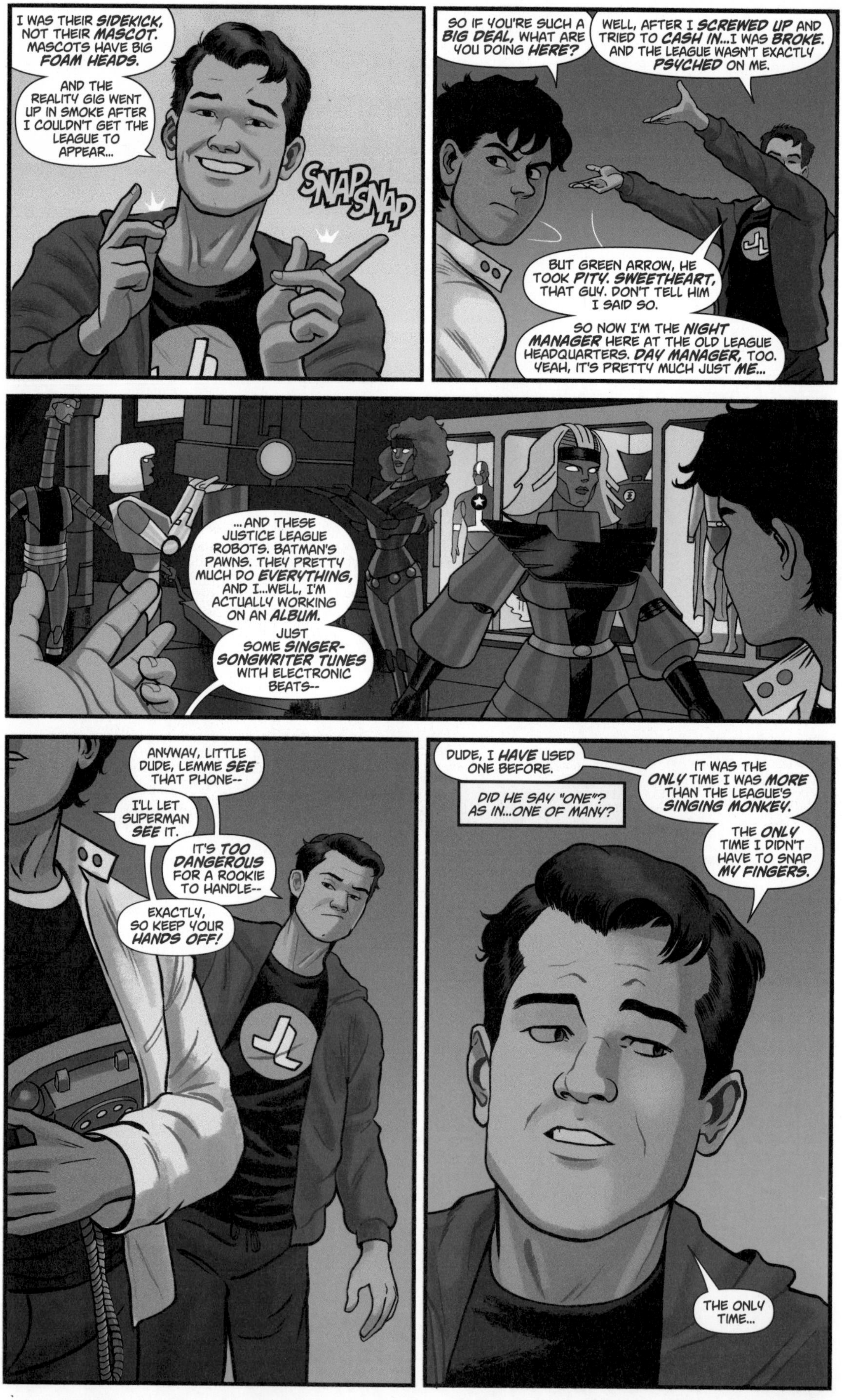
I WAS THEIR SIDEKICK, NOT THEIR MASCOT. MASCOTS HAVE BIG FOAM HEADS.
AND THE REALITY GIG WENT UP IN SMOKE AFTER I COULDN'T GET THE LEAGUE TO APPEAR...
SNAP SNAP
SO IF YOU'RE SUCH A BIG DEAL, WHAT ARE YOU DOING HERE?
WELL, AFTER I SCREWED UP AND TRIED TO CASH IN...I WAS BROKE. AND THE LEAGUE WASN'T EXACTLY PSYCHED ON ME.
BUT GREEN ARROW, HE TOOK PITY. SWEETHEART, THAT GUY. DON'T TELL HIM I SAID SO.
SO NOW I'M THE NIGHT MANAGER HERE AT THE OLD LEAGUE HEADQUARTERS. DAY MANAGER, TOO. YEAH, IT'S PRETTY MUCH JUST ME...
...AND THESE JUSTICE LEAGUE ROBOTS. BATMAN'S PAWNS. THEY PRETTY MUCH DO EVERYTHING, AND I...WELL, I'M ACTUALLY WORKING ON AN ALBUM.
JUST SOME SINGER-SONGWRITER TUNES WITH ELECTRONIC BEATS--
ANYWAY, LITTLE DUDE, LEMME SEE THAT PHONE--
I'LL LET SUPERMAN SEE IT.
IT'S TOO DANGEROUS FOR A ROOKIE TO HANDLE--
EXACTLY, SO KEEP YOUR HANDS OFF!
DUDE, I HAVE USED ONE BEFORE.
DID HE SAY "ONE"? AS IN...ONE OF MANY?
IT WAS THE ONLY TIME I WAS MORE THAN THE LEAGUE'S SINGING MONKEY.
THE ONLY TIME I DIDN'T HAVE TO SNAP MY FINGERS.
THE ONLY TIME...

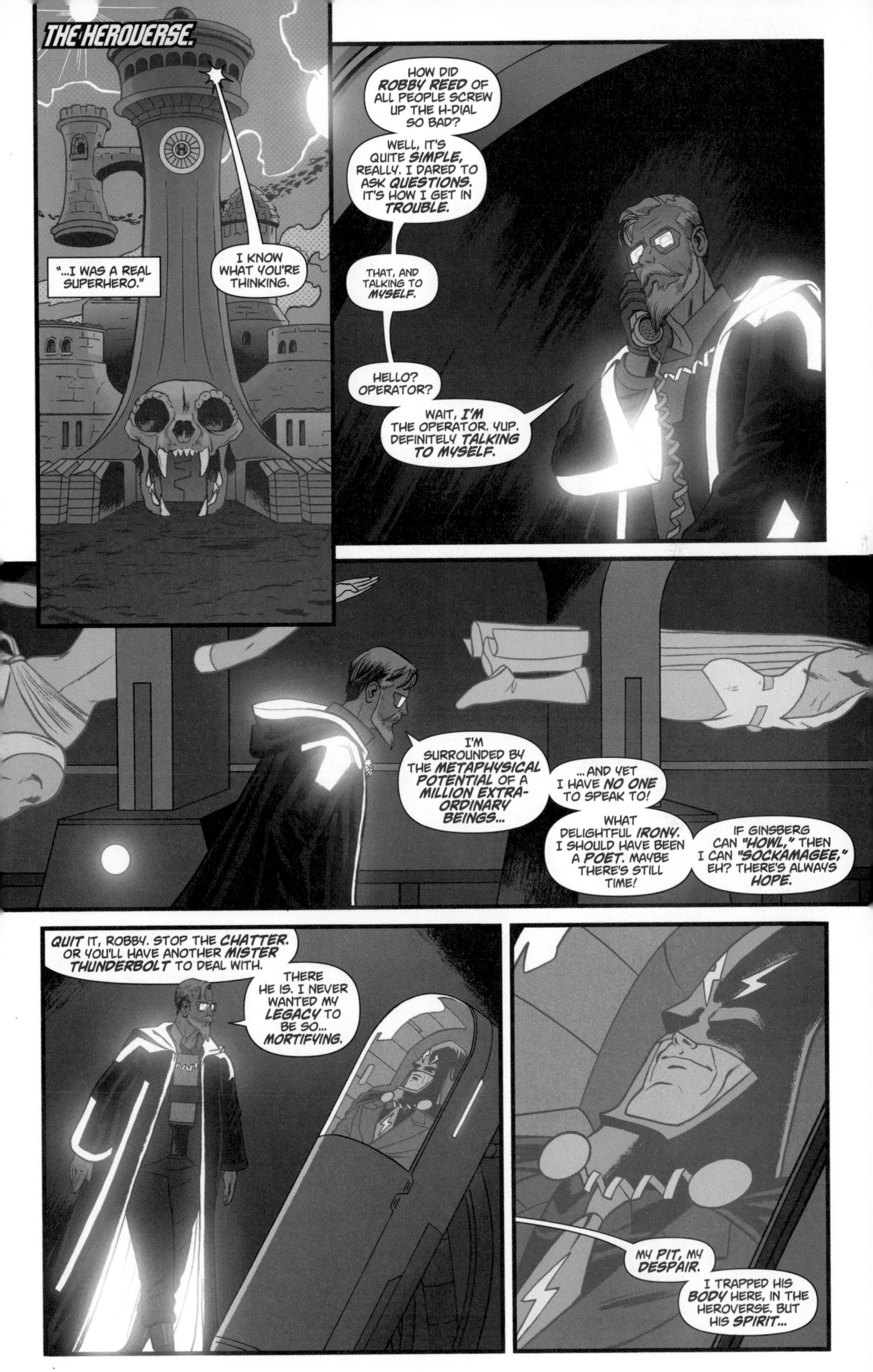
THE HEROVERSE.
"...I WAS A REAL SUPERHERO."
I KNOW WHAT YOU'RE THINKING.
HOW DID ROBBY REED OF ALL PEOPLE SCREW UP THE H-DIAL SO BAD?
WELL, IT'S QUITE SIMPLE, REALLY. I DARED TO ASK QUESTIONS. IT'S HOW I GET IN TROUBLE.
THAT, AND TALKING TO MYSELF.
HELLO? OPERATOR?
WAIT, I'M THE OPERATOR. YUP. DEFINITELY TALKING TO MYSELF.
I'M SURROUNDED BY THE METAPHYSICAL POTENTIAL OF A MILLION EXTRA-ORDINARY BEINGS...
...AND YET I HAVE NO ONE TO SPEAK TO!
WHAT DELIGHTFUL IRONY. I SHOULD HAVE BEEN A POET. MAYBE THERE'S STILL TIME!
IF GINSBERG CAN "HOWL," THEN I CAN "SOCKAMAGEE," EH? THERE'S ALWAYS HOPE.
QUIT IT, ROBBY. STOP THE CHATTER. OR YOU'LL HAVE ANOTHER MISTER THUNDERBOLT TO DEAL WITH.
THERE HE IS. I NEVER WANTED MY LEGACY TO BE SO... MORTIFYING.
MY PIT, MY DESPAIR.
I TRAPPED HIS BODY HERE, IN THE HEROVERSE. BUT HIS SPIRIT...

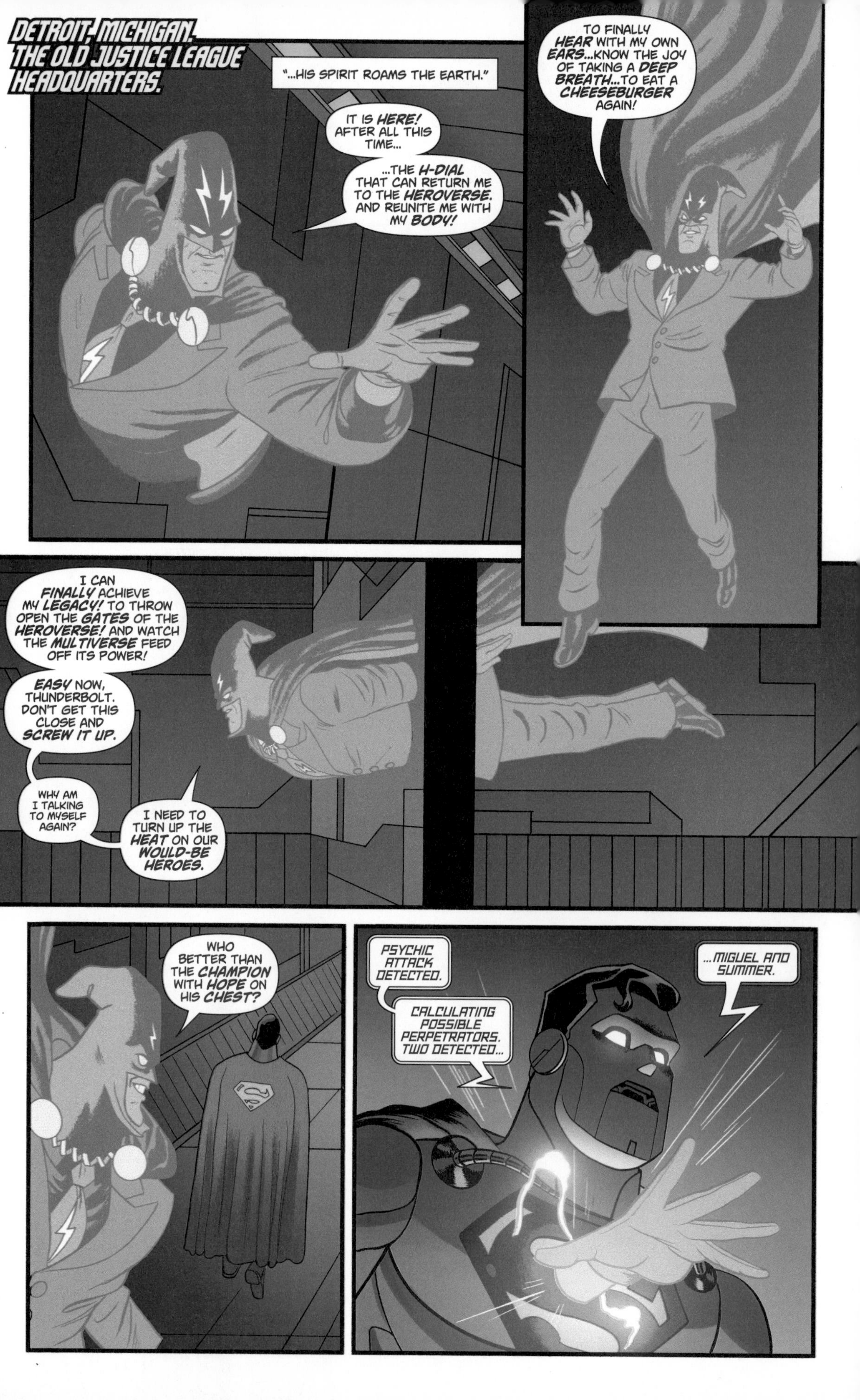

DETROIT, MICHIGAN. THE OLD JUSTICE LEAGUE HEADQUARTERS.
"...HIS SPIRIT ROAMS THE EARTH."
IT IS HERE! AFTER ALL THIS TIME...
...THE H-DIAL THAT CAN RETURN ME TO THE HEROVERSE. AND REUNITE ME WITH MY BODY!
TO FINALLY HEAR WITH MY OWN EARS...KNOW THE JOY OF TAKING A DEEP BREATH...TO EAT A CHEESEBURGER AGAIN!
I CAN FINALLY ACHIEVE MY LEGACY! TO THROW OPEN THE GATES OF THE HEROVERSE! AND WATCH THE MULTIVERSE FEED OFF ITS POWER!
EASY NOW, THUNDERBOLT. DON'T GET THIS CLOSE AND SCREW IT UP.
WHY AM I TALKING TO MYSELF AGAIN?
I NEED TO TURN UP THE HEAT ON OUR WOULD-BE HEROES.
WHO BETTER THAN THE CHAMPION WITH HOPE ON HIS CHEST?
PSYCHIC ATTACK DETECTED.
CALCULATING POSSIBLE PERPETRATORS. TWO DETECTED...
...MIGUEL AND SUMMER.

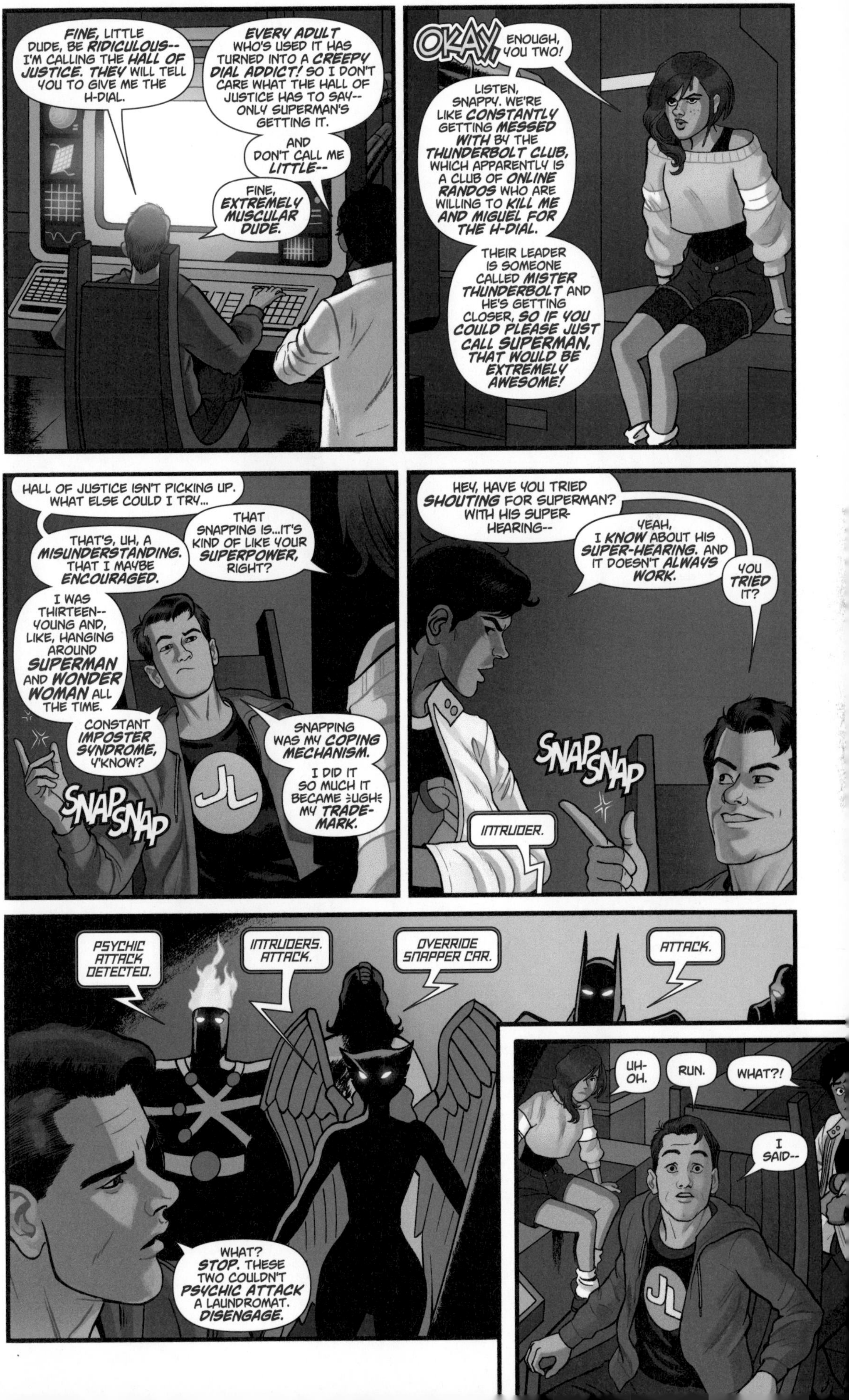
FINE, LITTLE DUDE, BE RIDICULOUS-- I'M CALLING THE HALL OF JUSTICE. THEY WILL TELL YOU TO GIVE ME THE H-DIAL.
EVERY ADULT WHO'S USED IT HAS TURNED INTO A CREEPY DIAL ADDICT! SO I DON'T CARE WHAT THE HALL OF JUSTICE HAS TO SAY-- ONLY SUPERMAN'S GETTING IT.
AND DON'T CALL ME LITTLE--
FINE, EXTREMELY MUSCULAR DUDE.
OKAY, ENOUGH, YOU TWO!
LISTEN, SNAPPY. WE'RE LIKE CONSTANTLY GETTING MESSED WITH BY THE THUNDERBOLT CLUB, WHICH APPARENTLY IS A CLUB OF ONLINE RANDOS WHO ARE WILLING TO KILL ME AND MIGUEL FOR THE H-DIAL.
THEIR LEADER IS SOMEONE CALLED MISTER THUNDERBOLT AND HE'S GETTING CLOSER, SO IF YOU COULD PLEASE JUST CALL SUPERMAN, THAT WOULD BE EXTREMELY AWESOME!
HALL OF JUSTICE ISN'T PICKING UP. WHAT ELSE COULD I TRY...
THAT SNAPPING IS...IT'S KIND OF LIKE YOUR SUPERPOWER, RIGHT?
THAT'S, UH, A MISUNDERSTANDING. THAT I MAYBE ENCOURAGED.
I WAS THIRTEEN-- YOUNG AND, LIKE, HANGING AROUND SUPERMAN AND WONDER WOMAN ALL THE TIME.
CONSTANT IMPOSTER SYNDROME, Y'KNOW?
SNAPPING WAS MY COPING MECHANISM.
I DID IT SO MUCH IT BECAME *UGH* MY TRADE-MARK.
SNAP SNAP
HEY, HAVE YOU TRIED SHOUTING FOR SUPERMAN? WITH HIS SUPER-HEARING--
YEAH, I KNOW ABOUT HIS SUPER-HEARING. AND IT DOESN'T ALWAYS WORK.
YOU TRIED IT?
SNAP SNAP
INTRUDER.
PSYCHIC ATTACK DETECTED.
INTRUDERS. ATTACK.
OVERRIDE SNAPPER CAR.
ATTACK.
WHAT? STOP. THESE TWO COULDN'T PSYCHIC ATTACK A LAUNDROMAT. DISENGAGE.
UH-OH.
RUN.
WHAT?!
I SAID--

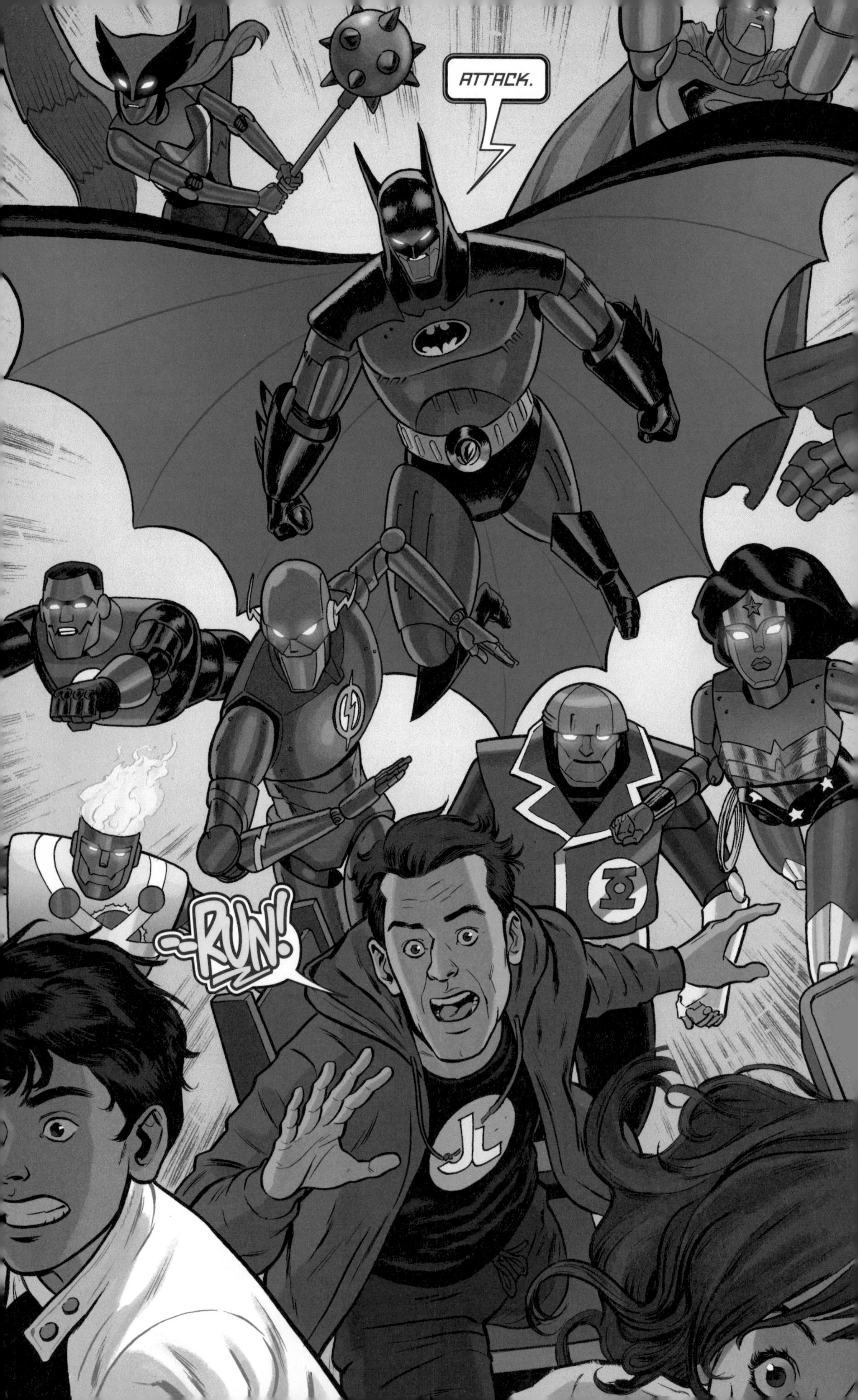
ATTACK.
--RUN!

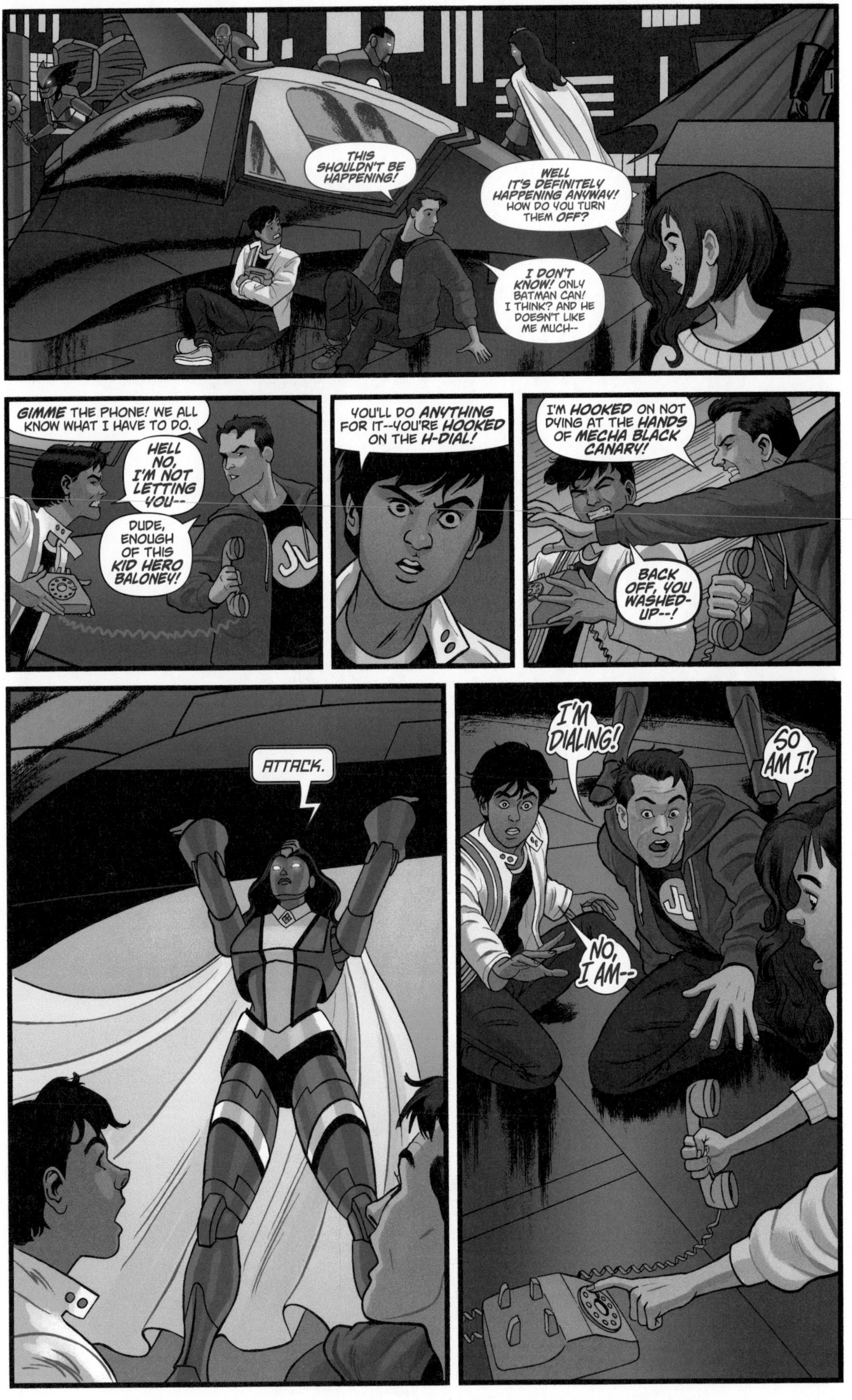
THIS SHOULDN'T BE HAPPENING!
WELL IT'S DEFINITELY HAPPENING ANYWAY! HOW DO YOU TURN THEM OFF?
I DON'T KNOW! ONLY BATMAN CAN! I THINK? AND HE DOESN'T LIKE ME MUCH--
GIMME THE PHONE! WE ALL KNOW WHAT I HAVE TO DO.
HELL NO, I'M NOT LETTING YOU--
DUDE, ENOUGH OF THIS KID HERO BALONEY!
YOU'LL DO ANYTHING FOR IT--YOU'RE HOOKED ON THE H-DIAL!
I'M HOOKED ON NOT DYING AT THE HANDS OF MECHA BLACK CANARY!
BACK OFF, YOU WASHED-UP--!
ATTACK.
I'M DIALING!
SO AM I!
NO, I AM--

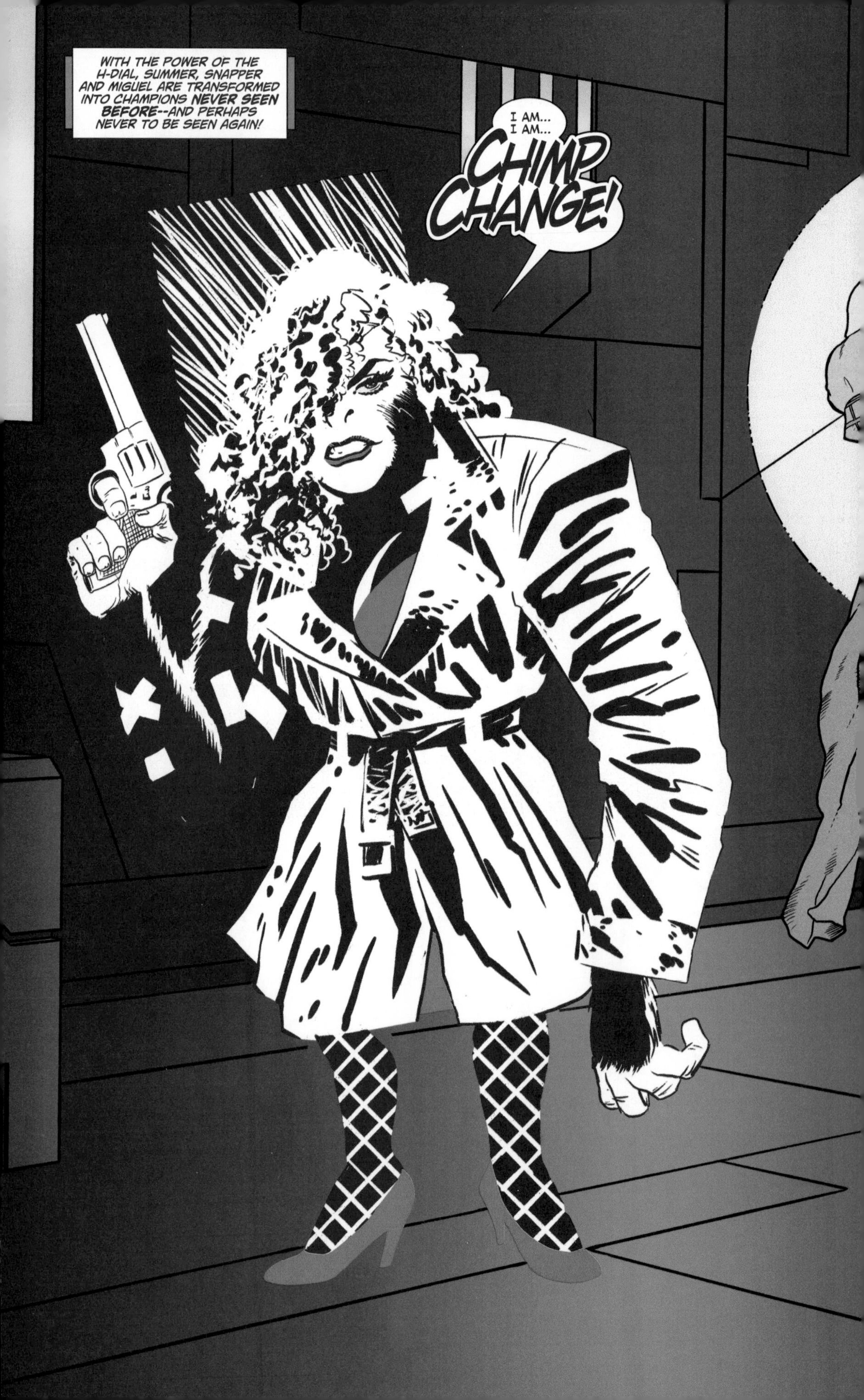
WITH THE POWER OF THE H-DIAL, SUMMER, SNAPPER AND MIGUEL ARE TRANSFORMED INTO CHAMPIONS NEVER SEEN BEFORE--AND PERHAPS NEVER TO BE SEEN AGAIN!
I AM... I AM...
CHIMP CHANGE!

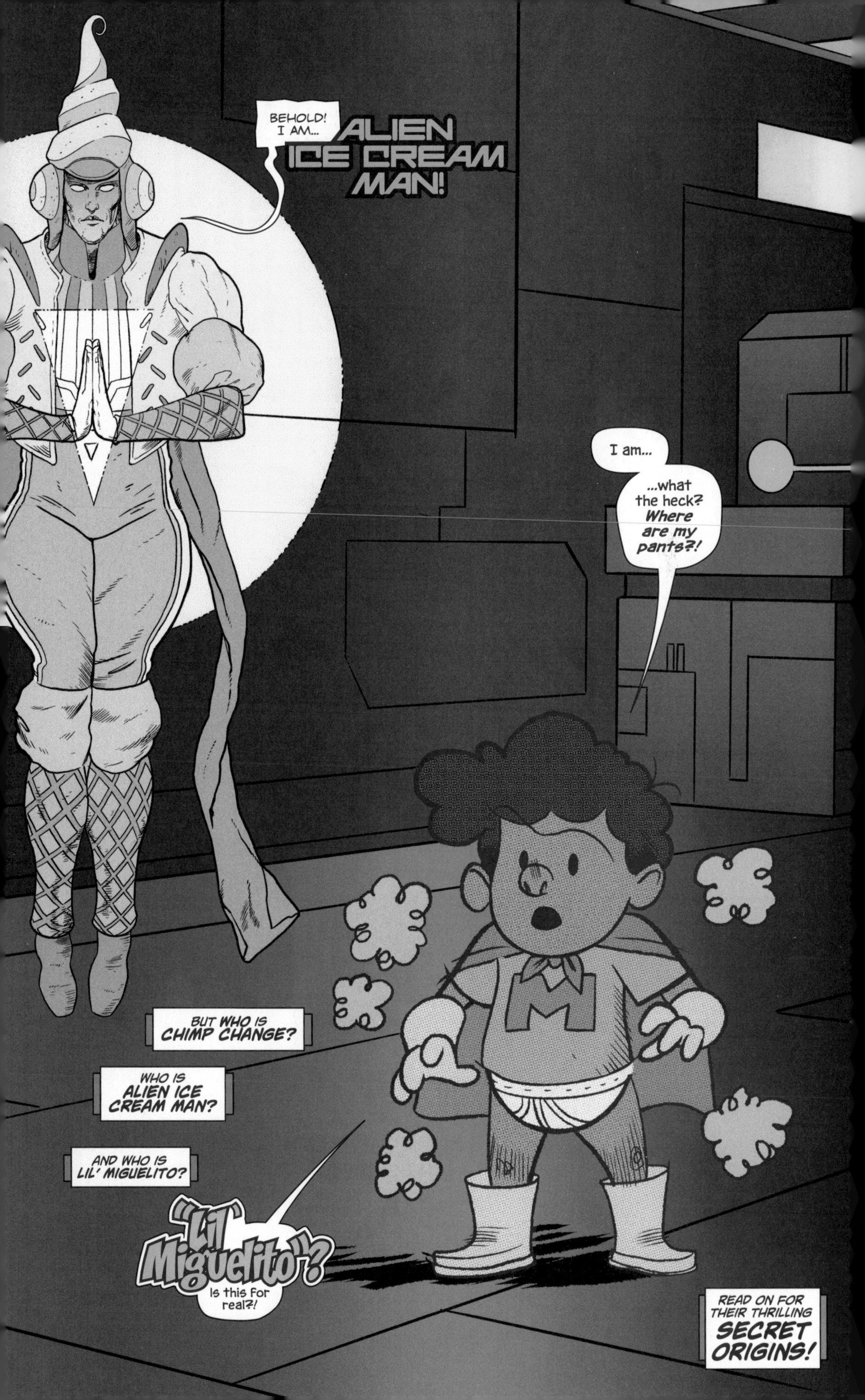
BEHOLD! I AM...
ALIEN ICE CREAM MAN!
I am...
...what the heck? Where are my pants?!
BUT WHO IS CHIMP CHANGE?
WHO IS ALIEN ICE CREAM MAN?
AND WHO IS LIL' MIGUELITO?
"Lil' Miguelito"? Is this for real?!
READ ON FOR THEIR THRILLING SECRET ORIGINS!

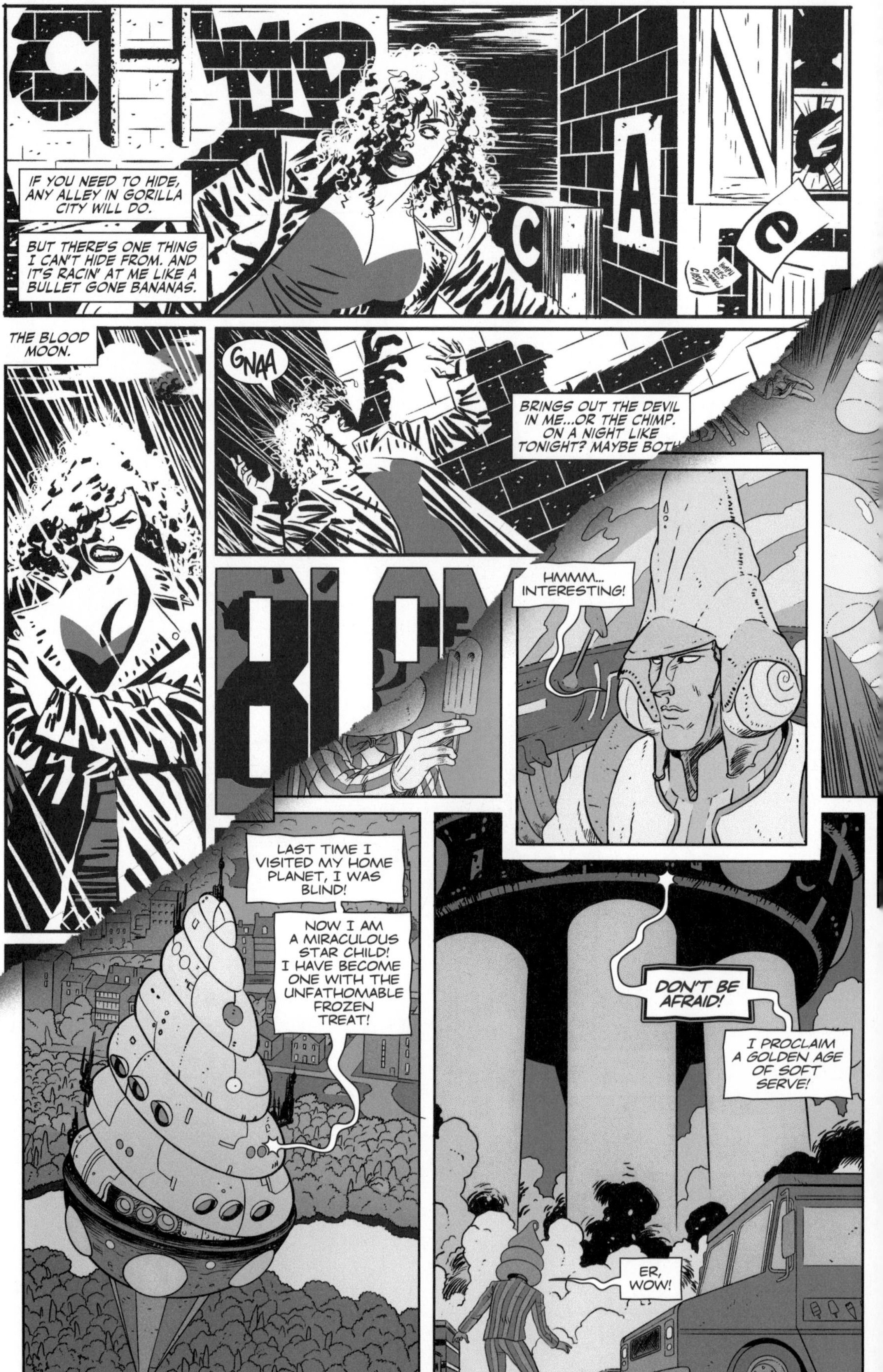
IF YOU NEED TO HIDE, ANY ALLEY IN GORILLA CITY WILL DO.
BUT THERE'S ONE THING I CAN'T HIDE FROM. AND IT'S RACIN' AT ME LIKE A BULLET GONE BANANAS.
THE BLOOD MOON.
GNAA
BRINGS OUT THE DEVIL IN ME...OR THE CHIMP. ON A NIGHT LIKE TONIGHT? MAYBE BOTH
HMMM... INTERESTING!
LAST TIME I VISITED MY HOME PLANET, I WAS BLIND!
NOW I AM A MIRACULOUS STAR CHILD! I HAVE BECOME ONE WITH THE UNFATHOMABLE FROZEN TREAT!
DON'T BE AFRAID!
I PROCLAIM A GOLDEN AGE OF SOFT SERVE!
ER, WOW!

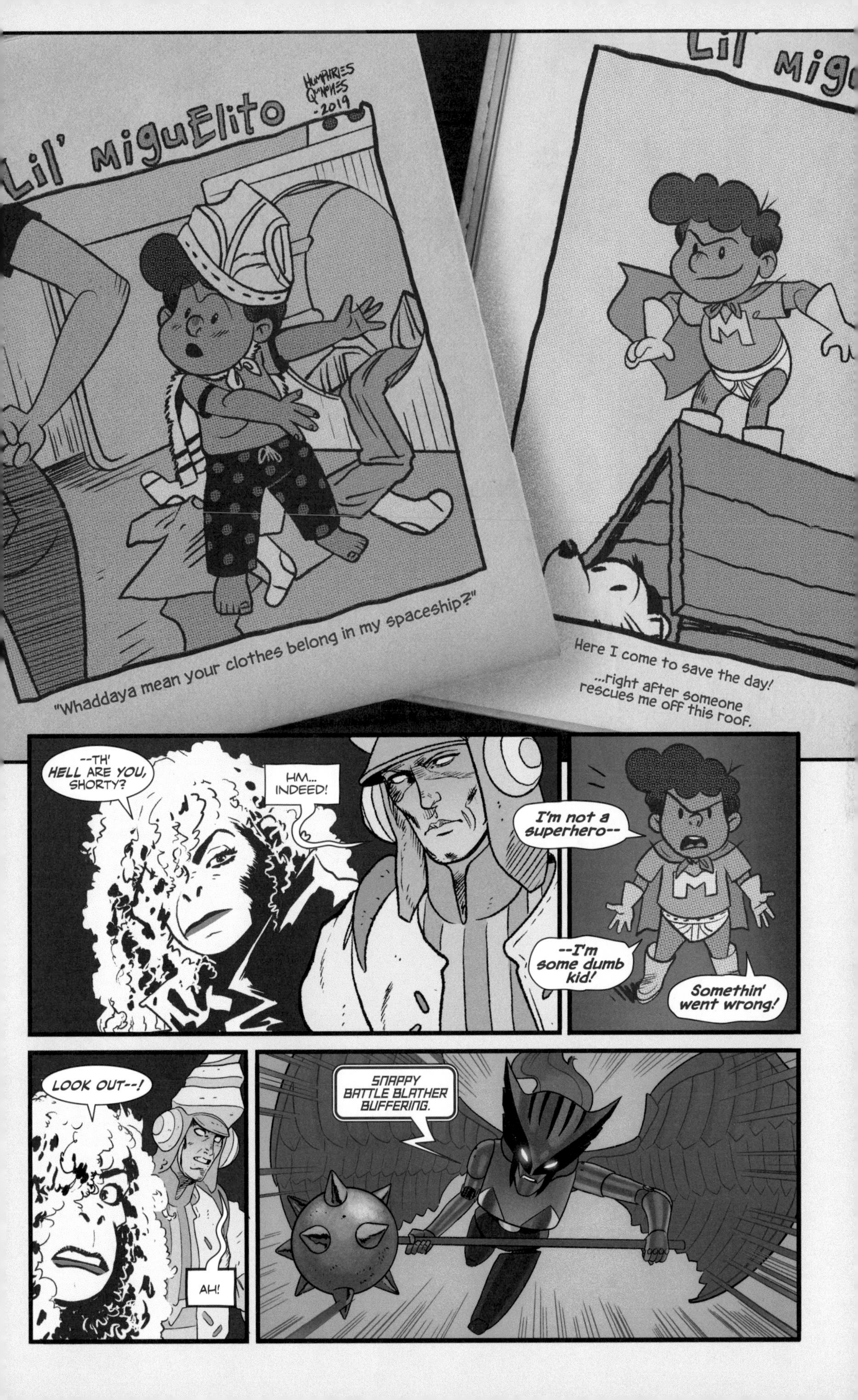
Lil' miguElito
Humphries Quiñones -2019
"Whaddaya mean your clothes belong in my spaceship?"
Lil' Migu
Here I come to save the day!
...right after someone rescues me off this roof.
--TH' HELL ARE YOU, SHORTY?
HM... INDEED!
I'm not a superhero--
--I'm some dumb kid!
Somethin' went wrong!
LOOK OUT--!
AH!
SNAPPY BATTLE BLATHER BUFFERING.

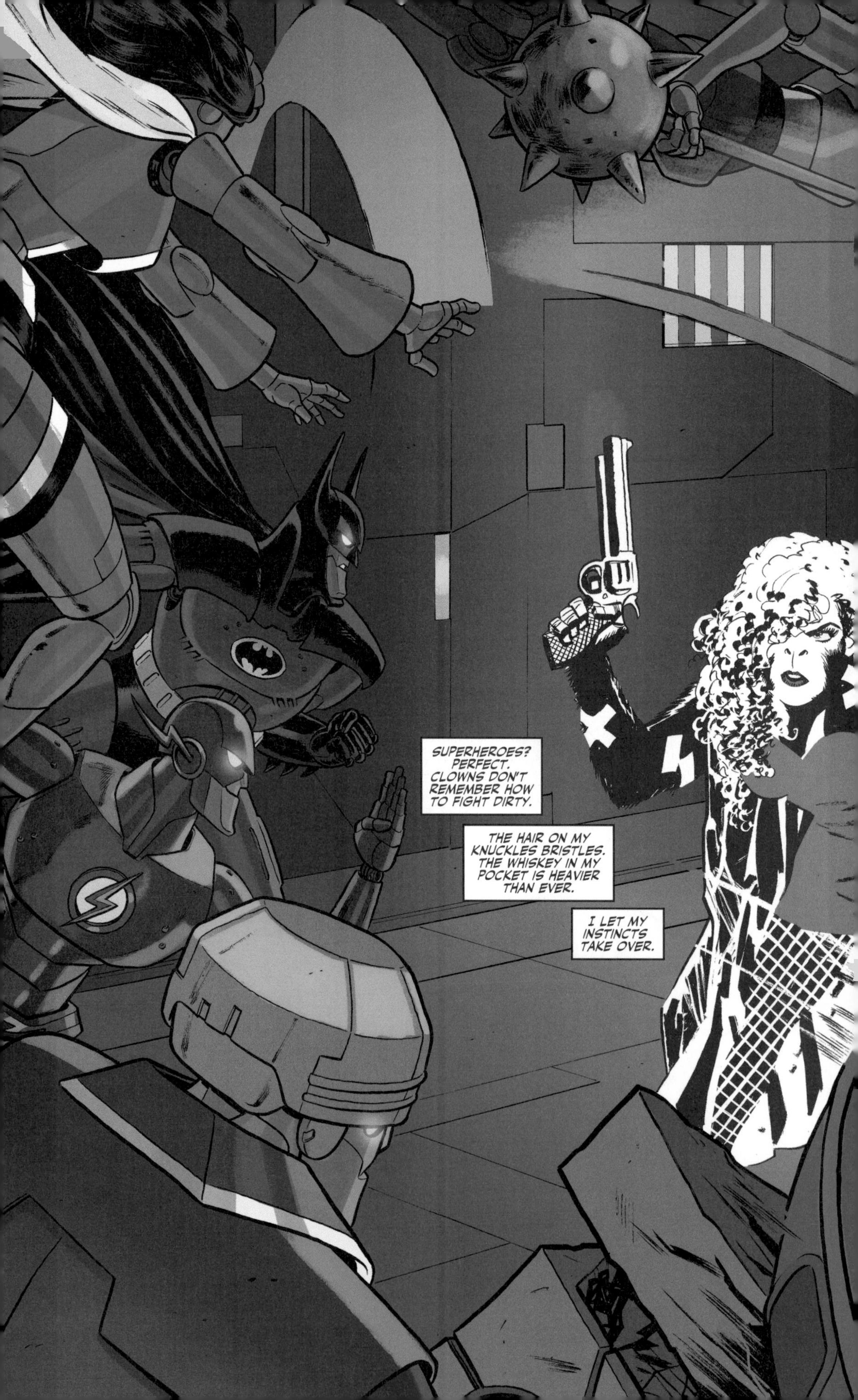

SUPERHEROES? PERFECT. CLOWNS DON'T REMEMBER HOW TO FIGHT DIRTY.
THE HAIR ON MY KNUCKLES BRISTLES. THE WHISKEY IN MY POCKET IS HEAVIER THAN EVER.
I LET MY INSTINCTS TAKE OVER.

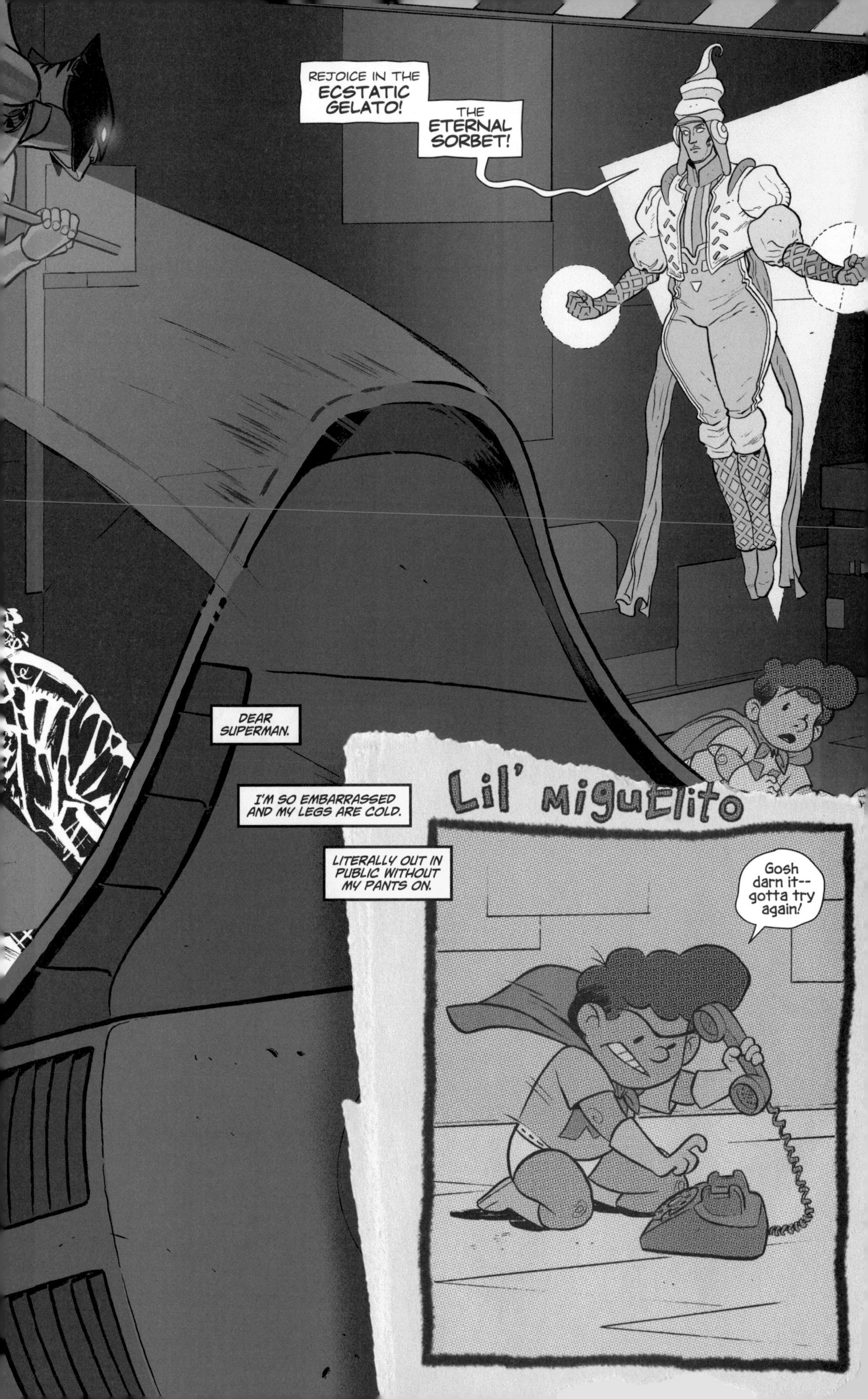
REJOICE IN THE ECSTATIC GELATO!
THE ETERNAL SORBET!
DEAR SUPERMAN.
I'M SO EMBARRASSED AND MY LEGS ARE COLD.
LITERALLY OUT IN PUBLIC WITHOUT MY PANTS ON.
Lil' migutlito
Gosh darn it-- gotta try again!

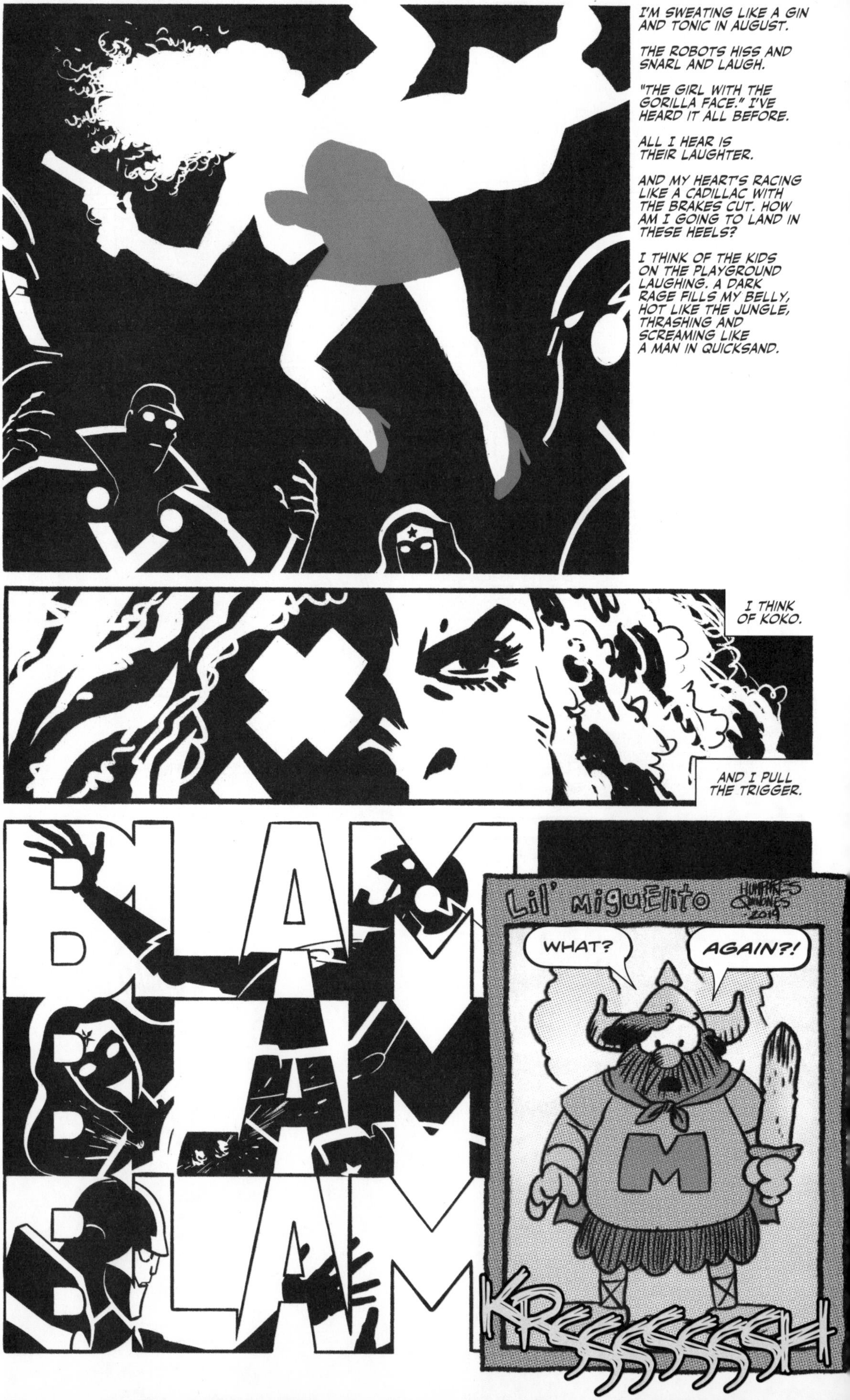
I'M SWEATING LIKE A GIN AND TONIC IN AUGUST.
THE ROBOTS HISS AND SNARL AND LAUGH.
"THE GIRL WITH THE GORILLA FACE." I'VE HEARD IT ALL BEFORE.
ALL I HEAR IS THEIR LAUGHTER.
AND MY HEART'S RACING LIKE A CADILLAC WITH THE BRAKES CUT. HOW AM I GOING TO LAND IN THESE HEELS?
I THINK OF THE KIDS ON THE PLAYGROUND LAUGHING. A DARK RAGE FILLS MY BELLY, HOT LIKE THE JUNGLE, THRASHING AND SCREAMING LIKE A MAN IN QUICKSAND.
I THINK OF KOKO.
AND I PULL THE TRIGGER.
BLAM
BLAM
BLAM
Lil' miguelito
HUMPHRIES QUIÑONES 2019
WHAT?
AGAIN?!
M
KRESSSSSSSH

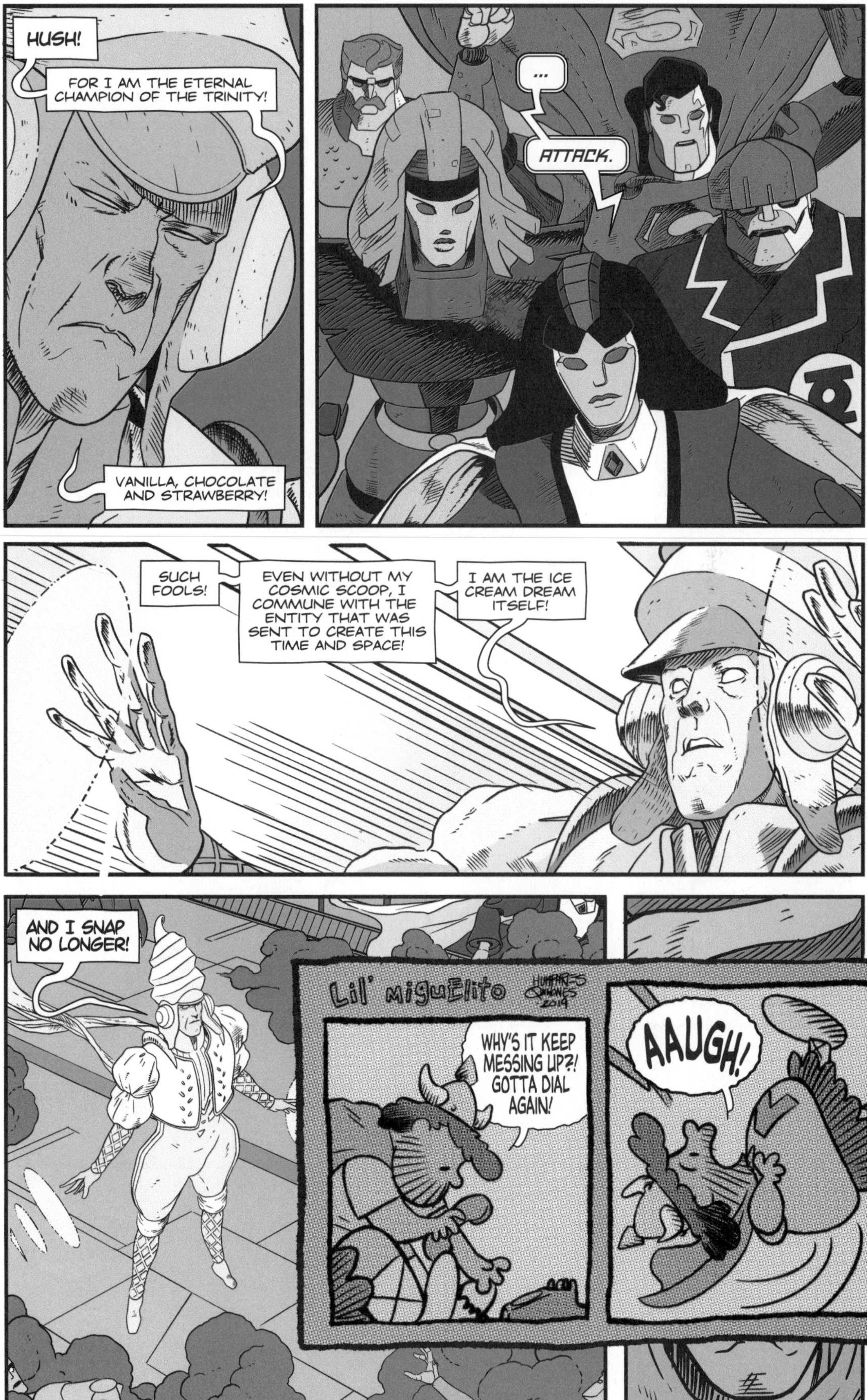
HUSH!
FOR I AM THE ETERNAL CHAMPION OF THE TRINITY!
VANILLA, CHOCOLATE AND STRAWBERRY!
...
ATTACK.
SUCH FOOLS!
EVEN WITHOUT MY COSMIC SCOOP, I COMMUNE WITH THE ENTITY THAT WAS SENT TO CREATE THIS TIME AND SPACE!
I AM THE ICE CREAM DREAM ITSELF!
AND I SNAP NO LONGER!
Lil' miguElito
HUMPHRIES QUIÑONES 2019
WHY'S IT KEEP MESSING UP?! GOTTA DIAL AGAIN!
AAUGH!

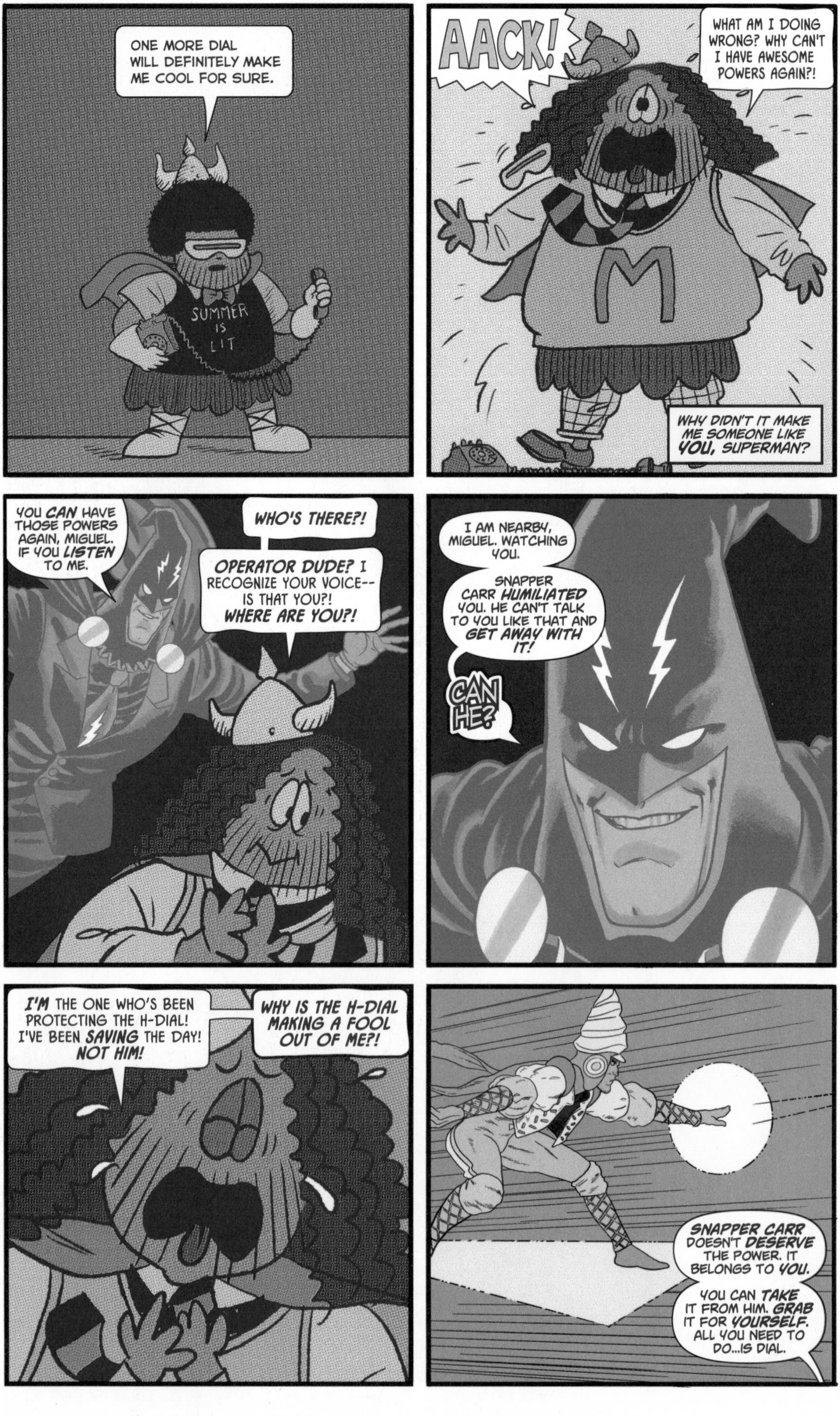
ONE MORE DIAL WILL DEFINITELY MAKE ME COOL FOR SURE.
SUMMER IS LIT
AACK!
WHAT AM I DOING WRONG? WHY CAN'T I HAVE AWESOME POWERS AGAIN?!
M
WHY DIDN'T IT MAKE ME SOMEONE LIKE YOU, SUPERMAN?
YOU CAN HAVE THOSE POWERS AGAIN, MIGUEL. IF YOU LISTEN TO ME.
WHO'S THERE?!
OPERATOR DUDE? I RECOGNIZE YOUR VOICE-- IS THAT YOU?! WHERE ARE YOU?!
I AM NEARBY, MIGUEL. WATCHING YOU.
SNAPPER CARR HUMILIATED YOU. HE CAN'T TALK TO YOU LIKE THAT AND GET AWAY WITH IT!
CAN HE?
I'M THE ONE WHO'S BEEN PROTECTING THE H-DIAL! I'VE BEEN SAVING THE DAY! NOT HIM!
WHY IS THE H-DIAL MAKING A FOOL OUT OF ME?!
SNAPPER CARR DOESN'T DESERVE THE POWER. IT BELONGS TO YOU.
YOU CAN TAKE IT FROM HIM. GRAB IT FOR YOURSELF. ALL YOU NEED TO DO...IS DIAL.

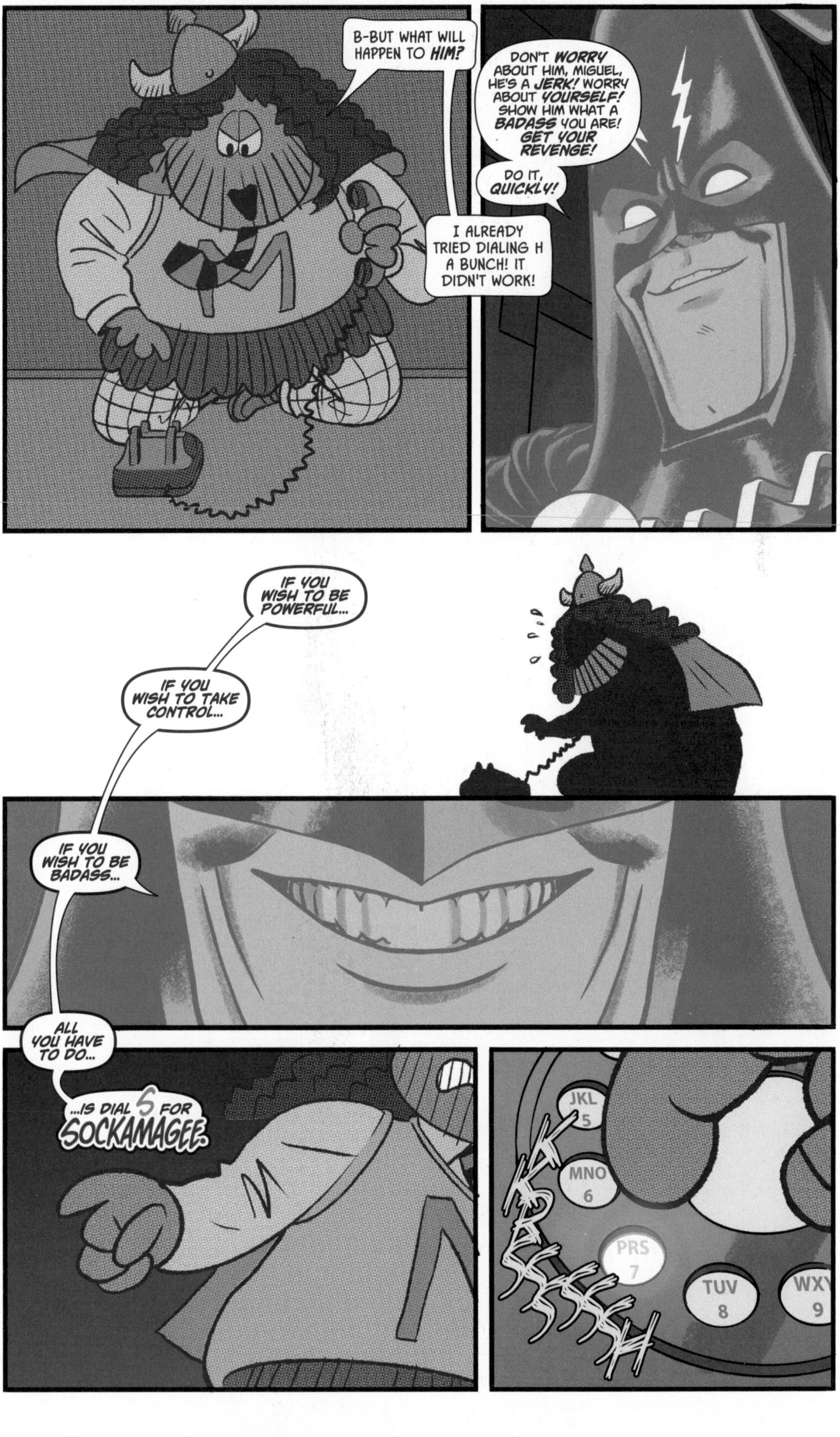
B-BUT WHAT WILL HAPPEN TO HIM?
I ALREADY TRIED DIALING H A BUNCH! IT DIDN'T WORK!
DON'T WORRY ABOUT HIM, MIGUEL, HE'S A JERK! WORRY ABOUT YOURSELF! SHOW HIM WHAT A BADASS YOU ARE! GET YOUR REVENGE!
DO IT, QUICKLY!
IF YOU WISH TO BE POWERFUL...
IF YOU WISH TO TAKE CONTROL...
IF YOU WISH TO BE BADASS...
ALL YOU HAVE TO DO...
...IS DIAL 5 FOR SOCKAMAGEE.
JKL 5
MNO 6
PRS 7
TUV 8
WXY 9
KRESSSSH

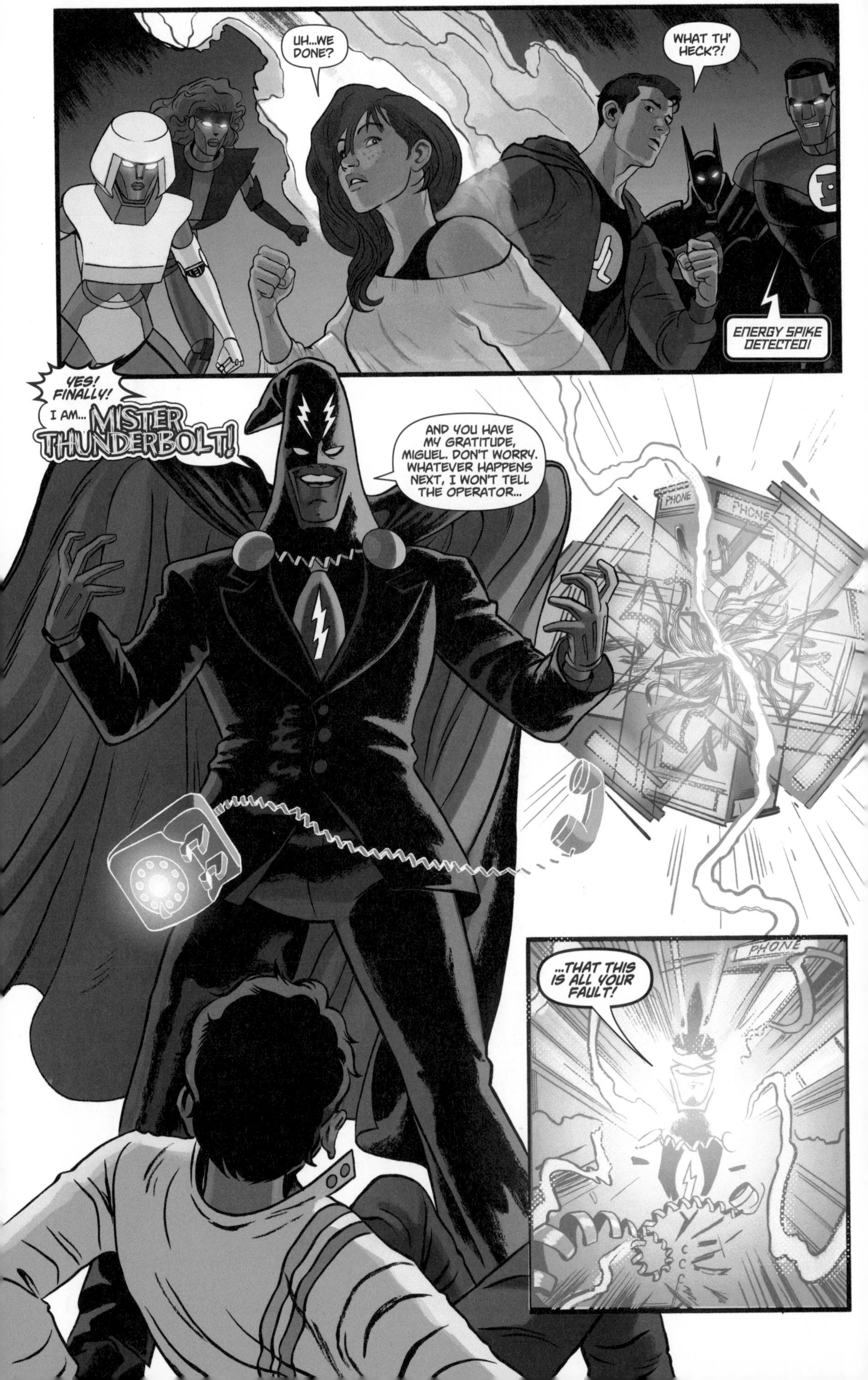
UH...WE DONE?
WHAT TH' HECK?!
ENERGY SPIKE DETECTED!
YES! FINALLY! I AM... MISTER THUNDERBOLT!
AND YOU HAVE MY GRATITUDE, MIGUEL. DON'T WORRY. WHATEVER HAPPENS NEXT, I WON'T TELL THE OPERATOR...
PHONE
PHONE
PHONE
...THAT THIS IS ALL YOUR FAULT!

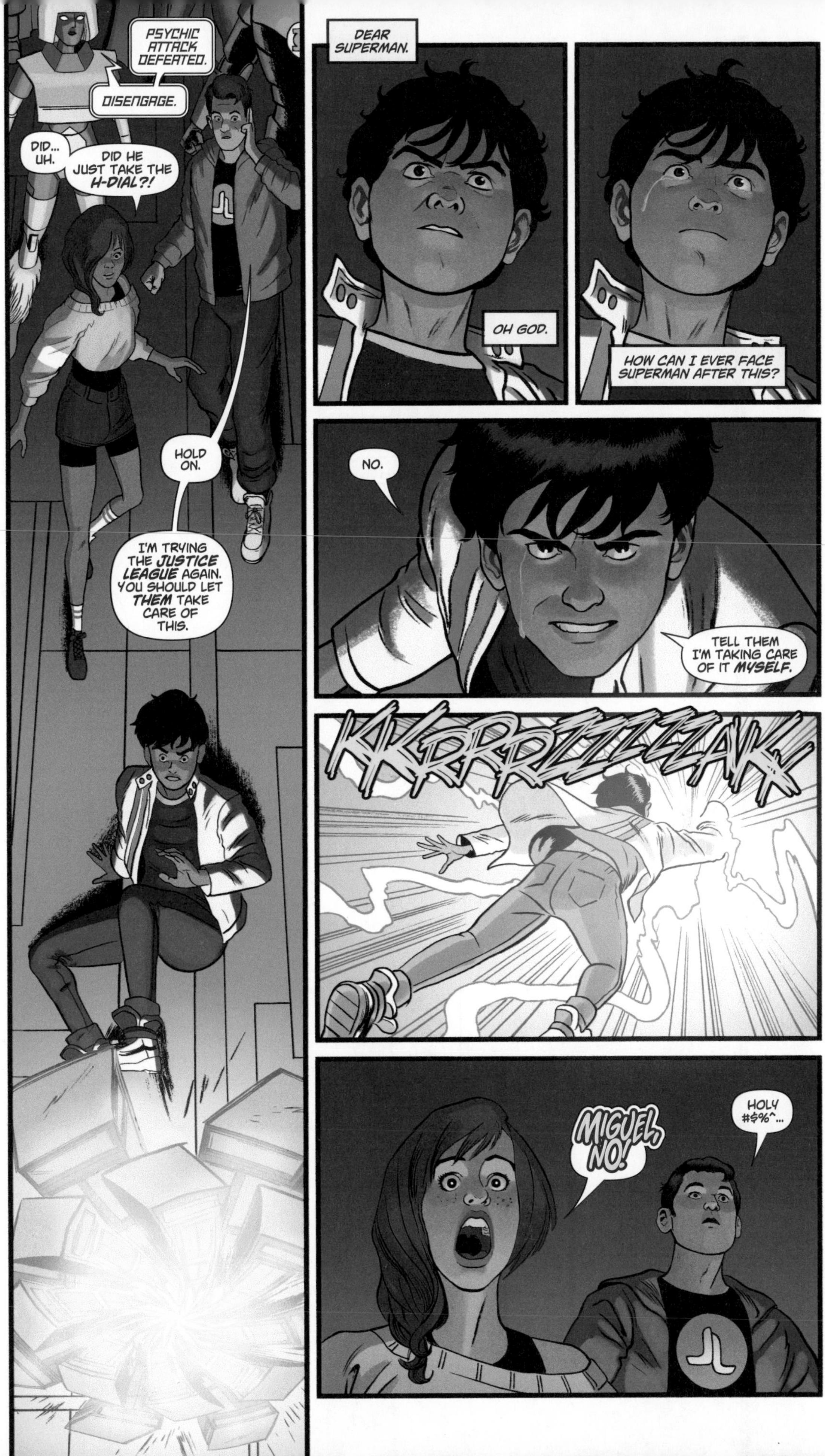
PSYCHIC ATTACK DEFEATED.
DISENGAGE.
DID... UH.
DID HE JUST TAKE THE H-DIAL?!
HOLD ON.
I'M TRYING THE JUSTICE LEAGUE AGAIN. YOU SHOULD LET THEM TAKE CARE OF THIS.
DEAR SUPERMAN.
OH GOD.
HOW CAN I EVER FACE SUPERMAN AFTER THIS?
NO.
TELL THEM I'M TAKING CARE OF IT MYSELF.
KKRRRZZZZAKK!
MIGUEL, NO!
HOLY #$%^...

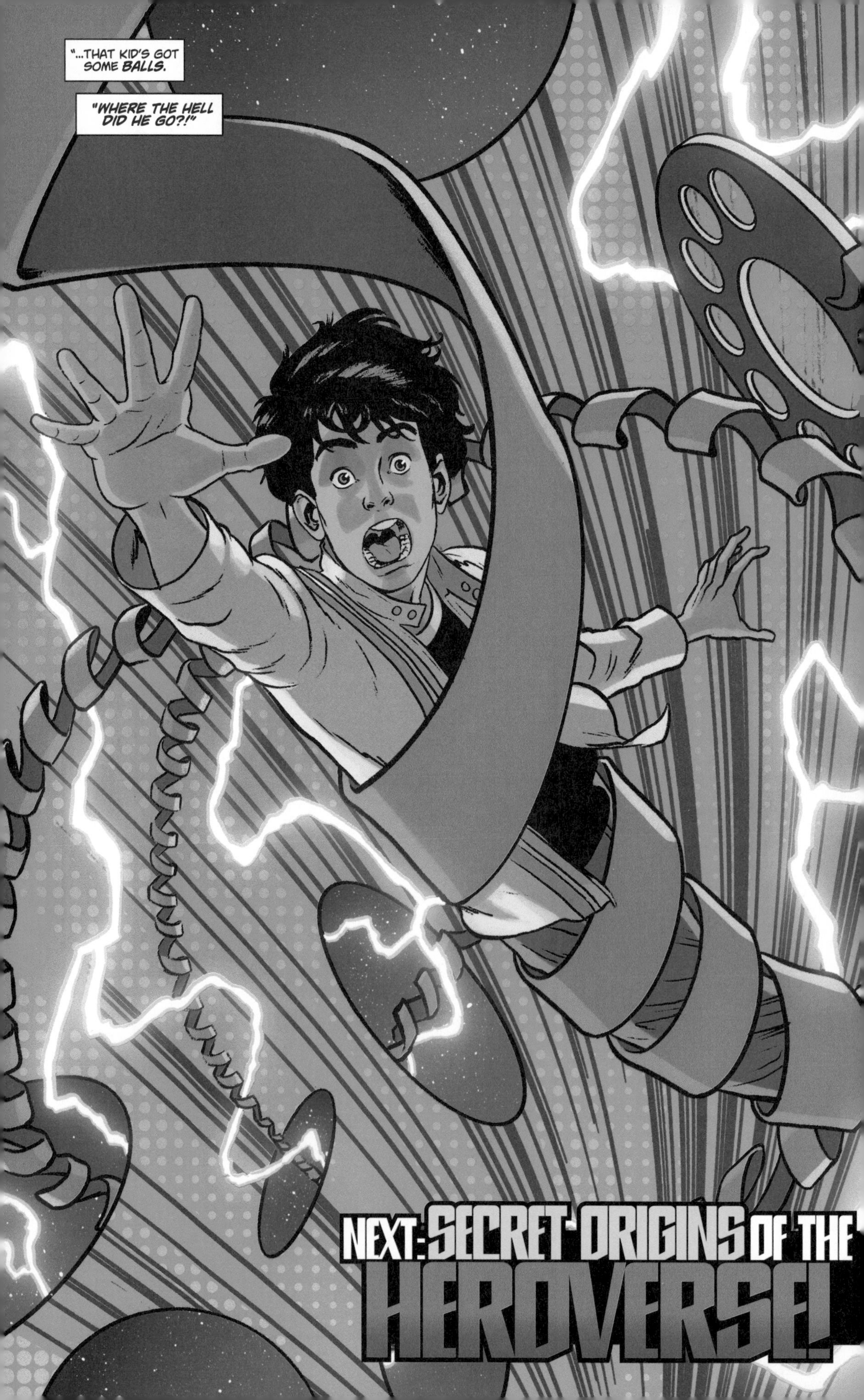
"...THAT KID'S GOT SOME BALLS.
"WHERE THE HELL DID HE GO?!"
NEXT: SECRET ORIGINS OF THE HEROVERSE!

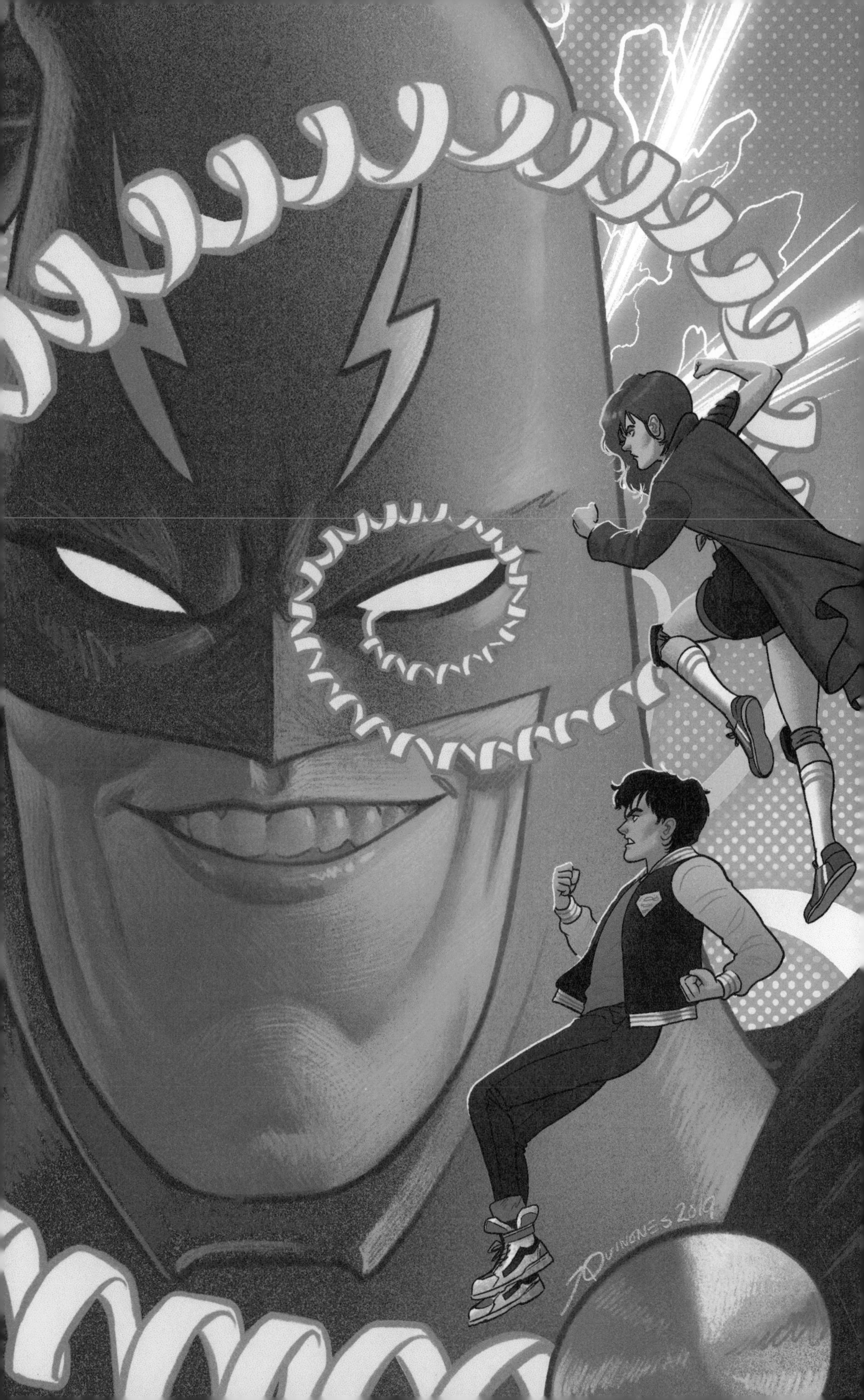
JQUINONES 2019

SECRET ORIGINS OF THE HEROVERSE

art by
JOE QUINONES

additional inks by
SCOTT HANNA and **MIKE ALLRED**

colors by
JORDAN GIBSON

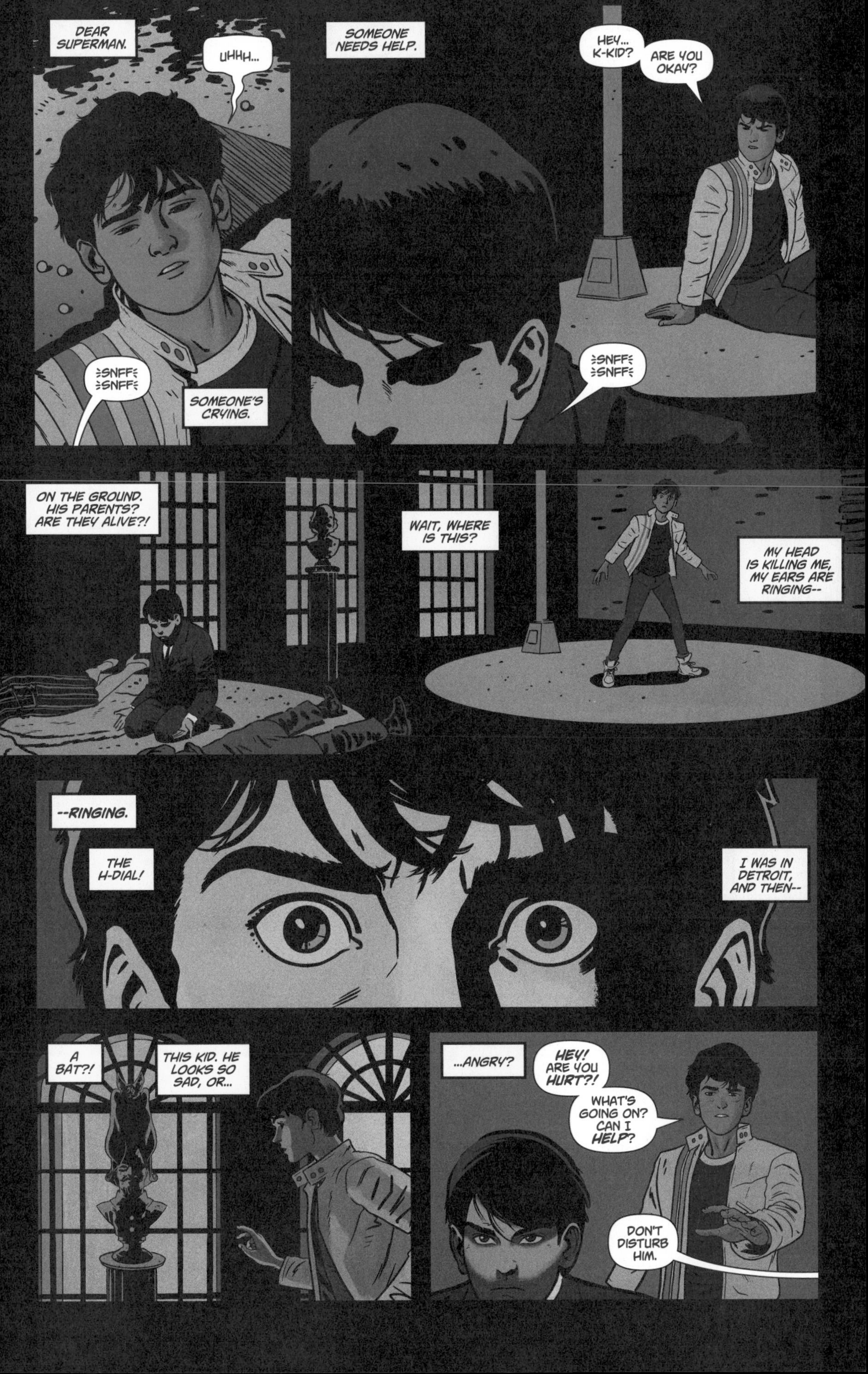
DEAR SUPERMAN.
UHHH...
SNFF SNFF
SOMEONE'S CRYING.
SOMEONE NEEDS HELP.
HEY... K-KID?
ARE YOU OKAY?
SNFF SNFF
ON THE GROUND. HIS PARENTS? ARE THEY ALIVE?!
WAIT, WHERE IS THIS?
MY HEAD IS KILLING ME, MY EARS ARE RINGING--
--RINGING.
THE H-DIAL!
I WAS IN DETROIT, AND THEN--
A BAT?!
THIS KID. HE LOOKS SO SAD, OR...
...ANGRY?
HEY! ARE YOU HURT?!
WHAT'S GOING ON? CAN I HELP?
DON'T DISTURB HIM.

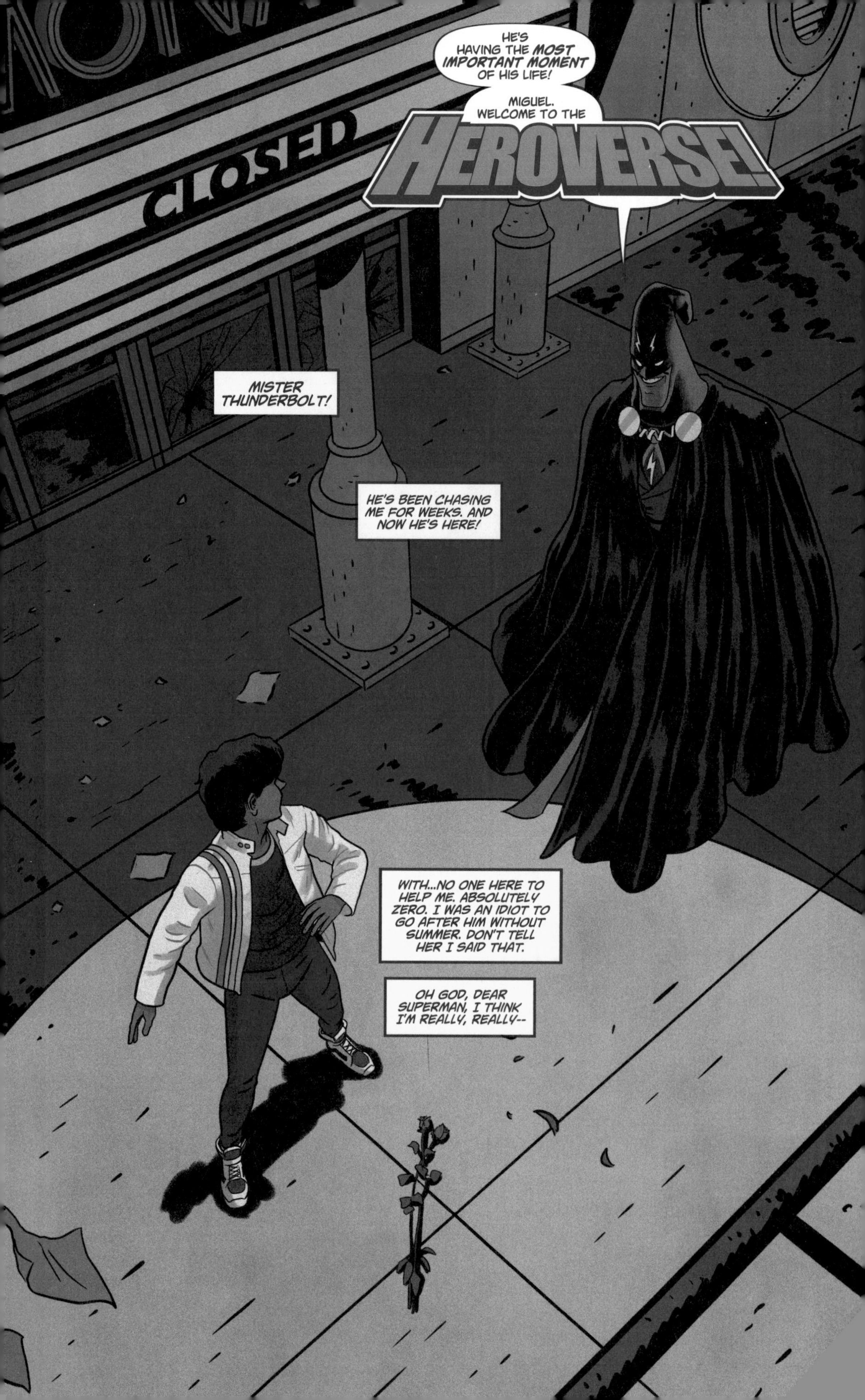
HE'S HAVING THE MOST IMPORTANT MOMENT OF HIS LIFE!
MIGUEL. WELCOME TO THE
HEROVERSE!
CLOSED
MISTER THUNDERBOLT!
HE'S BEEN CHASING ME FOR WEEKS. AND NOW HE'S HERE!
WITH...NO ONE HERE TO HELP ME. ABSOLUTELY ZERO. I WAS AN IDIOT TO GO AFTER HIM WITHOUT SUMMER. DON'T TELL HER I SAID THAT.
OH GOD, DEAR SUPERMAN, I THINK I'M REALLY, REALLY--

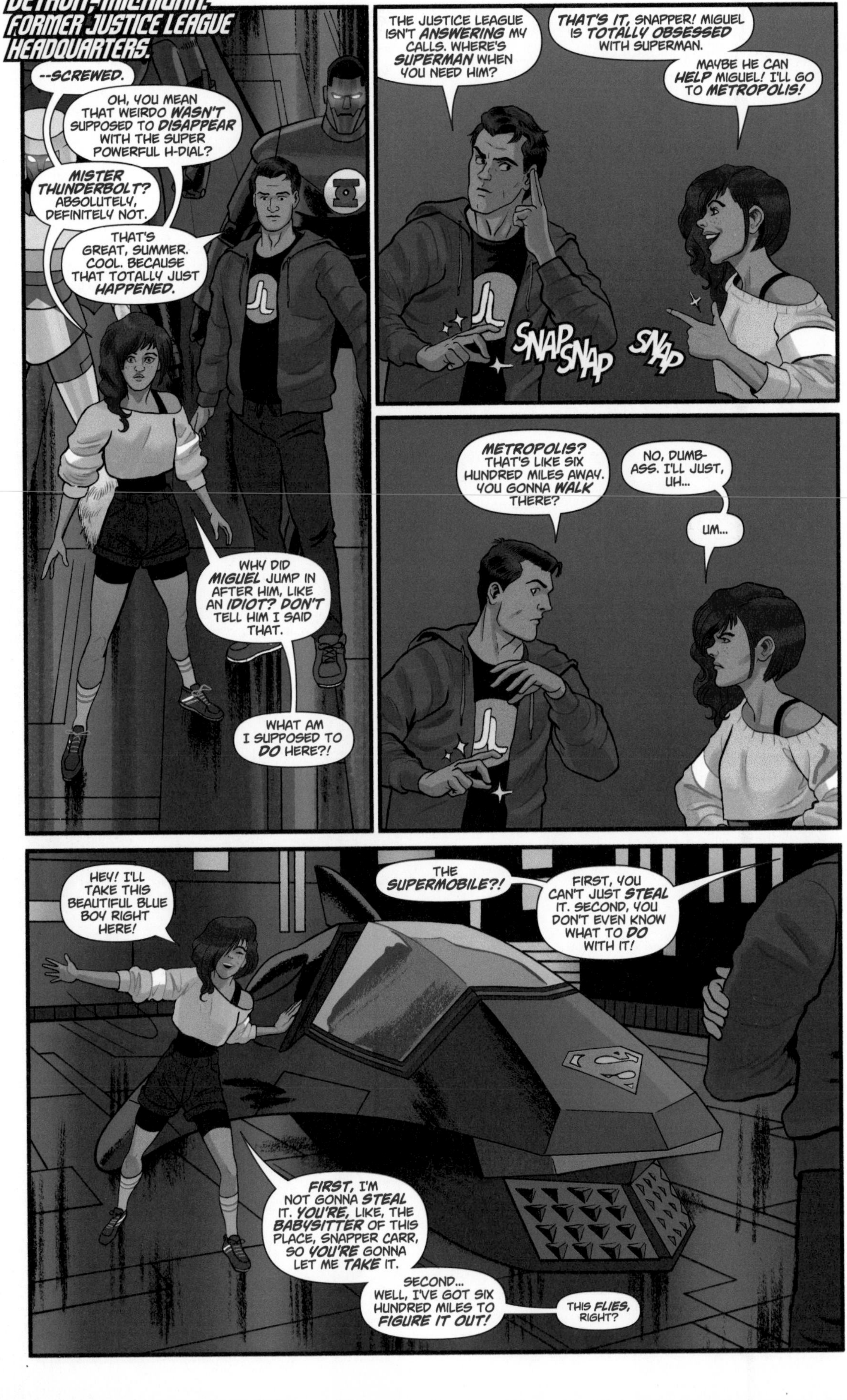

DETROIT, MICHIGAN. FORMER JUSTICE LEAGUE HEADQUARTERS.
--SCREWED.
OH, YOU MEAN THAT WEIRDO WASN'T SUPPOSED TO DISAPPEAR WITH THE SUPER POWERFUL H-DIAL?
MISTER THUNDERBOLT? ABSOLUTELY, DEFINITELY NOT.
THAT'S GREAT, SUMMER. COOL. BECAUSE THAT TOTALLY JUST HAPPENED.
WHY DID MIGUEL JUMP IN AFTER HIM, LIKE AN IDIOT? DON'T TELL HIM I SAID THAT.
WHAT AM I SUPPOSED TO DO HERE?!
THE JUSTICE LEAGUE ISN'T ANSWERING MY CALLS. WHERE'S SUPERMAN WHEN YOU NEED HIM?
THAT'S IT, SNAPPER! MIGUEL IS TOTALLY OBSESSED WITH SUPERMAN.
MAYBE HE CAN HELP MIGUEL! I'LL GO TO METROPOLIS!
SNAP SNAP
SNAP
METROPOLIS? THAT'S LIKE SIX HUNDRED MILES AWAY. YOU GONNA WALK THERE?
NO, DUMB-ASS. I'LL JUST, UH...
UM...
HEY! I'LL TAKE THIS BEAUTIFUL BLUE BOY RIGHT HERE!
THE SUPERMOBILE?!
FIRST, YOU CAN'T JUST STEAL IT. SECOND, YOU DON'T EVEN KNOW WHAT TO DO WITH IT!
FIRST, I'M NOT GONNA STEAL IT. YOU'RE, LIKE, THE BABYSITTER OF THIS PLACE, SNAPPER CARR, SO YOU'RE GONNA LET ME TAKE IT.
SECOND... WELL, I'VE GOT SIX HUNDRED MILES TO FIGURE IT OUT!
THIS FLIES, RIGHT?

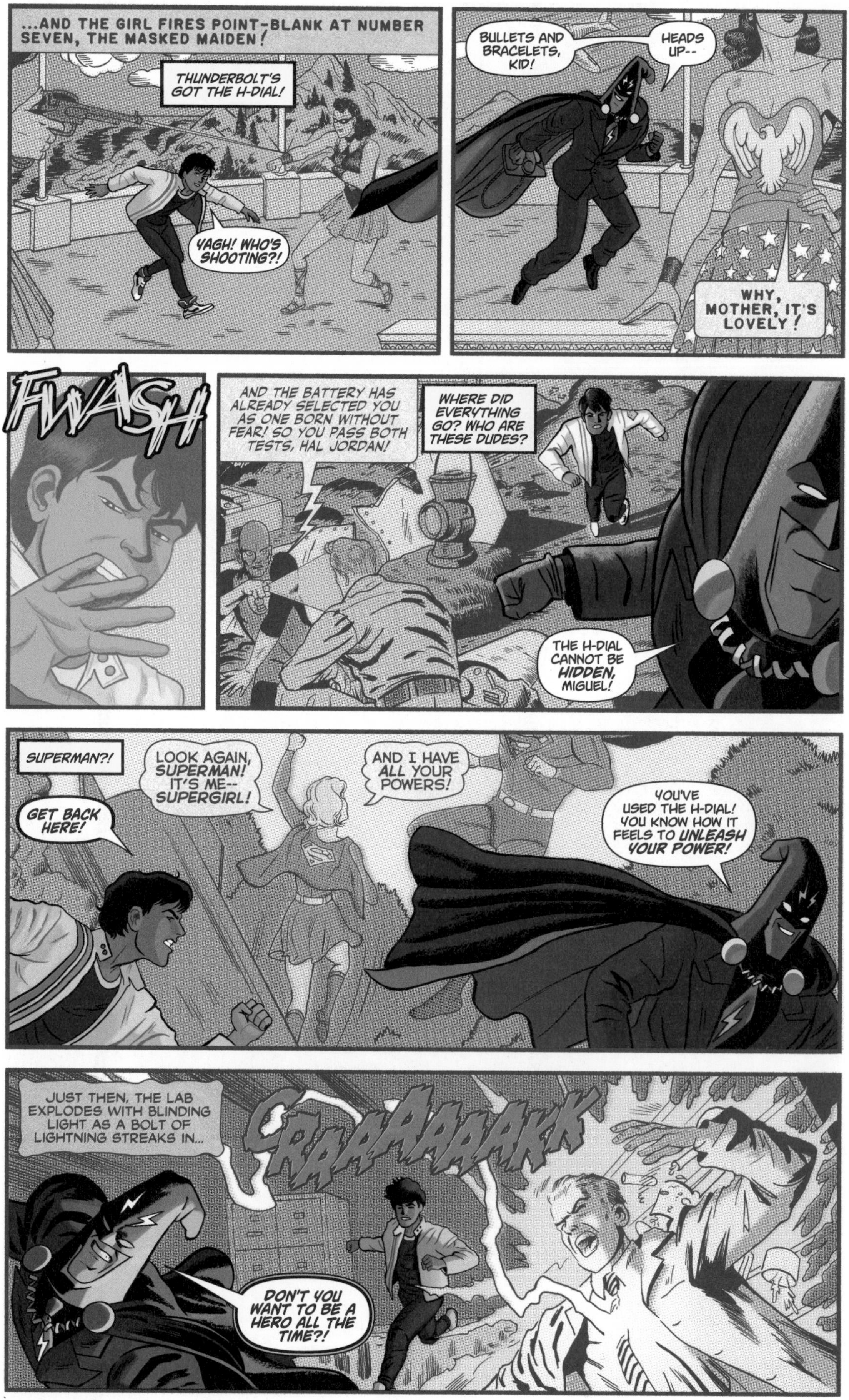
...AND THE GIRL FIRES POINT-BLANK AT NUMBER SEVEN, THE MASKED MAIDEN!
THUNDERBOLT'S GOT THE H-DIAL!
YAGH! WHO'S SHOOTING?!
BULLETS AND BRACELETS, KID!
HEADS UP--
WHY, MOTHER, IT'S LOVELY!
FWASH
AND THE BATTERY HAS ALREADY SELECTED YOU AS ONE BORN WITHOUT FEAR! SO YOU PASS BOTH TESTS, HAL JORDAN!
WHERE DID EVERYTHING GO? WHO ARE THESE DUDES?
THE H-DIAL CANNOT BE HIDDEN, MIGUEL!
SUPERMAN?!
LOOK AGAIN, SUPERMAN! IT'S ME-- SUPERGIRL!
AND I HAVE ALL YOUR POWERS!
GET BACK HERE!
YOU'VE USED THE H-DIAL! YOU KNOW HOW IT FEELS TO UNLEASH YOUR POWER!
JUST THEN, THE LAB EXPLODES WITH BLINDING LIGHT AS A BOLT OF LIGHTNING STREAKS IN...
CRAAAAAAAKK
DON'T YOU WANT TO BE A HERO ALL THE TIME?!

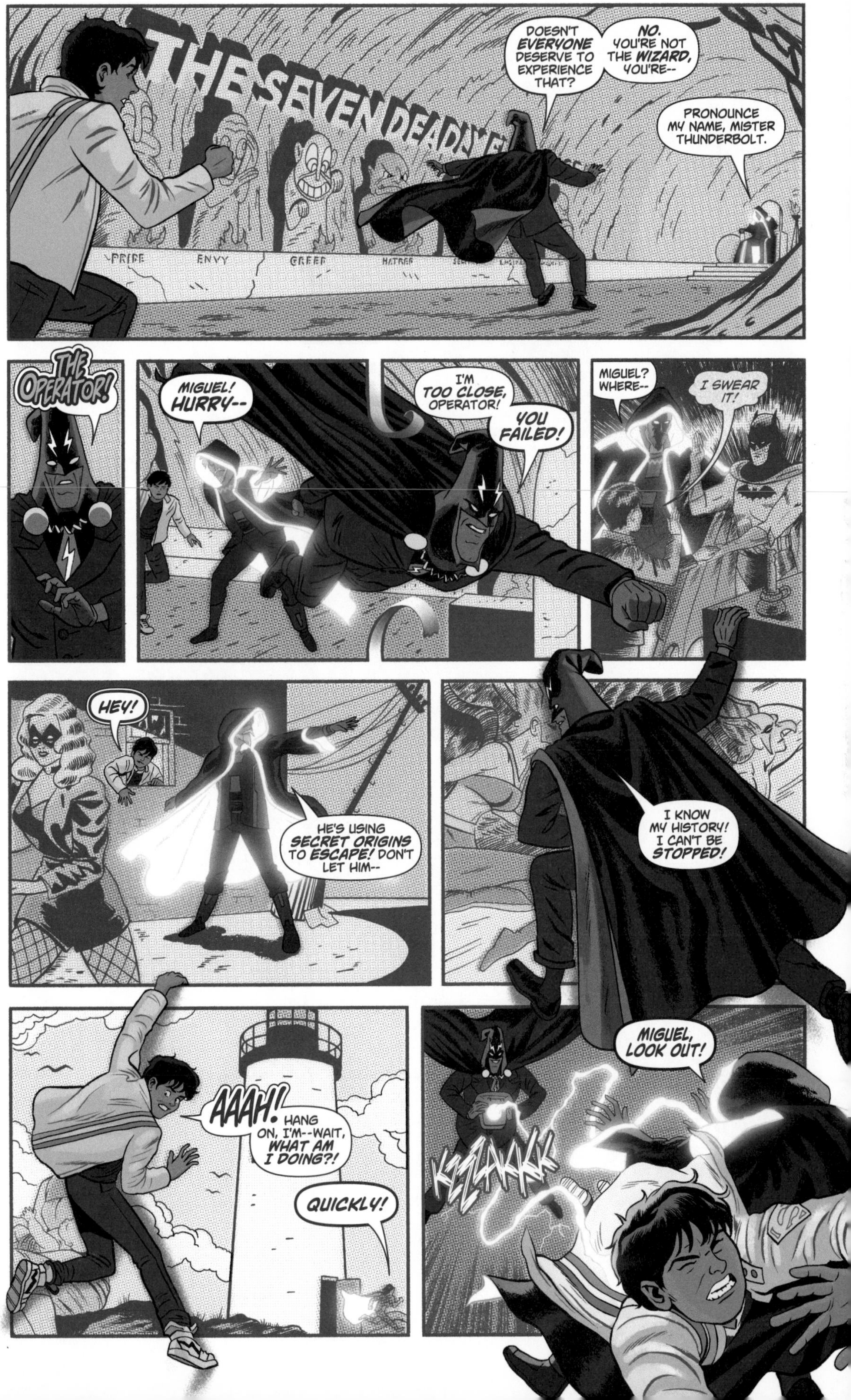
THE SEVEN DEADLY
PRIDE
ENVY
GREED
HATRED
DOESN'T EVERYONE DESERVE TO EXPERIENCE THAT?
NO. YOU'RE NOT THE WIZARD, YOU'RE--
PRONOUNCE MY NAME, MISTER THUNDERBOLT.
THE OPERATOR!
MIGUEL! HURRY--
I'M TOO CLOSE, OPERATOR!
YOU FAILED!
MIGUEL? WHERE--
I SWEAR IT!
HEY!
HE'S USING SECRET ORIGINS TO ESCAPE! DON'T LET HIM--
I KNOW MY HISTORY! I CAN'T BE STOPPED!
AAAH!
HANG ON, I'M--WAIT, WHAT AM I DOING?!
QUICKLY!
MIGUEL, LOOK OUT!
KZZAKKK

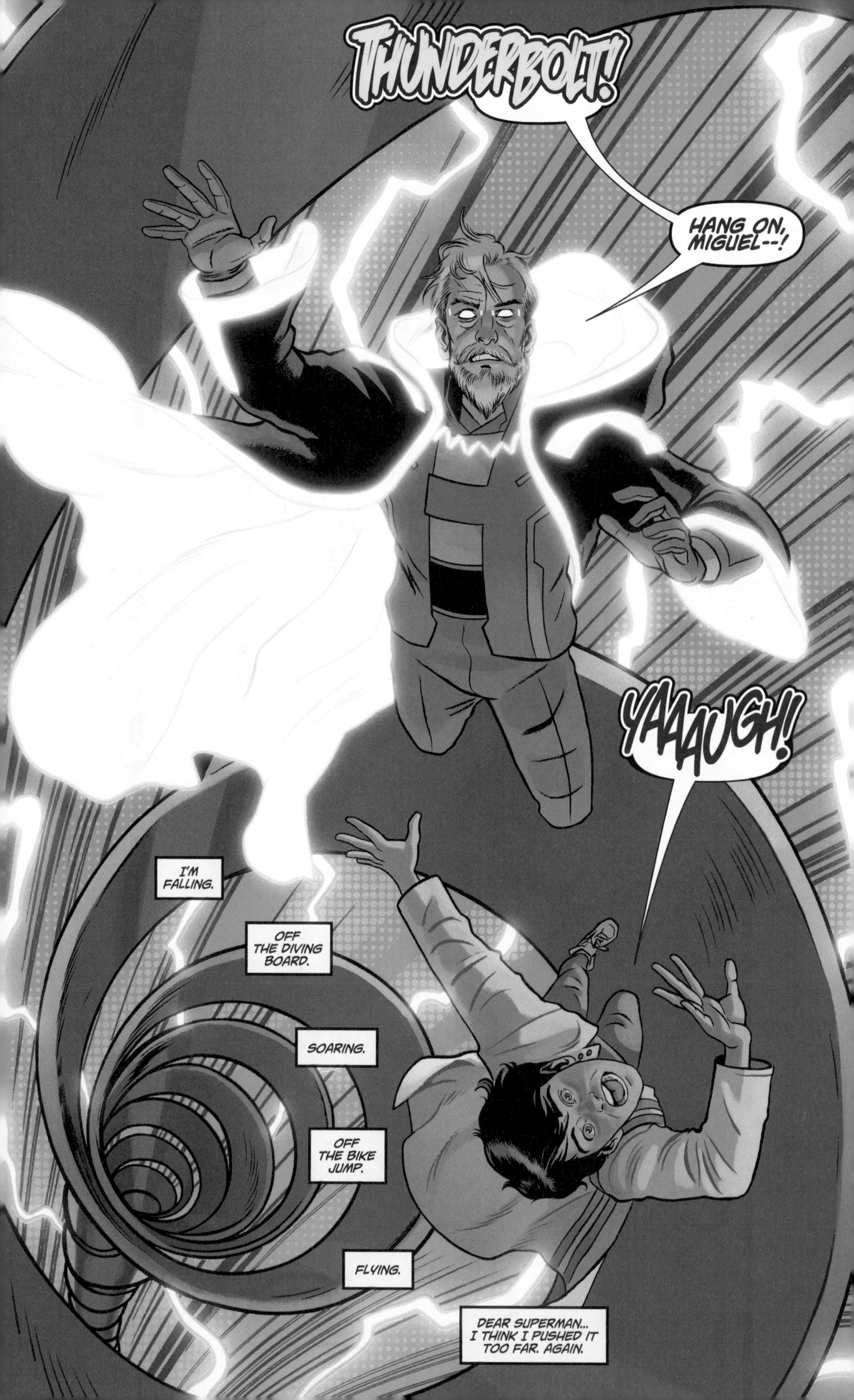
THUNDERBOLT!
HANG ON, MIGUEL--!
YAAAAUGH!
I'M FALLING.
OFF THE DIVING BOARD.
SOARING.
OFF THE BIKE JUMP.
FLYING.
DEAR SUPERMAN... I THINK I PUSHED IT TOO FAR. AGAIN.

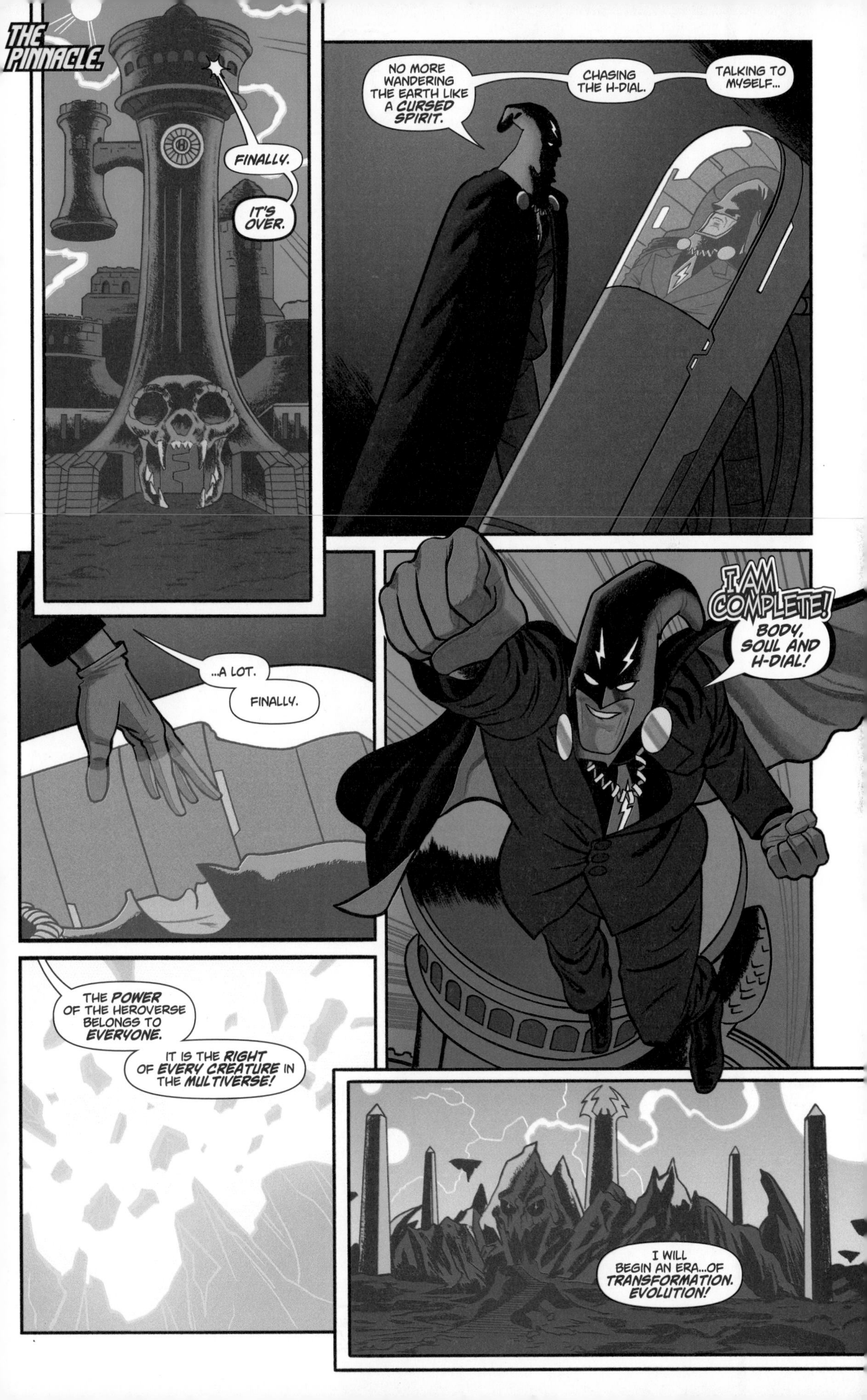
THE PINNACLE.
FINALLY.
IT'S OVER.
NO MORE WANDERING THE EARTH LIKE A CURSED SPIRIT.
CHASING THE H-DIAL.
TALKING TO MYSELF...
...A LOT.
FINALLY.
I AM COMPLETE!
BODY, SOUL AND H-DIAL!
THE POWER OF THE HEROVERSE BELONGS TO EVERYONE.
IT IS THE RIGHT OF EVERY CREATURE IN THE MULTIVERSE!
I WILL BEGIN AN ERA...OF TRANSFORMATION. EVOLUTION!

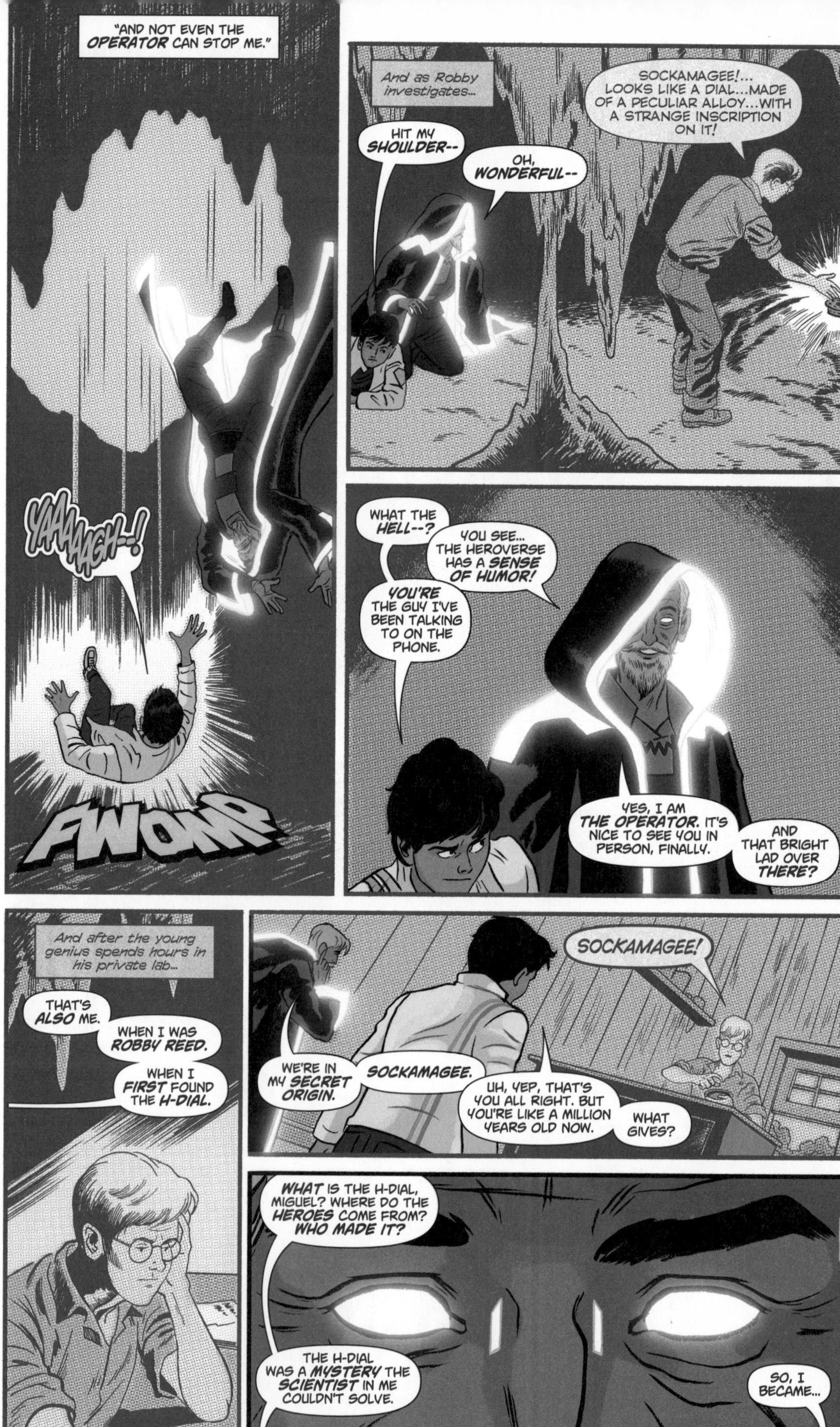

"AND NOT EVEN THE OPERATOR CAN STOP ME."
YAAAAAGH--!
FWOMP
And as Robby investigates...
HIT MY SHOULDER--
OH, WONDERFUL--
SOCKAMAGEE!... LOOKS LIKE A DIAL...MADE OF A PECULIAR ALLOY...WITH A STRANGE INSCRIPTION ON IT!
WHAT THE HELL--?
YOU SEE... THE HEROVERSE HAS A SENSE OF HUMOR!
YOU'RE THE GUY I'VE BEEN TALKING TO ON THE PHONE.
YES, I AM THE OPERATOR. IT'S NICE TO SEE YOU IN PERSON, FINALLY.
AND THAT BRIGHT LAD OVER THERE?
And after the young genius spends hours in his private lab...
THAT'S ALSO ME.
WHEN I WAS ROBBY REED.
WHEN I FIRST FOUND THE H-DIAL.
SOCKAMAGEE!
WE'RE IN MY SECRET ORIGIN.
SOCKAMAGEE.
UH, YEP, THAT'S YOU ALL RIGHT. BUT YOU'RE LIKE A MILLION YEARS OLD NOW.
WHAT GIVES?
WHAT IS THE H-DIAL, MIGUEL? WHERE DO THE HEROES COME FROM? WHO MADE IT?
THE H-DIAL WAS A MYSTERY THE SCIENTIST IN ME COULDN'T SOLVE.
SO, I BECAME...

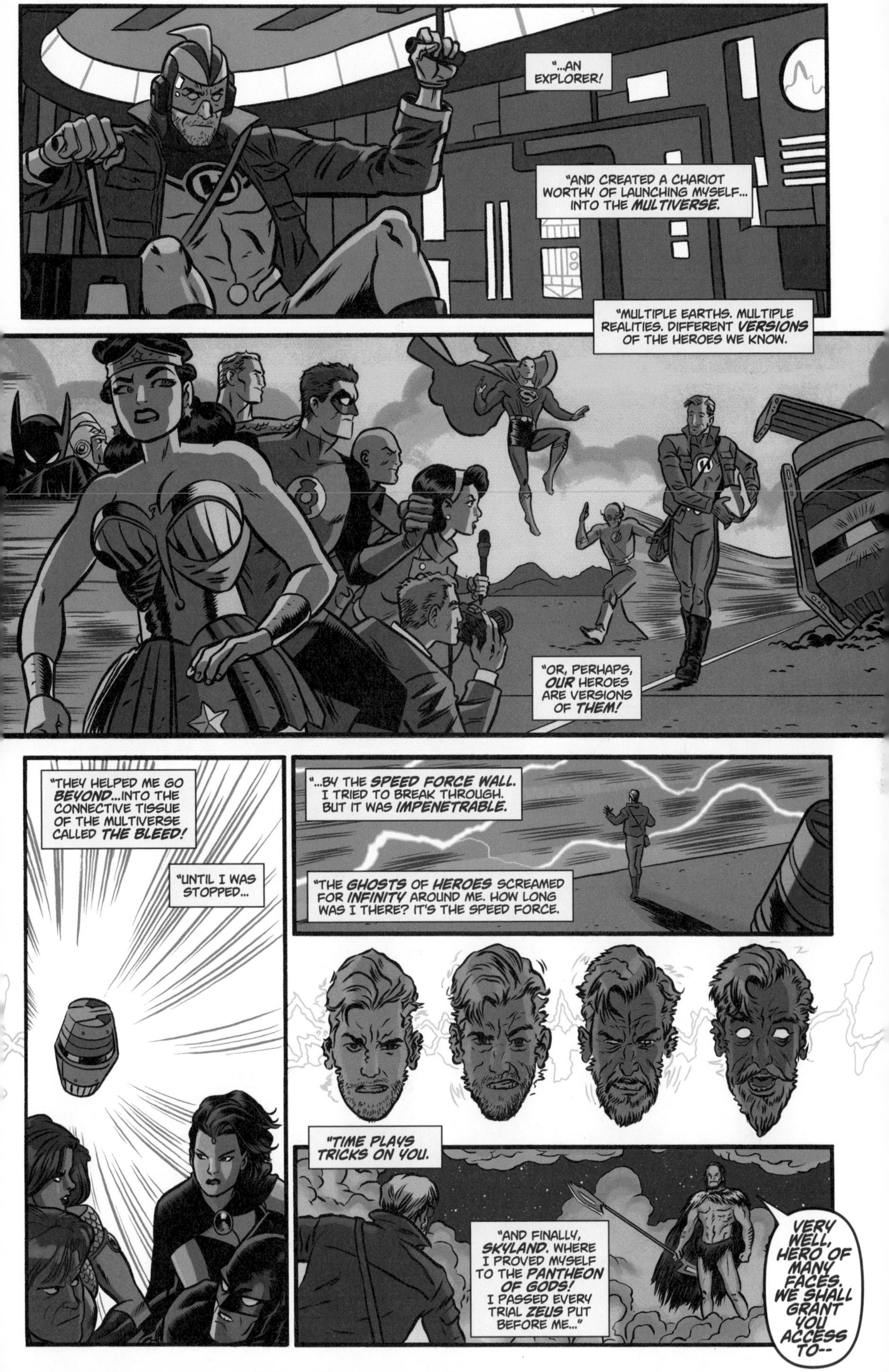
"...AN EXPLORER!
"AND CREATED A CHARIOT WORTHY OF LAUNCHING MYSELF... INTO THE MULTIVERSE.
"MULTIPLE EARTHS. MULTIPLE REALITIES. DIFFERENT VERSIONS OF THE HEROES WE KNOW.
"OR, PERHAPS, OUR HEROES ARE VERSIONS OF THEM!
"THEY HELPED ME GO BEYOND...INTO THE CONNECTIVE TISSUE OF THE MULTIVERSE CALLED THE BLEED!
"UNTIL I WAS STOPPED...
"...BY THE SPEED FORCE WALL. I TRIED TO BREAK THROUGH. BUT IT WAS IMPENETRABLE.
"THE GHOSTS OF HEROES SCREAMED FOR INFINITY AROUND ME. HOW LONG WAS I THERE? IT'S THE SPEED FORCE.
"TIME PLAYS TRICKS ON YOU.
"AND FINALLY, SKYLAND. WHERE I PROVED MYSELF TO THE PANTHEON OF GODS! I PASSED EVERY TRIAL ZEUS PUT BEFORE ME..."
VERY WELL, HERO OF MANY FACES. WE SHALL GRANT YOU ACCESS TO--

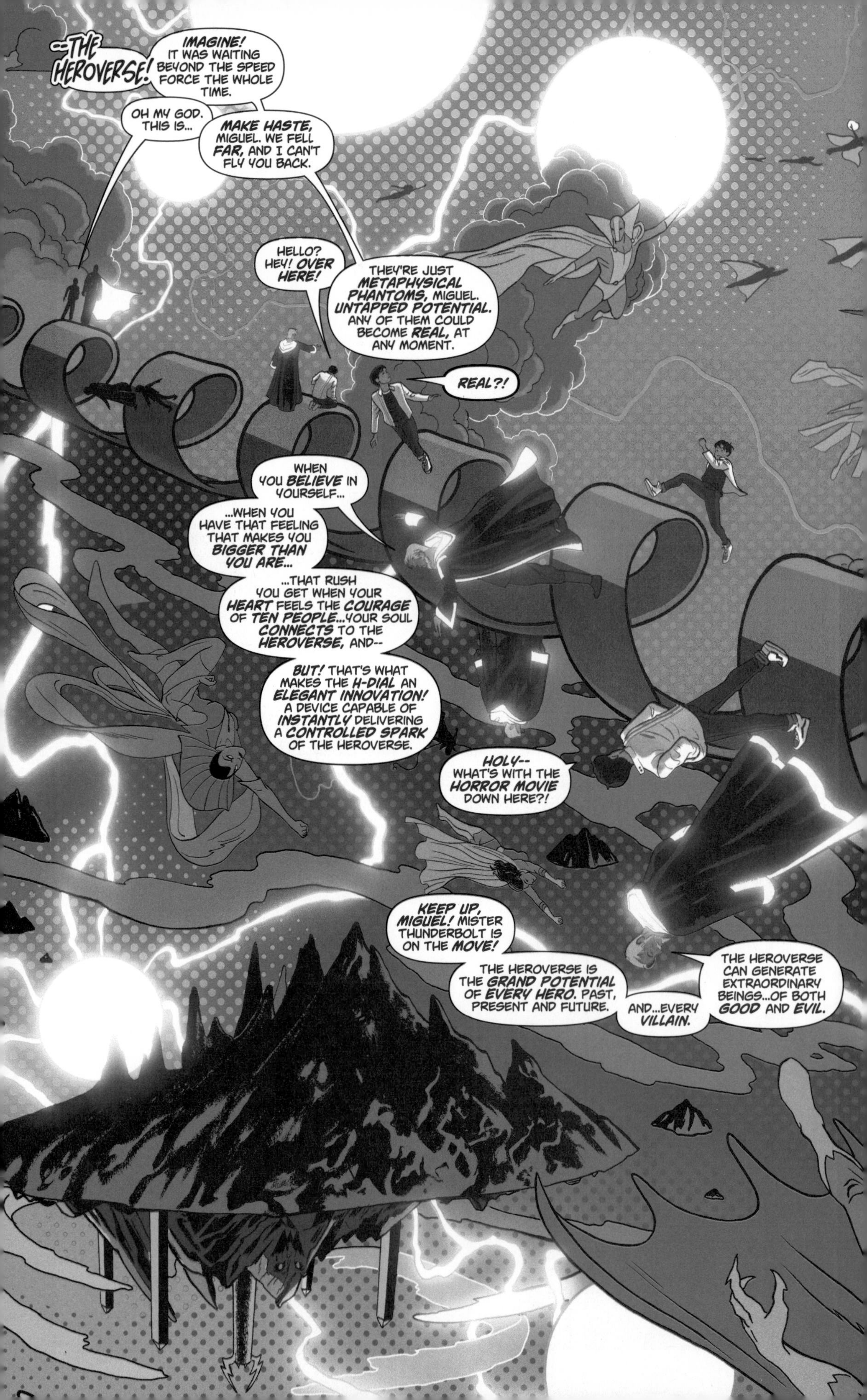
--THE HEROVERSE!
IMAGINE! IT WAS WAITING BEYOND THE SPEED FORCE THE WHOLE TIME.
OH MY GOD. THIS IS...
MAKE HASTE, MIGUEL. WE FELL FAR, AND I CAN'T FLY YOU BACK.
HELLO? HEY! OVER HERE!
THEY'RE JUST METAPHYSICAL PHANTOMS, MIGUEL. UNTAPPED POTENTIAL. ANY OF THEM COULD BECOME REAL, AT ANY MOMENT.
REAL?!
WHEN YOU BELIEVE IN YOURSELF...
...WHEN YOU HAVE THAT FEELING THAT MAKES YOU BIGGER THAN YOU ARE...
...THAT RUSH YOU GET WHEN YOUR HEART FEELS THE COURAGE OF TEN PEOPLE...YOUR SOUL CONNECTS TO THE HEROVERSE, AND--
BUT! THAT'S WHAT MAKES THE H-DIAL AN ELEGANT INNOVATION! A DEVICE CAPABLE OF INSTANTLY DELIVERING A CONTROLLED SPARK OF THE HEROVERSE.
HOLY-- WHAT'S WITH THE HORROR MOVIE DOWN HERE?!
KEEP UP, MIGUEL! MISTER THUNDERBOLT IS ON THE MOVE!
THE HEROVERSE IS THE GRAND POTENTIAL OF EVERY HERO. PAST, PRESENT AND FUTURE.
AND...EVERY VILLAIN.
THE HEROVERSE CAN GENERATE EXTRAORDINARY BEINGS...OF BOTH GOOD AND EVIL.

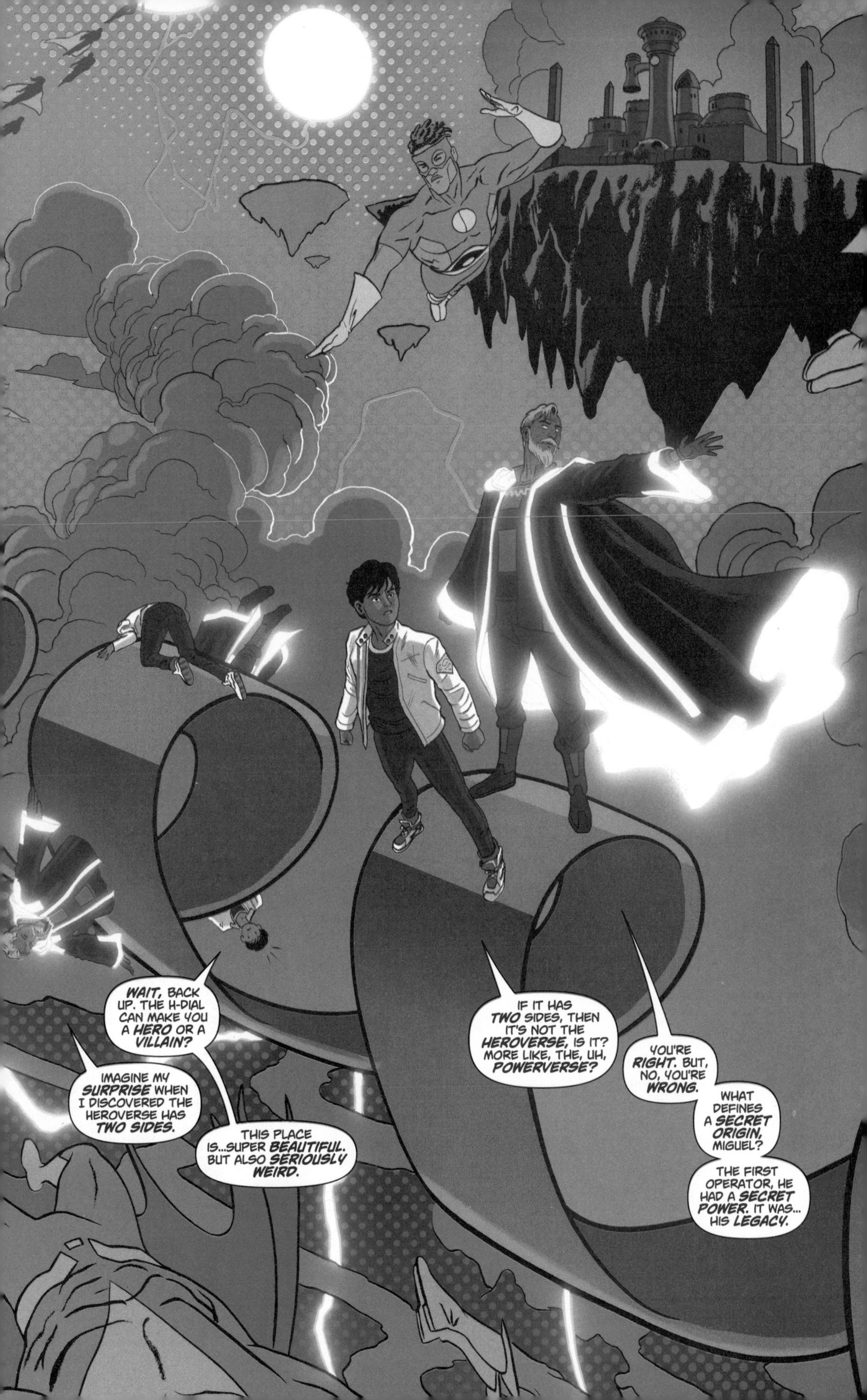
IMAGINE MY SURPRISE WHEN I DISCOVERED THE HEROVERSE HAS TWO SIDES.
WAIT, BACK UP. THE H-DIAL CAN MAKE YOU A HERO OR A VILLAIN?
THIS PLACE IS...SUPER BEAUTIFUL. BUT ALSO SERIOUSLY WEIRD.
IF IT HAS TWO SIDES, THEN IT'S NOT THE HEROVERSE, IS IT? MORE LIKE, THE, UH, POWERVERSE?
YOU'RE RIGHT. BUT, NO, YOU'RE WRONG.
WHAT DEFINES A SECRET ORIGIN, MIGUEL?
THE FIRST OPERATOR, HE HAD A SECRET POWER. IT WAS... HIS LEGACY.

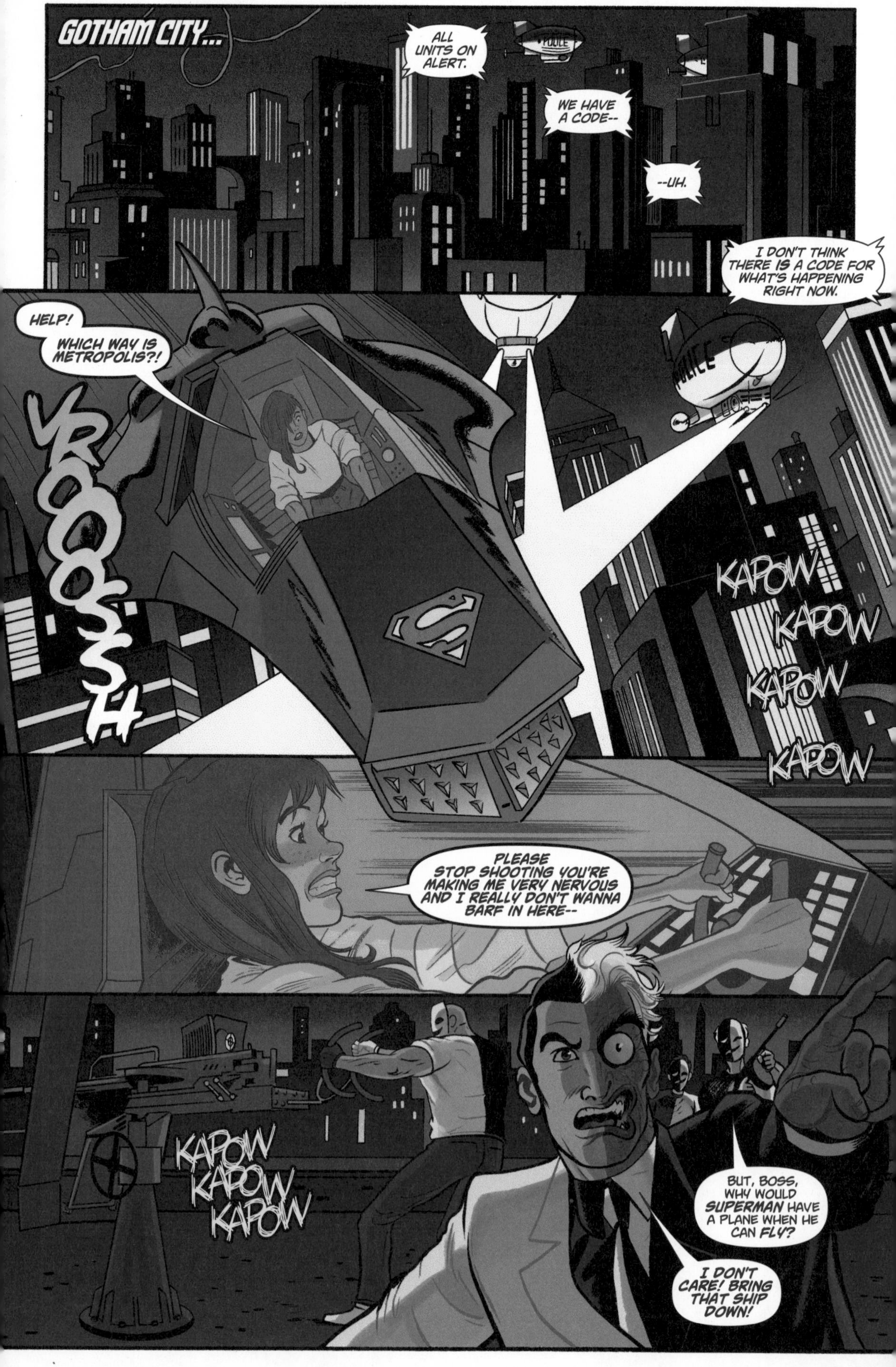
GOTHAM CITY...
ALL UNITS ON ALERT.
WE HAVE A CODE--
--UH.
I DON'T THINK THERE IS A CODE FOR WHAT'S HAPPENING RIGHT NOW.
HELP! WHICH WAY IS METROPOLIS?!
VROOOSH
KAPOW KAPOW KAPOW KAPOW
PLEASE STOP SHOOTING YOU'RE MAKING ME VERY NERVOUS AND I REALLY DON'T WANNA BARF IN HERE--
KAPOW KAPOW KAPOW
BUT, BOSS, WHY WOULD SUPERMAN HAVE A PLANE WHEN HE CAN FLY?
I DON'T CARE! BRING THAT SHIP DOWN!

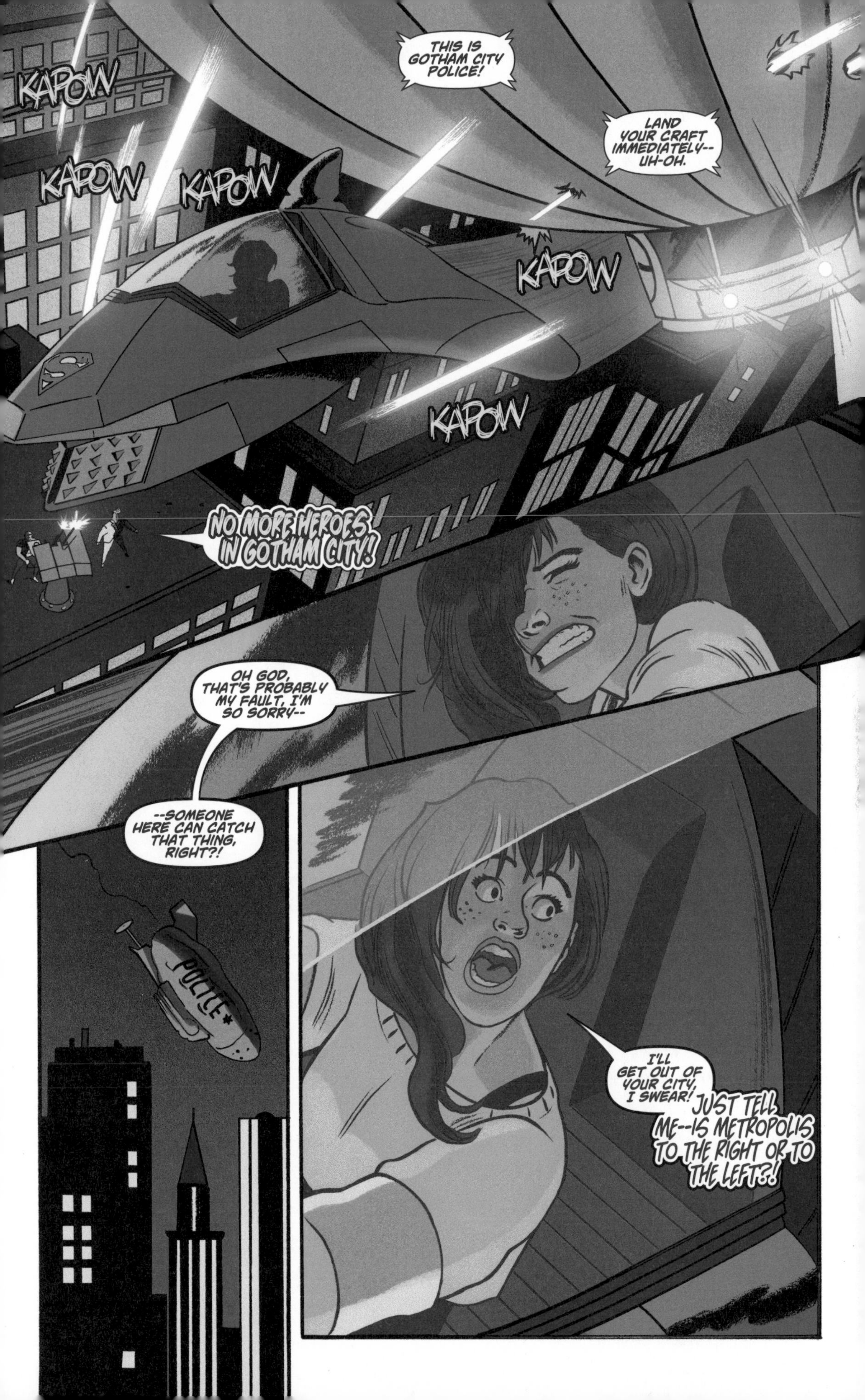
KAPOW
THIS IS GOTHAM CITY POLICE!
LAND YOUR CRAFT IMMEDIATELY-- UH-OH.
KAPOW
KAPOW
KAPOW
KAPOW
NO MORE HEROES IN GOTHAM CITY!
OH GOD, THAT'S PROBABLY MY FAULT, I'M SO SORRY--
--SOMEONE HERE CAN CATCH THAT THING, RIGHT?!
POLICE
I'LL GET OUT OF YOUR CITY, I SWEAR!
JUST TELL ME--IS METROPOLIS TO THE RIGHT OR TO THE LEFT?!

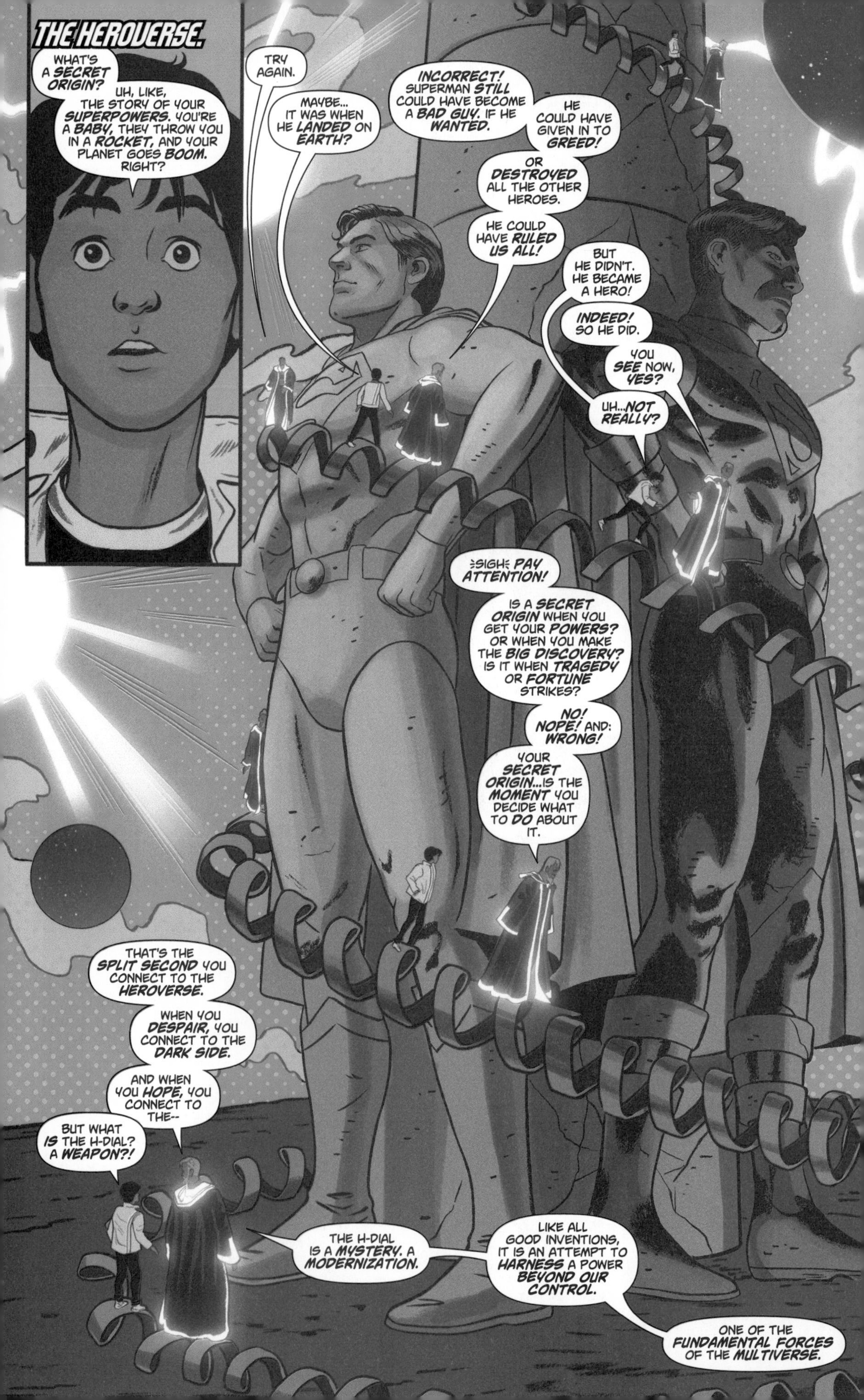
THE HEROVERSE.
WHAT'S A SECRET ORIGIN?
UH, LIKE, THE STORY OF YOUR SUPERPOWERS. YOU'RE A BABY, THEY THROW YOU IN A ROCKET, AND YOUR PLANET GOES BOOM. RIGHT?
TRY AGAIN.
MAYBE... IT WAS WHEN HE LANDED ON EARTH?
INCORRECT! SUPERMAN STILL COULD HAVE BECOME A BAD GUY. IF HE WANTED.
HE COULD HAVE GIVEN IN TO GREED!
OR DESTROYED ALL THE OTHER HEROES.
HE COULD HAVE RULED US ALL!
BUT HE DIDN'T. HE BECAME A HERO!
INDEED! SO HE DID.
YOU SEE NOW, YES?
UH...NOT REALLY?
SIGH PAY ATTENTION!
IS A SECRET ORIGIN WHEN YOU GET YOUR POWERS? OR WHEN YOU MAKE THE BIG DISCOVERY? IS IT WHEN TRAGEDY OR FORTUNE STRIKES?
NO! NOPE! AND: WRONG!
YOUR SECRET ORIGIN...IS THE MOMENT YOU DECIDE WHAT TO DO ABOUT IT.
THAT'S THE SPLIT SECOND YOU CONNECT TO THE HEROVERSE.
WHEN YOU DESPAIR, YOU CONNECT TO THE DARK SIDE.
AND WHEN YOU HOPE, YOU CONNECT TO THE--
BUT WHAT IS THE H-DIAL? A WEAPON?!
THE H-DIAL IS A MYSTERY. A MODERNIZATION.
LIKE ALL GOOD INVENTIONS, IT IS AN ATTEMPT TO HARNESS A POWER BEYOND OUR CONTROL.
ONE OF THE FUNDAMENTAL FORCES OF THE MULTIVERSE.

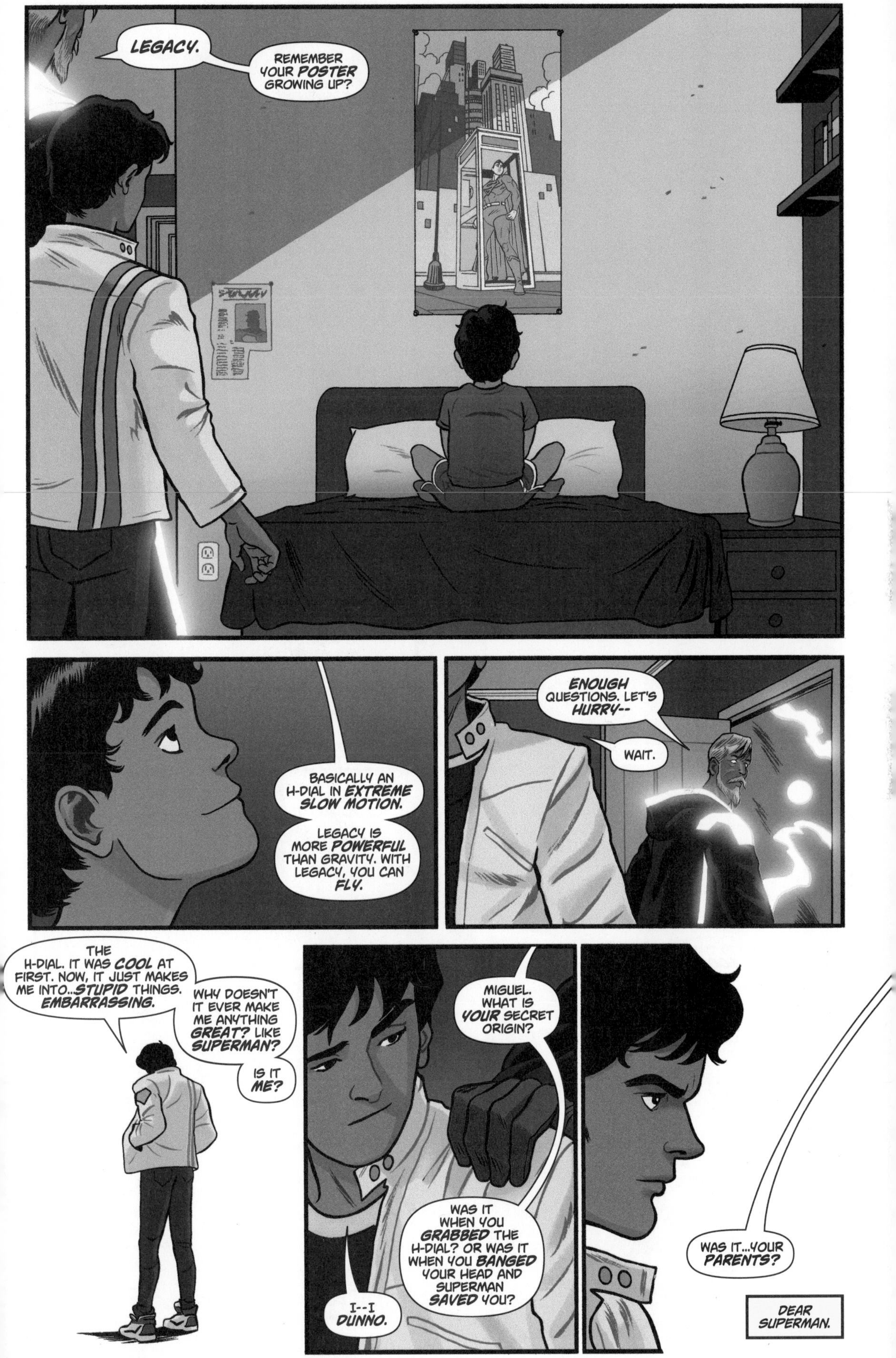
LEGACY.
REMEMBER YOUR POSTER GROWING UP?
BASICALLY AN H-DIAL IN EXTREME SLOW MOTION.
LEGACY IS MORE POWERFUL THAN GRAVITY. WITH LEGACY, YOU CAN FLY.
ENOUGH QUESTIONS. LET'S HURRY--
WAIT.
THE H-DIAL. IT WAS COOL AT FIRST. NOW, IT JUST MAKES ME INTO...STUPID THINGS. EMBARRASSING.
WHY DOESN'T IT EVER MAKE ME ANYTHING GREAT? LIKE SUPERMAN?
IS IT ME?
MIGUEL. WHAT IS YOUR SECRET ORIGIN?
WAS IT WHEN YOU GRABBED THE H-DIAL? OR WAS IT WHEN YOU BANGED YOUR HEAD AND SUPERMAN SAVED YOU?
I--I DUNNO.
WAS IT...YOUR PARENTS?
DEAR SUPERMAN.

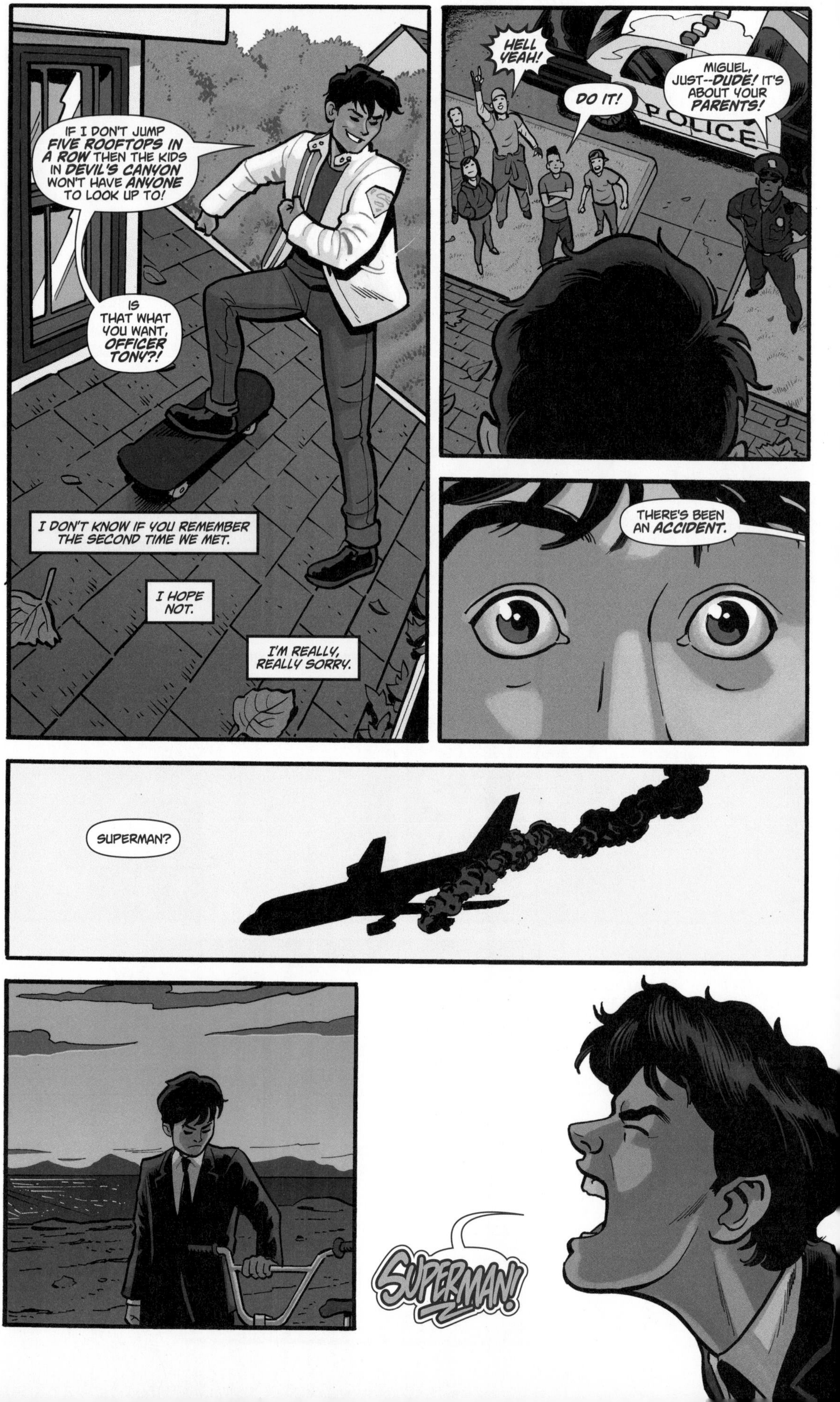
IF I DON'T JUMP FIVE ROOFTOPS IN A ROW THEN THE KIDS IN DEVIL'S CANYON WON'T HAVE ANYONE TO LOOK UP TO!
IS THAT WHAT YOU WANT, OFFICER TONY?!
I DON'T KNOW IF YOU REMEMBER THE SECOND TIME WE MET.
I HOPE NOT.
I'M REALLY, REALLY SORRY.
HELL YEAH!
DO IT!
MIGUEL, JUST--DUDE! IT'S ABOUT YOUR PARENTS!
POLICE
THERE'S BEEN AN ACCIDENT.
SUPERMAN?
SUPERMAN!

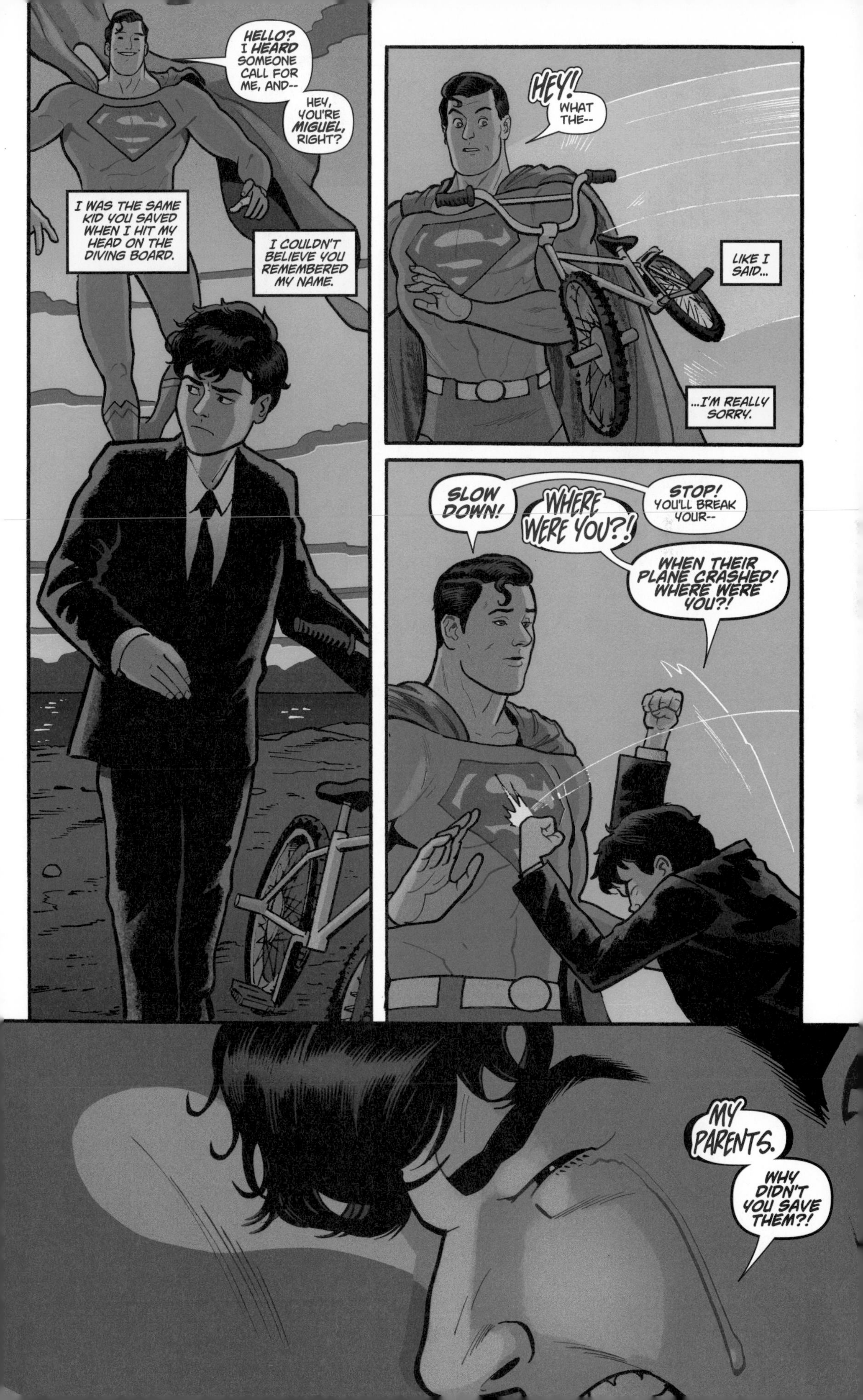
HELLO? I HEARD SOMEONE CALL FOR ME, AND--
HEY, YOU'RE MIGUEL, RIGHT?
I WAS THE SAME KID YOU SAVED WHEN I HIT MY HEAD ON THE DIVING BOARD.
I COULDN'T BELIEVE YOU REMEMBERED MY NAME.
HEY! WHAT THE--
LIKE I SAID...
...I'M REALLY SORRY.
SLOW DOWN!
STOP! YOU'LL BREAK YOUR--
WHERE WERE YOU?!
WHEN THEIR PLANE CRASHED! WHERE WERE YOU?!
MY PARENTS.
WHY DIDN'T YOU SAVE THEM?!

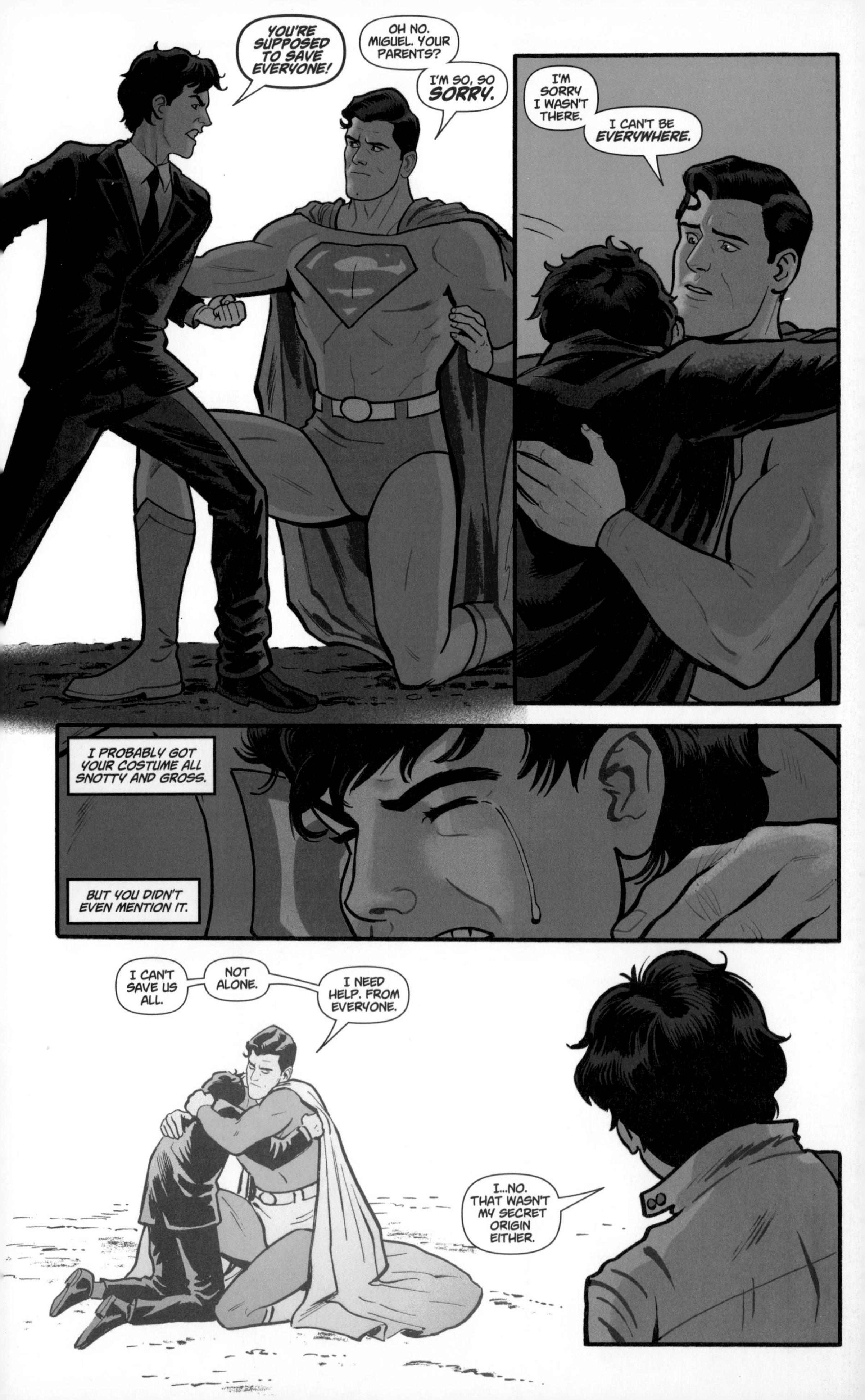
YOU'RE SUPPOSED TO SAVE EVERYONE!
OH NO. MIGUEL. YOUR PARENTS?
I'M SO, SO SORRY.
I'M SORRY I WASN'T THERE.
I CAN'T BE EVERYWHERE.
I PROBABLY GOT YOUR COSTUME ALL SNOTTY AND GROSS.
BUT YOU DIDN'T EVEN MENTION IT.
I CAN'T SAVE US ALL.
NOT ALONE.
I NEED HELP. FROM EVERYONE.
I...NO. THAT WASN'T MY SECRET ORIGIN EITHER.

WAIT! WHAT IF... I HAVEN'T HAD MY SECRET ORIGIN YET?!

KATHOOOOOOMM!

WAKE UP, MULTIVERSE!

FEEL THE FULL POTENTIAL OF THE HEROVERSE!

AND WE'LL START IN THE PLACE IT ALL BEGAN.

TIME TO DIAL--

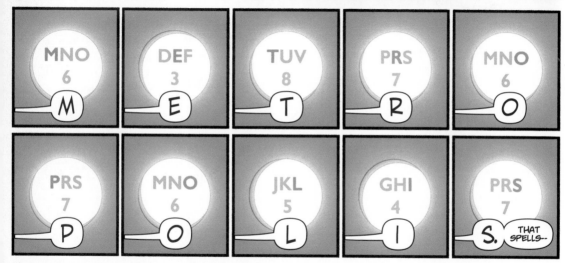

MNO 6 — M

DEF 3 — E

TUV 8 — T

PRS 7 — R

MNO 6 — O

PRS 7 — P

MNO 6 — O

JKL 5 — L

GHI 4 — I

PRS 7 — S.

THAT SPELLS--

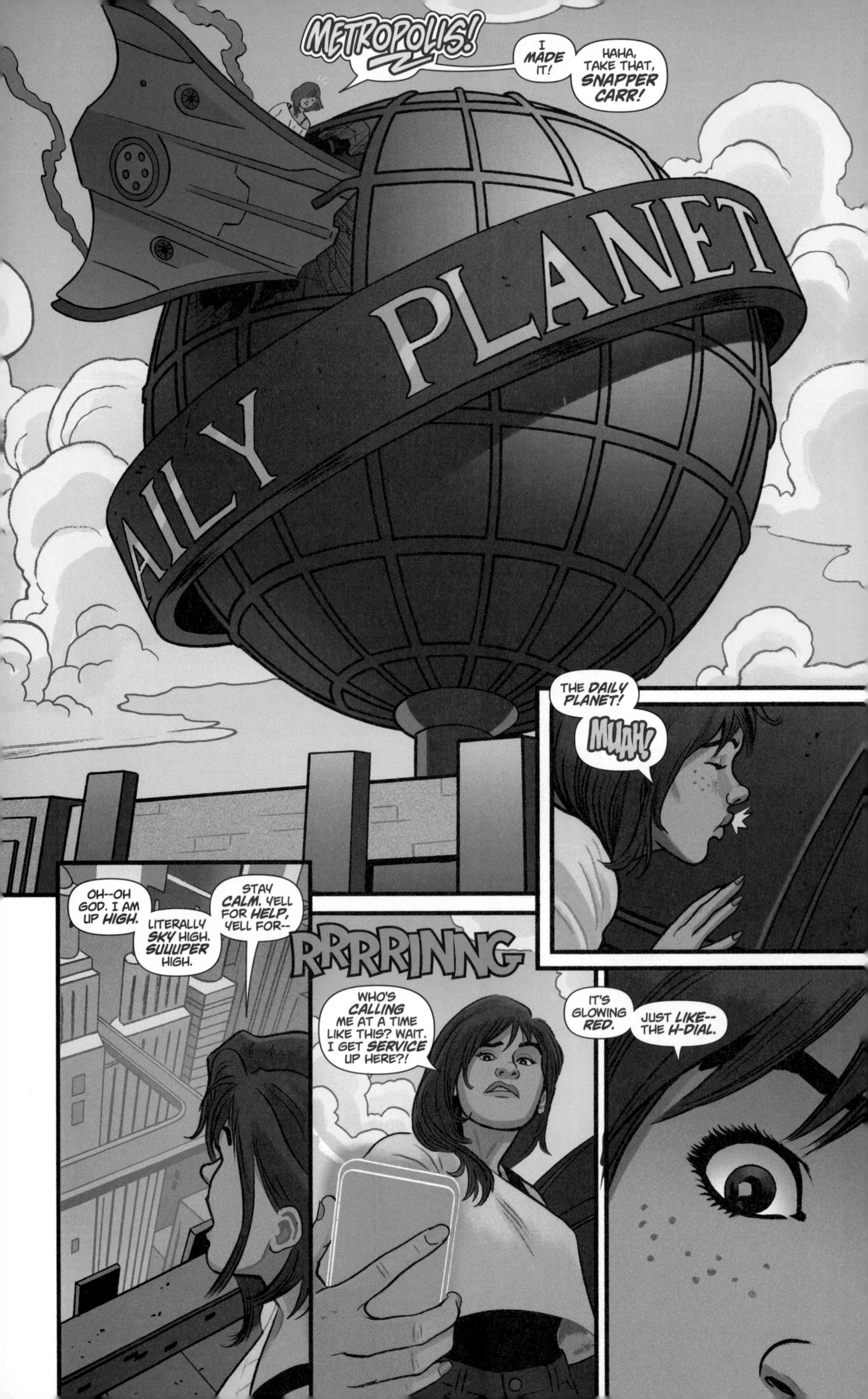
METROPOLIS!
I MADE IT!
HAHA, TAKE THAT, SNAPPER CARR!
DAILY PLANET
THE DAILY PLANET!
MUAH!
OH--OH GOD. I AM UP HIGH.
LITERALLY SKY HIGH. SUUUPER HIGH.
STAY CALM. YELL FOR HELP, YELL FOR--
RRRRINNG
WHO'S CALLING ME AT A TIME LIKE THIS? WAIT. I GET SERVICE UP HERE?!
IT'S GLOWING RED.
JUST LIKE-- THE H-DIAL.

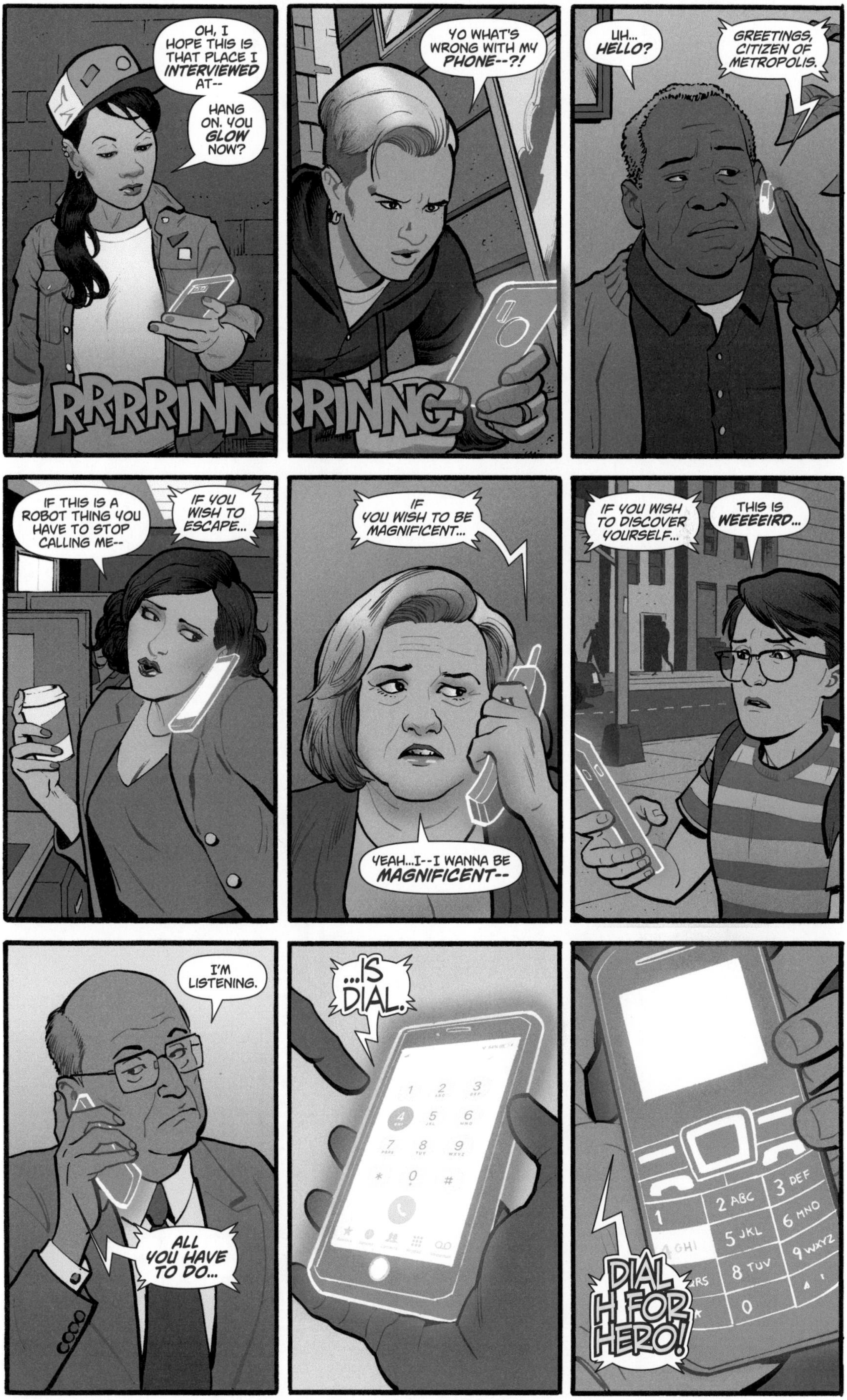
OH, I HOPE THIS IS THAT PLACE I INTERVIEWED AT--
HANG ON. YOU GLOW NOW?
RRRRINNG RRINNG
YO WHAT'S WRONG WITH MY PHONE--?!
UH... HELLO?
GREETINGS, CITIZEN OF METROPOLIS.
IF THIS IS A ROBOT THING YOU HAVE TO STOP CALLING ME--
IF YOU WISH TO ESCAPE...
IF YOU WISH TO BE MAGNIFICENT...
YEAH...I--I WANNA BE MAGNIFICENT--
IF YOU WISH TO DISCOVER YOURSELF...
THIS IS WEEEEIRD...
I'M LISTENING.
ALL YOU HAVE TO DO...
...IS DIAL.
DIAL H FOR HERO!

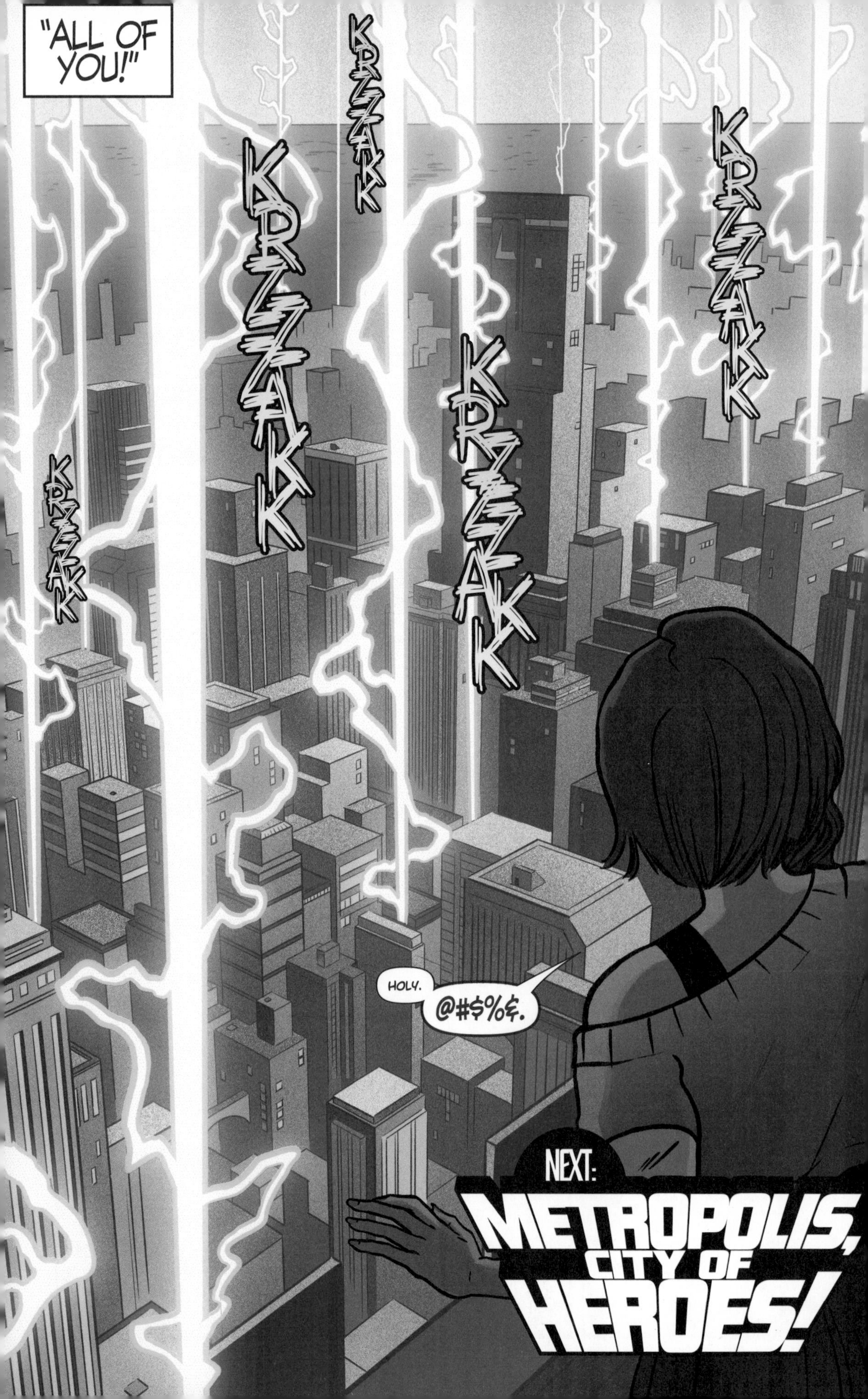
"ALL OF YOU!"
KRZZAKK
KRZZAKK
KRZZAKK
KRZZAK
KRZZAKK
HOLY.
@#$%&.
NEXT:
METROPOLIS, CITY OF HEROES!

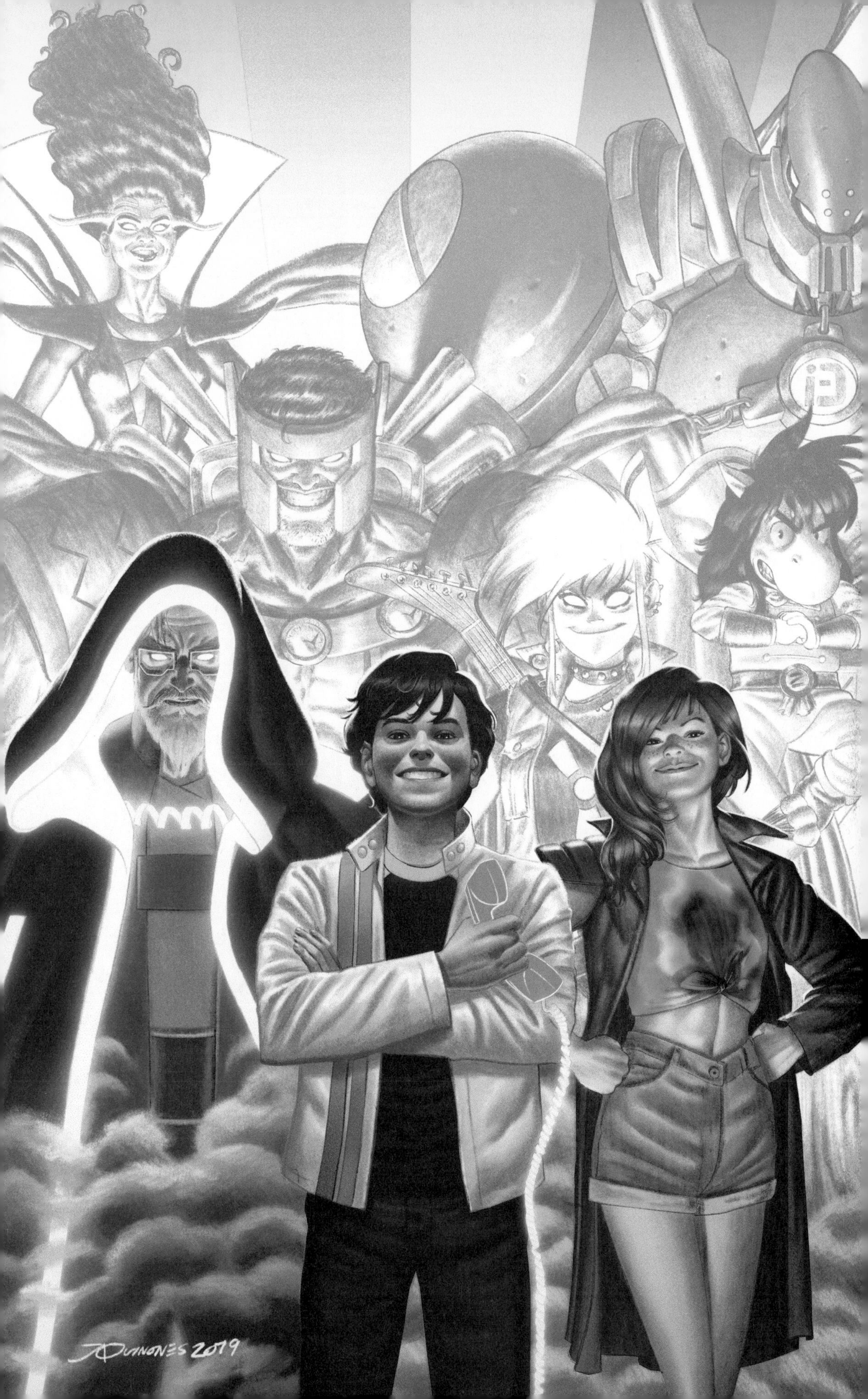
JQUINONES 2019

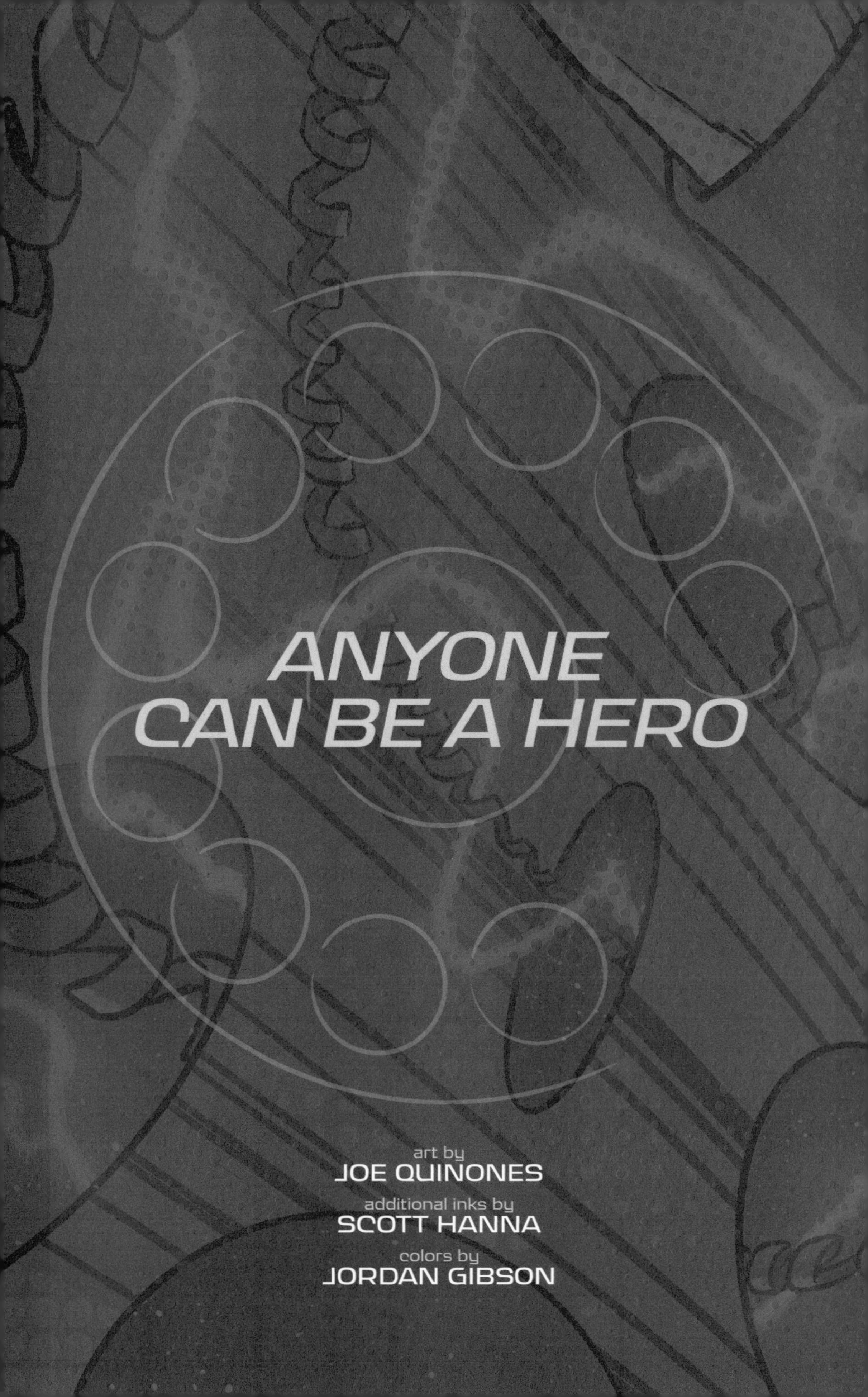

ANYONE CAN BE A HERO

art by
JOE QUINONES

additional inks by
SCOTT HANNA

colors by
JORDAN GIBSON

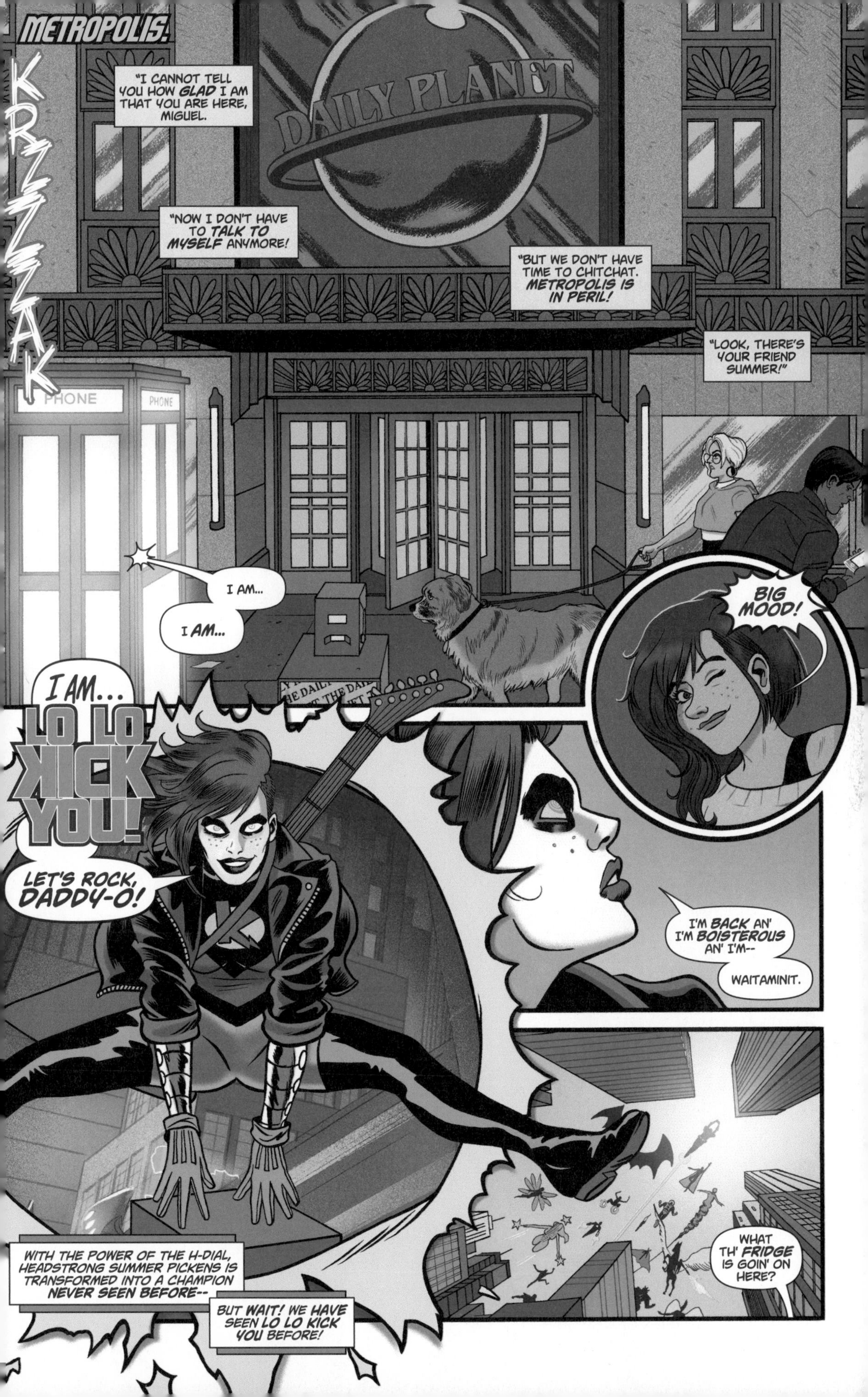
METROPOLIS:
KRZZZAK
DAILY PLANET
"I CANNOT TELL YOU HOW GLAD I AM THAT YOU ARE HERE, MIGUEL.
"NOW I DON'T HAVE TO TALK TO MYSELF ANYMORE!
"BUT WE DON'T HAVE TIME TO CHITCHAT. METROPOLIS IS IN PERIL!
"LOOK, THERE'S YOUR FRIEND SUMMER!"
PHONE
PHONE
I AM...
I AM...
BIG MOOD!
I AM... LO LO KICK YOU!
LET'S ROCK, DADDY-O!
I'M BACK AN' I'M BOISTEROUS AN' I'M--
WAITAMINIT.
WITH THE POWER OF THE H-DIAL, HEADSTRONG SUMMER PICKENS IS TRANSFORMED INTO A CHAMPION NEVER SEEN BEFORE--
BUT WAIT! WE HAVE SEEN LO LO KICK YOU BEFORE!
WHAT TH' FRIDGE IS GOIN' ON HERE?

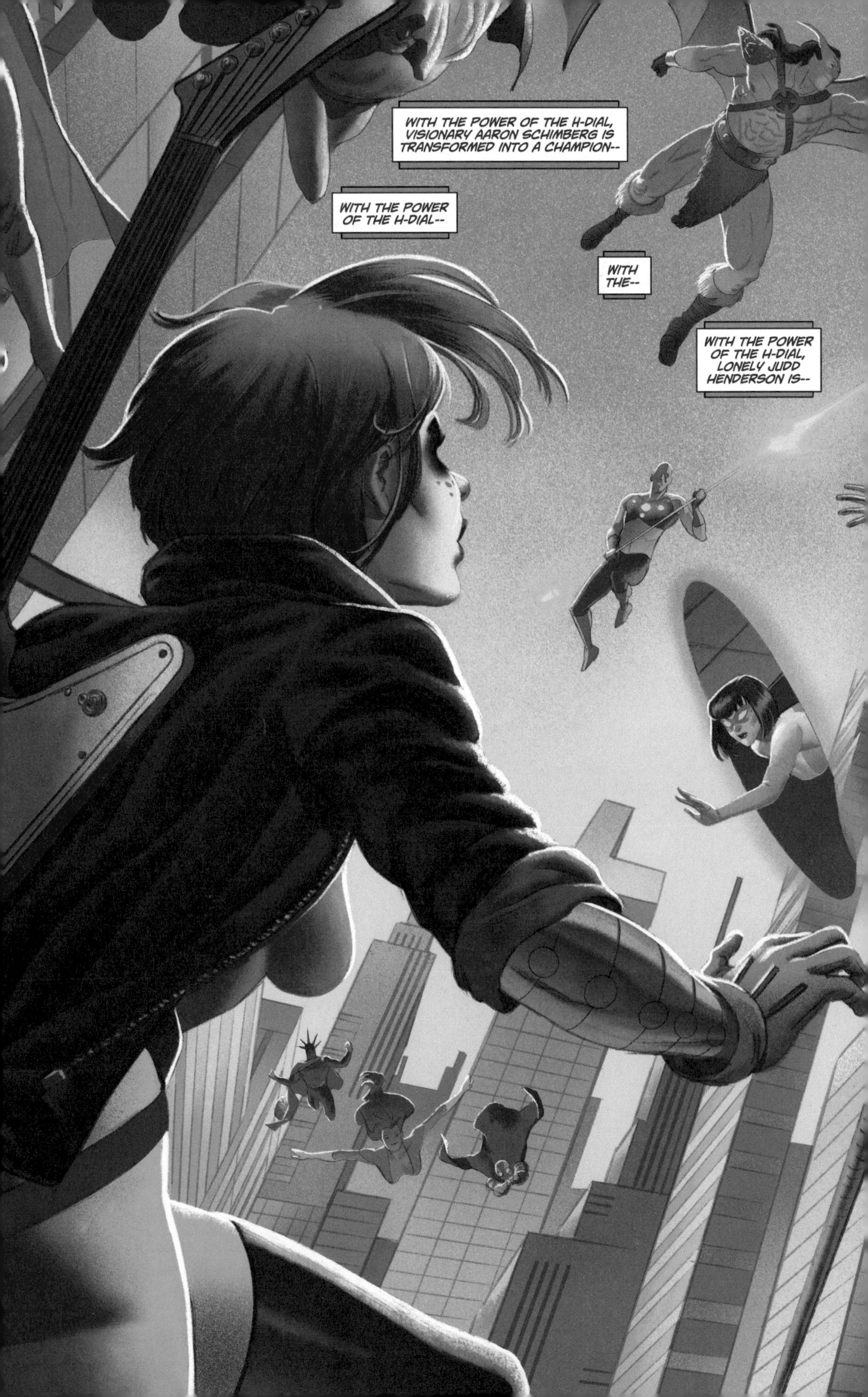
WITH THE POWER OF THE H-DIAL, VISIONARY AARON SCHIMBERG IS TRANSFORMED INTO A CHAMPION--
WITH THE POWER OF THE H-DIAL--
WITH THE--
WITH THE POWER OF THE H-DIAL, LONELY JUDD HENDERSON IS--

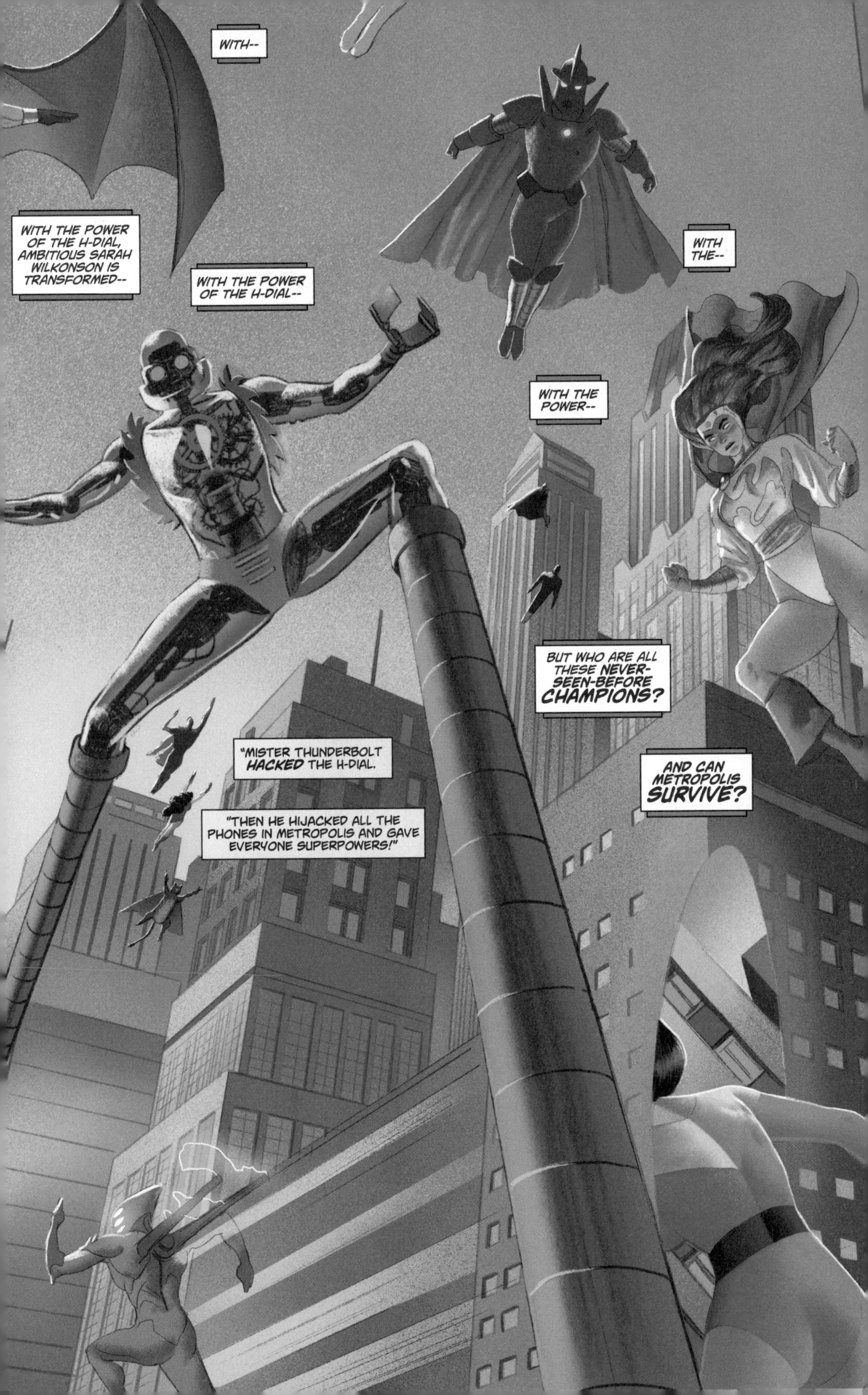
WITH--
WITH THE POWER OF THE H-DIAL, AMBITIOUS SARAH WILKONSON IS TRANSFORMED--
WITH THE POWER OF THE H-DIAL--
WITH THE--
WITH THE POWER--
BUT WHO ARE ALL THESE NEVER-SEEN-BEFORE CHAMPIONS?
AND CAN METROPOLIS SURVIVE?
"MISTER THUNDERBOLT HACKED THE H-DIAL.
"THEN HE HIJACKED ALL THE PHONES IN METROPOLIS AND GAVE EVERYONE SUPERPOWERS!"

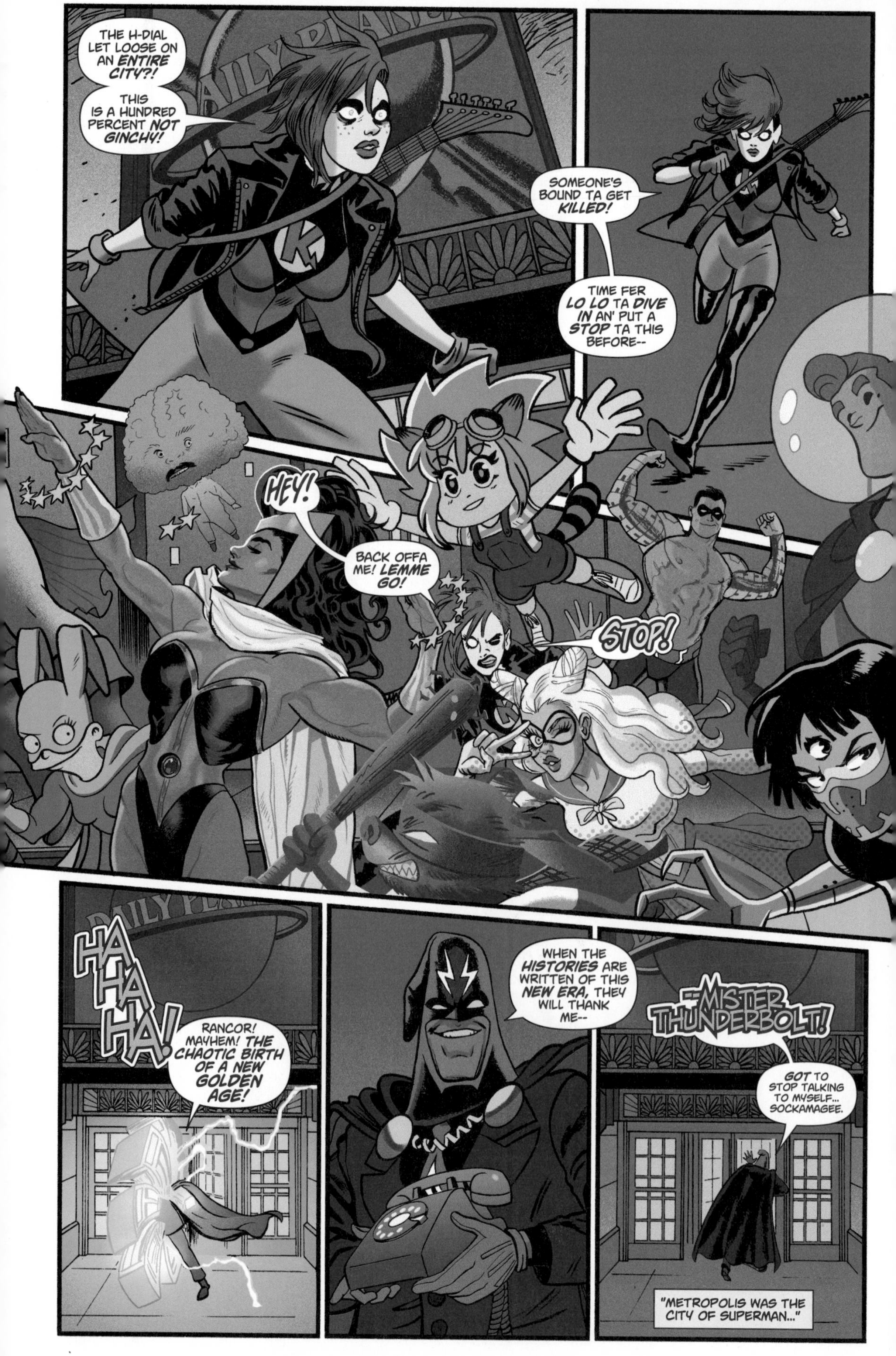
THE H-DIAL LET LOOSE ON AN ENTIRE CITY?!
THIS IS A HUNDRED PERCENT NOT GINCHY!
SOMEONE'S BOUND TA GET KILLED!
TIME FER LO LO TA DIVE IN AN' PUT A STOP TA THIS BEFORE--
HEY!
BACK OFFA ME! LEMME GO!
STOP!
HA HA HA!
RANCOR! MAYHEM! THE CHAOTIC BIRTH OF A NEW GOLDEN AGE!
WHEN THE HISTORIES ARE WRITTEN OF THIS NEW ERA, THEY WILL THANK ME--
--MISTER THUNDERBOLT!
GOT TO STOP TALKING TO MYSELF... SOCKAMAGEE.
"METROPOLIS WAS THE CITY OF SUPERMAN..."

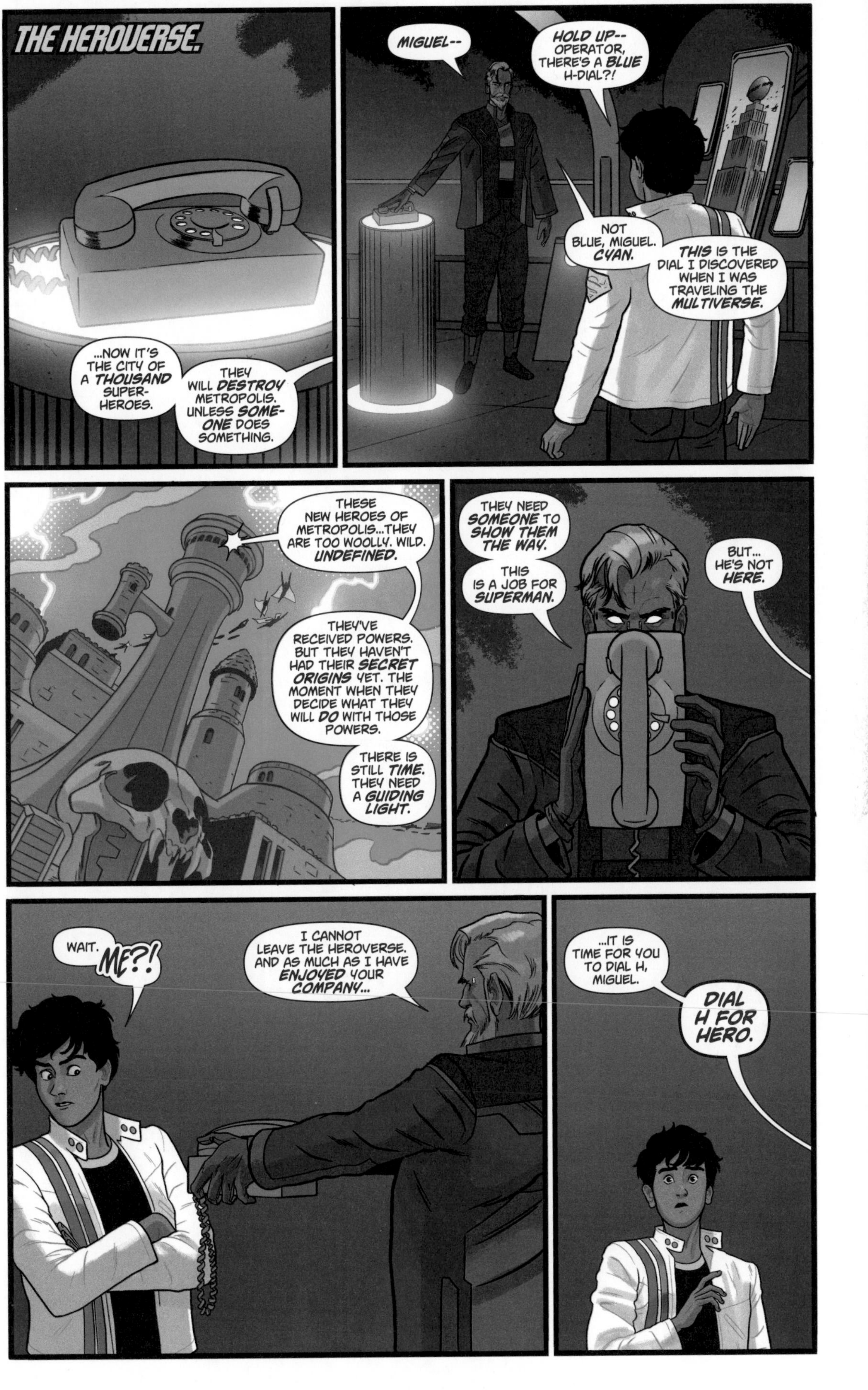
THE HEROVERSE.
...NOW IT'S THE CITY OF A THOUSAND SUPER-HEROES.
THEY WILL DESTROY METROPOLIS. UNLESS SOME-ONE DOES SOMETHING.
MIGUEL--
HOLD UP-- OPERATOR, THERE'S A BLUE H-DIAL?!
NOT BLUE, MIGUEL. CYAN.
THIS IS THE DIAL I DISCOVERED WHEN I WAS TRAVELING THE MULTIVERSE.
THESE NEW HEROES OF METROPOLIS...THEY ARE TOO WOOLLY. WILD. UNDEFINED.
THEY'VE RECEIVED POWERS. BUT THEY HAVEN'T HAD THEIR SECRET ORIGINS YET. THE MOMENT WHEN THEY DECIDE WHAT THEY WILL DO WITH THOSE POWERS.
THERE IS STILL TIME. THEY NEED A GUIDING LIGHT.
THEY NEED SOMEONE TO SHOW THEM THE WAY.
THIS IS A JOB FOR SUPERMAN.
BUT... HE'S NOT HERE.
WAIT. ME?!
I CANNOT LEAVE THE HEROVERSE. AND AS MUCH AS I HAVE ENJOYED YOUR COMPANY...
...IT IS TIME FOR YOU TO DIAL H, MIGUEL.
DIAL H FOR HERO.

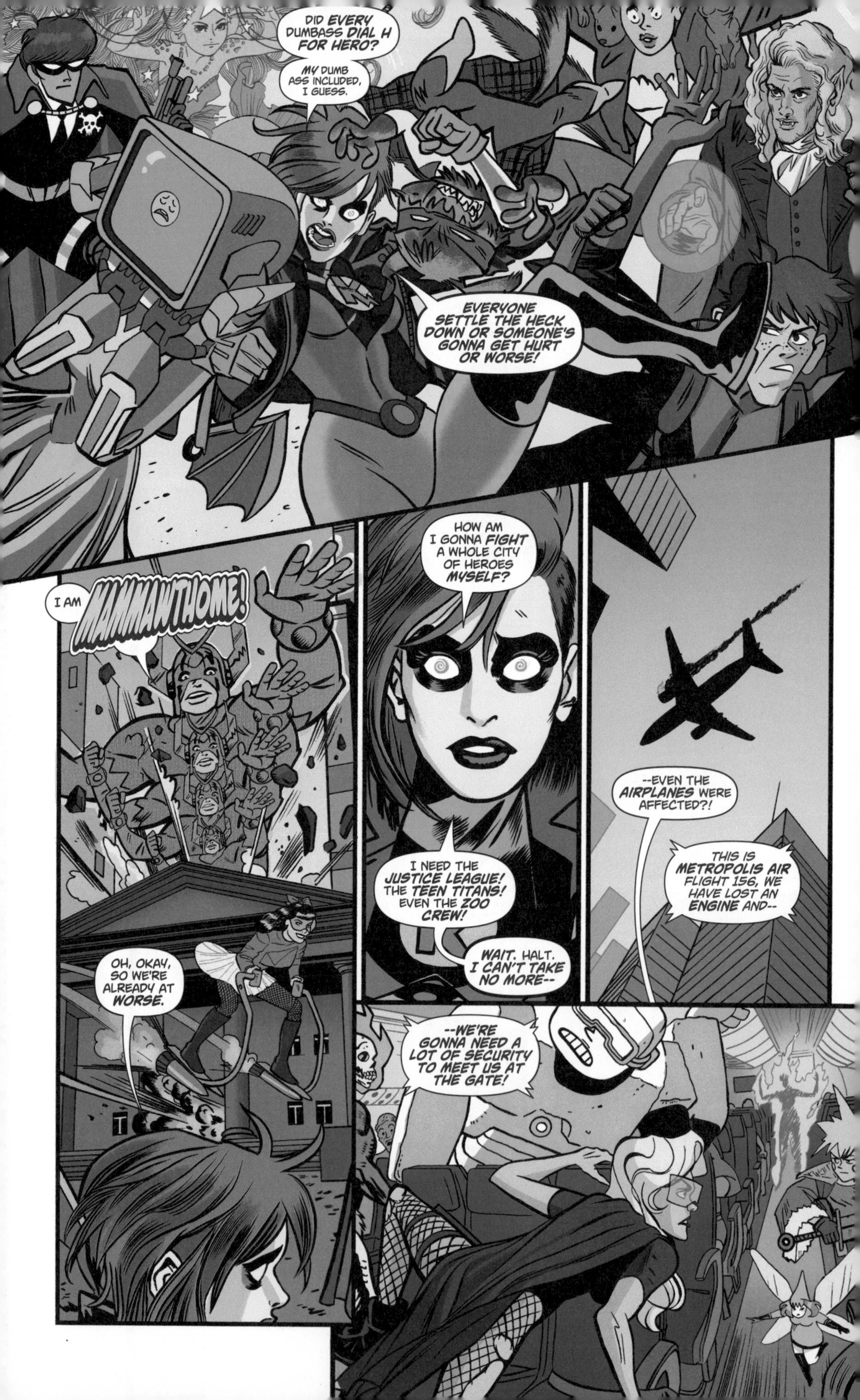
DID EVERY DUMBASS DIAL H FOR HERO?
MY DUMB ASS INCLUDED, I GUESS.
EVERYONE SETTLE THE HECK DOWN OR SOMEONE'S GONNA GET HURT OR WORSE!
I AM MAMMAWTHOME!
OH, OKAY, SO WE'RE ALREADY AT WORSE.
HOW AM I GONNA FIGHT A WHOLE CITY OF HEROES MYSELF?
I NEED THE JUSTICE LEAGUE! THE TEEN TITANS! EVEN THE ZOO CREW!
WAIT. HALT. I CAN'T TAKE NO MORE--
--EVEN THE AIRPLANES WERE AFFECTED?!
THIS IS METROPOLIS AIR FLIGHT 156, WE HAVE LOST AN ENGINE AND--
--WE'RE GONNA NEED A LOT OF SECURITY TO MEET US AT THE GATE!

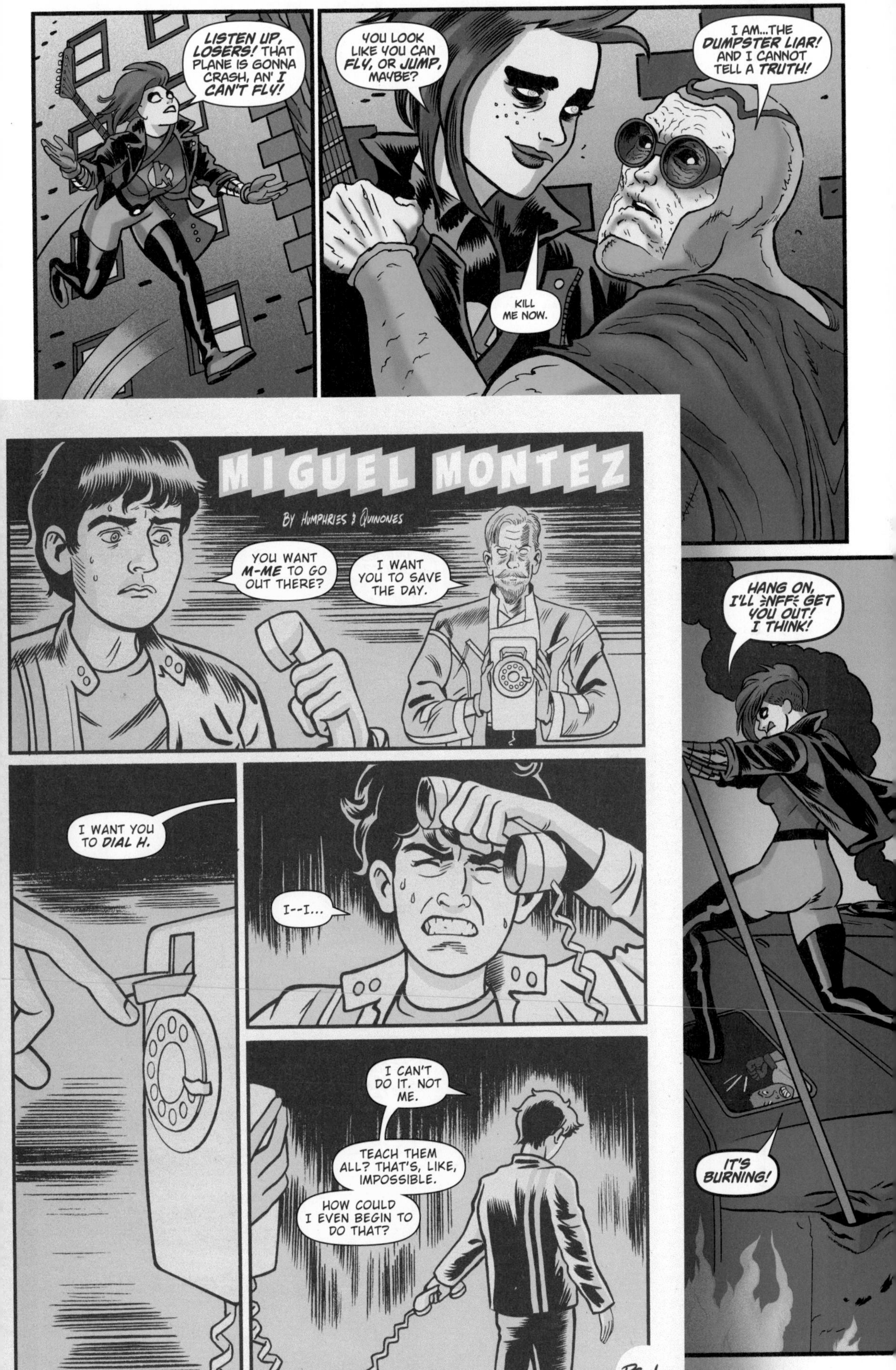
LISTEN UP, LOSERS! THAT PLANE IS GONNA CRASH, AN' I CAN'T FLY!
YOU LOOK LIKE YOU CAN FLY, OR JUMP, MAYBE?
I AM...THE DUMPSTER LIAR! AND I CANNOT TELL A TRUTH!
KILL ME NOW.
HANG ON, I'LL NFF GET YOU OUT! I THINK!
IT'S BURNING!
MIGUEL MONTEZ
BY HUMPHRIES & QUINONES
YOU WANT M-ME TO GO OUT THERE?
I WANT YOU TO SAVE THE DAY.
I WANT YOU TO DIAL H.
I--I...
I CAN'T DO IT. NOT ME.
TEACH THEM ALL? THAT'S, LIKE, IMPOSSIBLE.
HOW COULD I EVEN BEGIN TO DO THAT?
PG. 1

WAIT! STOP! WHO ARE YOU?! I MUST KNOW!

I'M THE FUZZY LOLLIPOP!

I'M BUSINESS AFFAIRS MAFIOSO! DO YOU WANNA--

HEY!

I NEED A BOZO WHO CAN FLY!

AND YOUR FLIRTING IS BAD!

HEY! MY FLIRT GAME IS SOUND!

DIDJA GO TO CLOWN COLLEGE FOR YOUR

NO ONE INSULTS MY HAIR!

HA-HA!

MIGUEL, LEFT TO THEIR OWN WHIMS, THEY WILL TEAR THE CITY APART.

THEN FIND SOMEONE ELSE! YOU'VE SEEN WHAT I TURNED INTO LAST TIME! I'M DUMB AND STUPID AND I'M...

I'M NOT LIKE SUPERMAN! THE H-DIAL KNOWS IT AND YOU KNOW IT!

I...CAUSED ALL OF THIS. MISTER THUNDERBOLT TRICKED ME, AND--I MESSED UP!

I CAN'T INSPIRE ANYBODY!

MIGUEL

I'M GONNA SCREW IT UP AGAIN.

I'M NOT A HERO.

PG. 2

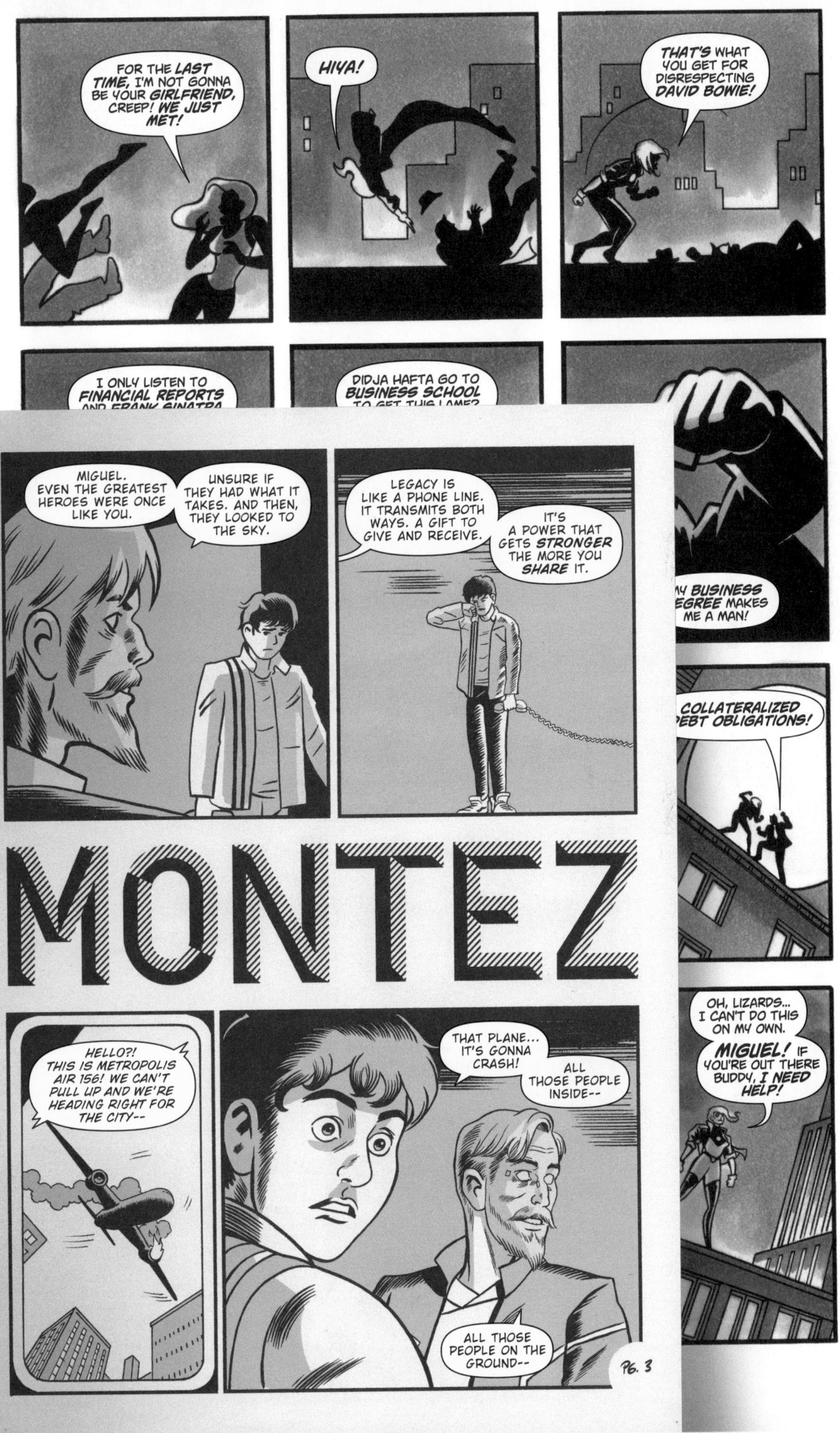

FOR THE LAST TIME, I'M NOT GONNA BE YOUR GIRLFRIEND, CREEP! WE JUST MET!
HIYA!
THAT'S WHAT YOU GET FOR DISRESPECTING DAVID BOWIE!
I ONLY LISTEN TO FINANCIAL REPORTS
DIDJA HAFTA GO TO BUSINESS SCHOOL
Y BUSINESS EGREE MAKES ME A MAN!
COLLATERALIZED EBT OBLIGATIONS!
OH, LIZARDS... I CAN'T DO THIS ON MY OWN.
MIGUEL! IF YOU'RE OUT THERE BUDDY, I NEED HELP!
MIGUEL. EVEN THE GREATEST HEROES WERE ONCE LIKE YOU.
UNSURE IF THEY HAD WHAT IT TAKES. AND THEN, THEY LOOKED TO THE SKY.
LEGACY IS LIKE A PHONE LINE. IT TRANSMITS BOTH WAYS. A GIFT TO GIVE AND RECEIVE.
IT'S A POWER THAT GETS STRONGER THE MORE YOU SHARE IT.
MONTEZ
HELLO?! THIS IS METROPOLIS AIR 156! WE CAN'T PULL UP AND WE'RE HEADING RIGHT FOR THE CITY--
THAT PLANE... IT'S GONNA CRASH!
ALL THOSE PEOPLE INSIDE--
ALL THOSE PEOPLE ON THE GROUND--
PG. 3

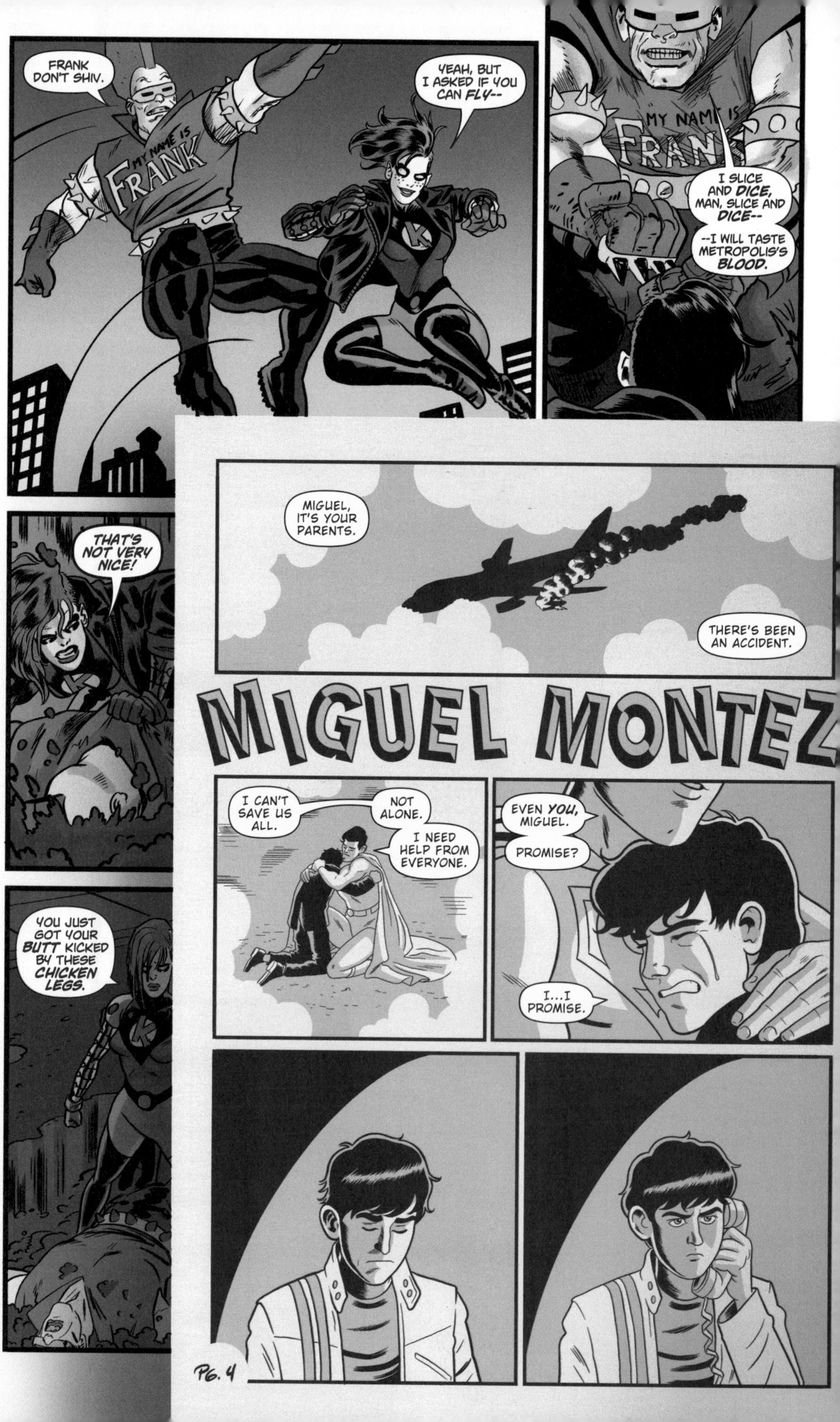

FRANK DON'T SHIV.
YEAH, BUT I ASKED IF YOU CAN *FLY*--
MY NAME IS FRANK
I SLICE AND *DICE*, MAN, SLICE AND *DICE*--
--I WILL TASTE METROPOLIS'S *BLOOD*.
THAT'S NOT VERY NICE!
YOU JUST GOT YOUR *BUTT* KICKED BY THESE *CHICKEN LEGS*.
MIGUEL, IT'S YOUR PARENTS.
THERE'S BEEN AN ACCIDENT.
MIGUEL MONTEZ
I CAN'T SAVE US ALL.
NOT ALONE.
I NEED HELP FROM EVERYONE.
EVEN *YOU*, MIGUEL.
PROMISE?
I...I PROMISE.
PG. 4

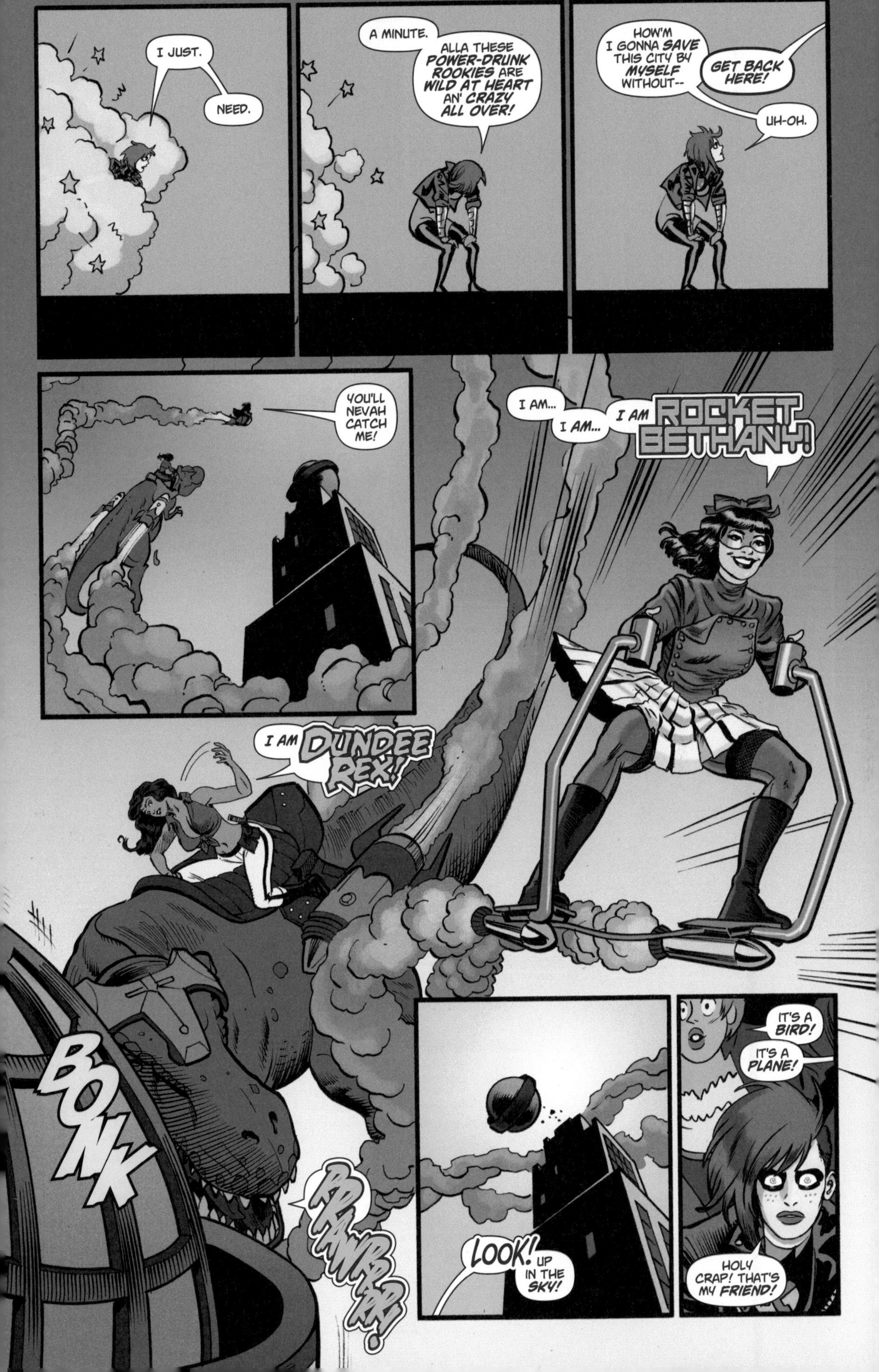
I JUST.
NEED.
A MINUTE.
ALLA THESE POWER-DRUNK ROOKIES ARE WILD AT HEART AN' CRAZY ALL OVER!
HOW'M I GONNA SAVE THIS CITY BY MYSELF WITHOUT--
GET BACK HERE!
UH-OH.
YOU'LL NEVAH CATCH ME!
I AM...
I AM...
I AM ROCKET BETHANY!
I AM DUNDEE REX!
BONK
RRAWRRR!
LOOK! UP IN THE SKY!
IT'S A BIRD!
IT'S A PLANE!
HOLY CRAP! THAT'S MY FRIEND!

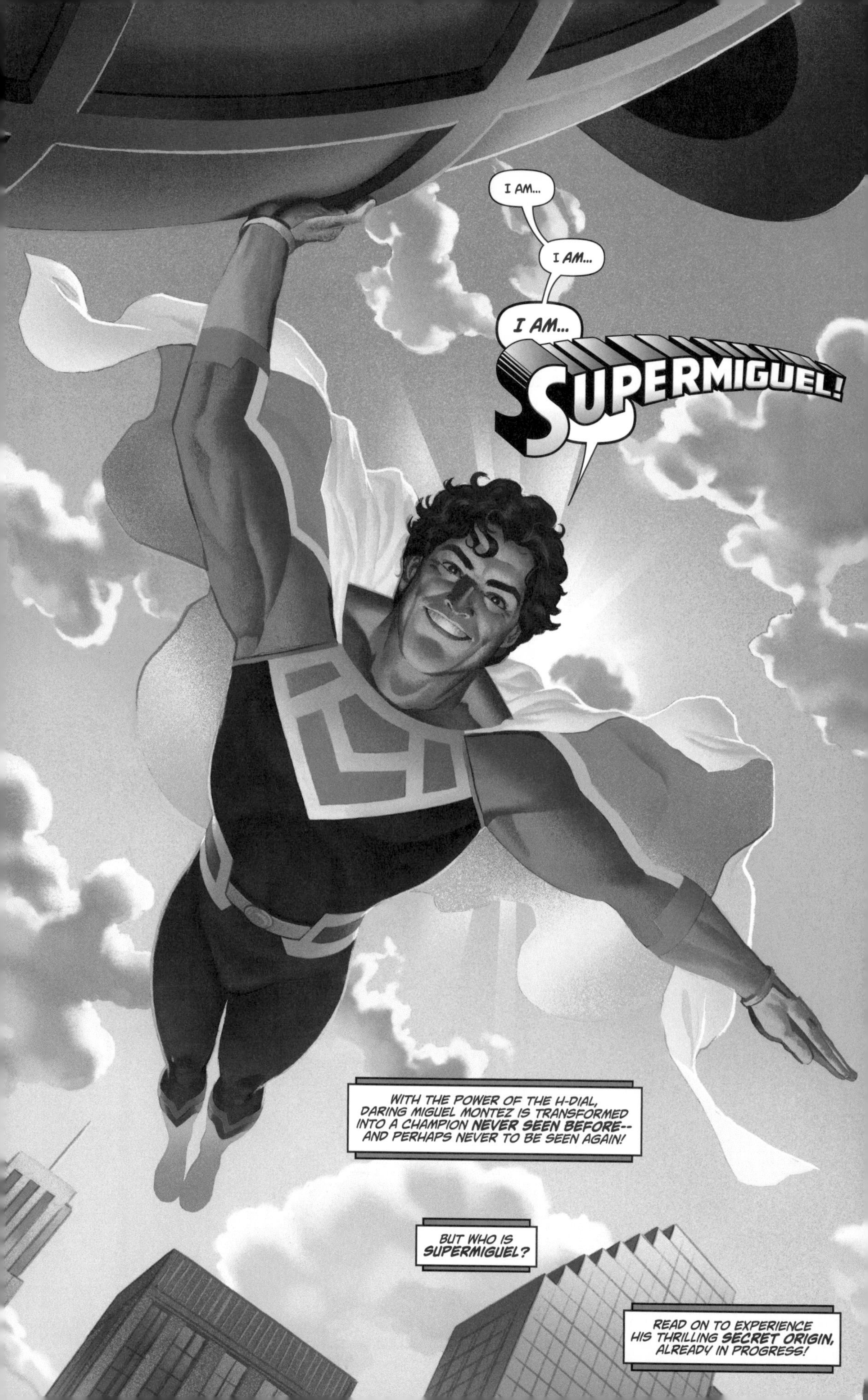

I AM...
I AM...
I AM...
SUPERMIGUEL!
WITH THE POWER OF THE H-DIAL, DARING MIGUEL MONTEZ IS TRANSFORMED INTO A CHAMPION NEVER SEEN BEFORE-- AND PERHAPS NEVER TO BE SEEN AGAIN!
BUT WHO IS SUPERMIGUEL?
READ ON TO EXPERIENCE HIS THRILLING SECRET ORIGIN, ALREADY IN PROGRESS!

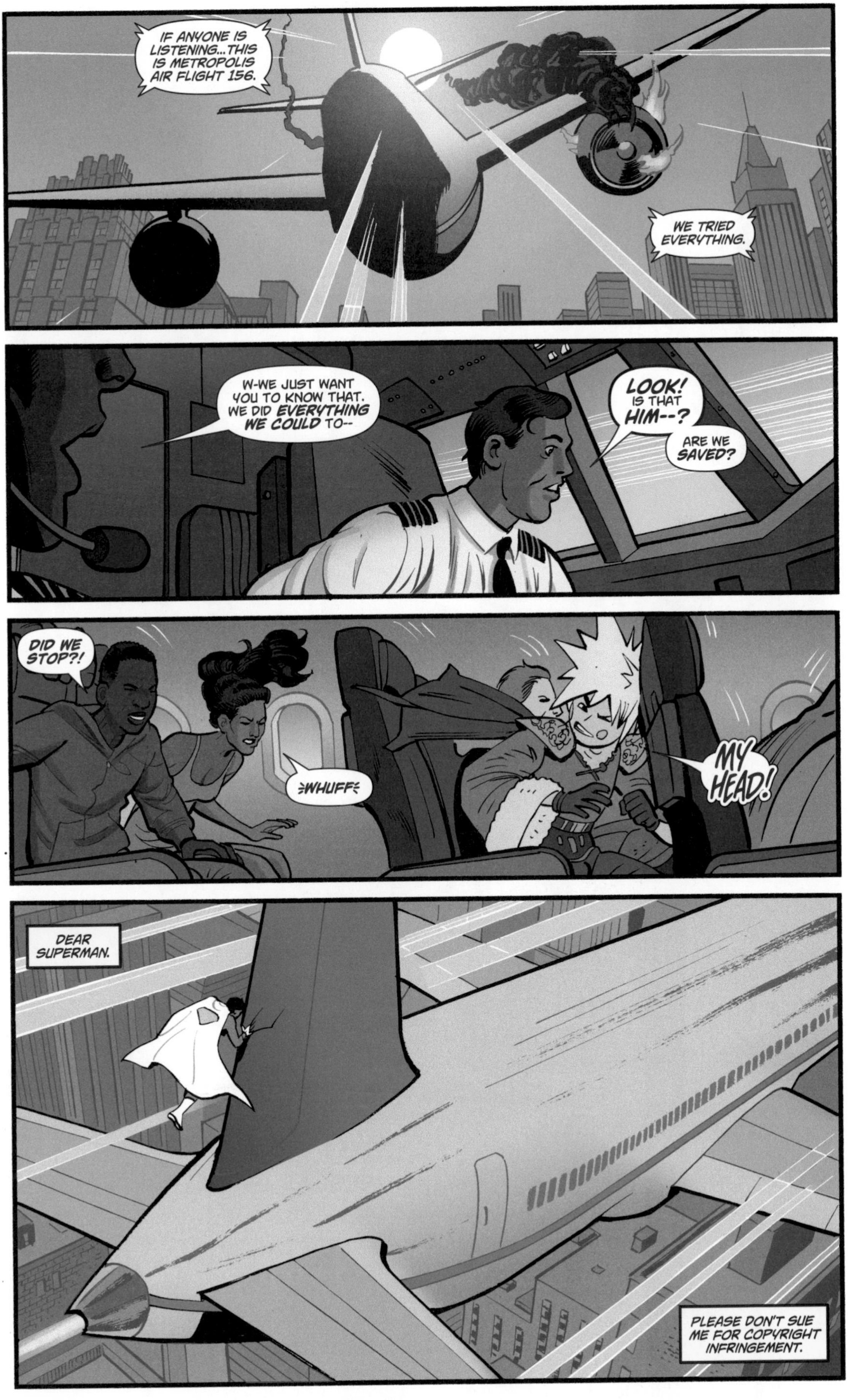
IF ANYONE IS LISTENING...THIS IS METROPOLIS AIR FLIGHT 156.
WE TRIED EVERYTHING.
W-WE JUST WANT YOU TO KNOW THAT. WE DID EVERYTHING WE COULD TO--
LOOK! IS THAT HIM--?
ARE WE SAVED?
DID WE STOP?!
WHUFF
MY HEAD!
DEAR SUPERMAN.
PLEASE DON'T SUE ME FOR COPYRIGHT INFRINGEMENT.

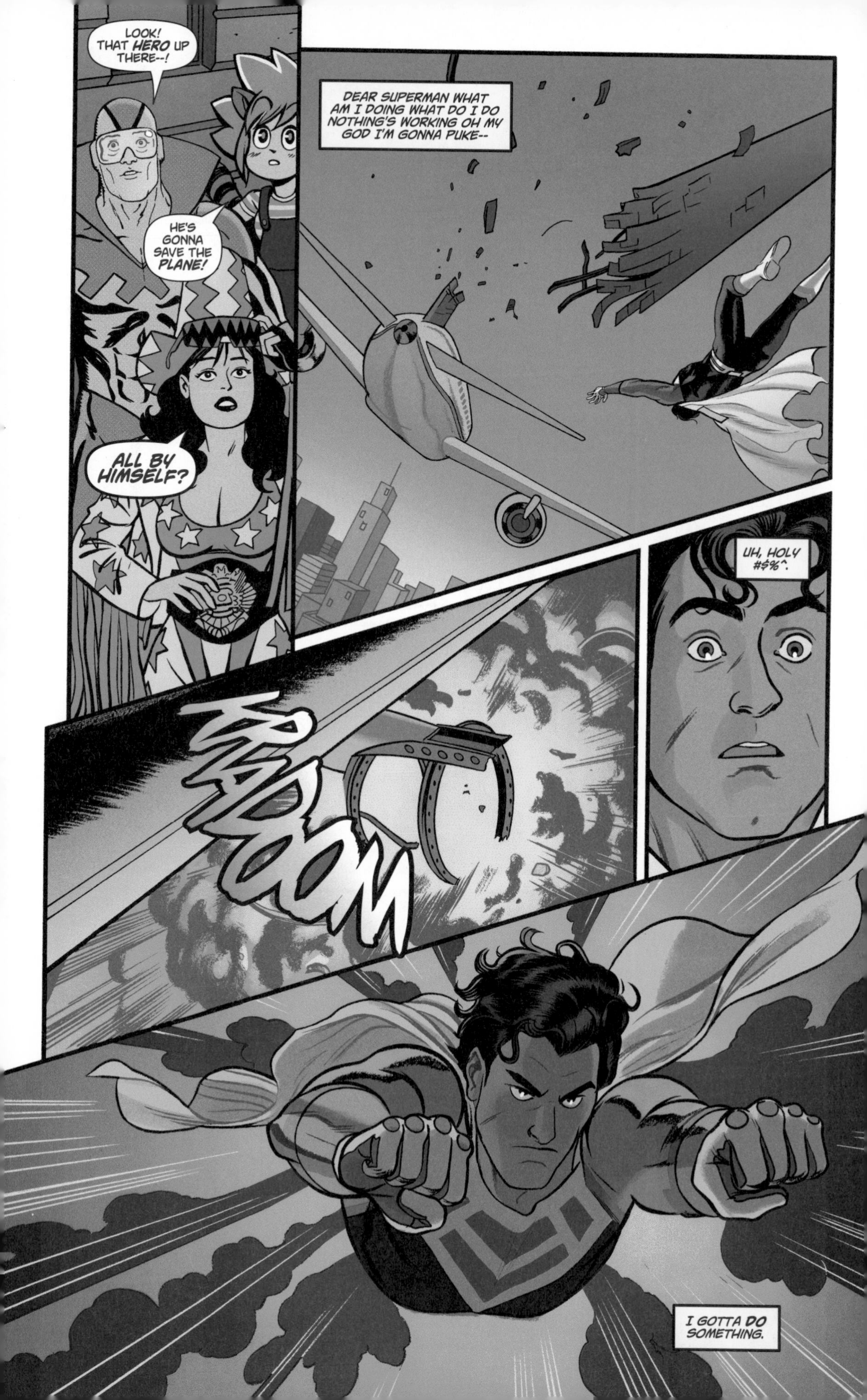
LOOK! THAT HERO UP THERE--!
HE'S GONNA SAVE THE PLANE!
ALL BY HIMSELF?
DEAR SUPERMAN WHAT AM I DOING WHAT DO I DO NOTHING'S WORKING OH MY GOD I'M GONNA PUKE--
UH, HOLY #$%^.
KRADOOM
I GOTTA DO SOMETHING.

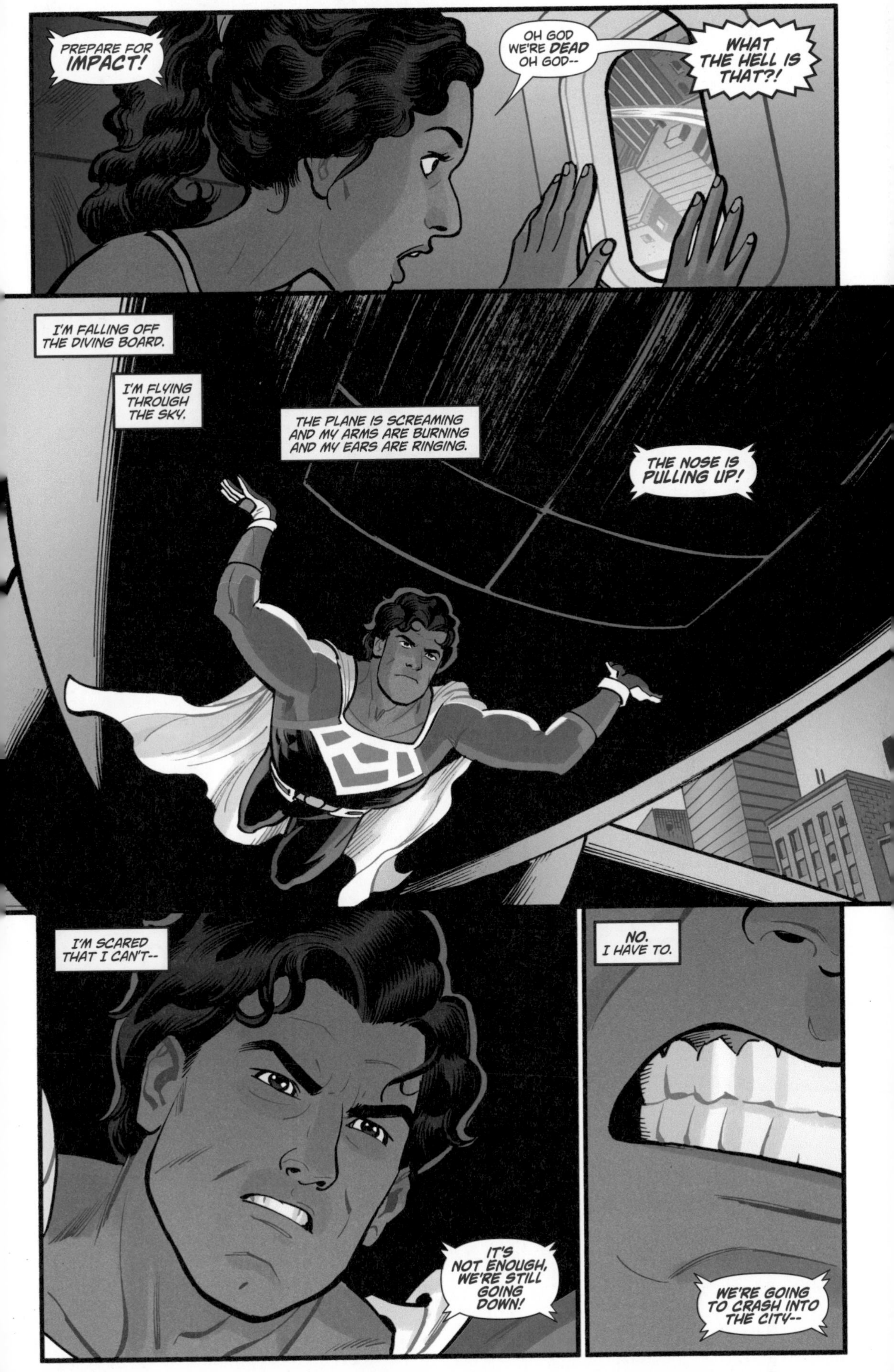
PREPARE FOR IMPACT!
OH GOD WE'RE DEAD OH GOD--
WHAT THE HELL IS THAT?!
I'M FALLING OFF THE DIVING BOARD.
I'M FLYING THROUGH THE SKY.
THE PLANE IS SCREAMING AND MY ARMS ARE BURNING AND MY EARS ARE RINGING.
THE NOSE IS PULLING UP!
I'M SCARED THAT I CAN'T--
IT'S NOT ENOUGH, WE'RE STILL GOING DOWN!
NO. I HAVE TO.
WE'RE GOING TO CRASH INTO THE CITY--

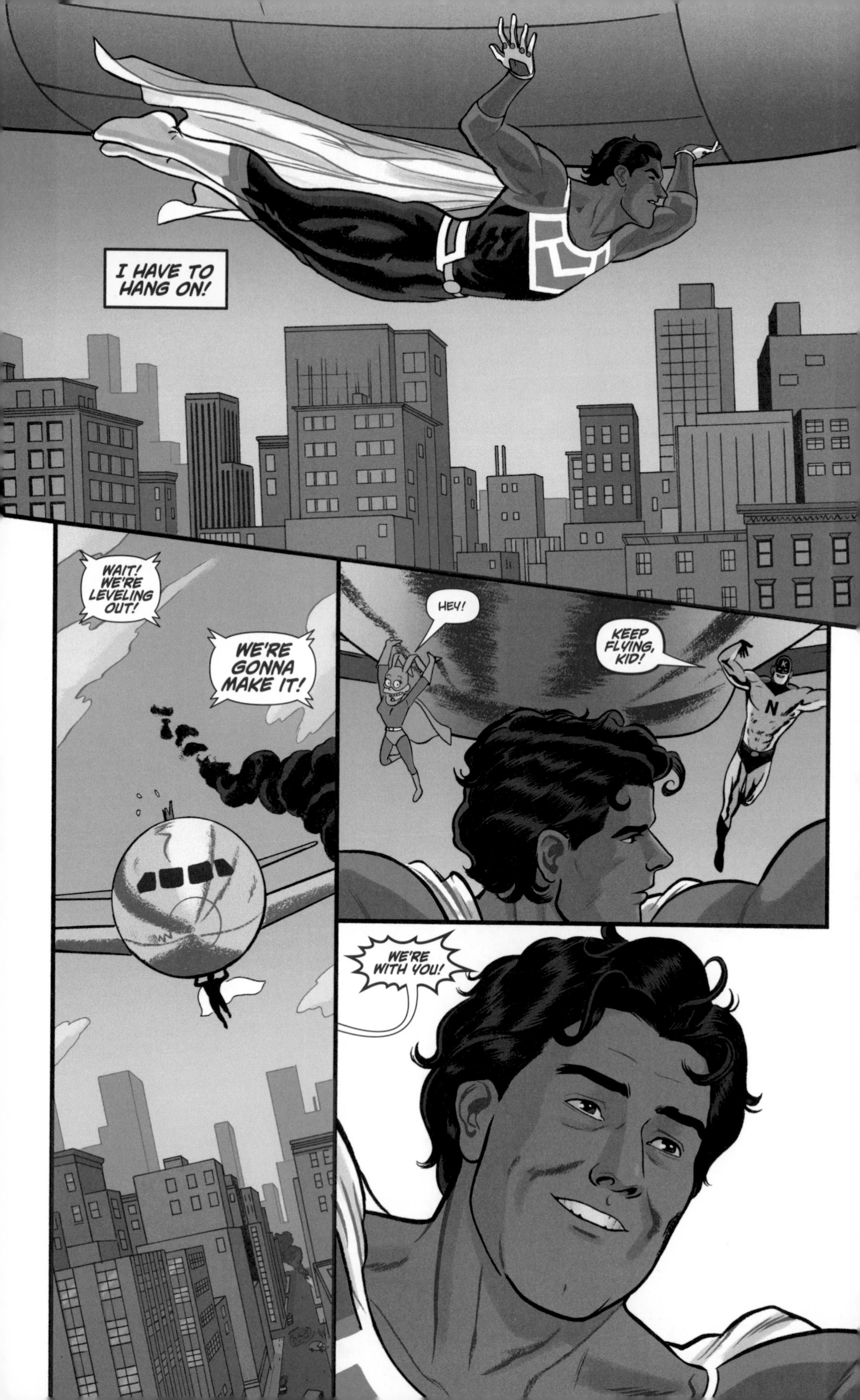
I HAVE TO HANG ON!
WAIT! WE'RE LEVELING OUT!
WE'RE GONNA MAKE IT!
HEY!
KEEP FLYING, KID!
WE'RE WITH YOU!

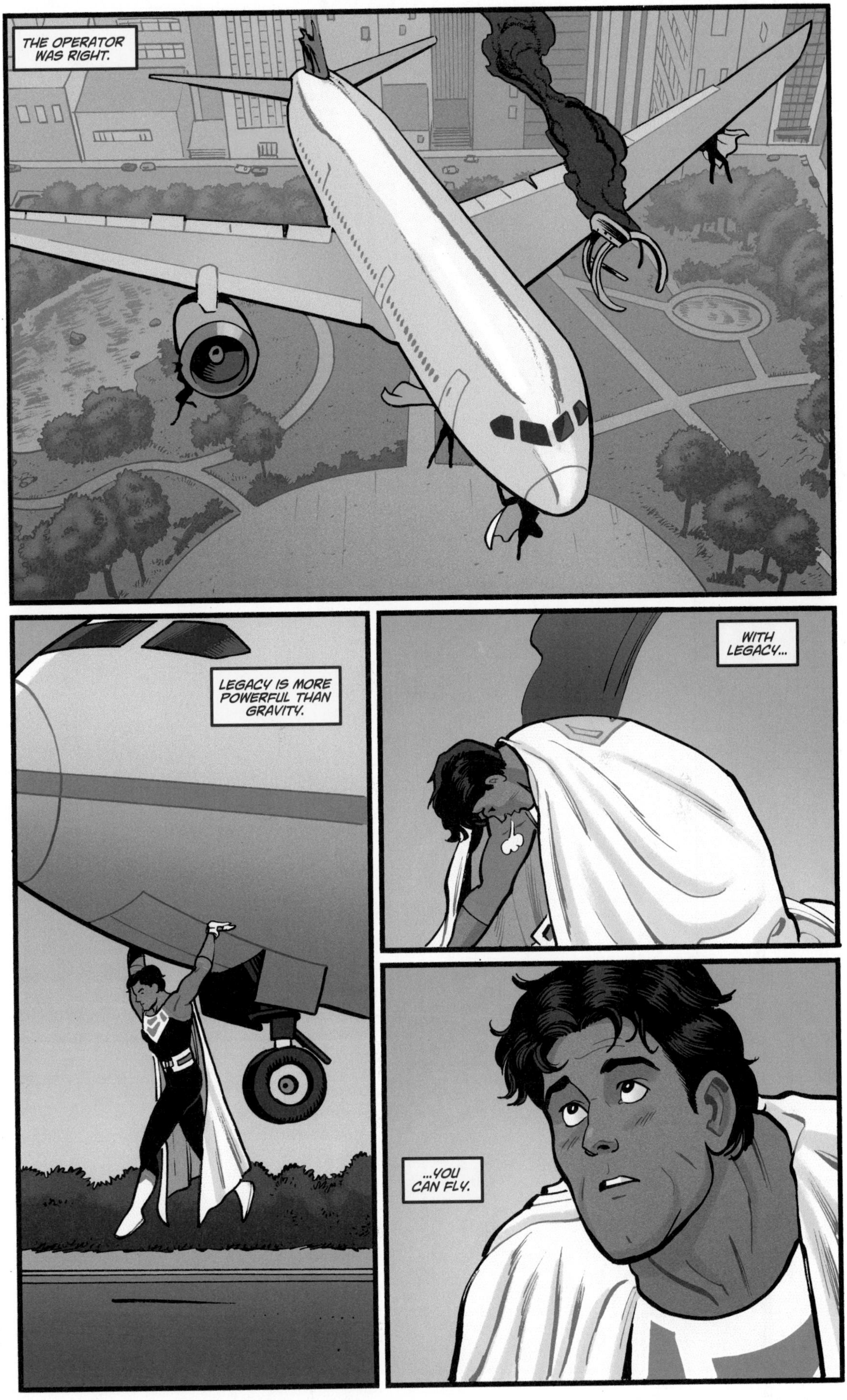
THE OPERATOR WAS RIGHT.
LEGACY IS MORE POWERFUL THAN GRAVITY.
WITH LEGACY...
...YOU CAN FLY.

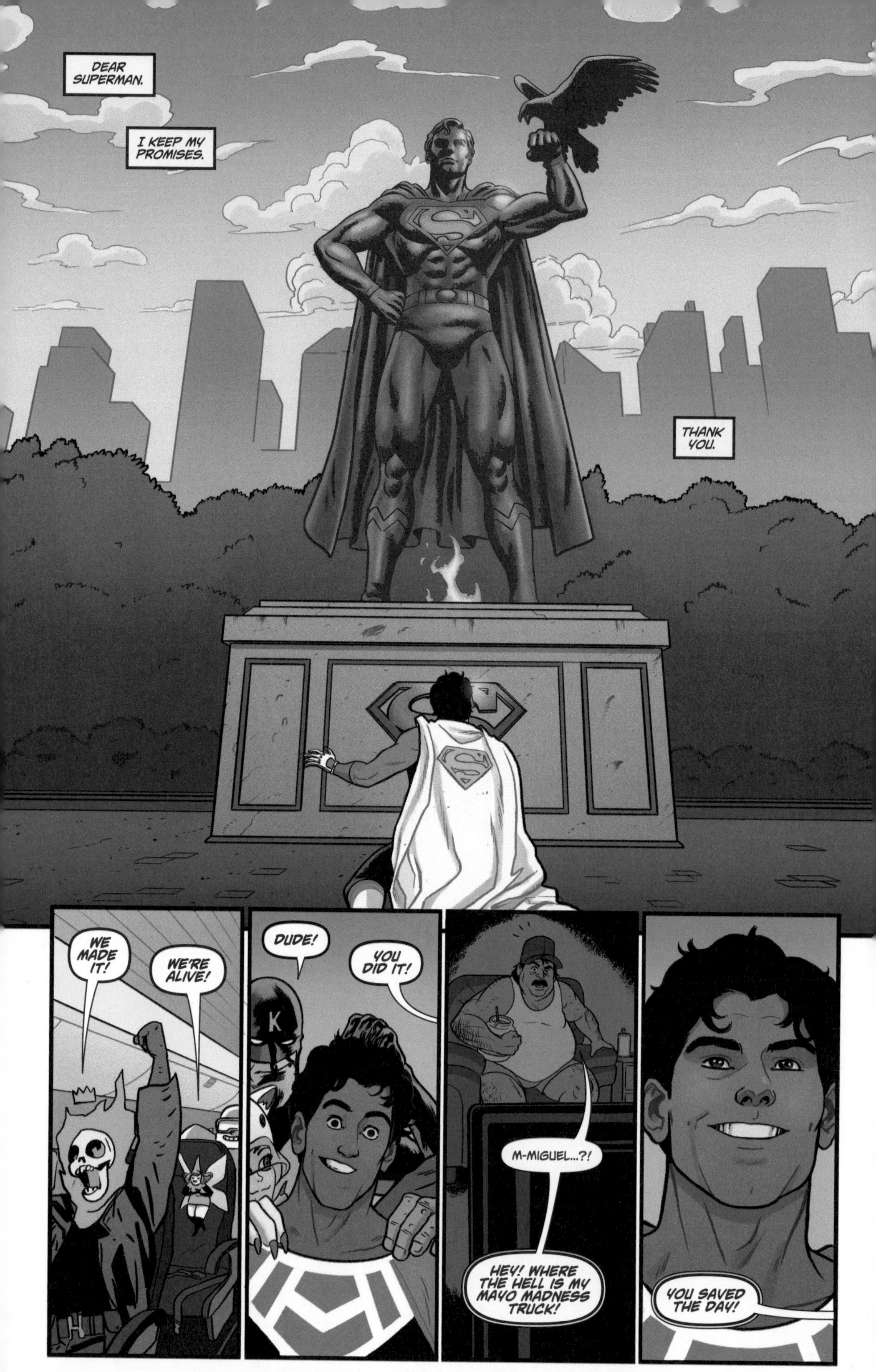
DEAR SUPERMAN.
I KEEP MY PROMISES.
THANK YOU.
WE MADE IT!
WE'RE ALIVE!
DUDE!
YOU DID IT!
M-MIGUEL...?!
HEY! WHERE THE HELL IS MY MAYO MADNESS TRUCK!
YOU SAVED THE DAY!

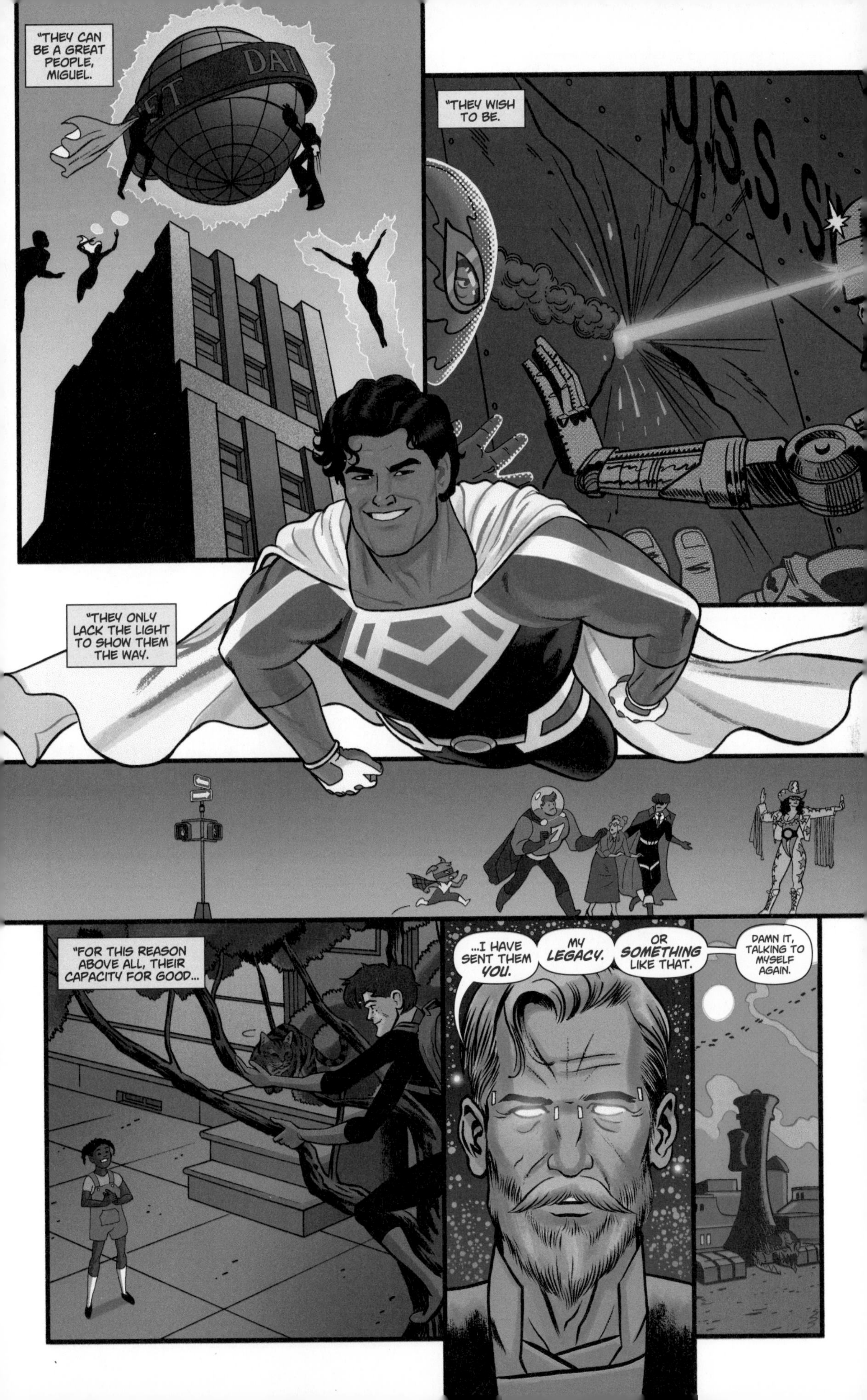
"THEY CAN BE A GREAT PEOPLE, MIGUEL.
"THEY WISH TO BE.
"THEY ONLY LACK THE LIGHT TO SHOW THEM THE WAY.
"FOR THIS REASON ABOVE ALL, THEIR CAPACITY FOR GOOD...
...I HAVE SENT THEM YOU.
MY LEGACY.
OR SOMETHING LIKE THAT.
DAMN IT, TALKING TO MYSELF AGAIN.

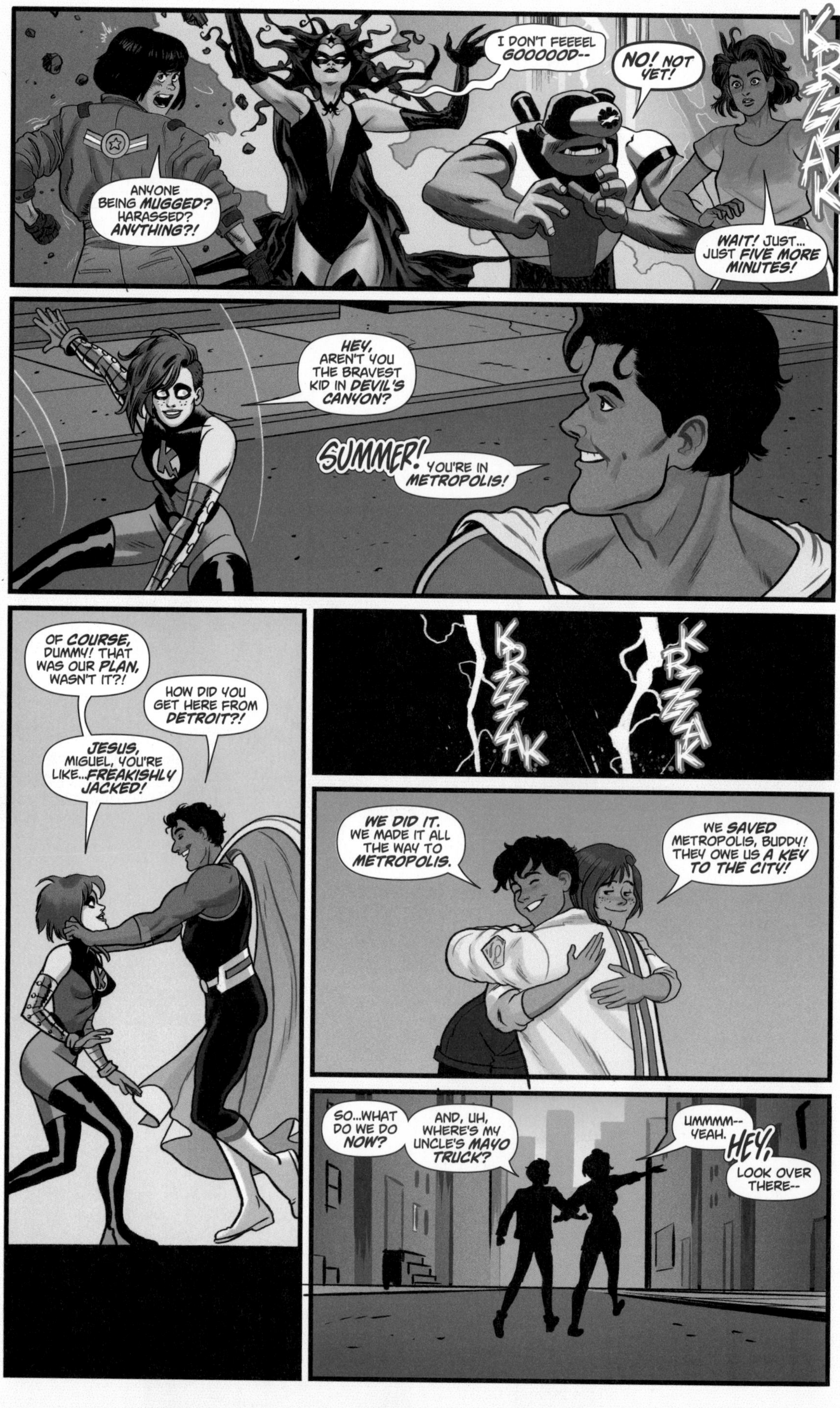
ANYONE BEING MUGGED? HARASSED? ANYTHING?!
I DON'T FEEEEL GOOOOOD--
NO! NOT YET!
KRZZZAK
WAIT! JUST... JUST FIVE MORE MINUTES!
HEY, AREN'T YOU THE BRAVEST KID IN DEVIL'S CANYON?
SUMMER! YOU'RE IN METROPOLIS!
OF COURSE, DUMMY! THAT WAS OUR PLAN, WASN'T IT?!
HOW DID YOU GET HERE FROM DETROIT?!
JESUS, MIGUEL, YOU'RE LIKE...FREAKISHLY JACKED!
KRZZZAK
KRZZZAK
WE DID IT. WE MADE IT ALL THE WAY TO METROPOLIS.
WE SAVED METROPOLIS, BUDDY! THEY OWE US A KEY TO THE CITY!
SO...WHAT DO WE DO NOW?
AND, UH, WHERE'S MY UNCLE'S MAYO TRUCK?
UMMMM-- YEAH.
HEY, LOOK OVER THERE--

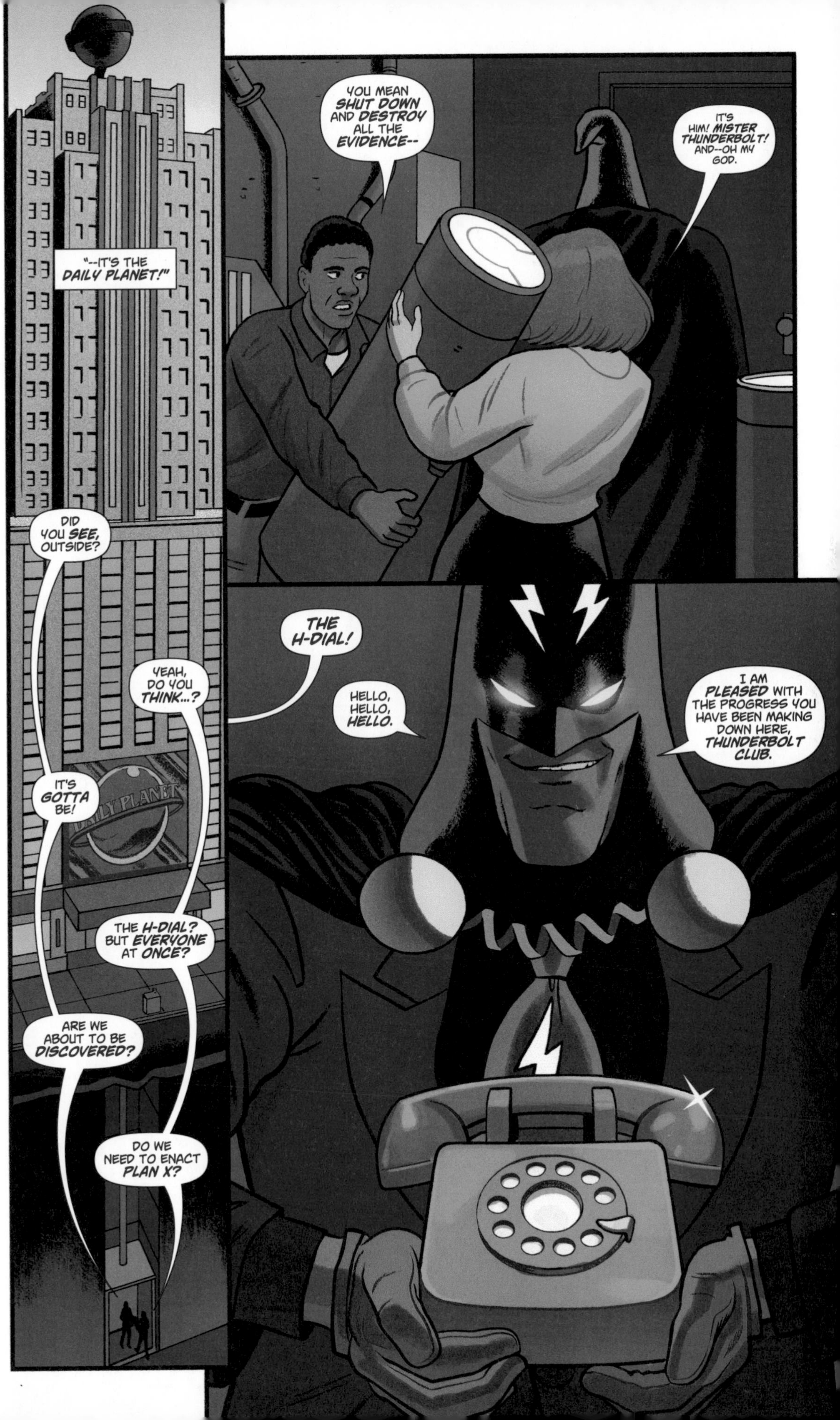
"--IT'S THE DAILY PLANET!"
DID YOU SEE, OUTSIDE?
YEAH, DO YOU THINK...?
IT'S GOTTA BE!
DAILY PLANET
THE H-DIAL? BUT EVERYONE AT ONCE?
ARE WE ABOUT TO BE DISCOVERED?
DO WE NEED TO ENACT PLAN X?
YOU MEAN SHUT DOWN AND DESTROY ALL THE EVIDENCE--
IT'S HIM! MISTER THUNDERBOLT! AND--OH MY GOD.
THE H-DIAL!
HELLO, HELLO, HELLO.
I AM PLEASED WITH THE PROGRESS YOU HAVE BEEN MAKING DOWN HERE, THUNDERBOLT CLUB.

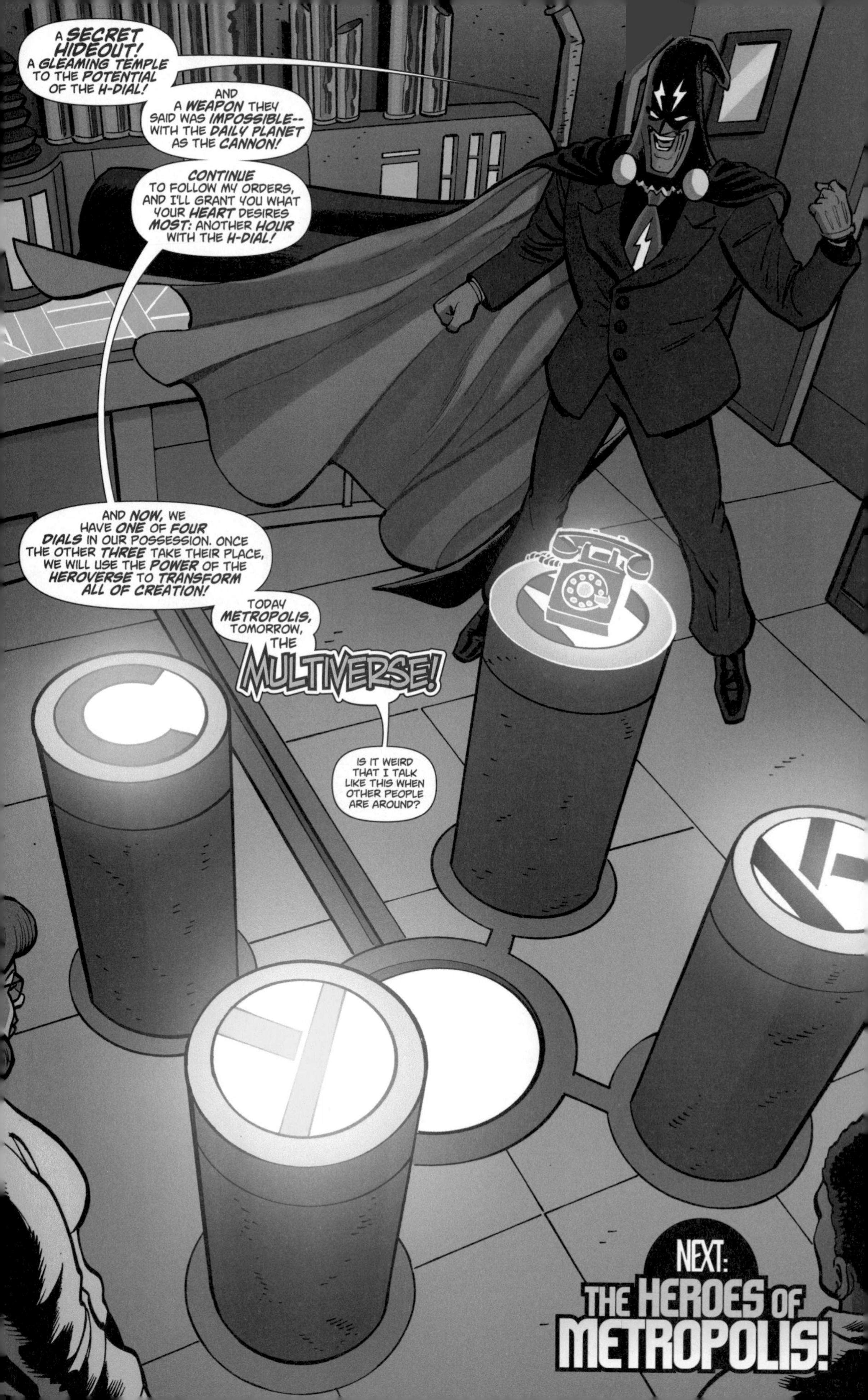
A SECRET HIDEOUT! A GLEAMING TEMPLE TO THE POTENTIAL OF THE H-DIAL!
AND A WEAPON THEY SAID WAS IMPOSSIBLE-- WITH THE DAILY PLANET AS THE CANNON!
CONTINUE TO FOLLOW MY ORDERS, AND I'LL GRANT YOU WHAT YOUR HEART DESIRES MOST: ANOTHER HOUR WITH THE H-DIAL!
AND NOW, WE HAVE ONE OF FOUR DIALS IN OUR POSSESSION. ONCE THE OTHER THREE TAKE THEIR PLACE, WE WILL USE THE POWER OF THE HEROVERSE TO TRANSFORM ALL OF CREATION!
TODAY METROPOLIS, TOMORROW, THE MULTIVERSE!
IS IT WEIRD THAT I TALK LIKE THIS WHEN OTHER PEOPLE ARE AROUND?
NEXT: THE HEROES OF METROPOLIS!

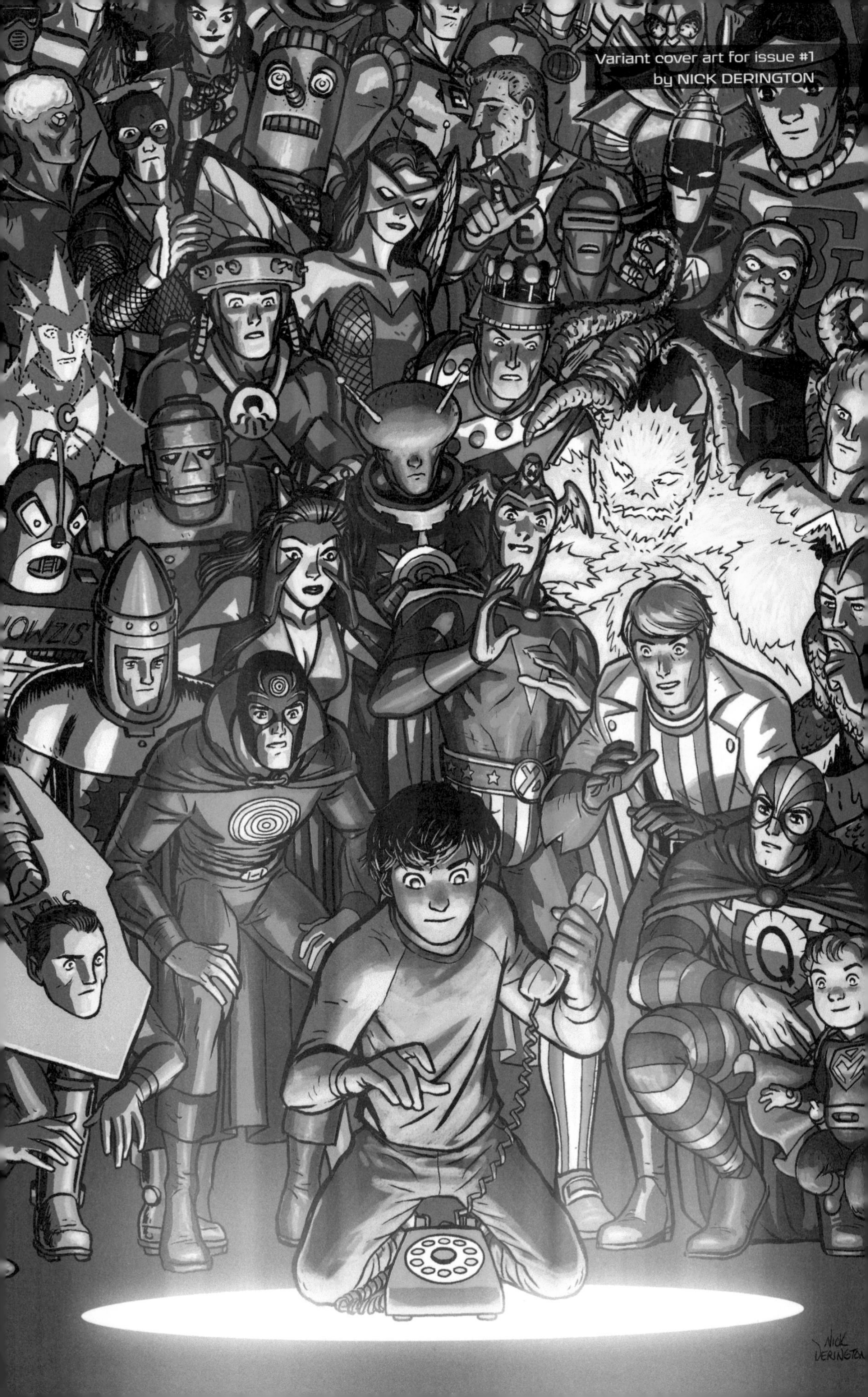
NICK
DERINGTON

Variant cover art for issue #1
by NICK DERINGTON

AFTERWORD

Hi! Brian Michael Bendis here—your Wonder Comics presenter person! I am here to share a little behind-the-scenes info on what happened with each one of this line's scrumptious new titles.

This is *Dial H for Hero*, and I should warn you, I am in love with my friend Sam Humphries and this is going to get a little mushy. But I figure now that you've read this amazing work and you're charmed and delighted with his voice, let me introduce you to the author.

You all know him as the dashing co-host of *DC Daily*, but he has also been diligently working for years as one of the best creators in the business. I fell in love with Sam the day I met him, which is what most people say when they meet him. We met at Marvel and became pals at the company's publishing retreats, where we discovered that there was a lot of overlap on the Venn diagram of our interests and passions for this business.

Sam went off to DC years before I even thought to do it. Part of what got me to DC was watching how much fun Sam was having. When the time came for me to meet my Kryptonian destiny, he was a huge help in making it happen. When Dan DiDio offered me the amazing opportunity to curate Wonder Comics, the thought bubble over my head read: Oh good! I get to make comics with Sam.

Even before this new line of books had a shape, I knew that Sam was definitely going to be involved with one of them. He didn't know this. He never asked me

for anything. But Sam was going to be part of this, no matter what.

Once Wonder Comics started to percolate, the first call began with me exclaiming, "Sam!" with such an excited breath of anticipation that Sam immediately matched my excitement and said, "Yeah?" And I said, "*Dial H for Hero*!"

There was a long pause. A decidedly long pause. Why? I thought Sam, with his glorious, idiosyncratic voice, was perfect for a new take on *Dial H for Hero*—or at least for the version that was in my head. I know there have been different incarnations over the years, ranging from the mostly campy to the mostly serious, but I imagined *my* vision of *Dial H for Hero* through the voice of Sam Humphries—and the comic in *my* head was *amazing*!

I deeply believe that *Dial H for Hero* is one of the greatest ideas in the history of popular culture—and lest you think I'm kidding, I put my name on it!

The original series debuted way back in *House of Mystery* #156 in a story written by Dave Wood and illustrated by comics legend Jim Mooney. The idea of Sam putting all of his magic inside this already amazing concept was one of my most inspired casting insights, and I knew when Sam heard it he would agree.

Sam said back to me: I don't know what this is. I never read it.

Sad trombones. I expected Sam to go, "Oh my God I love *Dial H for Hero*!" But

he did not. Instead he questioned our whole relationship and wondered why he even started being friends with me in the first place.

Usually, when a creator says they haven't had any interaction with a concept like this, that means they're not a fan, and I just tell myself that I was wrong and back off the whole thing. Sam took some pity on me, though, and decided to do a little research before he completely told me to go to hell. He dove into it and immediately saw what I saw: the unlimited, untapped potential of a brilliant hook. And—as you can tell because you've already read the first six issues—he *ran* with it.

I am so, so thrilled with this book. Behind the scenes, I was hesitant to even comment on it while it was being produced because I'm so happy with what Sam and Joe have made and I didn't want to jinx it.

I know I'm spending a lot of time talking about Sam and not about Joe Quinones. And that's only because I really do know Sam well and we've been through a lot of real-life stuff together.

I love Joe Quinones, too. Joe knows this. Or he does now. I worked with Joe at Marvel and I think he's one of the best illustrators working in any medium. What Joe Quinones might *not* know is that when the idea of Joe joining this book with Sam came up, I got so excited that I couldn't even think of another name. There was some balancing we

had to do with Joe's schedule—he is in demand—but we got him. And when that negotiation was going on I still couldn't conjure up anyone else for a Plan B. I just wanted Joe Quinones to do this book with Sam.

And I'm so deeply grateful that he brought his everything to this.

As of this writing, the six-issue experiment that was *Dial H for Hero* by Sam Humphries and Joe Quinones has been renewed. Six more issues are coming. And that's amazing.

That's because of Joe. That's because of Sam. And that's because of *you*.

I am so grateful that you rewarded us for this beautiful, magical, cosmic comic—Sam and Joe and everyone who contributed to its creation.

I have gotten more compliments about this book—particularly from inside Warner Bros.—than anything else in the Wonder Comics line. And I know it's because they can tell that it's being done by people who really love the magic of DC Comics and are doing everything they can to share that magic through one of the greatest ideas in the company's history.

My thanks to the entire creative and editorial team for making this all happen, and to you, for supporting the beautiful, generous voices in our medium.

Thank you, Sam. For everything.

BENDIS!
Portland, Oregon | 2019

CALL WAITING

Sketches and character designs by JOE QUINONES

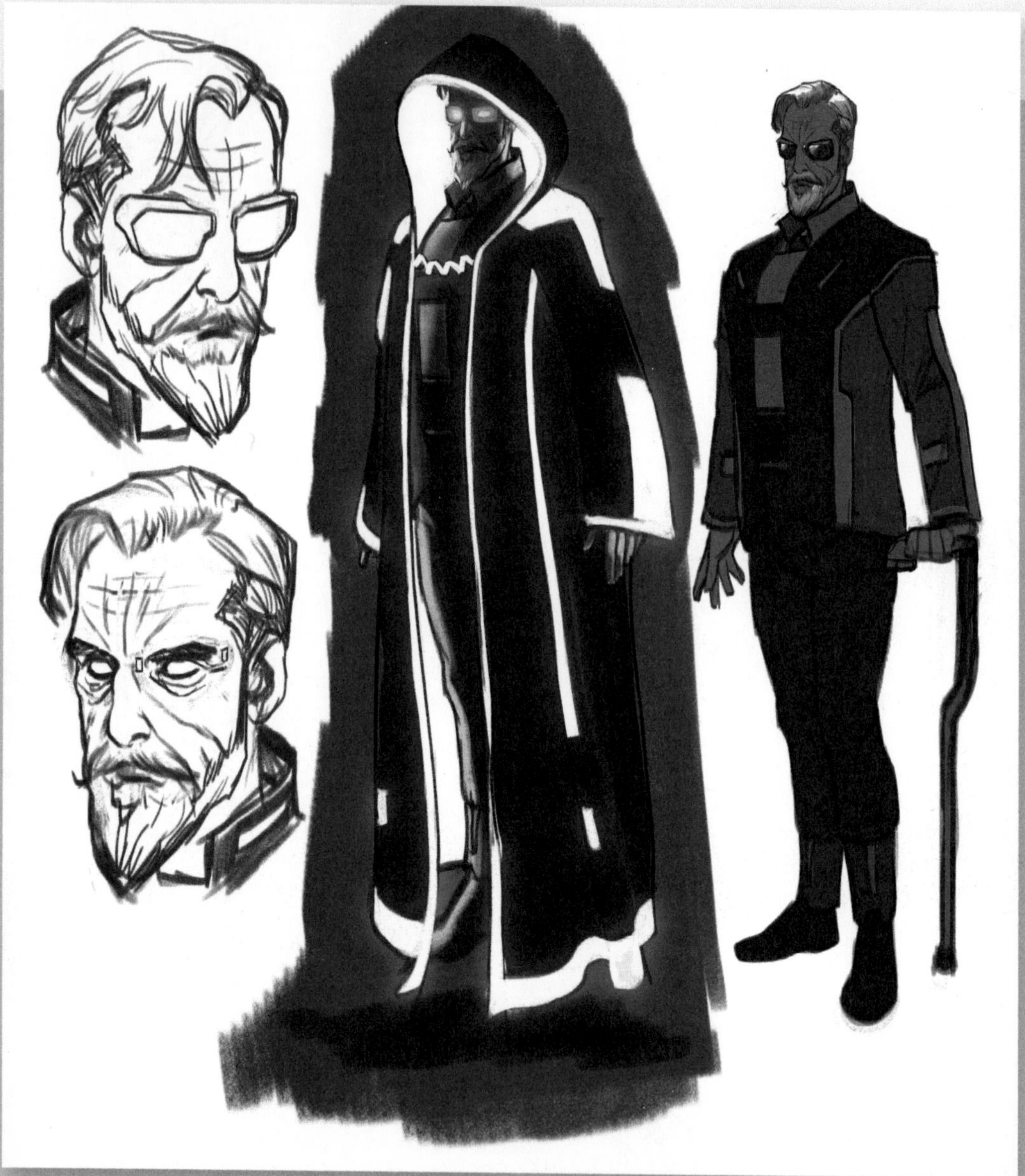

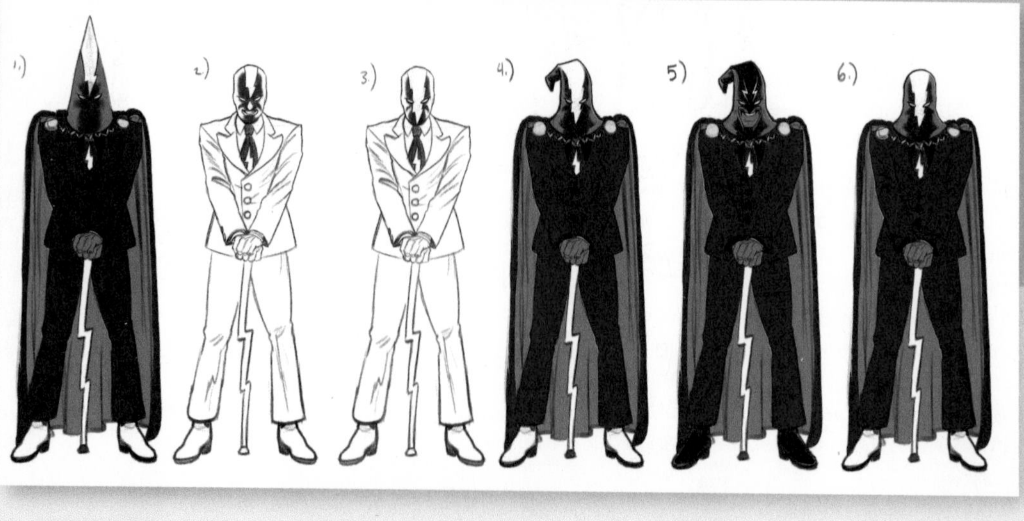
1.)
2.)
3.)
4.)
5)
6.)

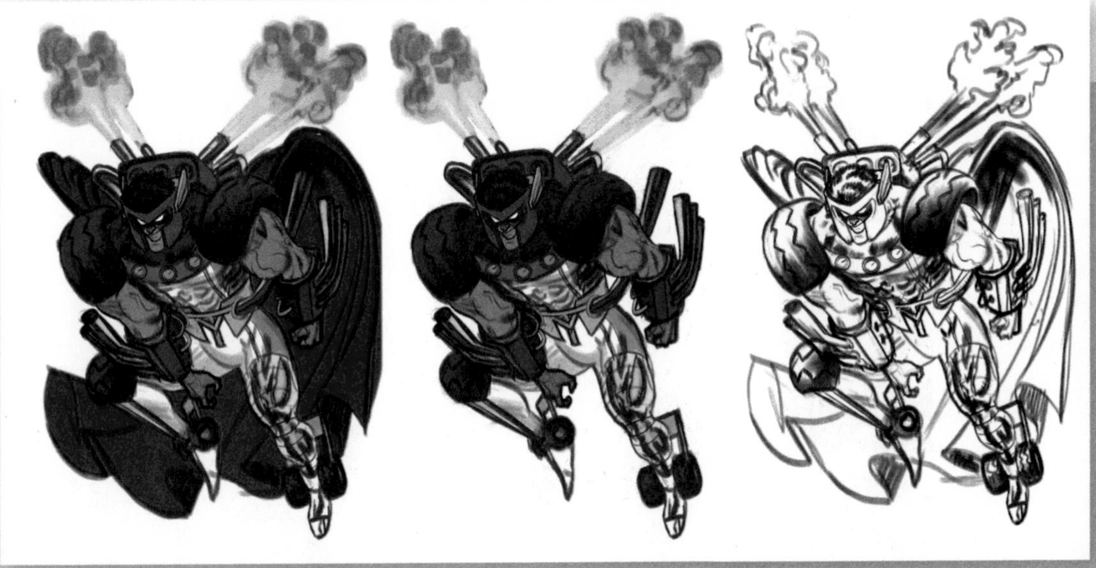

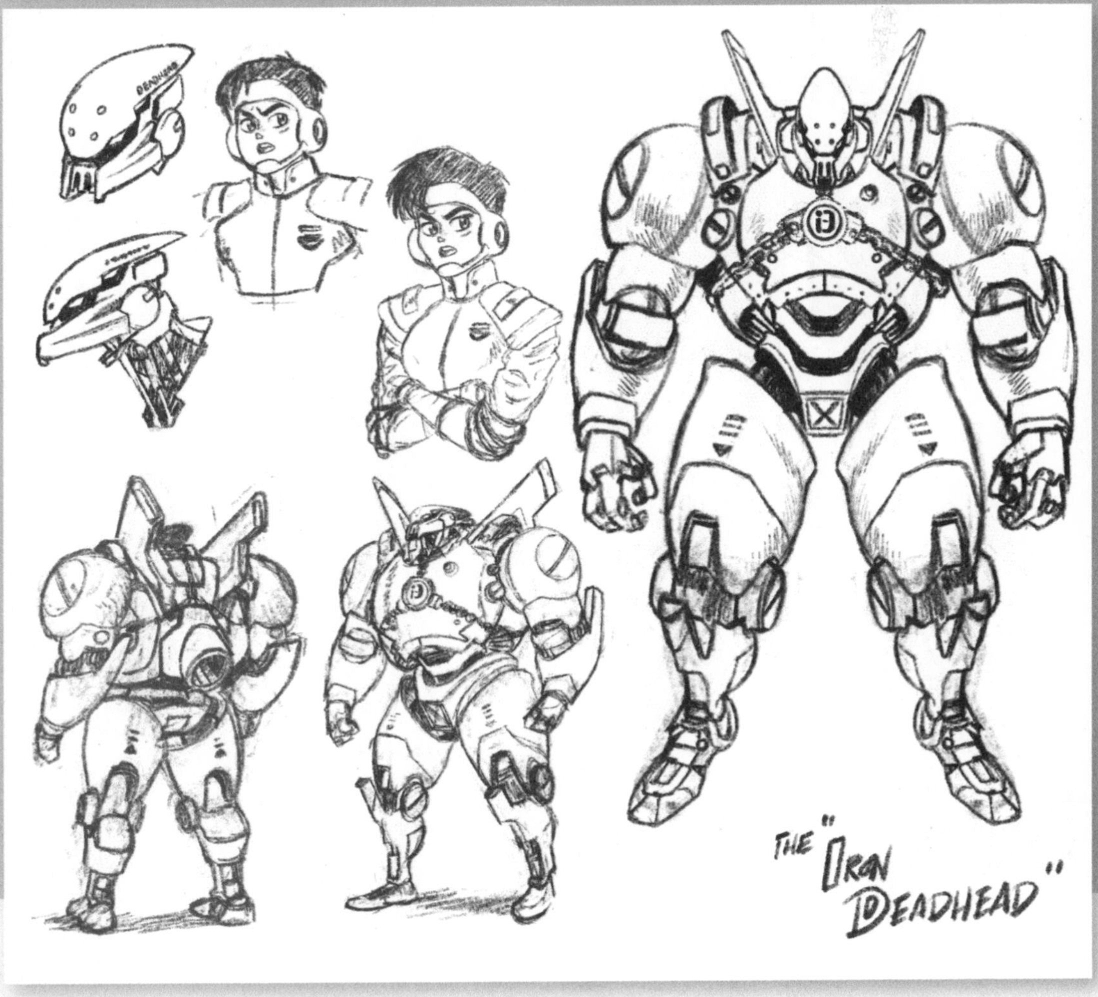
THE "IRON DEADHEAD"

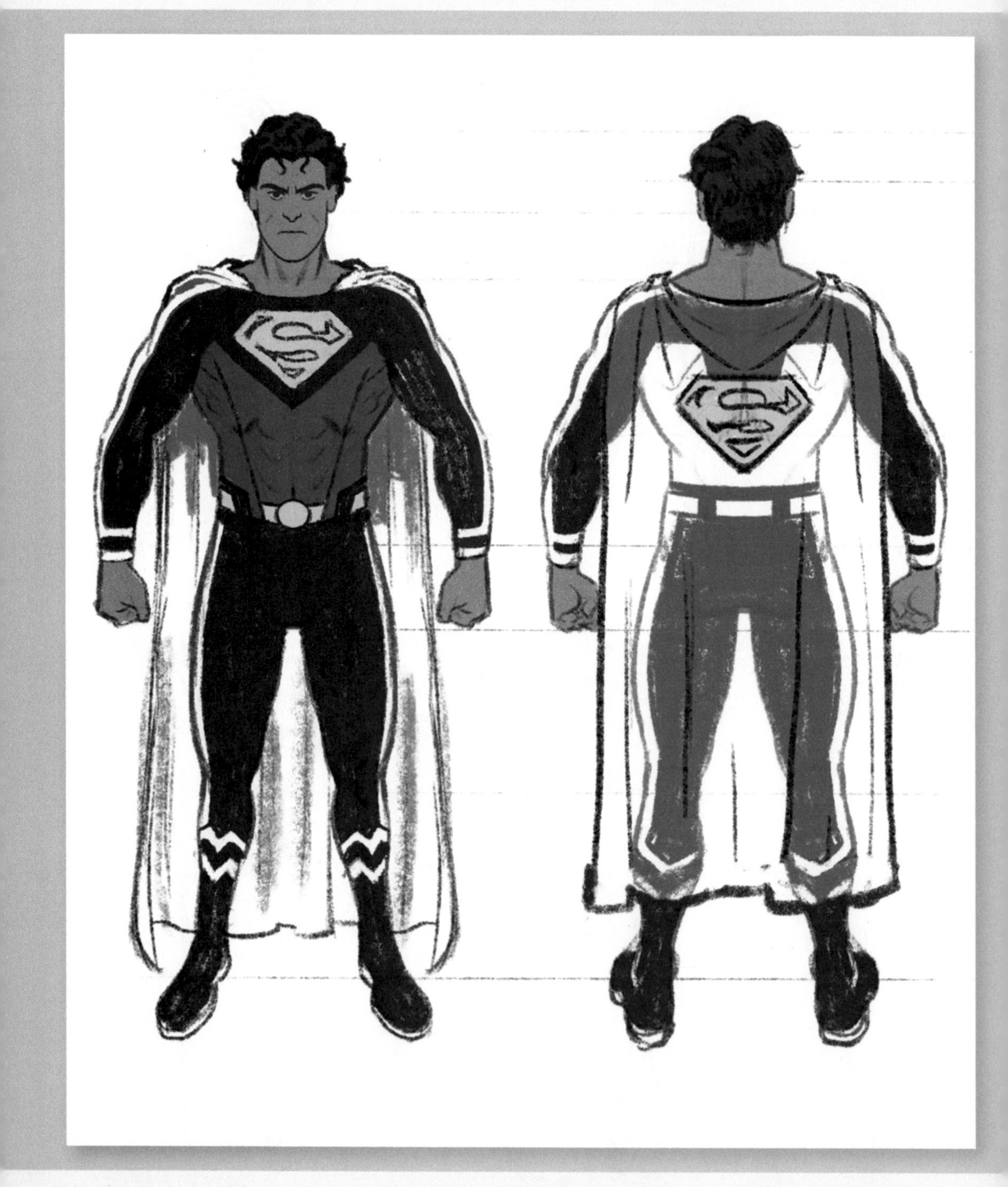

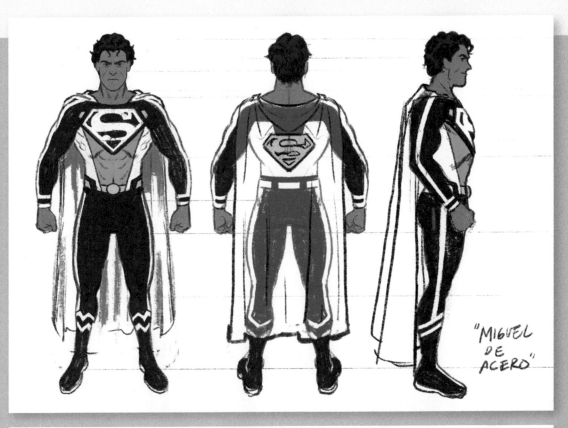

"MIGUEL
DE
ACERO"

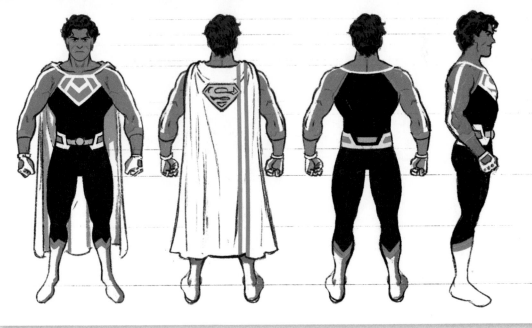

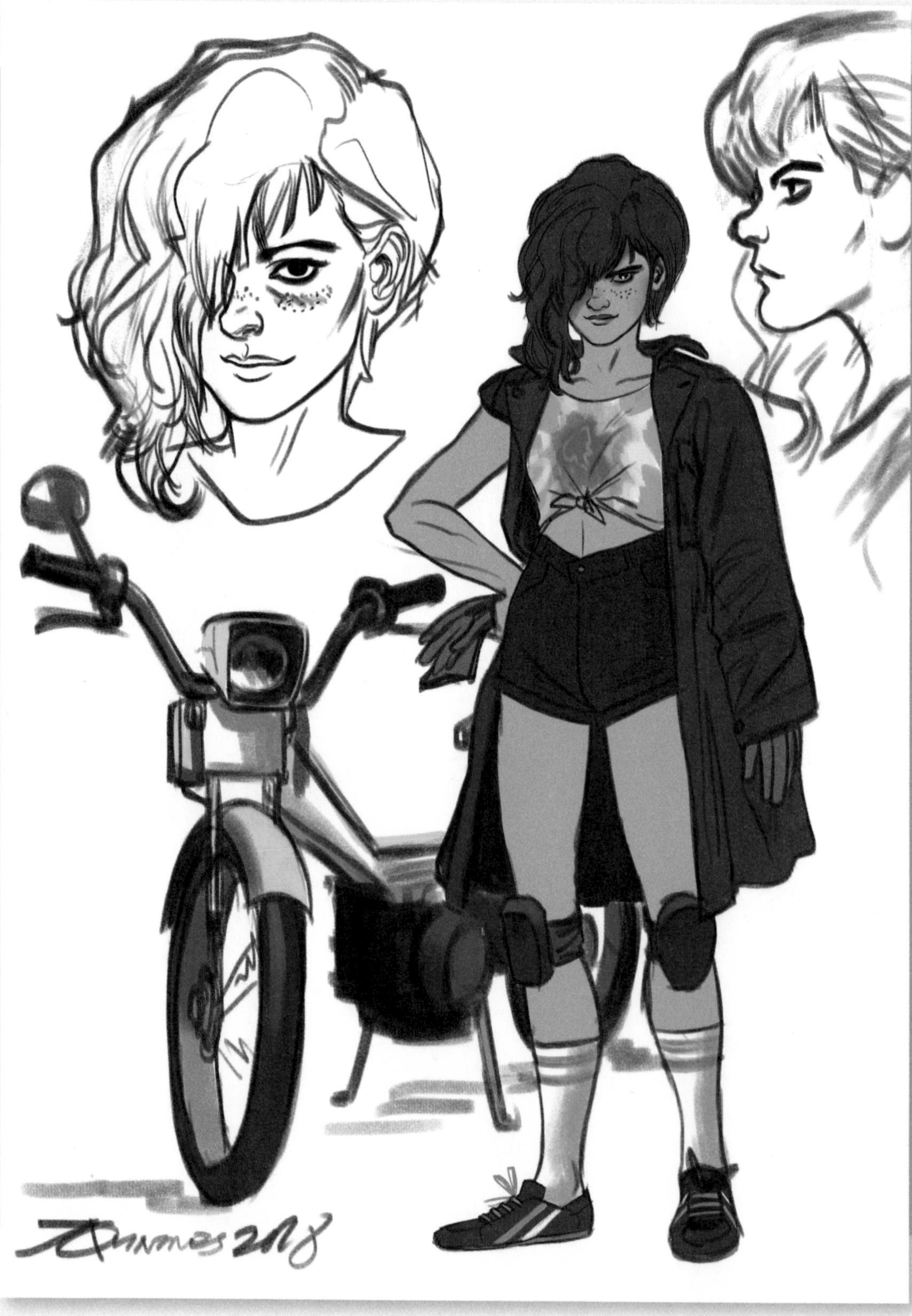

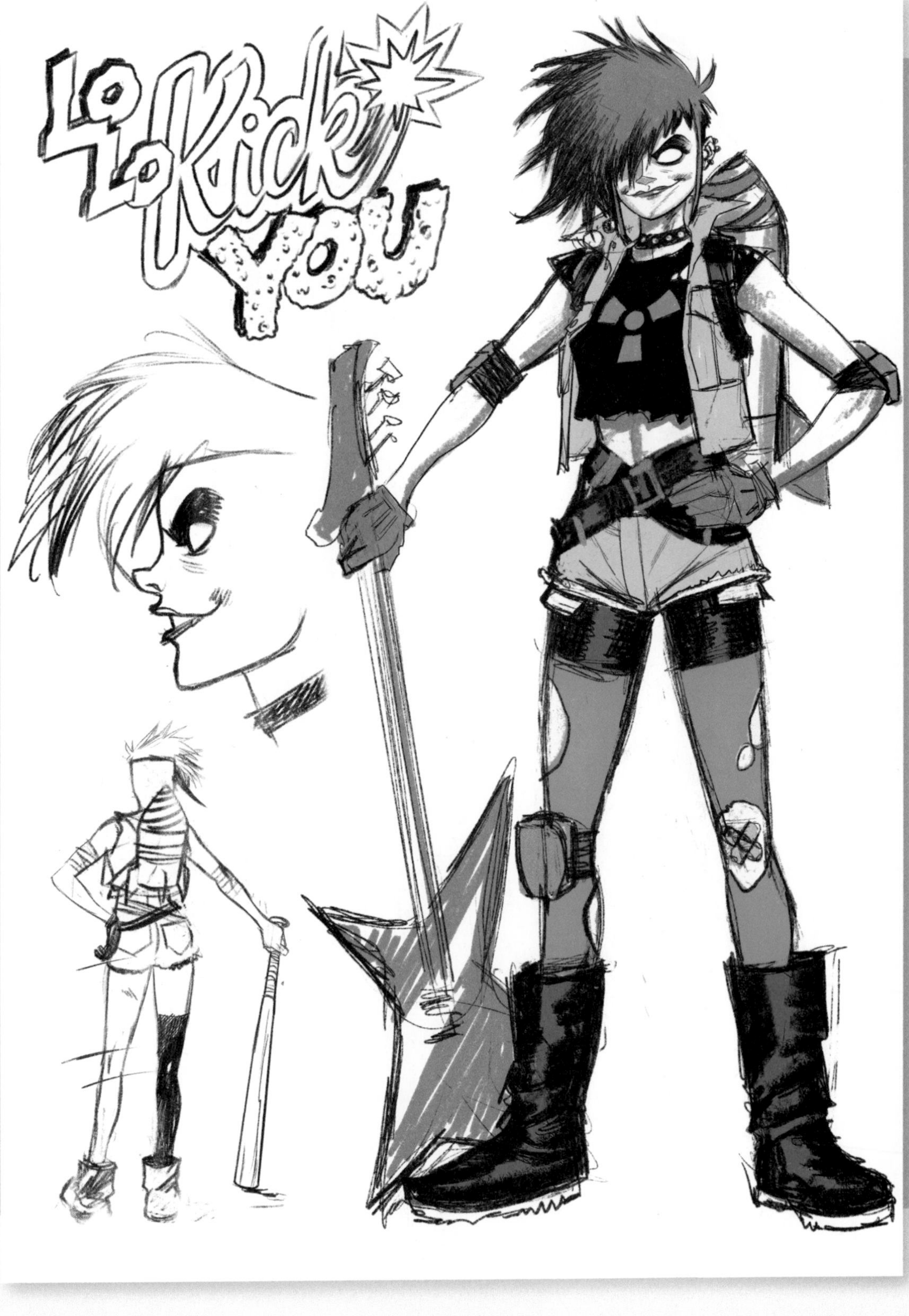
Lo Lo Kick YOU

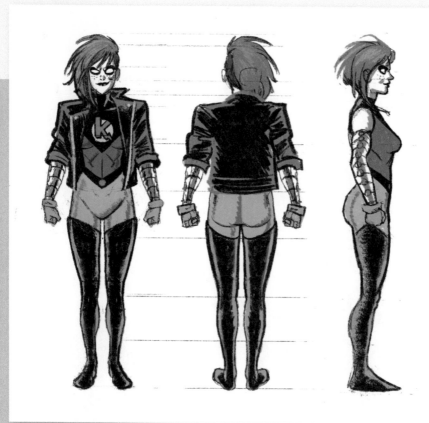
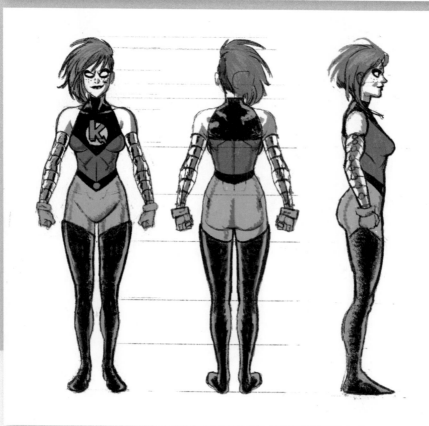

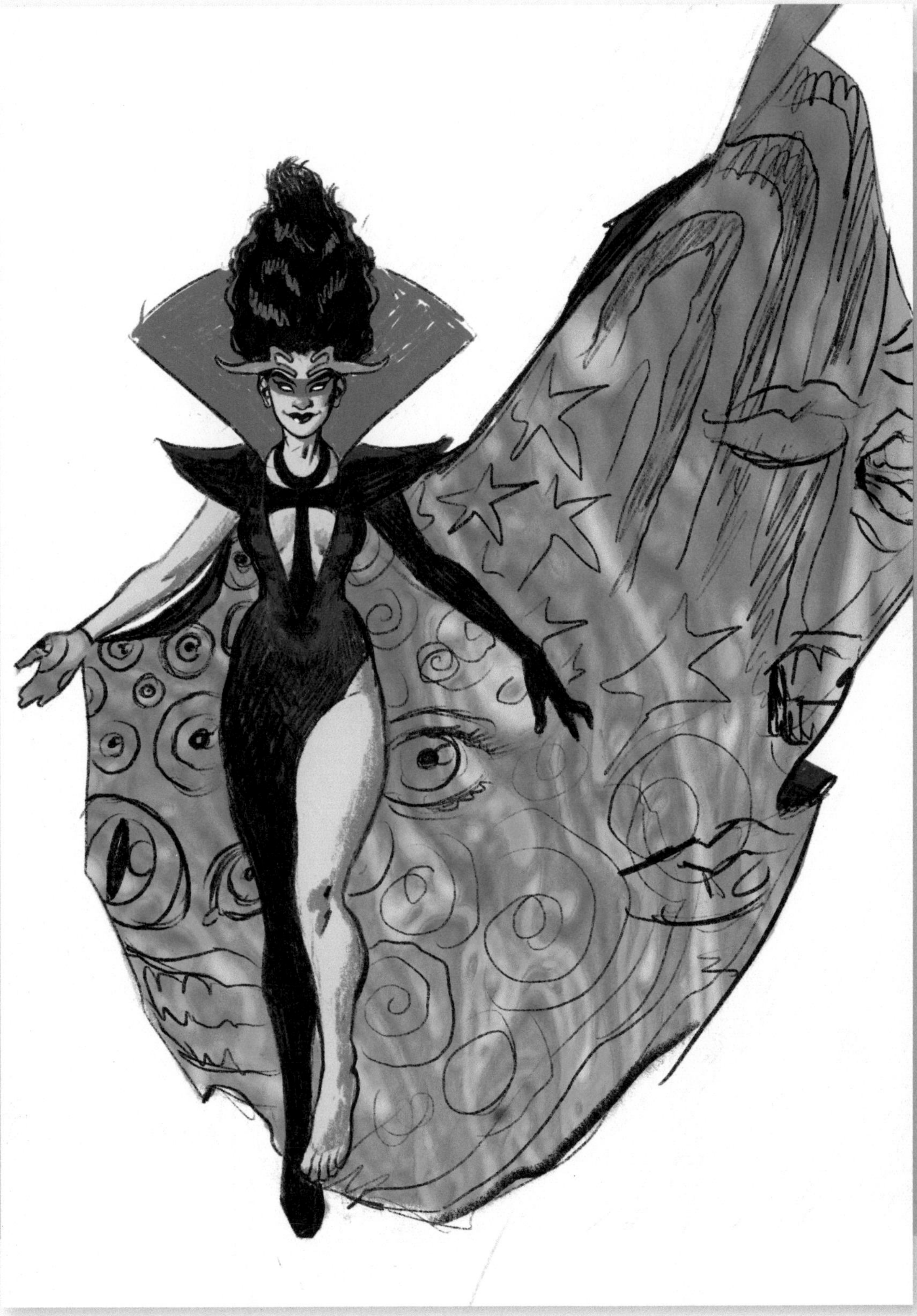

OFFICER GRANDLE